designing with web standards

jeffrey zeldman

New Riders

1249 Eighth Street, Berkeley, California 94710
An Imprint of Pearson Education

Designing with Web Standards

International Standard Book Number: 0-7357-1201-8

Library of Congress Catalog Card Number: 2001094556

Printed in the United States of America

First printing: May 2003

10 9 8 7

Trademarks

Warning and Disclaimer

Associate Publisher
Stephanie Wall

Production Manager
Gina Kanouse

Senior Product Marketing Manager
Tammy Detrich

Publicity Manager
Susan Nixon

Acquisitions Editor
Michael Nolan

Senior Development Editor
Jennifer Eberhardt

Senior Project Editor
Lori Lyons

Copy Editor
Karen Gill

Indexer
Lisa Stumpf

Proofreader
Nancy Sixsmith

Composition
Wil Cruz

Manufacturing Coordinator
Dan Uhrig

Interior Designer
Kim Scott

Cover Designer
Aren Howell

Table of Contents

Part III > Back End

About the Author

Jeffrey Zeldman is among the best-known web designers in the world. His personal site (www.zeldman.com) has welcomed more than sixteen million visitors and is read daily by thousands in the web design and development industry.

He is the publisher/creative director of A List Apart (www.alistapart.com), an online magazine "For People Who Make Websites," and the founder of Happy Cog (www.happycog.com), a design and consulting agency whose clients include Clear Channel Entertainment, Warner Bros. Pictures, Fox Searchlight Pictures, and The New York Public Library. In 1998, he co-founded The Web Standards Project (www.webstandards.org), a grassroots coalition of web designers and developers that helped end the Browser Wars by persuading Microsoft and Netscape to support the same technologies in their browsers.

Jeffrey is the author of *Taking Your Talent to the Web* (New Riders: 2001) and of numerous articles for A List Apart, Adobe, *Creativity*, Digital Web, *Macworld*, *PDN-Pix*, and other sites and print publications. He has been a juror for the Communication Arts Interactive Festival, the Art Directors Club of New York, the 5K, the Addy Awards, and the Radio Mercury Awards, and is an Advisory Board member of the Meet the Makers and i3Forum conferences.

He has lectured to groups including the American Institute of Graphic Arts (AIGA), The Columbia University Libraries, Los Alamos National Laboratories, The New York Public Library, The Public Library Association, and The New York State Forum for Information Resource Management, and at conferences including Builder, CMP, Seybold, SXSW Interactive, Web Design World, and Webvisions, among others. But what he really wants to do is direct.

About the Technical Reviewers

These reviewers contributed their considerable hands-on expertise to the entire development process for *Designing with Web Standards*. As the book was being written, these dedicated professionals reviewed all the material for technical content, organization, and flow. Their feedback was critical to ensuring that *Designing with Web Standards* fits our readers' need for the highest-quality technical information.

Eric A. Meyer has been working with the web since 1993. He is currently employed as a Standards Evangelist with Netscape Communications while living in Cleveland, Ohio—which is a much nicer city than you've been led to believe. A recognized name in the industry, Eric is often asked to speak at conferences on the subjects of web standards, cross-browser compatibility, CSS, and web design. A graduate of and former Webmaster for Case Western Reserve University, Eric coordinated the authoring and creation of the W3C's CSS1 Test Suite and has recently been pushing the limits of CSS-based design as far as he can. Eric is also the author of *Eric Meyer on CSS: Mastering the Language of Web Design* (New Riders), *Cascading Style Sheets: The Definitive Guide* (O'Reilly & Associates), *CSS2.0 Programmer's Reference* (Osborne McGraw-Hill), and the well-known CSS Browser Compatibility Charts.

J. David Eisenberg lives in San Jose, California with his kittens Marco and Zoë. He teaches HTML, XML, Perl, and JavaScript, and enjoys writing educational software and online tutorials.

David attended the University of Illinois, where he worked for the PLATO computer-assisted instruction project. He has also worked at Burroughs and Apple.

Thanks and Praise

I wrote this book, but many hands guided mine.

I am indebted to Jennifer Eberhardt at New Riders. Without her patience and persistence, this book would have stalled many times. Michael Nolan brought me to New Riders in 2000, for which I am grateful, and played a supporting role in the creation of this book. Chris Nelson encouraged me, and David Dwyer cleverly suggested I write this book when I had proposed instead a treatise to be called *The Little Orange Book of Web Design*.

In revising the text, I relied on the insights of two gifted technical editors. J. David Eisenberg is a teacher, a member of The Web Standards Project, and the author of *SVG Essentials* (`http://www.oreilly.com/catalog/svgess/`). Eric Meyer is a force behind Netscape's standards evangelism and the author of *Eric Meyer on CSS* (`http://www.ericmeyeroncss.com/`), whose title still embarrasses him. Both men are also my friends. You should be so lucky.

My thanks to the partners and colleagues with whom I was able to try out many of the techniques described in this book: Brian Alvey, Leigh Baker-Foley, Hillman Curtis, Nick Finck, Dennis James, Jamal Kales, Erin Kissane, Bruce Livingstone, Tanya Rabourn, Brad Ralph, Ian Russell, and Waferbaby. My gratitude also to Happy Cog's clients during the year I wrote this book, especially Steve Broback, Don Buckley, Eric Etheridge, Andrew Lin, Alec Pollak, and Randy Walker. Thanks for seeking the kind of work we do, indulging the occasional failed experiments, and paying those invoices.

Anything I've gotten right is largely due to Tantek Çelik, Joe Clark, Todd Fahrner, and (again) Eric Meyer. They know more than I ever will but think no less of me.

Without George Olsen and Glenn Davis there would not have been a Web Standards Project, and without the Project by now we would be coding every site fifteen ways. Thanks, gents, for helping to change the world.

I am grateful to every member of the Project's steering committee but wish to especially thank Tim Bray for the wit, Steven Champeon for keeping it on a higher plane, and Dori Smith for keeping it real. Thanks, too, to Rachel and Andrew for working so well with Macromedia and with its user community.

Jeffrey Veen may not realize it, but he helped me learn to relax as a public speaker and that enabled me to more effectively spread the message of web standards.

I learned from every supporter of The Web Standards Project and gained even more from its detractors, for it was their concerns that demanded an answer and their objections that helped shape the group's strategy between 1998 and 2002.

Thanks to the browser engineers who have worked so hard over the past three years, overcoming great odds and small budgets to truly deliver on the promise of web standards.

Thanks also to Janet Daly, Karl Dubost, Håkon Lie, Molly Holzschlag, Meryl Evans, and Michael Schmidt. And to Douglas Bowman, Owen Briggs, Chris Casciano, Eric Costello, Todd Dominey, Craig Saila, Christopher Schmitt, Mark Newhouse, and Waferbaby for pioneering CSS layouts. And to hundreds of web designers whose work invigorates and inspires us all. This book would double in size if I tried to list and thank you all, but you know who you are.

Special thanks to those designers whose work orbits a different planet from the one described in this book—people like Warren Corbitt, Joshua Davis, Matt Owens, and Lee Misenheimer. Your work challenges me to think twice about everything I do and believe as a web designer. There is room for both our visions.

I want to thank my father Maurice for co-authoring me and to wish him and his bride Katherine continued health, love, and happiness.

This book is for Carrie. I love you, Baby.

Tell Us What You Think

As the reader of this book, you are the most important critic and commentator. We value your opinion and want to know what we're doing right, what we could do better, what areas you'd like to see us publish in, and any other words of wisdom you're willing to pass our way.

Email: `errata@newriders.com`

Introduction

There was a time not that long ago when many drivers thought nothing of tossing empty bottles out the windows of their cars. Years later, these same citizens came to realize that littering was not an acceptable way to dispose of their trash. The web design community is now undergoing a similar shift in attitude, and web standards are key to this transformation.

The history of our medium has been to solve today's problems at tomorrow's expense. This book will show that the build-now, pay-later approach is no longer productive or necessary, and that today's problems can be solved *without* generating worse dilemmas downstream. It will also lay to rest the notion that designing with standards means leaving some users behind. In fact, it most often means just the opposite.

One Size Does Not Fit All

In this book, we'll examine some of the ways that standards can solve common problems of design and production. No book can cover every problem and solution, and another author's book might take an entirely different approach to any issue discussed in these pages. This book is biased toward meeting practical and immediate needs in a way that anticipates future requirements. The techniques and ideas advanced in this book have been tested and found useful in my agency's design and consulting practice, and these ideas, or variations on them, have been used on thousands of forward-looking sites.

Not every reader will immediately use every idea discussed in this book. If your style emphasizes tight grids, you might not cotton to rules-based design as described in Chapter 16, "A CSS Redesign." If your site must look great in 4.0 browsers, you might be interested in the hybrid techniques described in Chapters 8, "XHTML by Example: A Hybrid Layout (Part I)," through 10, "CSS in Action: A Hybrid Layout (Part II)," and indifferent to the pure CSS layout techniques discussed in Chapter 16.

Any thinking designer, developer, or site owner will endorse the *general* notions advanced in this book. Standards are vital to any medium. Because the software through which the web is viewed finally supports standards, it makes sense to learn about and correctly use them. Doing so saves time and money, reduces overhead, extends the usable life of our sites, and provides greater access to our content.

The latter point is important to anyone who wants to reach a wider, rather than a narrower, audience—particularly as nontraditional Internet access increases. It also has legal implications as more nations and more U.S. states create and begin to enforce accessibility regulations. Web standards and accessibility can help your site stay on the right side of these laws.

Theory Versus Practice

But some specific ideas and techniques advanced in this book are open to debate. If you are a hardcore standards geek (and I mean that in the nicest way possible), you might be unwilling to use XHTML until all browsers properly support sending XHTML documents as `application/xhtml+xml` instead of `text/html`. For details, see Ian Hickson's "Sending XHTML as Text/HTML Considered Harmful" (`http://www.hixie.ch/advocacy/xhtml`).

If you agree with Ian's view, you might choose to use HTML 4.01 for now, or you might want to configure your web server to send `application/xhtml+xml` to browsers that understand it and `text/html` to those that do not (http:// lists.w3.org/Archives/Public/www-archive/2002Dec/0005.html). In this book, I have avoided such issues because of my bias toward getting work done under present conditions—a bias I believe most of this book's readers will share.

Hybrid Layouts: On Their Way Out?

Likewise, some hardcore CSS fans might despise the idea of hybrid CSS/table layouts. Hybrid layout methods (Chapters 8 through 10) are offered for those who need them. Specifically, they are offered for designers whose work must look almost as good (and almost the same) in old, noncompliant browsers as it does in newer, more compliant ones.

We might not need these methods for long. As I write this page, ESPN.com has relaunched using CSS layout [**I.1**]. Ten million readers visit this sports site each day. When a site that big and that commercial adopts CSS layout techniques, the day of web standards is at hand. Although the site's initial use of standards was neither purist nor perfect, here is what art director Mike Davidson and his team got right:

- All CSS positioning. There are no tables for layout except in sponsored elements beyond the design team's control.

- No font tags.

- Bandwidth, bandwidth, bandwidth. Front-page markup and code weigh half of what they did before the relaunch while displaying a much richer page. (With more structural markup as discussed in Chapters 5, "Modern Markup," through 9, "CSS Basics," even greater bandwidth savings would be attained.)

- Only one style sheet for all browsers—no detection used or needed. The site looks more or less identical in all browsers that support `getElementById`, including Apple's new-for-2002 Safari browser, which is still in beta.

I.1
Are web standards too risky for commercial sites? ESPN.com didn't think so (www.espn.com). The vastly popular sports site relaunched with CSS layout in February 2003.

ESPN.com has attained significant benefits and delivered bandwidth savings to its readers by using many of the techniques advised in this book. But the site's first CSS incarnation does miss other ideas contained in this book (which, after all, had not yet been published when ESPN.com was redesigned with CSS). The site uses more browser detection than necessary. Its markup errs in the direction of presentation and does not validate. Accessibility could be better, and CSS could be more logical and more compact.

By the time you read this book, ESPN.com might have improved in some or all of these areas. But even if it hasn't yet done so, is the glass one quarter empty or three quarters full? Where ESPN.com leads, less brave and less popular commercial sites will surely follow. When a site with 10 million daily readers moves to CSS layout, it is a win for standards-based design and development methods.

A week before ESPN.com took the plunge, Netscape's DevEdge [**I.2**] was reborn as a standards showcase. The site had always provided solid information on web development—including tutorials on the proper use of standards—but its construction belied its content. With the standards-based redesign, the site began following its own advice and serving as a role model. Features included table-free, CSS layout; user-selectable styles; standards-based drop-down menus; and link URLs that print out for the reader's convenience via the CSS content property.

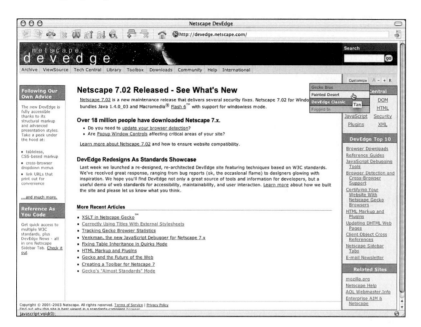

I.2

In February 2003, Netscape DevEdge followed its own advice and converted to standards-based layout and markup (`http://devedge.netscape.com/`).

A Continuum, Not a Set of Inflexible Rules

As this book will emphasize, web standards are a continuum, not a set of inflexible rules. In moving to web standards, you might not achieve perfect separation of structure from presentation (Chapter 2, "Designing and Building with Standards") in your first site or even your fifth. Your early efforts at accessibility (Chapter 14, "Accessibility Basics") might deliver only the minimum required by WAI Priority 1, and you might not get all of it exactly right.

The point is to begin. Fear of imperfection can immobilize the unwary in the same way that shame about our flab might keep us from going to the gym. But we won't begin to lose the excess avoirdupois until we make our first fumbling efforts at physical fitness. Likewise, our sites won't attain forward compatibility if we don't start *somewhere*. Deleting font tags might be where you start. Or you might replace nonstructural markup with meaningful <h…> and <p> tags. This is often an excellent place to begin, and as a consequence, this book will spend a fair amount of its time and yours considering modern markup and XHTML.

Show, Don't Sell

Designers sometimes bog down on the *selling* part of standards. Over the years, I have received hundreds of letters from designers who want to use standards, "but my client won't let me." If standards are a continuum, how can any client oppose at least some effort in their direction? For instance, even the most table-driven site can validate against HTML 4.01 or XHTML 1.0 Transitional and can be made to conform to U.S. Section 508 or WAI Priority 1 accessibility guidelines. No client would object to an error-free, accessible site.

What most designers concerned with selling standards are really saying is that they can't go as far as they would like to go on a particular project. For instance, they can't use pure CSS layout for a particular project because the client (or their boss) uses Netscape 4, whose CSS support is patchy at best. That might be true, but it is no reason not to write valid markup and correct CSS and use the Two-Sheet method described in Chapter 9 to deliver an acceptable and branded look and feel across multiple browser generations.

My agency is religious about web standards and accessibility but not about which methods we use or where they fall on an imaginary Standards Purity continuum. We use the method that best suits the project. To sell it, we do two things:

- In our proposals, we explicitly state which technologies will be used, keeping the description simple and straightforward. For instance, "XHTML 1.0 Transitional, a current standard, will be used for markup." After the client has agreed to the proposal and signed the contract, "permission" to use the indicated standard has been granted, and further hand wringing is not needed. Where a choice will impact the visual result in older browsers, this is also explicitly stated in the proposal.

- As work begins, in showing various stages to the client, we keep technological discussion to a minimum—even when dealing with a technologically savvy client. When delivering a redesign that is one-third the bandwidth of its predecessor and that retains formatting (even advanced formatting), no matter how many times it is changed or updated, we don't say, "CSS makes this possible." We say, "We've set up a system that protects formatting and is low bandwidth." If the client thinks we're smart and chooses to grant us more business, we can live with that.

Let Your Work Do the Selling for You

When Hillman Curtis, Inc. and Happy Cog collaborated on the Fox Searchlight Pictures site relaunch, our primary client contact was an experienced web designer and developer. Yet some of the hybrid CSS/table methods we used were new to him. "The site is so fast," he continually marveled, and we let him do so. We naturally included a style guide upon final delivery, and that style guide was explicit in its coverage of the site's technical aspects. But by that point, there was no need to sell what we had done because the results had already done the selling for us.

As you become known for doing this kind of work, clients will seek you out because of it, and you will have even less selling to do. Although Happy Cog is agnostic about hybrid versus pure CSS layouts, all my personal sites use CSS layout and increasingly so do my agency's smaller sites. We have even found it easier to do some design exploratory work in CSS instead of Photoshop; it's easier because it saves time and steps.

A recent project for our Clear Channel Entertainment client required several design variations, as most projects initially do. "By the way, these are CSS layouts," we informed the client. "I know that," he said. As these methods become normative (prompted in part by their adoption on commercial sites like ESPN.com, DevEdge, and Wired.com and on government and public sector sites as discussed in Chapter 4, "XML Conquers the World [And Other Web Standards Success Stories]"), they will increasingly go without saying—as using GIF or JPEG images presently goes without saying.

Selling In-House

I've described what happens at a for-hire web agency, but the same goes for in-house work. Try to avoid bogging down in discussions of baseline browsers and other old-school issues. Choose appropriate specifications, describe them briefly in the documentation your boss requires, and get busy.

Two years before writing this book, I lectured to a group of web developers at a large U.S. government organization. They were interested in web standards but bemoaned the agency's reliance on an old, noncompliant browser, which some believed made it impossible to use standards internally. (The belief was unfounded. Remember: Web standards are a continuum.)

While writing this introduction, I revisited the agency to deliver another little talk and found that the climate had changed. Most seats at the agency were now using Netscape 7. A few were still using Netscape 4 because some in-house applications had been built to take advantage of `document.layers`, the force behind Netscape 4's proprietary DHTML, and these applications were considered essential to some team members. But instead of throwing up their hands in defeat, attendees at the lecture wanted to discuss how they might migrate these applications to the W3C DOM.

The Smell of Change

Such changes are taking place everywhere, sometimes quickly and other times slowly. These changes will materialize anywhere thinking people face the task of creating or updating web content. Almost unnoticed amid economic and political worries and the grind of daily deadlines, our shared understanding of how the web works and how it should be built is undergoing a profound and continual metamorphosis. Web standards will soon be as widely discussed and studied as web usability and information architecture, and they will be considered every bit as essential as those disciplines—because they *are* every bit as essential to the health of our sites and of the medium in which we toil.

This book is large and has been crafted with care, yet it barely scratches the surface of what standards mean to the web. There is more to CSS, more to accessible, structured markup, and far more to the DOM than what this book or any single reference could convey. And as we've already mentioned, there are more ways to look at the issues we've covered than the way this author looks at them.

Put two designers in a room and you will hear three opinions. No two designers are likely to agree on every aspect of typography, branding, navigation, or color. The same is true of standards. There are as many disagreements in this realm as there are practitioners and theorists.

No book can deliver all things to all people, and this book is merely a pointer in the general direction of a journey whose path you must find for yourself. This book will have done its job if it helps you understand how standard technologies can work together to create forward-compatible sites—and provides a few tips to help you along your way.

I stumbled onto web standards after three years of designing sites the old-fashioned way, and it took me another five years to reach the understanding on which this book is based. You might disagree with any part of what I've said in these pages. I might disagree with some parts myself six months or two years from now. The point is not to bog down in differences or reject the whole because you're uncertain about one or two small parts. The point is to begin making changes that will help your projects reach the most people for the longest time, and often at the lowest cost.

If not now, when? If not you, who?

Part I

Houston, We Have a Problem

Before You Begin

This book is for designers, developers, owners, and managers who want their sites to cost less, work better, and reach more people—not only in today's browsers, screen readers, and wireless devices, but in tomorrow's, next year's, and beyond.

Most of us have gone a few rounds with the obsolescence that seems to be an inescapable part of the web's rapid technological advancement. Every time an improved browser version or new Internet device comes onto the scene, it seems to break the site we just finished producing (or paying for).

We build only to rebuild. Too often, we rebuild not to add visitor-requested features or increase usability, but merely to keep up with browsers and devices that seem determined to stay one budget-busting jump ahead of our planning and development cycles.

Even on those rare occasions in which a new browser or device merci-fully leaves our site unscathed, the so-called "backward-compatible" techniques we use to force our sites to look and behave the same way in all browsers take their toll in human and financial overhead.

We're so used to this experience that we consider it normative—the price of doing business on the web. It's a cost most of us can no longer afford (if we ever could).

Spiraling Costs, Diminishing Returns

Spaghetti code, deeply nested table layouts, `<font>` tags, and other redundancies double and triple the bandwidth required for our simplest sites. Our visitors pay the price by waiting endlessly for our pages to load. (Or they tire of waiting and flee our sites. Some wait patiently only to discover that when our site finally loads, it is inaccessible to them.)

Our servers pay the price by chugging out 60K per page view when 20 might suffice—and we pay our hosting companies (or increase our IT budgets) to keep up with the bandwidth our pages squander. The more visitors we attract, the higher the cost. To cope with our ad hoc front-end designs, our databases make more queries than they have to, further escalating our expense. Eventually we're forced to buy or lease additional servers to keep up with the demand— not of increased visitors but of excess markup and code.

Meanwhile, the hourly rates of the programmers we pay to code our sites six different ways (and to then write more code to serve the appropriate version to each visitor) can drive development costs so high we simply run out of money. A new browser or wireless device comes along, and with no cash left to cover the cost of coding for that browser or device, the cycle of obsolescence resumes.

Many of us have had the startling experience of visiting a site with a new browser, only to be told the site requires a "modern" browser that's much older than the one we're using. The site's owners and developers are not necessarily stupid or inconsiderate; they simply might have burned through their "perpetual upgrade" budget and have nothing left to give.

In other cases, the problem is not lack of funds but lack of knowledge or a misguided sense of what constitutes the best return on investment. Connected Earth, whose slogan is "How communication shapes the world," was recently redesigned at a reported cost of £1,000,000 (approximately $1.6 million U.S. at the time of this writing). Despite the funds lavished on the site's development, it is incompatible with nearly every modern browser on earth. It denies access to users of Mozilla [1], Netscape 6/7, and Opera [2]. Because the site is also incompatible with non-Windows operating systems, users of Internet Explorer for Macintosh are equally out of luck.

1

Despite a huge develop-ment budget, Connected Earth is incompatible with nearly all modern browsers. It excludes users of Mozilla (shown here), Netscape 6/7, and Opera on any platform, and users of Internet Explorer in Mac OS (`www.connected-earth.com`).

2

The same site as viewed (or more accurately, as not viewable) in Opera 7 for Windows XP. Connected Earth's technical problems could have been avoided by following the methods described in this book.

Whether a site has *grown* obsolete because the cost of perpetual recoding exceeded its budget, or the site was *born* obsolete thanks to outdated specifica-tions, the result is the same: the loss of an ever-increasing number of potential customers. After all, whether you're spending £1,000,000 or $1,000, the goal is to welcome visitors, not send them packing.

There is a solution.

Ending the Cycle of Obsolescence

Technologies created by the World Wide Web Consortium (see the sidebar, "What Is the W3C?") and other standards bodies and supported by most current browsers and devices now make it possible to design and build sites that will continue to work, even as those standards and browsers evolve. Battle-scarred industry veterans might be skeptical of this claim, but this book will show how it works.

This book will teach you how to escape the "build, break, rebuild" cycle, designing for the present and future web on and beyond the desktop, without excluding potential visitors and without wasting increasingly scarce time and money on short-sighted proprietary "solutions" that contain the seeds of their own obsolescence.

This is not a book for theorists or purists, but for practical people who need to get work done. It's for creative and business professionals who seek sensible advice and a range of proven techniques so that they can modify their skills and thinking and get on with the job of creating great websites that work for more visitors and customers.

Armed with this book, designers and developers will be able to quickly modify their existing practices to create websites that work in multiple browsers and devices instead of a handful, while avoiding perpetual obsolescence born of proprietary markup and coding techniques.

Site owners and managers who read this book will be able to stop wasting money on specs that only perpetuate the wasteful cycle. They will know how to write requirement documents that lead to forward-compatible sites.

What Is the W3C?

Created in 1994, the World Wide Web Consortium (W3C) (`http://www.w3.org/`) hammers out specifications and guidelines that are intended to promote the web's evolution and ensure that web technologies work well together. Roughly 500 member organizations belong to the consortium. Its director, Tim Berners-Lee (`http://www.w3.org/People/Berners-Lee/`), invented the web in 1989. Specifications developed by the W3C include HTML, CSS, XML, XHTML, and the standard Document Object Model (DOM), among many others.

For years, the W3C referred to such specs as "Recommendations," which might have inadvertently encouraged member companies such as Netscape and Microsoft to implement W3C specs less than rigorously. On its launch in 1998, The Web Standards Project (www.webstandards.org) relabeled key W3C Recommendations "web standards," a guerrilla marketing maneuver that helped reposition accurate and complete support for these specs as a vital ingredient of any browser or Internet device. (See the related sidebar, "What Is The Web Standards Project?")

Other standards bodies include the European Computer Manufacturers Association (ECMA), which is responsible for the language known as ECMAScript and more familiarly referred to as "standard JavaScript." See Chapter 3, "The Trouble with Standards," for details.

What Is Forward Compatibility?

What do we mean by forward compatibility? We mean that, designed and built the right way, any document that is published on the web can work across multiple browsers, platforms, and Internet devices—and will continue to work as new browsers and devices are invented. Open standards make this possible.

As an added attraction, designing and building with standards lowers production and maintenance costs while making sites more accessible to those who have special needs. (Translation: more customers for less cost, improved public relations, decreased likelihood of accessibility-related litigation.)

What do we mean by web standards? We mean structural languages like XHTML and XML, presentation languages like CSS, object models like the W3C DOM, and scripting languages like ECMAScript, all of which (and more) will be explained in this book.

Hammered out by committees of experts, these technologies have been carefully designed to deliver the greatest benefits to the largest number of web users. Taken together, these technologies form a roadmap for rational, accessible, sophisticated and cost-effective web development. (Site owners and managers: Don't worry yourselves over the technical chapters in this book. Just make sure your employees or vendors understand them.)

What do we mean by standards-compliant browsers? We mean products like Mozilla, Netscape 6+, MSIE5+/Mac, MSIE6+/Win, and Opera 7+ that understand and support XHTML, CSS, ECMAScript, and the DOM. Are these browsers perfect in their support for every one of these standards? Of course they're not. No software yet produced in any category is entirely bug free. Moreover, standards are sophisticated in themselves, and the ways they interact with each other are complex.

Nevertheless, modern browsers are solid enough that we can discard outdated methods, work smarter, and satisfy more users. And because standards are inclusive by nature, we can even accommodate folks who use old browsers and devices—but in a forward-compatible way.

No Rules, No Dogma

This is not a religious or dogmatic book. There is no "best" way to design a website, no one right way to incorporate standards into your workflow. This book will not advocate strict standards compliance at the expense of transitional approaches that might be better suited to particular sites and tasks. It will not oversell web standards by pretending that every W3C recommendation is flawless.

This book will tell you what you need to know to work around the occasional compliance hiccup in Internet Explorer, Netscape Navigator, and other modern browsers, and it will offer strategies for coping with the bad old browsers that might be used by some in your audience, including that stubborn guy in the corner office.

This book will not lie to you. Some proprietary methods and shortcuts are easier to use than some W3C specs. For instance, proprietary, IE-only scripting using Microsoft shortcuts such as innerhtml might be faster and easier than scripting for all browsers via the W3C standard DOM. Even so, from a business point of view, it makes more sense to code for all browsers rather than for one, and the DOM is the way to do that.

Likewise, even though we'll explore the benefits of structural markup and XHTML, we won't pretend that every tag on every page of every site always needs to be structural. And we won't tell you that every site must immediately move from HTML to XHTML—although we hope the advantages of XHTML will compel you to consider making that transition as soon as you can.

This book's author is known for advocating that web pages be laid out with Cascading Style Sheets (CSS) instead of traditional HTML tables whenever possible (whenever audience appropriate). The CSS standard solves numerous problems for developers and readers alike. CSS layout is the future and is already being used on many sites, from heavily trafficked corporate entities like Wired (www.wired.com) [3] to major search engines (www.alltheweb.com) to public sector and personal sites.

3

It's big. It's corporate. And it's built with web standards XHTML and CSS (www.wired.com).

But table layouts are far from dead, are still the right tool for many design jobs, and can be achieved without sacrificing standards compliance or forward compatibility. Although the advantages of CSS layout are undeniably appealing, it's your site and your choice.

In the minds of some standards purists, popular proprietary technologies like Flash and QuickTime have no place on the web. That attitude might be fine for theorists, but the rest of us have work to do, and technologies like Flash and QuickTime are the best tools for some jobs. This book won't have much to say about such technologies except in relation to markup and accessibility, but that's not because we dislike Flash or QuickTime; these technologies are simply outside this book's scope.

You might also have encountered web standards advocates who advise against using the proprietary GIF format, or accuse you of heresy if you choose to set your headlines in GIF text instead of in XHTML styled with CSS. XHTML headlines are often advisable and are sometimes the best choice. But in the real world, branding matters. A nicely kerned typeface rendered in the GIF (or non-proprietary PNG) format might be a better choice for your site than asking CSS to fetch Arial, Verdana, or Georgia from your visitors' System folders. It's your site. You call the shots.

Practice, Not Theory

We have nothing against the purists whose passion drives the creation of web standards. Quite the contrary: We admire such people immensely and are lucky enough to have befriended and learned from a number of them.

But this book is for working designers and developers and the clients and employers who pay for their expertise. Our exploration of web standards will be rooted in the context of design, content, and marketing issues. Our goal is to guide you through the world of web standards and to help you reach your own decisions—the only decisions with which any designer or client can ever be truly happy.

If this book contains one kernel of dogma, or holds one fixed, inflexible view, it's this: The cost of business as usual is too high. No one reading this book can afford to design today's websites with yesterday's piecemeal methods.

The old-school techniques had their place when some standards had yet to be written, whereas others were poorly supported in mainstream browsers. But that day is gone. Likewise, coding every site six ways might have seemed a reasonable practice when the Internet boom and grotesquely over-inflated budgets were at their height. But that day, too, is gone.

XHTML, XML, CSS, ECMAScript, and the DOM are here to stay. They are not ends in themselves, but components of a rational solution to problems that have plagued site owners and builders since the `<blink>` tag.

> ### What Is The Web Standards Project?
>
> Founded in 1998, The Web Standards Project helped end the browser wars by persuading Netscape, Microsoft, and other manufacturers to accurately and completely support specifications ("standards") that reduce the cost and complexity of development and ensure simple, affordable access for all. In addition to browser makers, the group now works with development tool manufacturers like Macromedia and with site owners and developers. The Web Standards Project is a grassroots coalition. Its activities are entirely voluntary and not for profit.

Is This Trip Really Necessary?

For websites to shed their traditional woes and move to the next level, designers and developers must learn to use web standards, and site owners and managers must be told how standards can help their business.

The revelation of web standards will not manifest itself on its own. Business owners are unlikely to scour the W3C website, decipher its pocket-protector-style documents, and intuitively grasp what cryptic acronyms like XHTML or CSS might mean to their profitability. Likewise, overworked designers and developers, struggling to make deadlines, have little time to trek through mailing lists and online tutorials in search of comprehensible explanations of changing web technologies.

To make the case for standards, this book had to be written. As cofounder of The Web Standards Project, the job fell to me. My name is Jeffrey. I carry a mouse. I also write in the editorial "we" except when absolutely necessary. It's a conceit I adopted when I began publishing websites in 1995. I (we) trust the reader will not be disturbed by this habit.

You'd probably rather read about graphics and motion design, new thinking in site architecture, and usability than about the changing technological under-pinnings of the web. I would rather write about those things. But our best efforts in design, architecture, and usability will be wasted if our sites stop working in Browser X or Device Y. There could be no filmmaking without industry-wide agreement on frame rates, lenses, and audio recording techniques. Likewise, the continued health of web design and development depends on the adoption of web standards. Without these standards, there can be no true usability and no coherent approach to design.

In terms of acceptance, the web got off to a faster start than any other medium ever introduced. But its commercial success preceded the development of industry standards, throwing all of us into the perilous position of creating products (websites) that were continually made obsolete by one proprietary browser or device innovation after another. We were all so busy producing that we had no time to question the way we worked. Today, if we intend to keep working and producing, we must question and modify our methods.

Web standards are the tools with which all of us can design and build sophisticated, beautiful sites that will work as well tomorrow as they do today. In this book, I'll explain the job of each standard and how all of them can work together to create forward-compatible sites. The rest is up to you.

—Jeffrey Zeldman
New York City
2003

chapter one

99.9% of Websites Are Obsolete

An equal opportunity disease afflicts nearly every site now on the web, from the humblest personal home pages to the multi-million-dollar sites of corporate giants. Cunning and insidious, the disease goes largely unrecognized because it is based on industry norms. Although their owners and managers might not know it yet, 99.9% of all websites are obsolete.

These sites might look and work all right in mainstream, desktop browsers whose names end in the numbers 4 or 5. But outside these fault-tolerant environments, the symptoms of disease and decay have already started to appear.

In modern versions of Microsoft Internet Explorer, Opera Software's Opera browser, Netscape Navigator, and Mozilla (the Open Source, Gecko-based browser whose code drives Navigator, CompuServe, AOL for OS X, AOL China, and other browsing environments), carefully constructed layouts have begun falling apart and expensively engineered behaviors have stopped working. As these leading browsers evolve, site performance continues to deteriorate.

In "off-brand" browsers, in screen readers used by people with disabilities, and in increasingly popular nontraditional devices from Palm Pilots to web-enabled cell phones, many of these sites have never worked and still don't, whereas others function marginally at best. Depending on needs and budget, site owners and developers have either ignored these off-brand browsers and devices or supported them by detecting their presence and feeding them customized markup and code, just as they do for "regular" browsers.

To understand the futility of this outdated industry practice and to see how it continually increases the cost and complexity of web development while never truly achieving its intended goal, we must examine modern browsers and see how they differ from the incompatible browsers of the past.

Modern Browsers and Web Standards

Throughout this book, when we refer to "modern" or "standards-compliant" browsers, we mean browsers that understand and support HTML and XHTML, Cascading Style Sheets (CSS), ECMAScript, and the W3C Document Object Model (DOM). Taken together, these are the standards that allow us to move beyond presentational markup and incompatible scripting languages and the perpetual obsolescence they engender.

As of this writing, such browsers include, among others, Mozilla 1.0 and higher; Netscape Navigator 6 and higher; Microsoft Internet Explorer 6 and higher for Windows; Microsoft Internet Explorer 5 and higher for Macintosh; and Opera Software's Opera 7 browser. For a chart that lists and compares the first wave of compliant browsers, please see, "Modern Browsers: The Good, the Bad, and the Ugly," in Part III of this book. Note that it is not an exhaustive list. Any attempt to list every standards-compliant browser would date this book faster than the Macarena. Although we will use the term "standards-compliant," please remember what we said before this chapter in this book's "Before You Begin" section: No browser is *perfectly* standards compliant or can be.

Lack of browser perfection is no reason to avoid standards. Millions of people currently use Internet Explorer 5 or 5.5 for Windows. From a standards point of view, those browsers are inferior to IE6/Windows, Netscape 6+, and so on. Does that mean if your audience includes IE5/Windows users you should forget about web standards? Does it mean you should tell IE5/Windows users to upgrade or get lost? We think not. Standards-oriented design and development need not and should not mean, "designing for the latest browsers only."

Likewise, using XHTML and CSS need not necessitate telling Netscape 4 users to go take a hike. A site properly designed and built with standards is unlikely to look pixel-for-pixel the same in Netscape 4 as it does in more compliant browsers. In fact, depending on your design method, it might look entirely different. And that's probably okay. We'll explain the why and how in Part II of this book, "Designing and Building."

New Code for a New Job

Modern browsers are not merely newer versions of the same old thing. They differ fundamentally from their predecessors. In many cases, they've been rebuilt from the ground up. Mozilla, Netscape 6/7, and related Gecko-based browsers are not new versions of Netscape Navigator 4. IE5+/Mac is not an updated version of IE4/Mac. Opera 7 is not based on the same code that drove earlier versions of the Opera browser. These products have been built with new code to do a new job: namely, to comply as nearly perfectly as possible with the web standards discussed in this book.

By contrast, the browsers of the 1990s focused on proprietary (Netscape-only, Microsoft-only) technologies and paid little heed to standards. Old browsers ignored some standards altogether, but that did not pose much of a development headache. If browsers didn't support the Portable Network Graphic (PNG) standard, for example, then developers didn't use PNG images. No problem. The trouble was, these old browsers paid lip service to some standards by supporting them partially and incorrectly. Slipshod support for standards as basic as HTML created an untenable web-publishing environment that led in turn to unsustainable production methods.

When a patient's appendix bursts, a qualified surgeon performs a complete appendectomy. Now imagine if, instead, a trainee were to remove half the appendix, randomly stab a few other organs, and then forget to sew the patient back up. We apologize for the unsavory imagery, but it's what standards support was like in old browsers: dangerously incomplete, incompetent, and hazardous to the health of the web.

If Netscape 4 ignored CSS rules applied to the `<body>` element and added random amounts of whitespace to every structural element on your page, and if IE4 got `<body>` right but bungled padding, what kind of CSS was safe to write? Some developers chose not to write CSS at all. Others wrote one style sheet to compensate for IE4's flaws and a different style sheet to compensate for the blunders of Netscape 4. To compensate for cross-platform font and UI widget differences, developers might also write different style sheets depending on whether the site's visitor was using Windows or a Mac (and too bad if the visitor was using Unix or Linux).

These CSS problems were a drop in the bucket, as was CSS. Browsers could not agree on HTML, on table rendering, or on scripting languages used to add interactivity to the page. There was no one right way to structure a page's content. (Well, there *was* one right way, but no browser supported it.) There was no one right way to produce the *design* of a page (well, there was, but no browser supported it) or to add sophisticated *behavior* to a site (eventually there was, but no old browser supported it).

Struggling to cope with ever-widening incompatibilities, designers and developers came up with the practice of authoring customized versions of (nonstandard) markup and code for each differently deficient browser that came along. It was all we could do at the time if we hoped to create sites that would work in more than one browser or operating system. It's the wrong thing to do today because modern browsers support the same open standards. Yet the practice persists, needlessly gobbling scarce resources, fragmenting the web, and leading to inaccessible and unusable sites.

The "Version" Problem

The creation of multiple versions of nonstandard markup and nonstandard code, each tuned to the nonstandard quirks of one browser or another, is the source of the perpetual obsolescence that plagues most sites and their owners. The goal posts are always receding, and the rules of the game are forever changing.

Although it's costly, futile, and nonsustainable, the practice persists even when it's unnecessary. Faced with a browser that supports web standards, many developers treat it like one that doesn't. Thus, they'll write detection scripts that sniff out IE6 and feed it Microsoft-only scripts even though IE6 can handle standard ECMAScript and the DOM. They then feel compelled to write separate detection scripts (and separate code) for modern Netscape browsers that can also handle standard ECMAScript and the DOM.

As the example suggests, much browser and device sniffing and much individual version creation is unnecessary in today's standards-friendly climate. In fact, it's worse than unnecessary. Even with constant updating—which not every site owner can afford—detection scripts often fail.

For instance, in Windows, the Opera browser identifies itself as Explorer. It does this mainly to avoid getting blocked by sites (such as many banking sites) that sniff for IE. But scripts written exclusively for IE browsers are likely to fail in the Opera browser. When Opera identifies itself as IE (its default setting upon installation) and when developers write IE-only scripts, site failure and user frustration loom large. Users have the option to change their User Agent (UA) string and force Opera to identify itself honestly instead of trying to pass for IE. But few users know about this option, and they shouldn't need to.

In addition to proprietary scripts, developers write presentational markup that doubles the bandwidth needed to view or serve a page while making that page less accessible to search engines and nontraditional browsers and devices. Such strategies often cause the very problem they were intended to solve: inconsistent rendering between one browser and another [1.1].

1.1
The MSN Game Zone (`zone.msn.com/blog.asp`) sports seven external style sheets and still doesn't render properly in most modern browsers. It also brags 14 scripts (most of them inline), including heavy-duty browser detection. And it still doesn't work. Throwing more versions of code at a problem rarely solves it.

With multiple versions come ever-escalating costs and conundrums. "DHTML" sites produced to the proprietary (and incompatible) scripting specifications of Netscape 4 and IE4 don't work in most modern browsers. Should the site owner throw more money at the problem, asking developers to create a fifth or sixth version of the site? What if there's no budget for such a version? Many users will be locked out.

Likewise, developers might expend tremendous time and resources spinning a "wireless" version of their site, only to discover that the wireless markup language they used has become obsolete, or that their wireless version fails in a popular new device. Some address the latter problem by spinning yet another version. Others publish embarrassing messages promising to support the new device "in the near future."

Even when they embrace standard web technologies like XHTML and CSS, designers and developers who cut their teeth on old-school methods miss the point. Instead of using standards to *avoid* multiple versions, many old-school developers create multiple, browser- and platform-specific CSS files that are almost always self-defeating [**1.1, 1.2**].

These practices waste time and money. Neither commodity has ever been abundant; both have been in especially short supply since the Western Economy began its millennial downturn. Worse still, these costly practices fail to solve the problem. Sites are still broken, and users are still locked out.

1.2
Content deep within the Adobe website (www.adobe.com) suffers from bungled leading that makes lines of text overlap. Instead of creating one or two linked style sheets that work for *all* browsers, the developers outsmarted themselves with browser- and platform-specific styles that interact poorly. (Adobe has corrected the problem since this book went to press.) Designers who cut their teeth on old-school methods miss the point that CSS and XHTML almost always remove the need for multiple versions.

Backward Thinking

Peel the skin of any major 2003-era site, from Amazon to Microsoft.com, from Sony to ZDNet. Examine their tortuous nonstandard markup, their proprietary ActiveX and JavaScript (often including broken detection scripts), and their ill-conceived use of CSS—when they use CSS at all. It's a wonder such sites work in any browser.

These sites work in yesterday's mainstream browsers because the first four to five generations of Netscape Navigator and Microsoft Internet Explorer did not merely tolerate nonstandard markup and browser-specific code; they actually encouraged sloppy authoring and proprietary scripting in an ill-conceived battle to own the browser space.

Often, nonstandards-compliant sites work in yesterday's browsers because their owners have invested in costly publishing tools that accommodate browser differences by generating multiple, nonstandard versions tuned to the biases of specific browsers and platforms, as described earlier in "The 'Version' Problem." The practice taxes the dial-up user's patience by wasting bandwidth on code forking, deeply nested tables, spacer pixels and other image hacks, and outdated or invalid tags and attributes.

What Is Code Forking?

Code is the stuff programmers write to create software products, operating systems, or pretty much anything else in our digital world. When more than one group of developers works on a project, the code might "fork" into multiple, incompatible versions, particularly if each development group is trying to solve a different problem or bend to the will of a different agenda. This inconsistency and loss of centralized control is generally regarded as a bad thing.

As used in this book, *code forking* refers to the practice of creating multiple versions of incompatible code to cope with the needs of browsers that do not support standard ECMAScript and the DOM (see "The 'Version' Problem").

At the same time, these multiple versions squander the site owner's bandwidth at a cost even the bean counters might be at a loss to calculate. The bigger the site and the greater its traffic, the more money that is wasted on server calls, redundancies, image hacks, and unnecessarily complex code and markup.

Hard numbers are hard to come by, but in general, if a site reduces its markup weight by 35%, it reduces its bandwidth costs by the same amount. An organization that spends $2,500 a year would save $875. One that spends $160,000 a year would save $56,000.

Yahoo's front page [**1.3**] is served millions of times per day. Each byte that is wasted on outdated HTML design hacks is multiplied by an astronomical number of page views, resulting in gigabytes of traffic that tax Yahoo's servers and add Pentagon-like costs to its overhead. If Yahoo would simply replace its deprecated, bandwidth gobbling <font> tags [**1.4**] with bandwidth-friendly CSS, the cost of serving each page would greatly diminish, and the company's profits would consequently rise. So why hasn't Yahoo made the switch?

We can only conclude that the company wishes its site to look exactly the same in 1995-era browsers that don't support CSS as it does in modern browsers that do. The irony is that no one beside Yahoo's management cares what Yahoo looks like. The site's tremendous success is due to the service it provides, not to the beauty of its visual design (which is nonexistent).

That this otherwise brilliant company wastes untold bandwidth to deliver a look and feel no one greatly admires says everything you need to know about the entrenched mindset of developers who hold "backward compatibility" in higher esteem than reason, usability, or their own profits.

Outdated Markup: The Cost to Site Owners

Suppose the code and markup on one old-school web page weighs in at 60K. Say that, by replacing outdated <font> tags and other presentational and proprietary junk with clean, structural markup and a few CSS rules, that same page can weigh 30K. (In my agency's practice, we can often replace 60K of markup with 22K or less. But let's go with this more conservative figure, which represents bandwidth savings of 50%.) Consider two typical scenarios, detailed next.

T1 Terminator

Scenario: A self-hosted small business or public sector website serves a constant stream of visitors—several hundred at any given moment. After cutting its page weight in half by converting from presentational markup to lean, clean, structural XHTML, the organization saves $1,500 a month.

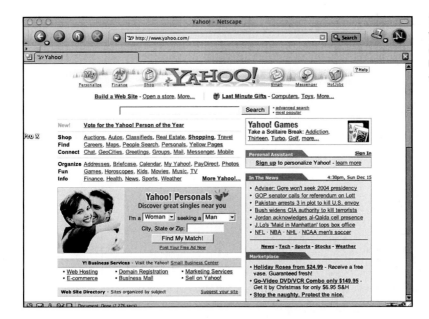

1.3
What Yahoo
(`www.yahoo.com`)
looks like—as plain as
white bread.

1.4
Peel Yahoo's skin
(view Source), and you'll
discover that the code
and markup used to
create this simple-
looking website are
unbelievably convoluted
and perplexing.

How it works: To serve its audience prior to the conversion, the self-hosted site requires two T1 lines, each of which is leased at a cost of U.S. $1,500 per month (a normal cost for a 1.544-megabit-per-second T1 line). After shaving file sizes by 50%, the organization finds it can get by just as effectively with a single T1 line, thus removing $1,500/month from its operating expenses. In addition to savings on bandwidth, there will also be fewer hardware expenses. The simpler the markup, the faster it's delivered to the user. The faster it's delivered, the less stress is placed on the server—and the fewer servers you need to buy, service, and replace. This is particularly true for servers that must cope with dynamic, database-driven content—that is, all commerce and most modern content sites.

Metered Megabytes

Scenario: As a commercially hosted site grows popular, its owners find themselves paying an unexpected file transfer penalty each month, to the tune of hundreds, or even thousands, of unexpected dollars. Cutting file sizes in half restores the monthly bill to a manageable and reasonable fee.

How it works: Many commercial hosting services allot their users a set amount of "free" file transfer bandwidth each month—say, up to 3GB. Stay below that number, and you'll pay your usual, monthly fee. Exceed it, and you must pay more. Sometimes *much* more.

In one infamous case, hosting company Global Internet Solutions slapped independent designer Al Sacui with $16,000 in additional fees after his noncommercial site, Nosepilot.com, exceeded its monthly file transfer allowance. It's an extreme case, and Sacui was able to avoid paying by proving that the host had changed the terms of service without notifying its customers (http://thewebfairy.com/gisol/), but only after a lengthy legal battle. Who wants to risk outrageous bills or protracted legal battles with an ornery hosting company?

Not every hosting company charges outrageous amounts for excess file transfers, of course. Pair.com, for instance, currently charges 1.5 cents a megabyte for overruns. A Pair-hosted small site with low traffic might save only $200/year. Larger sites with higher traffic have the most to save by reducing file sizes. Whether your site is large or small, visited by millions or just a handful of community members, the smaller your files, the lower your bandwidth, and the less likely you are to run afoul of your hosting company's file transfer costs. By the way, it's best to choose a hosting company that permits unlimited (also called "unmetered") file transfers rather than one that penalizes you for creating a popular site.

Condensed Versus Compressed Markup

After delivering a lecture on web standards, this author was approached by a developer in the audience who claimed that the bandwidth advantages of clean, well-structured markup didn't amount to a hill of beans for companies that compress their HTML.

In addition to *condensing* your markup by writing it lean and clean (that is, by preferring semantic structures to outdated "HTML design" methods), you can digitally *compress* your markup in some server environments. For instance, the Apache web server includes a mod_zip module that squeezes HTML on the server side. The HTML expands again in the user's browser.

The developer I spoke with gave this example: If Amazon.com wastes 40K on outdated font tags and other junk but uses mod_zip to compress it down to 20K, Amazon's bloated markup would represent less of an expense than my lecture (and this book) would suggest.

As it turns out, Amazon does not use mod_zip. In fact, the tool is used little on the commercial web, possibly due to the extra load required to compress pages before sending them. But that quibble aside, the smaller the file, the smaller it will compress. If you save money by compressing an 80K page down to 40K, you'll save even more by compressing a 40K page down to 20K. Savings in any given page-viewing session might seem small, but their value is cumulative. Over time, they can substantially reduce operating costs and might prevent additional expenses. (For instance, you might not need to lease additional T1 lines to cope with bandwidth overruns.)

Bandwidth savings are only one advantage to writing clean, well-structured markup, but they're one that accountants and clients appreciate, and they hold as true for those who compress their HTML as they do for the rest of us.

Backward Compatibility

What do developers mean by "backward compatibility?" If you ask them, they'll say they mean "supporting all our users." And who could argue with a sentiment like that?

In practice, however, "backward compatibility" means using nonstandard, proprietary (or deprecated) markup and code to ensure that every visitor has the same experience, whether they're sporting IE2 or Netscape 7. Held up as a Holy Grail of professional development practice, "backward compatibility" sounds great in theory. But the cost is too high and the practice has always been based on a lie.

There is no true backward compatibility. There is always a cut-off point. For instance, neither Mosaic (the first visual browser) nor Netscape 1.0 supports HTML table-based layouts. By definition, then, those who use these ancient browsers cannot possibly have the same visual experience as folks who view the web through slightly less ancient browsers like Netscape 1.1 or MSIE2.

Developers and clients who claim to strive for backward compatibility inevitably specify a "baseline browser" such as Netscape 3 and agree that that's the earliest browser their site will support. (Netscape 2 users are out of luck.) To fulfill their commitment of baseline browser support, developers layer their markup with a series of browser-specific, nonstandard hacks and workarounds that add weight to every page.

At the same time, developers write multiple scripts to accommodate the browsers they've chosen to support and use browser detection to feed each browser the code it likes best. In so doing, these developers further increase the girth of their pages, pump up the load on their servers, and ensure that the race against perpetual obsolescence will continue until they run out of money or go out of business.

Blocking Users Is Bad for Business

Whereas some companies undercut their own profitability trying to ensure that even the oldest browsers see their sites exactly as new browsers do, others have decided that only one browser matters. In a misguided effort to reduce expenses, an increasing number of sites are designed to work only in Internet Explorer, and sometimes only on the Windows platform, thus locking out 15–25% of their potential visitors and customers [**1.5, 1.6, 1.7, 1.8, 1.9**].

We won't pretend to understand the business model of a company that would say no to up to a quarter of its potential customers. And the sheer number of customers lost by this myopic approach should boggle the mind of any rational business owner or noncorporate agency with a mandate to serve the public. According to statistics compiled by NUA Internet Surveys (www.nua.ie/surveys/), more than 650.6 million people used the web as of September 2002. You do the math.

Say you don't mind losing up to 25% of the people who choose to visit your site. The "IE-only" approach still makes no sense because there's no guarantee that IE (or even desktop browsers as a category) will continue to dominate web space.

Some years before this book was written, Netscape's Navigator browser enjoyed a market share greater than Microsoft's Internet Explorer does today. At the time, conventional wisdom held that Netscape's was the only browser that mattered, and developers coded accordingly. Untold millions of dollars later, the market changed. Netscape-only sites were dumped in the digital landfill beside the Information Superhighway they rode in on.

Could the same fate lie in store for IE-only sites? Inconceivable as it seems, there's truly no telling. On the web, the only constant is change. Factor in the increasingly widespread use of nontraditional Internet devices, and the notion of designing to the quirks of any individual desktop browser at the expense of all other browsers and devices starts looking like the brain-dead business decision it is.

Besides, as this book will show, standards make it possible to design for all browsers and devices as easily and quickly as for just one. Between the spiraling cost of backward-compatible versioning and the futile shortsightedness of building for a single browser, web standards provide the only approach to development that makes a lick of sense.

Neither money-wasting versioning techniques nor the deliberate decision to support only one browser or platform will help today's sites work in tomorrow's browsers or thrive in the ever-changing world beyond the desktop. If these practices continue, costs and complexities will only escalate until just the largest companies can afford to build websites.

1.5
The home page of KPMG
(`www.kpmg.com`) as seen
in Navigator. Or rather,
as not seen in Navigator,
thanks to stupid, IE-only
code.

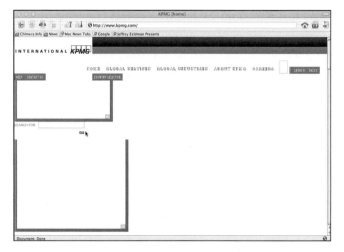

1.6
KPMG is equally useless
in Netscape 7. We guess
the company doesn't care
about those customers,
either.

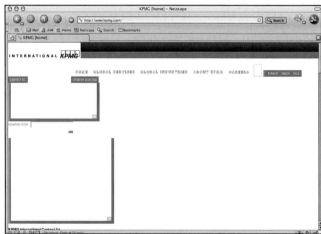

1.7
Well, if the site is for IE
only, let's try it in IE5
Macintosh Edition. Oops!
It doesn't work for those
users, either. (The site
works in IE5/Macintosh
about half the time and
fails the other half, for no
apparent reason.)

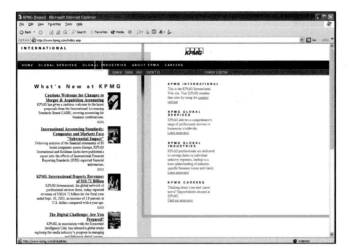

1.8
The same site as seen in IE6/Windows, where it finally deigns to work.

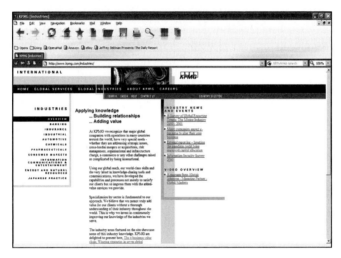

1.9
To be fair, the site kind of works in Opera 7 for Windows when Opera identifies itself as IE. (When Opera identifies itself as Opera, the site fails.)

In our efforts to deliver identical experiences across incompatible browsing environments—to make the web look like print and act like desktop software— we've lost sight of its true potential as a rich and multilayered medium accessible to all.

We lost it when designers and developers, scrambling to keep up with production demands during the short-lived Internet boom, learned nonstandard, browser-specific ways of creating sites, thus bringing us to our current pass whose name is obsolescence.

But the obsolescent period of web development is dying as you read these words, taking countless sites down with it. If you own, manage, design, or build websites, the bell tolls for you.

The Road to Stupidville

In early 1997, it was a common practice to write JavaScript for Netscape browsers and JScript (a JavaScript-like language) for Microsoft browsers. It was also common practice to use JavaScript (which worked only in Netscape) and ActiveX (which worked only in IE/Windows) to send each browser the code it needed. That's what we did for 3.0 browsers.

This practice didn't do a bit of good for "off-brand" browsers like Opera, and it didn't function correctly for users of Internet Explorer on the Macintosh platform, but it worked for "most" web users and quickly became the industry norm. If we wanted to create active web pages that did more than sit still and look pretty, we had no choice but to follow these procedures.

Late 1997 brought the 4.0 browsers from Netscape and Microsoft, each bragging of powerful "Dynamic HTML" (DHTML) capabilities that were, as you might have guessed, completely incompatible with each other. They were also incompatible with previous versions of themselves (what worked in Netscape 4 would not work in Netscape 3), not to mention being utterly incompatible with "off-brand" browsers that meekly supported basic specs like HTML instead of making up their own languages and attributes.

Was this any way to run an airline? Netscape and Microsoft thought so, and many designers and developers agreed. Those who disagreed had no choice but to grit their teeth and grind out the versions required to deliver an acceptably "professional" site.

How Do I Code Thee? Let Me Count the Ways.

There was DHTML for Netscape 4. There was incompatible DHTML for Internet Explorer 4, which pretty much only worked in Windows. There was non-DHTML JavaScript for Netscape 3 and non-DHTML Microsoft code for IE3. There might be additional code for off-brand and earlier browsers, or there might not be. In short, even the least interesting web page required more forks than a spaghetti restaurant.

Some developers limited themselves to two versions (one for IE4, and the other for Netscape 4) and demanded visitors get a 4.0 browser or get lost. Others, with smaller budgets, bet everything on one browser and generally lost that bet (if not their shirts).

The Web Standards Project, which launched shortly after the 4.0 browsers hit the market, estimated that the need to write four or more incompatible versions of every function added at least 25% to the cost of designing and developing any website—a cost typically borne by the client.

Some developers responded to this assessment with a self-satisfied shrug. The web was hot, hot, hot, and clients were willing to pay, pay, pay; so why should big web agencies worry about the high cost of multiple code and markup versions? Then the Internet bubble burst, web budgets shrank or froze, and agencies began downsizing or going under altogether. Suddenly, almost nobody could afford to fork over the cash for code forks.

While the industry was reeling from layoffs and closings, a new generation of browsers arrived that supported a common DOM—the one created by the W3C. What did this development mean? It meant versions were on the way out and a new era of standard-based design and development was finally at hand. And how did our economy-sobered industry respond to this long-desired news? By continuing to write code forks, developing for IE/Windows only, or switching to Macromedia Flash. For a business populated by visionaries, the web industry can be curiously myopic.

When Good Things Happen to Bad Markup

Early in a computer programmer's education, he or she learns the phrase "Garbage In, Garbage Out." Languages like C and Java don't merely encourage proper coding practice; they demand it.

Likewise, among the first things a graphic designer learns is that the quality of source materials determines the effectiveness of the end product. Start with a high-resolution, high-quality photograph, and the printed piece or web graphic will look good. Try to design with a low-quality snapshot or low-resolution web image, and the end result won't be worth viewing. You can turn a high-quality EPS into a suitably optimized web page logo, but you can't convert a low-resolution GIF into a high-quality web, print, or TV logo. Garbage in, garbage out.

But traditional mainstream browsers don't work the same way. Lax to the point of absurdity, they gobble up broken markup and bad links to JavaScript source files without a hiccup, in most cases displaying the site as if it were authored correctly. This laxity has encouraged front-end designers and developers to develop bad habits of which they are largely unaware. At the same time, it has persuaded middleware and backend developers to view technologies like XHTML, CSS, and JavaScript as contemptibly primitive.

Those who do not respect a tool are unlikely to use it correctly. Consider the following snippet, lifted from the costly e-commerce site of a company competing in a tough market, and reprinted here in all its warty glory:

```
<td width="100%"><ont face="verdana,helvetica,arial" size="+1"
color="#CCCC66"><span class="header"><b>Join now!</b></span>
</ont></td>
```

The nonsensical `<ont>` tag is a typo for the deprecated `<font>` tag—a typo that gets repeated thousands of times throughout the site, thanks to a highly efficient publishing tool. That error aside, this markup might look familiar to you. It might even resemble the markup on your site. In the context of this web page, all that's actually necessary is the following:

```
<h3>Join now!</h3>
```

Combined with an appropriate rule in a style sheet, the preceding simpler, more structural markup will do exactly what the cumbersome, nonstandard, invalid markup did, while saving server and visitor bandwidth and easing the transition to a more flexible site powered by XML-based markup. The same e-commerce site includes the following broken JavaScript link:

```
<script language=JavaScript1.1src=
"http://foo.com/Params.richmedia=yes&etc"></script>
```

Among other problems, the unquoted language attribute erroneously merges with the source tag. In other words, the browser is being told to use a nonexistent scripting language ("JavaScript1.1src").

By any rational measure, the site should fail, alerting the developers to their error and prompting them to fix it pronto. Yet until recently, the JavaScript on this site worked in mainstream browsers, thus perpetuating the cycle of badly authored sites and the browsers that love them. Little wonder that skilled coders often view front-end development as brain-dead voodoo unworthy of respect or care.

Junk Markup Might Be Hazardous to Your Site's Long-Term Health

But as newer browsers comply with web standards, they are becoming increasingly rigorous in what they expect from designers and developers, and thus increasingly intolerant of broken code and markup. Garbage in, garbage out is beginning to take hold in the world of browsers, making knowledge of web standards a necessity for anyone who designs or produces websites.

The damage is not irreparable. We can design and build websites a better way that works across numerous browsers, platforms, and devices, solving the problems of built-in obsolescence and user lockout while paving the way toward a far more powerful, more accessible, and more rationally developed web.

The cure to the disease of built-in obsolescence might be found in a core set of commonly supported technologies collectively referred to as "web standards." By learning to design and build with web standards, we can guarantee the forward compatibility of every site we produce.

"Write once, publish everywhere," the promise of web standards, is more than wishful thinking; it is being achieved today, using methods we'll explore in this book. Although today's leading browsers finally support these standards and methods, the message has not yet reached many working designers and developers, and new sites are still being built on the quicksand of nonstandard markup and code. This book hopes to change that.

The Cure

After a long struggle pitting designers and developers against the makers of leading browsers, we can finally employ techniques that guarantee the appearance and behavior of our sites, not simply in one manufacturer's browser, but in all of them.

Hammered out by the members of the World Wide Web Consortium (W3C) and other standards bodies and supported in current browsers developed by Netscape, Microsoft, Opera, and other companies, technologies like CSS, XHTML, ECMAScript (the standard version of JavaScript), and the W3C DOM enable designers to do the following:

- Attain more precise control over layout, placement, and typography in graphical desktop browsers while allowing users to modify the presentation to suit their needs.

- Develop sophisticated behaviors that work across multiple browsers and platforms.

- Comply with accessibility laws and guidelines without sacrificing beauty, performance, or sophistication.

- Redesign in hours instead of days or weeks, reducing costs and eliminating grunt work.

- Support multiple browsers without the hassle and expense of creating separate versions, and often with little or no code forking.

- Support nontraditional devices, from wireless gadgets and web-enabled cell phones fancied by teens and executives to Braille readers and screen readers used by those with disabilities—again without the hassle and expense of creating separate versions.

- Deliver sophisticated printed versions of any web page, often without creating separate "printer-friendly" page versions or relying on expensive proprietary publishing systems to create such versions.

- Separate style from structure and behavior, delivering creative layouts backed by rigorous document structure and facilitating the repurposing of web documents in advanced publishing workflows.

- Transition from HTML, the language of the web's past, to the more powerful XML-based markup of its future.

- Ensure that sites so designed and built will work correctly in today's standards-compliant browsers and perform acceptably in old browsers (even if they don't render pixel-for-pixel the same way in old browsers as they do in newer ones).

- Ensure that sites so designed will continue to work in tomorrow's browsers and devices, including devices not yet built or even imagined. This is the promise of forward compatibility.

- … and more, as this book will show.

Before we can learn how standards achieve these goals, we must examine the old-school methods they're intended to replace and find out exactly how the old techniques perpetuate the cycle of obsolescence. Chapter 2, "Designing and Building with Standards," reveals all.

chapter two

Designing and Building with Standards

How did designers and developers produce sites before web standards were created and before browsers supported them? Any which way they could. Consider Suck.com, one of the web's earliest and wittiest independent periodicals [2.1]. Suck possessed a sharp writing style and had the smarts to slap its daily content right on the front page, where readers couldn't miss it. It sounds obvious today, but in the mid-1990s, when Suck debuted, most sites buried their content behind splash pages, welcome pages, mission statements, and confusing "Table of Contents" pages.

Suck's straight-ahead emphasis on text felt refreshingly direct in an era when most commercial sites wrapped their content in overwrought, literal metaphors ("Step Up To Our Ticket Counter," "Enter the Web Goddess's Lair"). Likewise, Suck's spare, minimalist look and feel stood out at a time when many sites were over-designed exercises in metallic bevels and high-tech, Gothy glows, or non-designed messes flung together by systems administrators and self-taught HTML *auteurs*. Many sites at the time used every primitive device Netscape 1.1 offered the would-be layout artist, from the repeating background tile to the proprietary `<center>` tag, and some sites still revel in these techniques [2.2]. In a web where more was more, Suck stood out by daring to do less.

To achieve Suck's distinctively spare, content-focused appearance, co-creators Carl Steadman and Joey Anuff had to jump through hoops. HTML lacked design tools, and for good reason: As conceived by Tim Berners-Lee, the physicist who invented the web, HTML was a structured markup language (`http://www.w3.org/MarkUp/html-spec/`) derived from SGML, not a design language like Adobe's PostScript or the Cascading Style Sheets standard. (CSS had yet to be approved as a W3C recommendation, and once approved, it would take four long years before browsers supported the standard sufficiently close to spec.)

So how did Steadman and Anuff control their site's presentation? They did it with creativity, invention, and many rolls of digital duct tape.

2.1
Suck didn't. A decidedly bright site from the pioneering days of the commercial web (`www.suck.com`).

Jumping Through Hoops

To create the look of Suck, Steadman and Anuff wrote a Perl script that counted the characters in their text, inserting a `<p>` paragraph tag as a carriage return when a set number of characters had elapsed:

```
<p>One of the strange-but-truisms of
<p>minor peddling is that using the
<p>computer and other Fetish fodder
<p>somehow empowers children - plug
<p>in, log on, attend a good
<p>college on full scholarship, and
<p>get the hell out of the house.
```

The entire production was then wrapped in "typewriter" <tt> tags to force early graphical browsers (mainly Netscape 1.1) into styling the text in a monospace font like Courier or Monaco.

The result was rudimentary typographic control and a brute-force simulation of leading. Such HTML hacks offered the only way to achieve design effects in 1995. (The visual example shown in Figure 2.1 is from 1996, after a somewhat more graphic-intensive Suck redesign—still fairly minimalist. The original design is no longer available.)

Equally creative methods of forcing HTML to produce layout effects were widely practiced by web designers and were taught in early web design bibles by authors like Lynda Weinman and David Siegel. The creators of HTML clucked their tongues at this wholesale deformation of HTML, but designers had no choice as clients clamored for good-looking web presences.

Many designers still use methods like these in their daily work, and many books still teach these outdated—and in today's web, counterproductive—methods. One otherwise excellent web design book of 2002 straight-facedly advised its readers to control typography with font tags and "HTML scripts." Font tags have long been deprecated (W3C parlance for "please don't use this old junk") and HTML is not scriptable, but bad or nonsensical advice of this kind continues to appear in widely distributed web design tomes, thus perpetuating folly and ignorance.

The Cost of Design Before Standards

By creatively manipulating HTML, Suck had achieved a distinctive look, but at a double cost: The site excluded some readers and was tough for its creators to update.

In early Mom-and-Pop screen readers (audio browsers for the visually disabled), the voice that read Suck's text aloud would pause every few words in deference to the ceaseless barrage of paragraph tags, disrupting the flow of Suck's brilliantly argumentative editorials:

> One of the strange-but-truisms of ... [annoying pause]
>
> minor peddling is that using the ... [annoying pause]
>
> computer and other Fetish fodder ... [annoying pause]
>
> somehow empowers children—plug ... [annoying pause]

> in, log on, attend a good … [annoying pause]
>
> college on full scholarship, and … [annoying pause]
>
> get the hell out of the house.

Hard enough to parse under ideal conditions, Suck's convoluted sentence structures devolved into Zen incomprehensibility when interrupted by nonsemantic paragraph tags. These audio hiccups presented an insurmountable comprehension problem for screen reader users and made the site unusable to them.

If the HTML tricks that made the design work in graphical browsers thwarted an unknown number of readers, they also created a problem for Suck's authors each time they updated the site.

Because their design depended on Perl and HTML hacks, it was impossible to template. Hours of production work had to go into each of Suck's daily installments. As the site's popularity mushroomed, eventually leading to a corporate buyout, its creators were forced to hire not only additional writers but also a team of producers. The manual labor involved in Suck's production was inconsistent with the need to publish on a daily basis.

In a more perfect world, these difficulties would have been confined to the era in which they occurred. They would be anecdotes of early commercial web development. While admiring pioneering designers' ingenuity, we'd smile at the thought that development had ever been so screwy. But in spite of the emergence of standards, most commercial production still relies on bizarrely labor-intensive workarounds and hacks and continues to suffer from the problems these methods engender. The practice is so widespread that many designers and developers never even stop to think about it.

Modern Site, Ancient Ways

Leap from 1995 to 2001 and consider a contemporary website promoting The Gilmore Keyboard Festival (`www.thegilmore.com`) [**2.3**]. It's a pretty site, put together using labor-intensive table layout techniques that have long been industry norms.

2.3
The Gilmore Keyboard
Festival website
(www.thegilmore.com).
Lovely to look at, but
painful to update or
maintain.

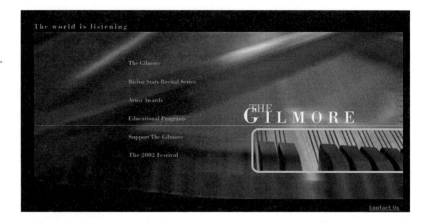

Aside from the fact that the Gilmore site makes assumptions about the size of the visitor's monitor and browser window, what's wrong with this picture? From the owner's point of view, the site hits a couple of sour notes:

- **Financial penalty of change**—If anything about the festival changes— for instance, if an additional Recital Series is added to this year's lineup— the site can't be updated via a simple text link. Nor can the web designers easily add additional links to the text GIF image map that serves as the site's navigational menu. The HTML table that combines the various image slices into an apparent whole [2.4] would burst apart if the size of any component image were to be altered.

  Thus, even the smallest changes to the site would incur a significant cost. The graphics would have to be redesigned, resliced, and reoptimized, and the table markup would have to be rewritten, along with associated image map markup and JavaScript code. When a task as basic as adding a link requires hours of work, you have to wonder if normative production methods have outlived their usefulness.

- **Exclusion of numerous potential visitors**—Less obvious, but no less important, the site as implemented is inaccessible to users of screen readers, text browsers, Palm Pilots, web-enabled cell phones, and those who use conventional browsers but turn off images. Such visitors will get absolutely nothing for their trouble, resulting in lost ticket sales or worse. Viewed in a nongraphical browsing environment [2.5], the page's total content reads as follows:

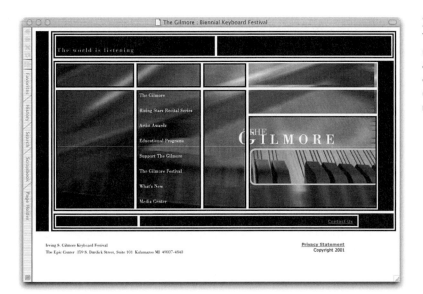

The same site, with CSS margins and borders added to reveal construction methods (and potential maintenance headaches).

[INLINE]

[INLINE] [INLINE]

[INLINE] [INLINE] [INLINE]

[INLINE] [USEMAP] [INLINE]

[INLINE]

Contact Us

[INLINE] Privacy Statement

Copyright 2001

Is "INLINE INLINE INLINE" the message The Gilmore's promoters hoped to convey? We doubt it. Is "INLINE INLINE INLINE" helpful to potential visitors? Clearly not.

Not every thwarted visitor takes this kind of frustration lying down. In theory, a disabled music lover might claim the site discriminated against him. We're not lawyers and don't mean to pick on this site, which was clearly created with the best of intentions.

2.5

In a nongraphical browser, The Gilmore provides no information, no text, no links, no nothin'. A free online Lynx emulator (www.delorie.com) was used to create this screen capture. To see how your web pages appear in a nongraphical environment, test them in Lynx, a Lynx emulator, or a screen reader like JAWS (or all three).

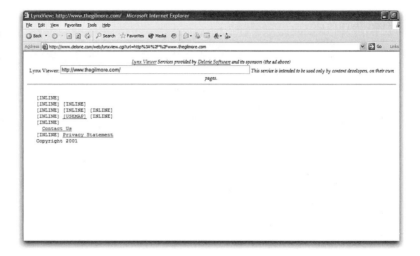

We're also not saying that images are bad or beauty is bad. To the contrary, images are vital, beauty is needed, and the creators of The Gilmore site have done a fine job of crafting an aesthetic online experience. That experience need not be inaccessible. This layout could look exactly as it does and be made accessible to all comers. But it hasn't been (yet).

Although unusually pretty, The Gilmore is quite typical in its design and construction methods. And the problems the site faces because of those methods are also typical. Most of us find that our carefully constructed table layouts break when the client wishes to make changes, as all clients do all the time. We either bill the client or eat the cost.

When budget limitations are severe—for instance, during an economic downturn—the client might request quick and dirty solutions that destroy the elegance and clarity of the existing presentation.

For instance, adding three raw hypertext links to the top or bottom of The Gilmore site would enable visitors to access newly created site sections, but it would also cause confusion. (Why, the visitor would wonder, are these links separated from the others? Are they more important than other links on the page? Less important?)

The addition of such links would also undo the site's carefully controlled aesthetic effects, diminishing the brand's image as a serious arts festival and thus lessening the site's value as a marketing tool.

Like the creators of The Gilmore website, many of us find that our old-school layouts don't travel well. They might look fine in the most popular browsers under "average" conditions and with "normal" preference settings. But beyond those normative conditions, our sites might cease to communicate. At the very least, such inaccessibility cuts off potential customers.

The Gilmore's owners and designers are not unique. They're following long-established industry norms. The problems these norms generate are the same problems faced by most websites today. They're the problems faced by any site crafted to the quirks of a few popular visual browsers instead of being designed to facilitate universal access via web standards. They are also the problems of any site that yokes presentation to structure by forcing HTML to deliver layouts.

Fortunately, there's another way to design and build websites—a way that solves the problems created by old-school methods without sacrificing the aesthetic and branding benefits the old methods deliver: web standards.

The Trinity of Web Standards

Figure 2.6 indicates how web standards solve the problems we've been discussing by breaking any web page into three separate components: structure, presentation, and behavior.

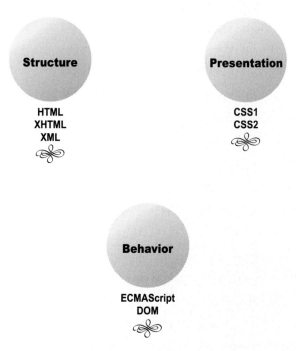

2.6
Structure, presentation, and behavior: the three components of any web page in the world of web standards.

Structure

A *markup language* (XHTML: `http://www.w3.org/TR/xhtml1`) contains text data formatted according to its structural meaning: headline, secondary headline, paragraph, numbered list, definition list, and so on.

On the web, this text would likely be part of a definition list `<dl>`. The subhead, "Structure," would be marked up as a definition title `<dt>`. The paragraph you're now reading would be wrapped in definition data `<dd>` tags:

```
<dl>
   <dt>
      Structure
   </dt>
   <dd>
   A <em>markup language</em> (<a href=http://www.w3.org/TR/
   xhtml1>XHTML</a>) contains text data formatted according
   to its structural meaning: headline, secondary headline,
   paragraph, numbered list, definition list, and so on.
   </dd>
   <dd>
   On the web, this text would likely be part of a definition
   list. The subhead, "Structure," would be marked up as a
   definition title. The paragraph you&#8217;re now reading
   would be wrapped in definition data tags.
   </dd>
</dl>
```

Alternately, the two paragraphs might be children of a single `<dd>` element:

```
<dl>Structure</dl>
<dd>
   <p>A <em>markup language</em> (<a href=http://www.w3.org/
   TR/xhtml1>XHTML</a>) contains text data formatted according
   to its structural meaning: headline, secondary headline,
   paragraph, numbered list, definition list, and so on.</p>
   <p>On the web, this text would likely be part of a
   definition list. The subhead, "Structure," would be marked
   up as a definition title. The paragraph you&#8217;re now
   reading would be wrapped in definition data tags.</p>
   </dd>
```

> ## The 411 on ’
>
> If you're one of the five people who will actually take the time to read the text in the XHTML examples, you might wonder what ’ means. Quite simply, it is the standard Unicode escaped character sequence for the typographically correct apostrophe. See Chapter 5, "Modern Markup," for more.

XML (`http://www.w3.org/TR/2000/REC-xml-20001006`), the extensible markup language, provides considerably more options than this, but for now we'll limit ourselves to XHTML, a transitional markup language and current W3C recommendation that works just like HTML in nearly every browser or Internet device.

When authored correctly (containing no errors, and no illegal tags or attributes), XHTML markup is completely portable. It works in web browsers, screen readers, text browsers, wireless devices—you name it.

The markup can also contain additional structures deemed necessary by the designer. For instance, content and navigation might be marked as such and wrapped in appropriately labeled tags:

```
<div id="content">[Your content here.]</div>
<div id="navigation">[Your navigational menu here.]</div>
```

The markup also contains embedded objects such as images, Flash presentations, or QuickTime movies, along with tags and attributes that present text equivalents for those who cannot view these objects in their browsing environment.

Presentation

Presentation languages (CSS1: `http://www.w3.org/TR/REC-CSS1`; CSS2: `http://www.w3.org/TR/REC-CSS2`) format the web page, controlling typography, placement, color, and so on.

In many cases, CSS can take the place of old-school HTML table layouts. In all cases, it replaces nonstandard font tags and bandwidth-wasting, outdated junk like this:

```
<td bgcolor="#FFCC00" align="left"
valign="top"><br><br><br> </td>
```

Such junk might be replaced by an unadorned table cell, by a table cell with a class attribute, or by nothing at all.

Because presentation is separated from structure, it is possible to change one without negatively affecting the other. For instance, you can apply the same layout to numerous pages or make changes to text and links without breaking the layout. You or your clients are free to change the XHTML at any time without fear of breaking the layout because the text is just text; it does not serve double duty as a design language.

Likewise, you can change the layout without touching the markup. Have readers complained that your site's typeface is too small? Change a rule in the global style sheet, and the entire site will reflect these changes instantly. Need a printer-friendly version? Write a print style sheet, and your pages will print beautifully, regardless of how they appear on the PC web browser screen. (We'll explain how these things work in Part II, "Designing and Building.")

Behavior

A standard object model (the W3C DOM at `http://www.w3.org/DOM/DOMTR#dom1`) works with CSS, XHTML, and ECMAScript 262 (`http://www.ecma.ch/ecma1/STAND/ECMA-262.HTM`), the standard version of JavaScript, enabling you to create sophisticated behaviors and effects that work across multiple platforms and browsers. No more Netscape-only JavaScript. No more IE/Windows-only ActiveX and JScript (as described in Chapter 1, "99.9% of Websites Are Obsolete").

Depending on the site's goals and audience, designers and developers can seize all the power of web standards by fully separating structure from presentation and behavior. Or they might choose to create *transitional* sites combining old and new—for instance, blending simple XHTML table layouts with CSS control of typography, margins, leading, and colors.

Into Action

If Suck were alive and well today, web standards like XHTML and CSS would allow the staff to concentrate on writing. A basic XHTML template would deliver the document structure. CSS would control the look and feel without requiring additional design work per-issue, aside from the preparation of article-specific images. Paragraph tags would be properly used to denote the beginnings and ends of paragraphs, not to force vertical gaps between each line of text. (CSS would do that job.)

In graphical browsers like IE, Mozilla/Netscape, and Opera, style sheets would ensure that Suck looked as its designer intended. Structured XHTML would deliver Suck's content not only to these browsers but also to personal digital assistants (PDAs), screen readers, and text browsers without the accompanying nonstructural hiccups of fake paragraphs and similar hostages to markup-as-a-design-tool.

As a content-focused site, Suck.com would make a prime candidate for a strict XHTML/CSS makeover in which substance and style would be delivered via the appropriate technology: CSS for layout and XHTML for structured content. But Suck could also benefit from a transitional approach: simple XHTML tables for the positioning of primary content areas and CSS for the rest.

The creators of The Gilmore site could not benefit from templating—at least, not on the site's front page as it is currently designed. But they could deliver their existing layout with CSS, conserving bandwidth while enabling the design team to change one section of the page without reworking the entire layout.

The Gilmore could use the CSS background property to position its primary image as a single JPEG file instead of a dozen image slices [2.4] and could easily overlay one or more menu graphics using any of several time-tested CSS positioning methods, including some that work in 4.0 browsers whose support for CSS is incomplete.

The creators of The Gilmore could also use valid XHTML and accessibility attributes including alt, title, and longdesc to ensure that the site's content would be accessible to all instead of meaningless to many [2.5]. Less graphic-intensive inner site pages could be delivered via transitional (CSS plus tables) or stricter (pure CSS) methods.

Benefits of Transitional Methods

Transitional methods that comply with XHTML and CSS would be a vast improvement over what we have today and would solve the problems discussed so far. With transitional techniques—CSS for typography, color, margins, and so on and XHTML tables for basic layout—you increase usability, accessibility, interoperability, and long-term viability, albeit at the cost of more work and expense (and in most cases, more bandwidth) than a nontable, pure-CSS approach.

Happy Cog (www.happycog.com), my web agency's business site, is a transitional one [**2.7, 2.8, 2.9**]. It combines XHTML table layout techniques with CSS1 and CSS2 and simple DOM-based scripting. The site complies with the XHTML 1.0 Transitional and CSS standards, and it's compatible with the accessibility requirements of Section 508 and WAI Priority 1 Guidelines (more about those guidelines in Part II).

By complying with XHTML, CSS, and Section 508, the Happy Cog site ensures its long-term viability as browsers and standards evolve. By using some old-school methods (chiefly table layouts), it manages to look good in new browsers [**2.7**] and reasonably presentable in Browser-Wars-era user agents like Netscape 4 [**2.8**], whose support for CSS is pitifully incomplete. (User agent sounds like something from a James Bond movie, but it's actually W3C parlance for browsers and other Internet devices.) At the same time, Happy Cog's use of simple structural markup and accessibility techniques allows its content to reach nongraphical browsers [**2.9**], screen readers, and emerging wireless devices.

The transitional strategy employed by Happy Cog provides forward and backward compatibility and is an entirely appropriate tactic for many sites today. But to reap the greatest benefits of designing and building with web standards takes a fundamental change in thinking and methodology.

The goal of streamlining production, preserving the integrity and portability of content, and delivering the appropriate level of design to differently enabled user agents is not only the way things *should* work, but it's also the way they *can* and *do* work today—when you design and build with standards.

The ability to separate structure from presentation and behavior is the corner-stone of this new design approach. It is the way all sites will be designed in the future (unless they are Flash-only sites), and it is already being used on hard-core, forward-compatible sites, such as the ones we're about to examine.

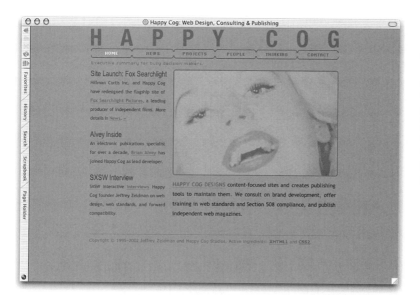

2.7
Happy Cog, this author's business site (www.happycog.com), is an exercise in *transitional* forward compatibility, combining streamlined XHTML table layouts with CSS and the DOM. When viewed in a modern browser, its proper presentation is fully revealed.

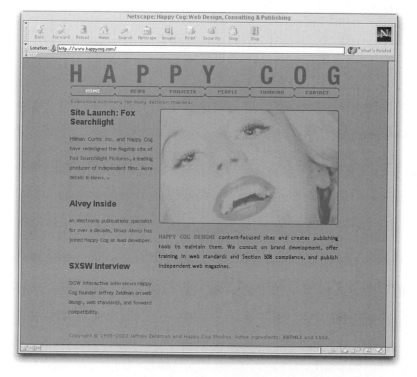

2.8
Opened in an old browser (Netscape 4) whose support for CSS is iffy at best, most of Happy Cog's presentation comes through intact. Several subtleties of the design are lost, but we don't mind and neither will most Netscape 4 users, who are accustomed to a certain lack of polish on most sites they visit.

2.9
Happy Cog once again—
this time as viewed in
Lynx, a text-only browser.
As it should be, the site's
content is fully accessible
when separated from
the visual presentation.
Compare and contrast
with Figure 2.5, where
none of The Gilmore
site's content is accessible
beyond the graphical
desktop browser. Happy
Cog is no smarter or
better intended than The
Gilmore; we're just using
standards to ensure that
our site is accessible, and
The Gilmore isn't doing
so (yet).

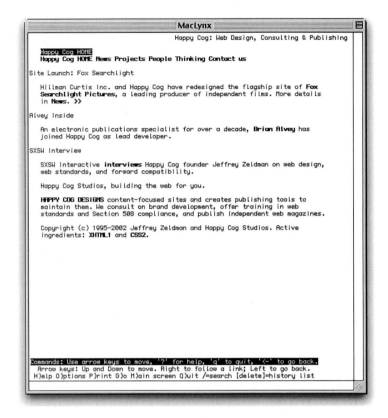

The Web Standards Project: Portability in Action

The Web Standards Project (WaSP) [2.10] launched in 1998 to persuade
Netscape, Microsoft, and other browser makers to thoroughly support the
standards discussed in this book. It took time, persistence, and strategy (a.k.a.
yelling, whining, and pleading), but eventually browser makers bought into
The WaSP's view that interoperability via common standards was an absolute
necessity if the web was to move forward.

Lip Service

One of the ironies of the struggle for standards compliance in browsers
was that Netscape and Microsoft are W3C members who have contributed
significantly to the creation of web standards, yet had to be bullied into fully
supporting the very technologies they helped to create. Go figure.

After browsers finally began meaningfully supporting standards (see Chapter 3, "The Trouble with Standards"), The Web Standards Project relaunched in 2002 to encourage designers and developers to learn about and harness the power of these hard-won technologies. To denote the enlargement of the group's mission from bully pulpit to educational resource, the site was rewritten and redesigned.

As expected, the site looks nice in standards-compliant browsers [2.10]. It also looks acceptable in older, less-compliant browsers [2.11]. But the site transcends the PC-based browsing space without requiring additional or alternative markup, code, or device detection. (Look, Ma, no versions!)

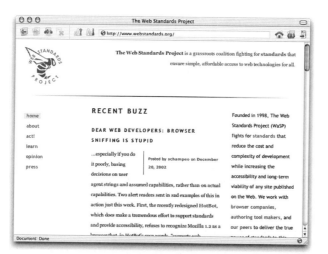

2.10
The Web Standards Project's home page as seen in Chimera, a Gecko-based browser for Mac OS X (www.webstandards.org). Its CSS layout looks the same in all modern, standards-compliant browsers. But wait, there's more!

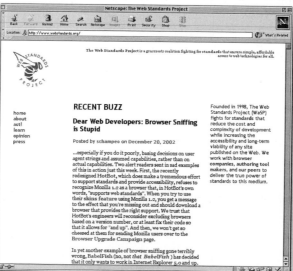

2.11
The same site looks decent and works acceptably in Netscape 4, our poster child for non-standards-compliance. A special "Netscape 4 version" was not needed.

2.12

(left) The same site on a different day, as seen in a Palm Pilot. Look, Ma, no WAP! Screenshot courtesy of Porter Glendinning (www.serve.com/apg/).

2.13

(right) The same site as seen in Microsoft's PocketPC. Screenshot courtesy of Anil Dash (www.dashes.com/anil/).

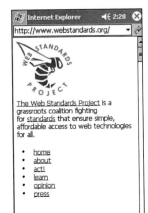

2.14

Webstandards.org again, this time as viewed in Apple's long-discontinued Newton handheld. Screenshot courtesy of Grant Hutchinson (www.splorp.com).

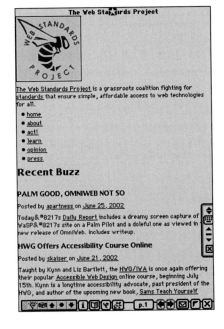

One Document Serves All

The Web Standards Project is built with XHTML 1.0 Strict. CSS is used for layout. There is no Palm version or WAP version. Multiple versions are not needed; when you design and build with standards, one document serves all.

Figure **2.12** shows `webstandards.org` as seen in a Palm Pilot. Figure **2.13** shows how it looks in Microsoft's PocketPC. Most uncannily of all, Figure **2.14** shows the site working just as fine as you please on a Newton handheld, Apple's long-discontinued predecessor to the Palm Pilot. Grant Hutchinson, who captured the Newton screenshot, told us: "There's nothing like viewing a modern site using a piecemeal browser on a vintage operating system."

That should be music to the ears of any designer or site owner who wants to reach the greatest number of visitors with the least effort. Strict compliance with XHTML and intelligent use of CSS frees designers and developers from the need to create multiple versions.

Notice in Figures **2.12** through **2.14** that the DHTML menu that shows up on the left side of the screen in a desktop web browser turns into an ordinary bulleted list at the top of a Palm, PocketPC, or Newton display. How is that magic accomplished? Simple. The DHTML menu actually *is* a bulleted (unordered) list. CSS alters its appearance in compliant desktop browsers. The menu changes from page to page via ordinary Server Side Includes (SSI).

A List Apart: One Page, Many Views

A List Apart (`www.alistapart.com`), this author's online magazine "for people who make websites," converted to CSS-only layout in February 2001. The design [**2.15**] was adapted from the site's branded "HTML Minimalist" look and feel, which had previously been accomplished via HTML tables.

A Source of Inspiration

All style sheets used on A List Apart (and at zeldman.com, for that matter) are open source, free for your use and adaptation when creating your own sites. To find a site's style sheets, select View Source in your browser, make a note of the CSS file locations referenced in the `<head>` of the document, and then cut and paste that file location into your browser's address bar. For instance, if the XHTML in the `<head>` of the document reads like this:

```
<style type="text/css" media="all">
@import "/styles/basic.css ";
</style>
```

  or

```
<link rel="StyleSheet"
href="/styles/basic.css"
type="text/css" media="screen" />
```

you'll type `http://www.domain.com/ styles/basic.css` into your browser's address bar. Most browsers will display the style sheet as ordinary text that you can cut and paste into your HTML editor or download to your hard drive.

To save time, you might prefer to visit `www.favelets.com` and install the View CSS Style Sheets bookmarklet into your browser's toolbar. You can then immediately load any site's style sheets into new browser windows with one click.

I created the ALA CSS redesign in collaboration with Todd Fahrner and Tantek Çelik, both of whom participate in the W3C's CSS working groups. Fahrner is a CSS expert and a steering committee member of The Web Standards Project. Çelik is a browser engineer employed by Microsoft, the creator of Favelets, and the whiz behind the Tasman rendering engine that drives the IE5+ Macintosh edition. (See "Modern Browsers: The Good, the Bad, and the Ugly," in this book's Back End section for details on rendering engines and standards compliance.)

ALA readers who dislike the site's default text treatment can switch to a larger, more legible typeface via a style sheet switcher developed by Paul Sowden. ALA Issue No. 126 (`www.alistapart.com/issues/126/`) explains how the switcher works and provides open source code you can use and adapt to create style sheet switchers for your websites. (See Chapter 15, "Working with DOM-Based Scripts," and Chapter 16, "A CSS Redesign," for more information.)

Figure **2.15** shows A List Apart as it looks in CSS-compliant browsers like IE5+, Mozilla, Netscape 6+, and Opera 5+. In other environments, the site takes on a completely different appearance.

Figure **2.16** shows the same site when viewed in a non-CSS-compliant browser—in this case, Netscape Navigator 4. The site is still perfectly legible and usable.

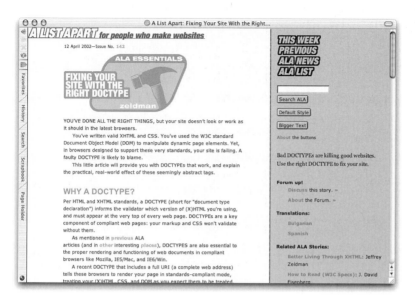

2.15
A List Apart, the author's online magazine for web designers, as seen in a CSS-compliant browser (`www.alistapart.com`). ALA switched to CSS-only layout in February, 2001. Hundreds of other sites soon followed suit.

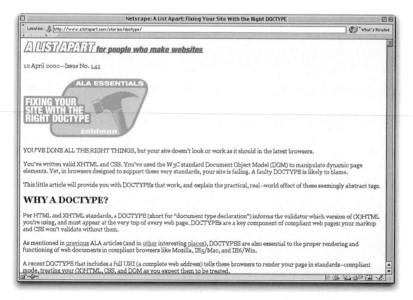

2.16
The same site as seen in a 4.0 browser. No CSS layout, no problem. The site is still readable and usable.

Indeed, some readers might prefer it this way; immediately following our CSS redesign, Netscape 4 usage by ALA visitors temporarily *increased*. It seems these visitors preferred a plain page their browser could handle to the previous layout whose gymnastics only underscored Netscape 4's weaknesses. Those who hold that standards hurt users of old browsers might consider this story an indicator of just the opposite: When properly used, standards help everyone.

In Figure **2.16**, you'll notice that the navigational sidebar seems to have disappeared. Actually, it has simply moved to the bottom of the page. The text appears in the face and size dictated by the user's preferences. No browser detection is used to deliver this simplified format. Instead, the style sheet that controls the site's onscreen appearance is linked in such a way that noncompliant browsers ignore it. (We'll explain how that works in Part II, "Designing and Building.")

No tables or other nonstructural junk get in the way of the content. The only "design" concession used in the markup is a background color attribute applied to the <body> tag so that the header graphics will match the rest of the page in non-CSS browsers.

Design Beyond the Screen

Last but not least, Figure **2.17** shows what an A List Apart article looks like when printed. As you can see, the sidebar has been removed, fonts and colors have been optimized for printing, and the URL of every link is usefully displayed, whether said URL appears on the screen version or not.

This magic is accomplished via a separate print style sheet designed by Eric Meyer, working from an earlier print style sheet developed by Todd Fahrner and this book's author. Meyer is a CSS expert and the author of *Eric Meyer on CSS* (New Riders, 2002). His ALA article, "Going to Print" (www.alistapart.com/ stories/goingtoprint/), explains the rationale and techniques for creating a print style sheet, and we'll be discussing similar techniques in Part II of this book.

The important concept to grasp for now is that with a single, lightweight document—a print style sheet—A List Apart no longer needs to produce separate, "printer-friendly" versions. In all probability, neither will your sites. A possible exception: Sites that use multipage article formats, like www.wired.com or the O'Reilly Network (www.oreilly.com), will still require a printer-friendly page simply to stitch the whole story together into a single document. But they, too, can still benefit from using a print style sheet, obviously, because the output of that stitched-together page can use a print style sheet.

Let's review the benefits reaped by the two sites we've just looked at.

2.17
From web to print: ALA articles become printer friendly on-the-fly, thanks to print style sheets.

Time and Cost Savings, Increased Reach

If designing and building with standards means you no longer need to create multiple versions of every site, it's easy to see that time and cost savings can be enormous:

- No more Netscape-only versions
- No more IE-only versions
- No more "basic" versions for old browsers
- In many cases, no more WAP or WML versions

- In many cases, no more printer-friendly versions
- No more browser and platform sniffing, and no more straining of the server to fetch various browser or device-optimized components

Much as they might want to accommodate users of wireless and other nontraditional devices, many organizations simply cannot afford to build separate wireless or plain-text versions. Thanks to the XHTML and CSS standards, they don't have to. Without lifting a finger, these organizations will still reach new readers and customers, whose numbers are legion.

Strict standards compliance also provides a huge head start on solving the accessibility problem. If your site works in a Palm Pilot, it most likely works in a screen reader like Jaws, although, of course, you need to test to be sure, and you might need to do a bit more work to be truly accessible. We'll discuss accessibility and Section 508 in Chapter 14, "Accessibility Basics," and in other sections of Part II.

Where We Go from Here

Markup languages based on XML (see Chapter 4, "XML Conquers the World [And Other Web Standards Success Stories]") will make today's web look like kindergarten. But we can't get to tomorrow's web by following yesterday's design and development norms.

There are two ways forward: transitional forward compatibility (a savory blend of traditional and standards-based techniques) and strict forward compatibility based on complete (or near-complete) separation of structure, presentation, and behavior.

Transitional forward compatibility accepts the reality of today's mixed browsing environment. It's well suited to projects where branding is a priority and noncompliant browsers make up a significant portion of your audience. Strict forward compatibility, as its name implies, hews closer to the spirit of standards, is the most forward-compatible approach, and provides the greatest benefits when used in appropriate contexts. Let's look more closely at what these approaches entail.

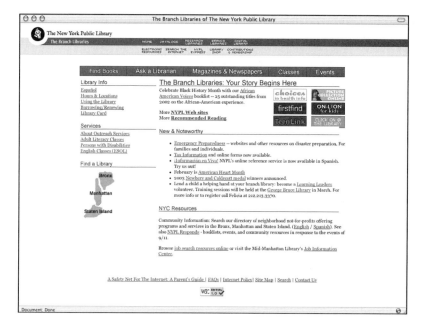

2.18
The New York
Public Library
(www.nypl.org/branch/)
takes a transitional approach
to web standards: valid
XHTML with light use of
tables for layout, WAI Priority
1 accessibility, and CSS for
typography, margins, and
colors. Both forward and
backward compatible, transitional forward compatibility
is an easy standards conversion and an appropriate
one for many organizations.

Transitional Forward Compatibility

Ingredients

- Valid XHTML for markup. (HTML 4.01 can also be used.)

- Valid CSS for control of typography, color, margins, and so on.

- Light use of XHTML tables for layouts, avoiding deep nesting by letting
  CSS do some of the work.

- Optionally: Structural labels applied to significant table cells (facilitates
  CSS and scripting and helps with next year's transition to table-less
  CSS layout).

- DOM-based JavaScript/ECMAScript, possibly with code forking to
  accommodate 4.0 versions of IE and Navigator.

- Accessibility attributes and testing.

Recommended for

Transitional forward compatibility is recommended for sites visited by a
high percentage of 4.0 and older browsers that simply aren't up to the job of
adequately supporting CSS, let alone the DOM. Also recommended for those
occasions in which tables do a better job of layout delivery than CSS. The
transitional approach is used by the branch libraries of The New York Public

Library [2.18] to accommodate a huge installed base of Netscape 4 users while still complying with the XHTML and CSS standards, with an eye toward accessibility and long-term viability.

Benefits

- Rational backward compatibility: Sites can be made to look reasonably good even in crummy old browsers. They will always look better in newer, more compliant browsers, and that's okay. (One might argue it is even more than okay because it subtly encourages holdouts to get with the times.)

- Forward compatibility: Sites will continue to work in future browsers and devices.

- Begins paving the way for your eventual transition to XML-based markup and pure CSS layout.

- Fewer maintenance problems in today's browsers as junk markup and proprietary code are removed.

- Increased accessibility; decreased accessibility-related problems with their attendant loss of customers and risk of litigation.

- Partially restores document structure to documents. (We say "partially" because markup still includes some design structures.)

- Begins restoring elegance, clarity, and simplicity to markup, with consequent reduction in file sizes, resulting in less wasted bandwidth and lower delivery, production, and maintenance costs.

Downside

- Structure and presentation are still yoked together, making it harder and more costly to update/maintain sites.

- For the same reason (the yoking together of structure and presentation), it will be harder and more costly to roll sites so designed into future, XML-based content-management systems. This is unlikely to be a problem for small, designy sites (brochure sites), but it might be more of a sticking point for large-scale content and commerce sites containing hundreds or thousands of dynamically generated pages.

Strict Forward Compatibility

Ingredients

- Full separation of structure from presentation and behavior.

- Valid CSS used for layout. Tables used only for their original purpose: the presentation of tabular data such as that found in spreadsheets, address books, stock quotes, event listings, and so on.

- Valid XHTML 1.0 Strict or Transitional used for markup.

- Emphasis on structure. No presentational hacks in markup (Strict) or as few as possible presentational hacks in markup (Transitional).

- Structural labeling/abstraction of design elements. ("Menu" rather than "Green Box.")

- DOM-based scripting for behavior. Limited code forking only if and when necessary.

- Accessibility attributes and testing.

Recommended for

Strict forward compatibility is recommended for any site that is not visited by a high percentage of noncompliant (typically 4.0 and earlier) browsers. Strict allows noncompliant browsers to access content, but it's usually less successful in delivering branding and behavior to those old browsers.

Benefits

- Forward compatibility: Increased interoperability in existing and future browsers and devices (including wireless devices).

- Stronger transition toward more advanced forms of XML-based markup.

- Reaches more users with less work.

- No versioning.

- Fewer (if any) accessibility problems. The content of sites so designed is generally accessible to all.

- Restores elegance, simplicity, and logic to markup.

- Restores document structure to documents.

- Faster, easier, less expensive production and maintenance. Because sites cost less to produce and maintain, low budgets can avoid strain, while higher budgets (if available) can be put into writing, design, programming, art, photography, editing, and usability testing.

- Easier to incorporate into dynamic publishing and template-driven, content-management systems.

- CSS layout makes possible some designs that cannot be achieved with HTML tables.

- Sites will continue to work in future browsers and devices.

Downside

- Sites are likely to look quite plain in old browsers.

- Browser support for CSS is imperfect. Some workarounds might be required.

- Some techniques that are easy to achieve with HTML tables are hard (or impossible) to pull off using CSS layout. Some designs might need to be rethought.

- Some otherwise compliant browsers (Opera prior to Version 7, for instance) might choke on DOM-based behaviors.

- DOM-based behaviors will not work in 4.0 and earlier mainstream browsers or in screen readers, text browsers, and most wireless devices. You'll need to use <noscript> tags and CGI to deliver alternative functionality to these browsers and devices.

Part II explains how standards work (individually and collectively) and offers tips and strategies to solve design and business problems related to various types of web development. But before we delve in, let's pause to consider some questions that might already have occurred to you.

If standards increase interoperability, enhance accessibility, streamline production and maintenance, reduce wasted bandwidth, and lower costs, why aren't all designers and developers using web standards correctly and consistently on every site they create?

Why aren't all clients clamoring for standards compliance the way inmates in old prison movies rattle tin cans against the bars of their cells? Why was it even necessary for us to write a book like this and for you to read it, let alone beg your clients, colleagues, bosses, and vendors to read it? Why aren't web standards more widely understood and used?

By a strange coincidence, our next chapter addresses that very question.

chapter three

The Trouble with Standards

Web standards hold the key to accessible, cost-effective web design and development, but you wouldn't know it from surveying significant commercial and creative sites of the past few years. In this chapter, we'll explore some of the reasons why web standards have not yet been incorporated into the normative practice of all design shops and in-house web divisions and are not yet obligatory components of every site plan or request for proposal.

If you would prefer to read web standards success stories, turn to Chapter 4, "XML Conquers the World (And Other Web Standards Success Stories." If you're sold on standards and are ready to roll up your sleeves, skip ahead to Chapter 5, "Modern Markup." But if you need help selling standards to your colleagues—or if you simply want to understand how an industry can attain standards without using them—this chapter is for you.

Lovely to Look At, Repulsive to Code

In mid-2002, with six others from the new media community, I served on the judging committee of the Eighth Annual Communication Arts Interactive Awards (www.commarts.com), arguably the most prestigious design competition in the industry. The sites and projects submitted in competition were among the year's most skillfully developed and designed.

We judges initially spent 10 weeks reviewing thousands of websites and CD-ROMs, narrowing the field to hundreds of finalists from which fewer than 50 would be selected as winners. The final judging took place in the Bay Area, where the seven of us were sequestered for a week. Until winners were chosen, we could not leave. At week's end, we had chosen 47 winning projects and had thereby been released from bondage.

To celebrate the end of the judging (and with it, my newfound freedom), I met a San Francisco friend for dinner. The competition intrigued my pal, who knew a little something about web development himself.

My friend asked, "Did you take off points if the sites were not standards-compliant?"

I blinked. "None of them were standards-compliant," I said.

It was a fact. Of thousands of submitted sites, not one had been authored in valid, structural HTML. Many of these sites were visually arresting [3.1] and skillfully programmed [3.2]; several offered compelling, well-written content; and a few were startlingly original. But not one had a clue about valid structural markup, compact CSS, or standards-based scripting.

More than half the submitted sites had been developed entirely in Flash. Most of the rest worked only in 4.0 browsers, only in IE4, or only in Netscape 4. A few worked only in Windows. Of the hundreds of finalists, most of them lavishly (and expensively) produced, and each of them in its own way representing the industry's best professional efforts, not one had the slightest use for web standards.

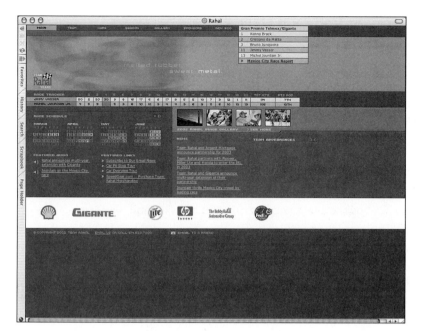

3.1
Team Rahal, Inc.
(`www.rahal.com`), one of
the winners of the Eighth
Annual Communication
Arts Festival, is beautiful,
impressive, and
nonstandards-compliant.

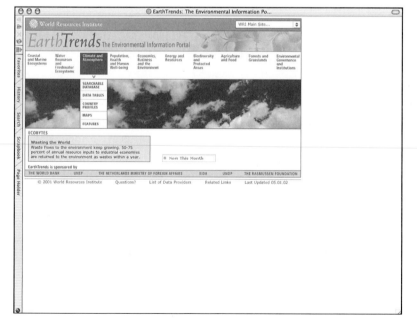

3.2
World Resources
Institute (`http://
earthtrends.wri.org/`),
another visually striking
competition winner, is
cleverly programmed;
but it, too, makes little use
of web standards.

Common Goals, Common Means

The websites submitted to Communication Arts were wildly diverse in their creative and marketing objectives, but most shared certain underlying goals—the same goals as your sites and mine. We all want our sites to attract their targeted audience, encourage participation, be easy to understand and use, and say all the right things about our organization, product, or service, not only in words, but also in the way the site looks and works.

Most of us would like to get the best value for the money in our budgets. We want our sites to work for as many people and in as many environments as possible. We hope to avoid bogging down in browser and platform incompatibilities and to stay at least one jump ahead of the swinging scythe of technological change.

Most of us hope to create a site that will work well into the future without continual, costly technological tinkering as described in Chapter 2, "Designing and Building with Standards." We would rather spend our limited time updating content and adding services than recoding our sites every time a new browser or device comes along.

Standards are the key to achieving these goals. So why haven't they taken the development community by storm?

Perception Versus Reality

For one thing, as with accessibility (see Chapter 14, "Accessibility Basics"), many designers hold the mistaken belief that web standards are somehow hostile or antithetical to the needs of good graphic design. For another, those who create standards are not in the business of *selling* them; the visually and architecturally pedestrian sites of W3C or ECMA [**3.3**] hold little inspirational appeal for graphic stylists and consumer-oriented designers. And the unprofessional appearance of W3C or ECMA does little to combat the myth that standards are antithetical to visual design. Only beautifully designed sites that use standards [**3.4**] can overturn that false perception.

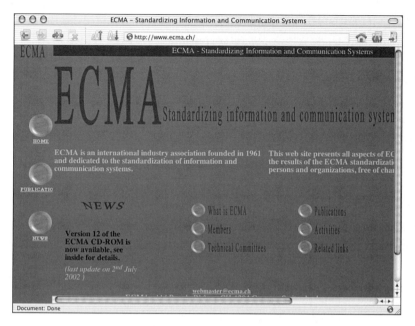

3.3

ECMA (European Computer Manufacturers Association) is a bona fide standards body and home to many great minds. Unfortunately, none of those great minds possess even the barest competence in consumer-friendly writing, graphic design, or site architecture. Thus, the ECMA site (`www.ecma.ch`) is unlikely to inspire designers to learn about ECMAScript or other standards. (Contrast it with Figures 3.1 and 3.2, which represent the kind of appearance that inspires visual designers. You'll read more about ECMA later in this chapter.)

3.4

Kaliber 10000 (K10k), an avidly read design portal (`www.k10k.net`), is constructed with valid XHTML, CSS, and the W3C Document Object Model (DOM). Although not the first to embrace these standards, K10k's use of them is important, for it shows the design community that standards can support good graphic design.

Then, too, designers and developers who've taken the time to learn the Heinz 57 varieties of proprietary scripting and authoring might see little reason to learn anything new—or might be too busy learning JSP, ASP, or .NET to even think about changing their fundamental front-end techniques. Those who depend on WYSIWYG editors to do their heavy lifting have a different reason for not using standards. Namely, they depend on WYSIWYG editors; therefore, they're likely unaware that leading WYSIWYG editors now support standards. Many highly skilled developers use WYSIWYG tools like Dreamweaver and GoLive, of course, but so do many semi-skilled workers who would be powerless to create even a basic web page if denied access to said tools.

Finally, it is only relatively recently that mainstream browsers have offered meaningful standards compliance. Many web professionals are so used to doing things the hard way that they haven't noticed that browsers have changed. Let's examine this last reason first.

2000: The Year That Browsers Came of Age

With the release in March 2000 of IE5 Macintosh Edition, the world (or at least that portion of the world that uses Macs) finally got more than a teasing taste of web standards. IE5/Mac supported XHTML, ECMAScript, nearly all of the CSS1 specification, much of CSS2, and most of the DOM. IE5/Mac was also able to display raw XML, although it's not clear why anyone would want to do so. (See Chapter 5 for more about this, or visit Bugzilla at `http://bugzilla.mozilla.org/show_bug.cgi?id=64945` to see some of the approaches that *uber*-geeks have taken to the problem of displaying raw XML in browsers.)

IE5/Mac: Switching and Zooming

IE5/Mac was so attuned to standards that it varied its display and performance according to the `<!DOCTYPE>` listed at the top of a web page's markup—a technique called *DOCTYPE switching*, to be discussed in greater detail in Chapter 11, "Working with Browsers Part I: DOCTYPE Switching and Standards Mode." Put simply, with the right DOCTYPE, a page would display and function as web standards said it should. With an old or partial DOCTYPE (or none), the page would render in backward-compatible "Quirks" mode, to avoid breaking non-standards-compliant sites—that is, to be kind to 99.9% of commercial sites on the web, at least for now [3.5].

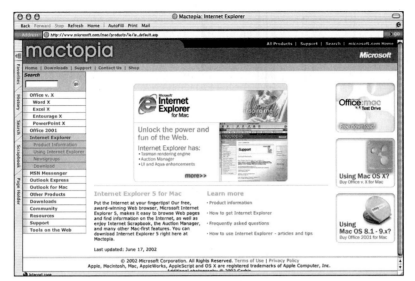

3.5
Hello, world, it's IE5 Macintosh Edition, the first browser to get most web standards mostly right, and one whose innovations found their way into competitive products (www.microsoft.com). Some of those innovations eventually even made their way into IE for Windows. But not all of them, unfortunately.

IE5/Mac also included a feature called Text Zoom [**3.6**] that enabled users to magnify or shrink any web text, including text set in pixels via CSS, thus solving a long-standing accessibility problem. Prior to IE5/Mac, only Opera Software's Opera browser allowed users to shrink or magnify all web text, including text set in pixels. Opera did this by "zooming" the entire page, graphics and all—an innovative approach to the occasionally epic conflict between what a designer desires and what a user might need [**3.7**, **3.8**, **3.9**].

3.6
IE5/Mac's Text Zoom at work. At the touch of a command key or the click of a drop-down menu, users can enlarge (or reduce) the text on any web page, whether that text is set in pixels, points, centimeters, or any other relative or absolute unit. Images on the page are unaffected—only the text size is changed. Text Zoom soon found its way into Netscape, Mozilla, Chimera, and other leading standards-compliant browsers. Alas, maddeningly, three years after IE for Macintosh introduced Text Zoom, IE for Windows still does not offer this essential accessibility feature.

3.7

PixelSurgeon
(www.pixelsurgeon.com/
news/), a leading design
portal and sister site to K10k
[3.4], as viewed in Opera
Software's Opera 7 browser
at actual size.

3.8

The same site magnified
by 200% via Opera's
innovative Page Zoom
feature. For visually
impaired users, Page
Zoom provides a way
to read small graphic
buttons and any other
text gifs whose minuscule
fonts might otherwise
pose an accessibility
problem.

3.9

The same site again, this
time magnified by 500%
via Opera's Page Zoom.
For designers, this Opera
feature provides a way to
more closely study a site's
visual elements without
the hassle of first saving
them as screen captures
and then opening them
in Photoshop.

Netscape's Bold Move

A flood of standards-compliant browsers followed the release of IE5/Mac. Netscape 6 and its open source code parent Mozilla supported XML, XHTML, CSS, ECMAScript, and the DOM across all computing platforms. It, too, used DOCTYPE switching and offered Text Zoom, and it was designed from the ground up to be a fully compliant browser.

To achieve full standards compliance, at WaSP's urging, Netscape had boldly junked its existing Navigator/Communicator 4.0 browser and every scrap of legacy code that had gone into it, restarting from a clean slate. Building a new browser from scratch took far longer than upgrading an existing browser. Netscape lost considerable market share during the years of Mozilla/ Netscape 6 development—which began in 1998 but did not produce a commercial product until late 2000 (and arguably, did not produce a *viable* commercial product until 2002).

These managers and engineers were not crazy. They obviously believed, as WaSP did, that the new browser would be finished in about a year. When one year became two and then three, the managers and engineers hung in there with a heroic, if increasingly baffling, determination to see the job through to the end.

Many companies would have abandoned such a project, shrugged their shoulders, and released a nonstandard 5.0 browser built on legacy code rather than sacrifice additional time and market share to a fiercely single-minded competitor like Microsoft. Although shareholders might disagree, Netscape's management and engineers deserve thanks and credit for placing interoper- ability and the future health of the web ahead of short-term benefits and their own self interest.

The Floodgates Open

Opera 6 came next—no DOCTYPE switching and no DOM, but fine support for most other standards. Opera eschewed DOCTYPE switching because, alone among commercial browsers, Opera had always sought to display pages according to W3C spec. Therefore, Opera's makers saw no reason to offer a backward-compatible "quirks" mode. (Opera 5 and 6 did not support the standard W3C DOM, but Opera 7, released in 2002, does.)

Finally, Microsoft released IE6 for Windows, a browser that mostly caught up with its Macintosh product's accurate CSS rendering; that offered strong support for XML, ECMAScript, and the DOM; and joined IE5/Mac, Mozilla, and Netscape 6+ in providing DOCTYPE switching. (On the browser's release, the Windows-centric trade press finally noticed DOCTYPE switching and gave IE6/Windows the credit for it.)

IE6/Windows failed to implement Text Zoom, but Text Zoom, although highly desirable from the point of view of accessibility and user friendliness, is an innovation, not a standard. IE6/Windows got CSS fixed-attachment backgrounds wrong, and it also suffered (and still does) from a bug that can break CSS layouts that use the `float` property (see Chapter 16, "A CSS Redesign"). Even so, IE6/Windows was a highly compliant, well-made browser, and its IE5.x/Windows predecessor came close enough to be worked with—or around.

None of these browsers was perfect (no software is), but each was a major achievement that demonstrated genuine commitment to interoperability via standards. No one, least of all The Web Standards Project, had believed these companies would come so far or do so much. With leading browsers finally attaining a kind of parity in their standards compliance, designers and developers were free to use CSS layout and other standards-based techniques.

2000–2001: The Standards Vanguard

A vanguard of designers and developers boldly began employing CSS layout and other standards-based techniques, including DOM-based scripting, prior to the release of IE6/Windows. Some did this by creating workarounds that forced IE5/Windows to render CSS accurately and turned off CSS in 4.0 browsers because said browsers could not render it accurately. Others took a layered approach, giving all browsers *something* to look at while reserving the "full" design for newer, more compliant browsers. This millennial design vanguard will be discussed in Chapter 4. Its workarounds and strategies will be covered in Part II, "Designing and Building."

Too Little, Too Late?

The release of solidly compliant mainstream browsers was great news for web users and builders. But by the time the glad tidings arrived, many designers and developers were convinced that web standards were a pipe dream, and many had ceased even trying to implement them correctly. It's not hard to understand why. The perception was years in the making.

CSS: The First Bag Is Free

The CSS1 spec had been issued around Christmas of 1996. A few months later, IE3 debuted, including rudimentary CSS support among its features. CSS support (entirely missing in Netscape 3) gave Microsoft's browser its first whiff of credibility at a time when Netscape Navigator dominated the web. IE3 supported just enough CSS to let you dump your nonstandard <font> tags and begin experimenting with margins, leading, and other rudiments of CSS layout. Excited by what they saw on Microsoft demo pages [**3.10**] touting its new browser's capabilities, many designers took their first plunge into CSS design—and soon came up gasping for air.

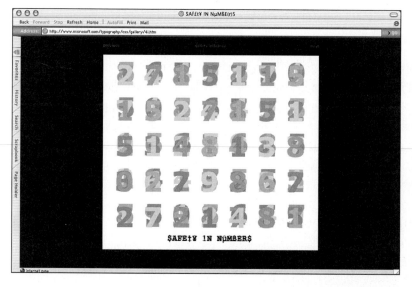

3.10
A page from Microsoft's 1998 CSS gallery (http://www.microsoft.com/typography/css/gallery/). Overlapping type and all other design effects were created entirely in CSS—no GIF images, no JPEGs. IE3 could display these effects; Netscape 3 (then the market leader) could not. The gallery's CSS used incorrect values required by IE3's imperfect CSS engine, and its overall standards compliance was nil, but the genie was out of the bottle. Having glimpsed what CSS might do, many of us never looked back.

IE3's CSS support was a bold first step, but like all first steps, it was buggy and incomplete. Those authoring CSS for the first time exulted in the creative freedom it offered but quickly bogged down in early IE bugs that could make a page unusable. For instance, under certain circumstances, images on a CSS-driven page would sit *on top* of text instead of alongside it. To get an idea of what this was like, place your hand on this paragraph and try to read it through your flesh. Unless you're Claude Rains, you'll have a tough time.

The workaround to this early CSS rendering bug in IE 3 was to place every image and paragraph in its own table cell, thus doubling the weight of your page while defeating the purpose of CSS (to control layout without tables and without excess bandwidth). Designers soon concluded that CSS was not ready for prime time—a determination that seemed reasonable given the absence of any CSS support in market-leading Netscape 3.

Bad Browsers Lead to Bad Practices

Then came the 4.0 browsers. Although still buggy and incomplete, IE4 greatly improved on IE3's CSS support. Netscape 4 offered CSS for the first time in a last-minute implementation so broken and foul it set adoption of CSS back by at least two years.

To be fair, Netscape 4's CSS support was far better than IE3's had been (`http://www.webreview.com/style/css1/leaderboard.shtml`). But while almost nobody today uses IE3, tens of millions still use Netscape 4. Thus, many site owners feel compelled to support Netscape 4—and mistake "support," which is a good thing, with "pixel-perfect sameness and identical behavior," which is a bad thing because it ties developers' hands and forces them to write bad code and dumb markup.

The Curse of Legacy Rendering

Among Netscape 4's chief CSS failings were legacy renderings and lack of inheritance.

Designed to abstract presentation from structure, CSS makes no assumptions about how elements are supposed to be displayed or even what markup language you're going to use, although browsers and other user agents typically do make those assumptions. (Some modern browsers use CSS to enforce their assumptions and allow the designer's style sheets to override them.) By default in most browsers, without CSS, the `<h1>` heading would be big and bold, with vertical margins (whitespace) above and below.

CSS lets you change that. With CSS, `<h1>` can be small, italic, and margin-free if it suits the designer to make it so. Alas, not in Netscape 4, which adds its default legacy renderings to any CSS rule the designer specifies. If the CSS says there shall be no whitespace below the headline, Netscape 4 will go ahead and stick whitespace down there anyway.

When designers applied CSS to standard HTML markup, they quickly discovered that IE4 mainly did what they asked it to do, whereas Netscape 4 made a mess of their layouts.

Some designers abandoned CSS. Others (sadly including me) initially worked around the problem by eschewing structural markup, using constructions like `<div class="headline1">` instead of `<h1>`. This solved the display problem at the expense of document structure and semantics, thereby placing short-term gain ahead of long-term viability and leading to numerous problems down the road. Said problems have now come home to roost.

This author has long since abandoned the practice of wholesale document structural deformation, but a huge proportion of designers and developers still write junk markup in the name of backward compatibility with Netscape 4. This normative practice is fatally flawed, creating usability problems while stymieing efforts to normalize and rationalize data-driven workflows.

Content management systems, publishing tools, and visual web editors (a.k.a. WYSIWYG editors) developed during the 4.0 browser era are littered with meaningless markup that vastly increases the difficulty and expense of bringing sites into conformance with current standards or preparing legacy content for XML-driven databases. On large sites created by multiple designers and developers, each designer might use different nonstandard tags, making it impossible to gather all the data and reformat it according to a more useful scheme. (Imagine a public library where books were indexed, not by the Dewey Decimal System, but according to the whims of Joe, Mary, and various other cataloguers, each making up their own rules as they went along.)

Outside the realm of graphical browsers, structurally meaningless markup also makes pages less usable. To a Palm Pilot, web phone, or screen reader user, `<div class="headline1">` is plain text, not a headline. Thus, we buy or build content management systems that swap one set of tags for another when a single set of standard tags would serve. Or we force Palm Pilot, web phone, and screen reader users to view nonstructural markup and guess at our meanings.

We can thank Netscape 4 (and our own willingness to accommodate its failings) for miring us in this mess. No wonder those Netscape and Mozilla engineers kept working on the four-year-long Mozilla project. They really had no worthwhile legacy product to fall back on.

Inherit the Wind

Netscape 4 also failed to understand and support inheritance, the brilliant underlying concept that gives CSS its power. CSS streamlines production and reduces bandwidth by enabling general rules to percolate down the document tree unless the designer specifies otherwise.

For instance, in CSS, you can apply a font face, size, and color to the body selector, and that same face, size, and color will show up in any "child" of the body tag, from <h1> to <p> and beyond—but not in Netscape 4. In Netscape 4, 2 + 2 = 2 + 2, not 4.

Knowledgeable developers worked around the browser's lack of support for inheritance by writing redundant rules:

```
body, td, h1, p    {font-family: verdana, arial, helvetica,
sans-serif;}
```

In the preceding example, the td, h1, and p selectors are redundant because any compliant browser automatically styles those "child" elements the same way as the "parent," body element.

Slightly less knowledgeable developers spelled out their rules in full, thus creating even more redundancy while wasting even more bandwidth:

```
body   {font-family: verdana, arial, helvetica, sans-serif;}
td     {font-family: verdana, arial, helvetica, sans-serif;}
h1     {font-family: verdana, arial, helvetica, sans-serif;}
p      {font-family: verdana, arial, helvetica, sans-serif;}
```

… and so on. It was a waste of user and server bandwidth, but it got the job done. Other developers concluded that CSS didn't work in Netscape 4 (they had a point) or that CSS was flawed. (They were wrong, but the perception became widespread.)

Netscape 4 had other CSS failings—enough to fill the Yellow Pages of a major metropolis—but these are enough to paint the picture, and they were also enough to delay widespread adoption of the CSS standard.

Miss Behavior to You

Along with CSS snafus, early browsers could not agree on a common way to facilitate sophisticated behavior via scripting. Every scriptable browser has an Object Model stating what kinds of behaviors can be applied to objects on the page. Netscape 4 sported a proprietary `document.layers` model. IE4 countered with its own proprietary `document.all` model. Neither browser supported the W3C DOM, which was still being written. Developers who wanted to apply sophisticated (or even basic) behaviors to their sites had to code two ways to cover these two browsers. Supporting earlier browsers (backward compatibility) required more code and more hoop jumping, as described in Chapter 2.

Prior browsers could not even agree on a common scripting language. Early on, Netscape invented JavaScript, promising to release it as a standard so that other browser makers could support it. But for some years, despite their promise, Netscape held onto the secret of JavaScript, viewing it as a competitive advantage. (If Navigator remained the only browser that supported JavaScript, why would anyone develop for a less powerful competitive browser, so Netscape reasoned. In their place, Microsoft would likely have done the same. In fact, Microsoft did the same thing with their proprietary ActiveX technology.)

To compete, Microsoft reverse-engineered JavaScript, changing it along the way, which is inevitable in any reverse-engineering project. The resulting language worked like JavaScript but not *exactly* like JavaScript. The new language was just different enough to louse you up. Microsoft called their scripting language JScript. Meanwhile, Microsoft cooked up a separate technology they called ActiveX, which was supposed to provide seamless functionality in all versions of their IE browser but really only worked correctly on the Windows platform, where it is still used to do things like fill in for missing plug-ins.

JScript, JavaScript, ActiveX: In the name of cross-browser and backward compatibility, developers found themselves dancing with multiple partners, none of whom seemed to be listening to the same tune—and clients paid the piper in the form of ever-escalating development and testing costs.

Standardized Scripting at Long Last

Eventually, ECMA ratified a standard version of JavaScript that they modestly called ECMAScript (www.ecma.ch/ecma1/STAND/ECMA-262.HTM). In time, the W3C issued a standard DOM. Ultimately, Netscape and Microsoft supported both—but not before years of hellish incompatibility had turned many developers into experts at proprietary, incompatible scripting techniques and Object Models and persuaded many site owners that web development would always be a Balkanized affair. Hence, the "IE-only" site, the broken detection script, and in some cases the abandonment of web standards in favor of proprietary solutions like Flash.

By the way, if you wonder what ECMA stands for, don't bother trying to find out on the organization's hideous and confusing site ⌊3.3⌋. For what it's worth, ECMA is the European Computer Manufacturers Association, and it's also a bona fide standards body, unlike the W3C, which labels the technologies it develops "recommendations" rather than "standards." Confusing sites and bewildering labels are another reason standards have had difficulty achieving widespread acceptance on the modern web.

Confusing Sites, Bewildering Labels

Behold the CSS2 specification as presented by the W3C [3.11]. CSS2 is a powerful standard presentation language created to facilitate the needs of designers, but you wouldn't know it from gazing at this page. It's about as uninspiring a presentation as you've seen since your Uncle Carl showed you the personal site he threw together one afternoon using Microsoft FrontPage and a $50 image editor.

Ignoring a gnawing feeling of dread, you attempt to read and comprehend the spec in spite of its unappealing appearance. After all, the W3C is made up of scientists, not graphic designers. All that matters are the words, right? Twenty minutes into your reading experience, cross-eyed and weeping, you surf to an online computer store and buy Macromedia Flash.

To be fair, not only is the W3C not in the business of graphic design, usability consulting, or information architecture, but it's also not in the business of writing designer-friendly tutorials. The W3C site is a series of accurate technical documents created by leading thinkers and expert technologists—and that's all it was ever supposed to be.

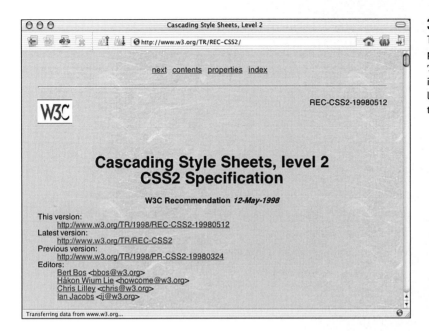

3.11
The CSS 2 specification per W3C (`www.w3.org/ TR/REC-CSS2/`): An inspiring presentation language whose presentation here is anything but.

In "How to Read W3C Specs" (`www.alistapart.com/stories/readspec/`), O'Reilly author and WaSP steering committee member (and one of this book's technical editors) J. David Eisenberg explains it this way: "When you seek answers, you're looking for a user manual or user reference guide; you want to *use* the technology. That's not the purpose of a W3C specification. The purpose of a 'spec' is to tell programmers who will implement the technology, what features it must have, and how they are to be implemented. It's the difference between the owner's manual for your car and the repair manuals."

By definition, the W3C speaks to engineers, not the public. It's not trying to explain or sell the standards it creates. As noted earlier, it doesn't even call them "standards," although that's what they are. (Actually, in recent press materials and on parts of the W3C site, the Consortium has begun using the "s" word instead of the more passive "recommendations." This is a good thing.)

Unlike a corporation, the W3C is not reimbursed for its efforts when you use a web standard, and it discourages its member companies from patenting (`http://www.w3.org/TR/2002/WD-patent-policy-20021114/`) or charging royalties for web standards or components thereof.

Academics Versus Economics

Detached from the dog-eat-dog, dog-buys-other-dog's-company-only-to-put-it-out-of-business world, the W3C inhabits a contemplative space where it can focus on the web's potential instead of its competitive pressures. W3C activities are of geeks, by geeks, and for geeks, and its site reflects the group's emphasis on science over style or consumer-friendly ease of use.

The trouble is, designers, developers, and site owners care greatly about style and care even more about consumer-friendly ease of use. On their own sites, they would never intentionally publish difficult, arcane text that confuses readers; never willfully stick their most important content in out-of-the-way places; and never deliberately present their content in an unaesthetic, non-branded setting that encourages visitors to click the Back button.

Psychologically, people who care about branding, aesthetics, clarity, and ease of use and who spend their day struggling to bring these attributes to their own web projects are unlikely to believe that an amateurish-looking site filled with arcane technical documents holds the key to their future. So what do these people trust? They trust slick presentations from corporate giants.

Consortia Suggest, Companies Sell

In the West, when we face a business or creative problem, we tackle it by opening a software application, and we look to market-leading corporations to deliver the products we need. Site owners check the health of their business by opening Microsoft Excel-formatted spreadsheets. Designers create logos in Adobe Illustrator and animations in Macromedia Flash, and they prepare images and web layouts in Adobe Photoshop. For every problem, there's a software category, for every category, a leader.

Although pioneering web designers and developers learned to create pages in Notepad and SimpleText, many who came later relied on visual editing products (WYSIWYG tools) to handle their authoring chores. As proprietary scripting languages and incompatible Object Models made development ever more complex, products like Macromedia Dreamweaver and Adobe GoLive helped many pros create sites that worked while hiding the underlying complexities. How would you support multiple browsers? Push the right button, and the software would do it for you.

These category-leading visual editors were sophisticated and powerful. But until recently, the code and markup they generated had little to do with web standards. Like developers, Dreamweaver and GoLive wrote browser-specific scripts and nonsemantic markup structures.

Dreamweaver MX and GoLive 6 are far more compliant than previous versions (see "Web Standards and Authoring Tools" in Chapter 4), although they still require developer knowledge. And where do their users turn for knowledge? They turn to the attractive, well-written product sites that serve as online user manuals and foster the development of Dreamweaver and GoLive communities. We'll have more to say about such sites in just a moment.

Product Awareness Versus Standards Awareness

As companies were striving to deliver "push-button easy" solutions to the problems of front-end design, the same thing was happening on the back end and in the middle. Proprietary publishing tools and database products from big brands like IBM, Sun, Lotus, and Microsoft and tough little companies such as Allaire (now part of Macromedia) offered needed functionality at a time when standards like XML and the DOM were still being hammered out in committee.

You don't build your car from scratch. Why build your website that way? Sign here, buy now, and if anything doesn't work, we'll fix it in the next upgrade. To deadline-driven developers, the pitch made sense, for the same reason it had once made sense to treat HTML as a design tool: namely, meeting client needs right now.

Thus, product awareness rather than standards awareness dominated the thinking of many web developers and especially of many web designers. For every designer or developer who checked out W3C specs, there were 10 who got their information from the websites of Netscape, Microsoft, Macromedia [**3.12**], Adobe [**3.13**], and other major (and smart) companies.

Unlike w3.org, these sites are created to serve consumers (professional designers and developers), to deepen the bond between company and customer, and to enhance the corporate brand. Thus, these sites tend to be well (or at least adequately) designed per corporate branding specs, and their tutorials are written and edited for easy comprehension by a professional audience.

3.12

Like the W3C,
Macromedia creates
invaluable tools for
designers and developers
(www.macromedia.com).
Unlike the W3C,
Macromedia *sells* these
tools and works hard to
foster engagement with
the design community
and to speak that
community's language
on its website.

3.13

Like its rival
Macromedia, Adobe
(www.adobe.com)
continually interacts with
its users, finding out what
they want most and
changing its products
accordingly. Also like its
rival, Adobe works hard
to "speak designers'
language" on its website.
Contrast this figure with
Figures 3.3 and 3.11.

Needless to say, such tutorials emphasize the efficacy of the company's products. When these companies mention web standards, it's likely to be in passing or in connection with claims that their product is more compliant than a competitor's. After all, the goal of such sites is to make you value the product you just bought and be willing to buy next year's upgrade.

In short, many web professionals—designers and developers as well as their clients and employers—know quite a lot about proprietary solutions and quite a bit less about web standards. Nor do many realize, except perhaps tangentially, that aligning themselves exclusively with any single company or product line might lock them into an ever-increasing cycle of expense: from necessary upgrades to costly customization to training, consulting, and beyond. After all, that's simply how business works.

One particular product deserves special mention, and it gets it directly below.

The F Word

Of all the competing proprietary solutions that corporations have tried to sell, none has succeeded as brilliantly as Macromedia Flash [**3.14**]. The product began as a humble plug-in called FutureSplash that allowed designers to embed vector-based graphics and animations on their pages.

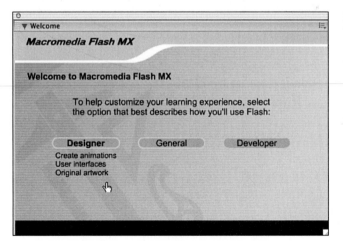

3.14
Welcome to Macromedia Flash! The Flash authoring environment might be rich, deep, and complex, but Macromedia does all it can to guide designers and developers by the hand as they begin to climb the product's steep learning curves.

Designers paid little attention to FutureSplash, but Macromedia, being the smart company that it is, immediately recognized its potential. Macromedia bought the plug-in and its associated authoring tool, renamed it Flash, and rebuilt it into a richly flexible authoring environment driven by a powerful JavaScript-like programming language called ActionScript.

Macromedia also managed to foster a cult of Flash development.

The Value of Flash

While the incompatible scripting languages and Object Models of the 4.0 browsers wreaked havoc and drove up costs, Flash 4 and its powerful scripting language worked equally well in Navigator, IE, and Opera and nearly as well in Mac OS, Linux, and UNIX as it did in Windows. For many designers, it was adios to HTML, botched 4.0 browser CSS, and rat's nests of incompatible code, and *hello baby* to Flash.

Spinning logos, tedious "loading" screens, and endless, unwanted "intros" initially gave Flash a bad name among users. But juvenile abuse of the new tool's power eventually gave way to sophisticated user experiences created by the likes of One9ine [**3.15**], Juxt Interactive [**3.16**], and other high-end shops. Less talented and less innovative agencies hastily hopped on the Flash bandwagon, often producing far less engaging sites, but you can't blame bad carpentry on the hammer and nails. Flash was eating the rich application space the way Microsoft's browser was eating Netscape's lunch.

Although appropriate to many projects, Flash was wrong for countless others that used it anyway, and Flash 4 suffered from woeful usability and accessibility problems that bothered users tremendously without seeming to be noticed by developers and clients. Among the product's most vocal critics was Jakob Nielsen (`http://www.useit.com`) of the Nielsen Norman consulting group.

In 2002, Macromedia addressed its problems by greatly improving the accessibility and usability features of its upgraded Flash MX product and by hiring Nielsen as a consultant, thereby changing his tune. (If Microsoft and Netscape had shown the same smarts and hired *their* harshest critics, this author would be lolling about on a private beach instead of toiling at this book—but I digress.)

In capable hands, Flash facilitates rich interactive experiences that would be difficult to emulate using standard markup, CSS, SVG (Scalable Vector Graphics), and the DOM.

3.15
Place a powerful tool in the hands of extremely gifted visual designers, and what do you get? You get rich user experiences that are hard to match. One9ine (`www.one9ine.com`) is a New York City-based shop whose high-end design work is executed almost entirely in Flash.

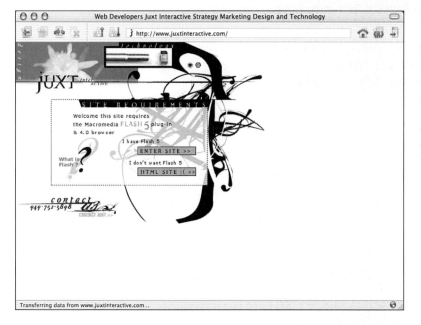

3.16
California-based Juxt Interactive (`www.juxtinteractive.com`) is another of the Flash pioneers whose supremely artful user experience designs helped bury the notion that Flash was a gimmick capable only of creating annoying "intros."

SVG for You and Me

SVG is an XML application and standard vector language capable of animation and scripting and fully compatible with other web standards. But as of
this writing, no popular browser natively supports SVG, and its use requires
a plug-in, just as Flash does. (The W3C's Amaya browser supports SVG to a
limited extent, and some flavors of Mozilla can be compiled with partial SVG
support, but these environments are far from the mainstream.)

Currently, if you want to create complex, application-like interfaces, it's easier
to do so in Flash, with its huge installed base and single development environment. One day it might make more sense to create such applications using a
combination of XML, XHTML, CSS, ECMAScript, SVG, and the DOM.

The Trouble with Flash

The principal problem with Flash is that it is inappropriate for many content
and commerce sites. Yet developers use it in these inappropriate situations
because Flash facilitates snazzy presentations that make clients feel they're
getting bang for their buck—and because, successful or not, Flash sites look
good in the company's portfolio.

News sites, portals, shopping sites, institutional sites, community sites,
magazines, directories, and others that emphasize text or involve practical
interactivity are still best served with XHTML, CSS, and other standards. Yet
many developers sell Flash instead, not because it serves the project's goals,
but because they get off on it, and the resulting work attracts new clients. It's
roughly the equivalent of ad agencies pushing work that doesn't sell in hopes
of racking up creative awards.

The Other Trouble with Flash

The other problem with Flash is that some designers are so enamored of it that
they've forgotten how to use web standards—if they ever knew in the first place.
As a result, one finds Flash presentations embedded in sites that work only in
one or two browsers. The Flash files themselves would work in any browser that

contained the plug-in, but the sites have been so miserably authored that many users are unable to access the Flash content. There are even Flash sites that require IE merely to load a Flash presentation. This is like demanding that you use a Zenith (and not a Sony) simply to access your cable TV feed.

When called upon to create a "traditional" standards-based site, these shops use the old methods whose problems we've described in this book, often turning the job over to their junior teams, so senior designers and developers can continue to focus on Flash projects. It's as if the web has stood still since these shops discovered Flash.

XML, XHTML, CSS, and the DOM are not dull technologies for junior teams and beginners, but mature and powerful standards capable of delivering rich user experiences. I have no problem with shops that specialize in beautiful, usable, highly functional Flash work. I would just like to see the same care and attention paid to the other 90% of design and development. But I don't have to sell you. You bought this book.

Compliance Is a Dirty Word

The other obstacle to widespread acceptance of web standards is the mistaken belief that standards will somehow diminish creativity, tie the developer's hands, or result in lessened user experiences vis-á-vis old-school, proprietary methods. Where does this mistaken notion come from?

It might come from developers who tried using web standards in 4.0 and older browsers and were rightfully displeased with the results. But the days of poor standards compliance are gone.

The Power of Language to Shape Perceptions

The phrase "web standards" might be at fault. The Web Standards Project coined the phrase as an act of propaganda. We sought a set of words that would convey to browser makers exactly what was at stake—a set of words whose underlying ethical imperative would remind browser makers of their commitment to technologies they had helped to create and pledged to support. We needed a phrase that would convey to developers, clients, and tech journalists the urgent importance of reliable, consistently implemented, industry-wide technologies. "Recommendations" didn't cut it. "Standards," we felt, did.

We had no budget and few hopes, yet somehow we succeeded. Today, companies like Netscape, Microsoft, Adobe, and Macromedia strive for standards compliance and brag of it as an expected and desired feature—like four-wheel drive. But although those companies "get it," many in the design community do not. Some mistake "web standards" for an imposed and arbitrary set of design rules (just as some think of usability that way—as do some usability consultants, unfortunately). It should be explained to these designers that web standards have nothing to do with external aesthetic guidelines or commandments.

If not the phrase, "web standards," perhaps the word "compliance" might be at fault. Designers want to comply with their creative visions, not with a complex set of technological rules. They should be told that those rules have nothing to do with the look and feel of any site; they merely enable browsers to deliver what the designer has created. Likewise, clients want to comply with corporate or institution-driven site goals based on marketing requirements and user analysis. Again, web standards can only help by ensuring that sites work for more people on more platforms.

The Inspiration Problem

Designers and clients might be turned off by the lack of visual inspiration (sometimes bordering on hostility to design and branding) found on some sites that discuss web standards or brag about their compliance with one or more W3C specifications. We'll encounter the same problem when we discuss accessibility. (Some accessibility sites are downright ugly, but the problem lies with those sites' designers, not with accessibility, which carries no visual penalty. The same is true for web standards, even if the look and feel of the W3C website or of ECMA is unlikely to motivate designers to get busy learning about XML and CSS2.)

The Wthremix contest [3.17], launched in December of 2002, sought to generate some of that missing aesthetic interest. The founders explained their goals this way:

> The W3C creates powerful standards and guidelines that make web development more rational and enhance user experience. Technologies like XML, CSS, XHTML, the DOM, and guidelines like the Web Accessibility Initiative can help us create more powerful sites that work better for all. But the W3C is composed of super-geeks, not consumer-oriented designers, developers, writers, and information specialists.

As a result, the W3C's powerful technologies and guidelines are trapped in a sprawling site that is less attractive and less usable than it might be. We wondered if the W3C's website could be transformed into one that is better looking, better organized, better branded, and much easier to use and understand. Hence this contest.

The Contest

Wthremix is a design challenge for coders and a coding challenge for designers. Here's the idea: Create a redesign of the W3C home page. Design an intuitive layout and navigation, organize the content with the user in mind, and create an aesthetic that reflects the importance and influence of the institution. Show us what you think the W3C home page should look like, how it should communicate to its users and, to make your point, use valid tableless XHTML and CSS, and meet WAI accessibility level 1.

3.17
The Wthremix contest launched in December 2002 challenged designers and coders to redesign the W3C's website (`http://w3mix.web-graphics.com/`).

Other Problems

Some might mistrust web standards because of bad experiences with the buggy first version of Netscape 6 or a few bugs still unfixed in IE6 over a year after that browser was released.

Others, intrigued by the promise of web standards, might have converted a site from HTML to XHTML, only to discover that their layouts suddenly looked different in Netscape 6+, Mozilla, and IE6. In Chapter 11 we'll explain why that happens and the simple, quick fixes that can get your site back on course. But if you don't know about those simple, quick fixes, you might be mistrustful of web standards and might want to bury your head in the sand and persevere in the obsolete, non-standard methods that used to work so well in yesterday's browsers.

Don't give in to the dark side. Although ignorance and prejudice are as rampant in web design as in any other human endeavor, web standards are here to stay—and this book is here to help.

chapter four

XML Conquers the World (And Other Web Standards Success Stories)

Before we go any further, it's worth countering the previous chapter's bad vibes by discussing the ways web standards have established firm footholds in and beyond the Internet. Despite the misunderstandings that stymie their adoption in some quarters, web standards are winning the day on many fronts and are rapidly changing technology, business, and publishing on and *off* the web.

In this chapter, we'll take a first look at the most successful web standard since HTML: Extensible Markup Language (XML). XML is an all-embracing data format that's been almost universally adopted and adapted to meet complex needs. We'll discover how XML helps software products remain viable in a rapidly changing market, solves the problems of today's data-driven businesses, and has given rise to a new generation of interoperable web applications and services.

We'll also see how web standards have facilitated détente and encouraged cooperation between arch competitors in the browser business. We'll learn how professional web authoring tools that once ignored standards have come to embrace them. And we'll see how the personal sites of forward-thinking designers and developers have fostered wider acceptance of CSS layout, XHTML markup, and conformance with Web Accessibility Initiative (WAI) and Section 508 accessibility guidelines.

Each of these success stories shares a common core: Standards are gaining acceptance because they work. The more these standards are accepted, the harder and better they will work and the smoother the road will be before us all.

The Universal Language (XML)

Chapter 3, "The Trouble with Standards," described how poor compliance in early browsers persuaded many designers and developers that standards were a pipe dream, leading some to cling doggedly to counterproductive, obsolete methods, and others to embrace Flash to the exclusion of HTML, CSS, and JavaScript. Reading that chapter might have convinced you that web standards face an uphill battle in terms of acceptance and correct usage. Then what are we to make of XML?

The Extensible Markup Language standard (www.w3.org/TR/2000/REC-xml-20001006), introduced in February 1998, took the software industry by storm [4.1]. For the first time, the world was offered a universal, adaptable format for structuring documents and data, not only on the web, but everywhere. The world took to it as a lad in his Sunday best takes to mud puddles.

XML and HTML Compared

Although it's based on the same parent technology that gave rise to good old HTML (and just like HTML, it uses tags, attributes, and values to format structured documents), XML is quite different from the venerable markup language it's intended to replace.

HTML is a basic language for marking up web pages. It has a fixed number of tags and a small set of somewhat inconsistent rules. In HTML, you must close some tags, mustn't close others, and might or might not want to close still others, depending on your mood. This looseness makes it easy for anyone to create a web page, even if they don't quite know what they're doing—and that, of course, was the idea.

Name	Date Modified	Size	Kind
508_rules.xml	5/20/02, 1:32 PM	180 KB	eXten...ument
800 x 600.xml	4/22/02, 4:07 AM	12 KB	eXten...ument
1024 x 768.xml	4/22/02, 4:07 AM	12 KB	eXten...ument
1152 x 768.xml	4/22/02, 4:07 AM	12 KB	eXten...ument
1280 x 1024.xml	4/22/02, 4:07 AM	12 KB	eXten...ument
ActionsPanel.xml	3/5/02, 9:16 PM	108 KB	eXten...ument
ActionsPanel.xml	3/5/02, 9:16 PM	108 KB	eXten...ument
AlbumData.xml	1/2/03, 5:00 PM	4 KB	Text ...cument
AsCodeHints.xml	3/5/02, 9:16 PM	4 KB	eXten...ument
AsCodeHints.xml	3/5/02, 9:16 PM	4 KB	eXten...ument
AsColorSyntax.xml	3/5/02, 9:16 PM	20 KB	eXten...ument
AsColorSyntax.xml	3/5/02, 9:16 PM	20 KB	eXten...ument
ASP JavaScript.xml	12/19/02, 11:32 PM	12 KB	Text ...cument
ASP JavaScript.xml	5/20/02, 1:28 PM	12 KB	eXten...ument
ASP VBScript.xml	5/20/02, 1:28 PM	16 KB	eXten...ument
ASP VBScript.xml	12/19/02, 11:32 PM	16 KB	Text ...cument
ASP.NET CSharp.xml	5/20/02, 1:28 PM	12 KB	eXten...ument
ASP.NET CSharp.xml	12/19/02, 11:32 PM	12 KB	Text ...cument
ASP.NET VB.xml	12/19/02, 11:32 PM	16 KB	Text ...cument
ASP.NET VB.xml	5/20/02, 1:28 PM	16 KB	eXten...ument
BBEdit.xml	5/20/02, 1:30 PM	36 KB	eXten...ument
bookmarks.xml	1/2/03, 5:02 PM	8 KB	Text ...cument
catalog.xml	11/17/00, 3:24 PM	4 KB	Text ...cument
CFCsMenus.xml	5/20/02, 1:29 PM	4 KB	eXten...ument
CodeColoring.xml	12/19/02, 11:32 PM	144 KB	Text ...cument
CodeColoring.xml	5/20/02, 1:28 PM	144 KB	eXten...ument
codehints.xml	5/20/02, 1:32 PM	4 KB	eXten...ument
CodeHints.xml	5/20/02, 1:28 PM	324 KB	eXten...ument
Colors.xml	12/19/02, 11:32 PM	8 KB	Text ...cument
Colors.xml	5/20/02, 1:28 PM	8 KB	eXten...ument
com.apple.pmcache.xml	12/16/02, 10:01 PM	104 KB	Text ...cument
com.epson.printer.C40Series.xml	9/3/02, 10:51 PM	16 KB	Text ...cument
com.epson.printer.C60Series.xml	9/3/02, 10:51 PM	16 KB	Text ...cument
com.epson.printer.C80Series.xml	9/3/02, 10:51 PM	16 KB	Text ...cument

Maci...HD ▸ System ▸ Library ▸ Fram...rks ▸ Appli...ork ▸ Versions ▸ A ▸
Fram...rks ▸ Print...ork ▸ Versions ▸ A ▸ Resources ▸ com....xml

4.1

"Mommy, there's XML on my computer!" Run a quick search on an average Macintosh, and you'll find hundreds of XML files. Some store operating system preferences, whereas others drive printers. Still others are essential components of applications including Acrobat, iPhoto, iTunes, Eudora, Internet Explorer, Mozilla, Chimera, Flash MX, Dreamweaver MX, and more. XML is a web standard that goes way beyond the web.

It was a fine idea in the early days, when the web needed basic content and not much else. But in today's more sophisticated web, where pages are frequently assembled by publishing tools and content must flow back and forth from database to web page to wireless device to print, the lack of uniform rules in HTML impedes data repurposing. It's easy to convert text to HTML, but it's difficult to convert data marked up in HTML to any other needed format.

Likewise, HTML is merely a formatting language, and not a particularly self-aware one. It contains no information about the content it formats, again limiting your ability to reuse that content in other settings. And, of course, HTML is strictly for the web.

XML-based markup, by contrast, is bound by consistent rules and is capable of traveling far beyond the web. When you mark up a document in XML, you're not merely preparing it to show up on a web page. You're encoding it in tags that can be understood in any XML-aware environment.

One Parent, Many Children

Specifically, XML is a language for creating other languages. As long as they adhere to its rules, librarians are free to create XML markup whose custom tags facilitate the needs of cataloging. Music companies can create XML markup whose tags include artist, recording, composer, producer, copyright data, royalty data, and so on. Composers can organize their scores in a custom XML markup language called MusicML. (To avoid carpal tunnel syndrome, we will refer to "creating XML markup" as "writing XML" from here on.)

These custom XML languages are called *applications*, and because they are all XML, they are compatible with each other. That is, an XML parser can understand all these applications, and the applications are able to easily exchange data with one another. Thus, data from a record company's XML database can end up in a library's catalog of recordings without human labor or error and without bogging down in software incompatibilities.

An Essential Ingredient of Professional and Consumer Software

This power to format, understand, and exchange data has made XML as ubiquitous as Coca-Cola™. XML not only stores content housed in online and corporate databases, but it also has become the lingua franca of database programs like FileMaker Pro and of much nondatabase-oriented software, from high-end design applications to business products like Microsoft Office and OpenOffice, whose native file formats are XML-based.

Apple's UNIX-based Macintosh OS X operating system stores its preferences in XML. Print design powerhouses Quark XPress 5.0 and Adobe InDesign 2.0 import and export XML and support the creation of XML-based templates. Visual web editors such as Macromedia Dreamweaver MX and Adobe GoLive 6 are likewise XML-savvy, making it easier (or at least possible) to bounce data back and forth between the printed page, the web layout, and the database that runs your online store or global directory.

Not content to merely parse XML, some products are actually made of the stuff. Macromedia Dreamweaver MX is built with XML files that are available to the end user [4.2, 4.3, 4.4], making it possible to modify the program by rolling up your shirtsleeves and editing these files (www.alistapart.com/stories/dreamweaver/). Customizing Dreamweaver in this way and selling these customized versions to Dreamweaver-using colleagues has become something of a cottage industry.

4.2
Dreamweaver MX, a popular web development tool, is made up of files whose formats will be familiar to web developers. Under the hood, Dreamweaver MX is composed of XML files...

4.3
...along with GIF, HTML, and JavaScript files. Like the files on a website, Dreamweaver's components are organized in subdirectories.

4.4
Savvy Dreamweaver users can edit these files to customize the product. Here, a user is changing Dreamweaver's default keyboard shortcuts by editing an XML file called menus.xml.

Consumer software loves XML, too. The Personal Information Manager on your PC, Mac, or PDA reads and writes XML or can be made to do so via third-party products such as the Ælfred XML parser for the Palm Pilot (www.xml.com/pub/r/216). When your digital camera time-stamps a snapshot and records its dimensions, file size, and other such information, it most likely records this data in XML. Each time your dad emails you those pipe-clobbering 7MB vacation photos, he's likely sending you XML-formatted data along with the beauty shots of lens caps at sunset.

Even hobbyist image-management software like Apple's iPhoto [4.5] understands XML. When you print a snapshot of little Oscar's first encounter with a puppy, Oscar's flushed cheeks and the pooch's bright eyes come out right thanks to print presets stored as XML data by the Macintosh OS X operating system.

More Popular Than MTV

Why has XML seized the imagination of so many disparate manufacturers and found its way into their products? XML combines standardization with *extensibility* (the power to customize), *transformability* (the power to convert data from one format to another), and relatively seamless data exchange between one XML application or XML-aware software product and another.

As an open standard unencumbered by patents or royalties, XML blows away outdated, proprietary formats with limited acceptance and built-in costs. The W3C charges no fee when you incorporate XML into your software product or roll your own custom XML-based language. Moreover, acceptance of XML is viral. The more vendors who catch the XML bug, the faster it spreads to other vendors, and the easier it becomes to pass data from one manufacturer's product to another's.

Plus, XML works. Gone are the days when your office mates considered you a guru if you were able to beat plain, tab-delimited text out of one product and import it into another (often with some data loss and much manual reformatting). XML helps vendors build products whose interoperability empowers consumers to work smarter, not harder. Consumers respond with their pocketbooks.

4.5
Apple's consumer-friendly iPhoto software (www.apple.com/iphoto/), a free component of its OS X operating system, uses XML to organize photo library data, remember print presets, and more.

Not a Panacea, But Plays One on TV

We're not saying that XML is a panacea for all software problems. The data in a JPEG is much better expressed in binary format than as text. Nor are we claiming that every software package on the market "gets" XML, although most professional applications and many consumer products do, and their numbers are continually growing. We're not even saying that all software that claims to support XML does so flawlessly. But flawlessly implemented or not, XML has transformed the software industry along with the workplace.

Even the makers of products that don't support XML seem to believe they should. In April 2002, distressed by lackluster sales and a fragmented middleware market, a group of interactive television and technology providers banded together under the banner of the iTV Production Standards Initiative. Its mission: to unveil and shore up support for an XML-based standard intended to "allow producers to write interactive content once and distribute it to all major set-top box and PC platforms" (www.allnetdevices.com/developer/news/2002/04/09/itv_firms.html).

Sound familiar? It's exactly what The Web Standards Project had to say about W3C standards during the browser wars of the mid- to late 1990s.

Builds Strong Data Five Ways

On the web, XML is increasingly the format of choice for IT professionals, developers, and content specialists who must work with data housed in large corporate or institutional systems. Choosy mothers choose XML for five reasons, many of which will be familiar from the preceding discussion:

- Like ASCII, XML is a single, universal file format that plays well with others.

- Unlike ASCII (or HTML), XML is an intelligent, self-aware format. XML not only holds data; it can also hold data *about* the data (metadata), facilitating Search and other functions.

- XML is an *extensible* language, capable of being customized to suit the needs of any institution, company, or business or academic category, and of generating additional XML-based languages that perform specific tasks, such as data syndication or the delivery of web services.

- XML is based on rules that ensure consistency as data is transferred to other databases, transformed to other formats, or manipulated by other XML applications.

- Via additional XML protocols and XML-based helper languages, XML data can be automatically transferred to a wide variety of formats, from web pages to printed catalogs and annual reports. This transformational power is the stuff developers could only dream about before XML came along. Nor do corporate bean counters fail to appreciate the cost-saving efficiencies that XML facilitates.

A Mother Lode of Inventions

The next four examples and the lessons that follow from them will suggest the depth of XML acceptance on the web and illustrate how the continual emergence of new XML-derived languages and protocols solves problems that once daunted even the brainiest developers.

Extensible Stylesheet Language Transformations (*www.w3.org/TR/xslt*)

This XML-based markup language can extract and sort XML data and format it as HTML or XHTML, ready for immediate online viewing. If you prefer, XSLT can transform your data to PDF or text or use it to drive a continuously update-able chart or similar business image rendered in the Scalable Vector Graphics

(SVG) format. XSLT can even do all these things simultaneously. For a hands-on tutorial, see J. David Eisenberg's "Using XML" (`www.alistapart.com/stories/usingxml/`).

Resource Description Framework (*www.w3.org/RDF/*)

This XML-based language provides a coherent structure for applications that exchange metadata on the web. In practical terms, RDF integrates library catalogs and directories; collects and syndicates news, software, and all kinds of content; and facilitates communication and sharing between various types of collections (such as personal photo and music collections, to steal an example from the write-up on W3C's site). The power of RDF can also drive software. If you happen to have the Mozilla browser available on your desktop, open its folders and sniff around. You'll find RDF (and CSS) files that help the browser do its job. Specifically, dig around in the profile folders. Each profile has its own set of XML-based files.

Rich Site Summary (*http://backend.userland.com/rss092*)

Rich Site Summary (RSS) is a lightweight XML vocabulary for describing websites, originally developed by Dan Libby to populate AOL/Netscape's "My Netscape" portal. After AOL lost interest in it in April 2001, Dave Winer's UserLand Software Company carried the spec forward. Today, RSS is used by thousands of sites, making it among the most widely accepted XML formats on the web today [4.6].

4.6
The weblog, or personal periodical, at Splorp.com offers an XML RSS feed, enabling the site's content to be easily syndicated (`www.splorp.com`). By the way, the site claims that "Splorp is the sound of scooping lasagna." Now you know.

XML-RPC (*www.xmlrpc.com*)

Another UserLand Software innovation, XML-RPC is "a spec and a set of implementations that allow software running on disparate operating systems [and] …in different environments to make procedure calls over the Internet." Among other things, XML-RPC can be used to automate site management tasks in web publishing tools.

Web Publishing Tools for the Rest of Us

As this brief survey shows, what XML-aware software products described earlier in this chapter do at a price, XML-based languages do for free in the hands of clever developers. In turn, these developers often create new products to facilitate the needs of their fellow designers, developers, and authors.

Personal publishing software like Movable Type (`www.movabletype.org`), used by HTML-savvy and nontechnically oriented publishers alike to maintain web journals, news sites, and web logs, employs XML-RPC to facilitate site management and XML RSS to automatically syndicate and distribute content to other XML-aware sites [4.7]. While Movable Type grants its users the power to publish, XML gives Movable Type the ability to exist.

Movable Type is but one of several publishing products that use XML to manage and syndicate content. Others include Radio UserLand [4.8], UserLand Frontier (`http://frontier.userland.com/`), and Pyra Software's Blogger (`www.blogger.com`). These products are continually growing in popularity, as a second wave of personal publishers, including those who missed the initial web "revolution," discover the joy of sharing their thoughts online.

Thus, as personal publishing spreads, so does XML—not only among sophisticated developers but also among those who've never heard of the XML standard and would be hard pressed to write XML (or sometimes, even HTML) on their own.

What's sauce for independents is sauce for market leaders. Flash MX imports, exports, and works with XML, thereby adding the business benefits of standards-based data exchange to the proprietary creative power of Macromedia's widely used design tool. Developers can use the same XML data to drive Flash and non-Flash versions of a site, saving time and expense while making better use of resources.

At Your Service(s)

The logic of XML drives the emerging web services market, too. The XML-based Simple Object Access Protocol (`www.develop.com/soap/`) facilitates informa-tion exchange in a decentralized, platform-independent network environment, accessing services, objects, and servers, and encoding, decoding, and process-ing messages. The underlying power of XML allows SOAP to cut through the complexity of multiple platforms and products.

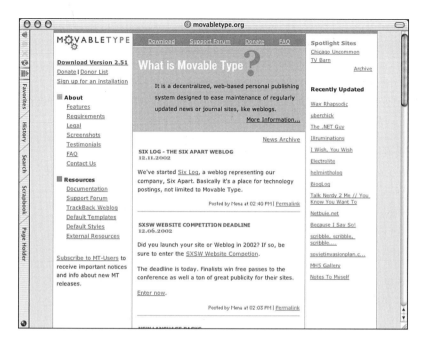

4.7

Movable Type, a convenient web publishing tool, uses XML derivatives to facilitate site management and make content available to other XML-aware sites (www.movabletype.org).

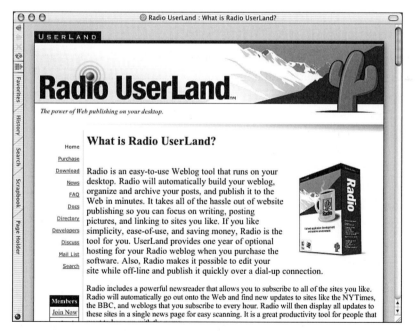

4.8

Radio UserLand (http://radio.userland.com/) uses XML derivatives like SOAP to "take all of the hassle out of website publishing so you can focus on writing, posting pictures, and linking to sites you like."

SOAP is only one protocol in the burgeoning world of web services (www.w3.org/2002/ws/), a category that big companies like IBM (www-106.ibm.com/developerworks/webservices/) and Microsoft (www.microsoft.com/net/) hope to own. Small, independent, and open source developers offer a competing vision of decentralized web services, where no single company dominates. David Rosam defines web services like this:

> Web Services are reusable software components based on XML and related protocols that enable near zero-cost interaction throughout the business ecosystem. They can be used internally for fast and low-cost application integration or made available to customers, suppliers, or partners over the Internet. [Source: www.dangerous-thinking.com/stories/2002/02/16/webServicesDefined.html]

XML drives most web services protocols, and its built-in interoperability is largely what makes such services possible. As long as XML is free to all, there's no reason that any company (however large and powerful) need dominate the category.

XML Applications and Your Site

XML is the language on which Scalable Vector Graphics (www.w3.org/TR/SVG/) and Extensible Hypertext Markup Language (www.w3.org/TR/2002/REC-xhtml1-20020801/) are based. Illustrators who export their client's logo in the SVG format and web authors who compose their pages in XHTML are using XML, whether they know it or not.

The rules that are common to all forms of XML help these formats work together and with other kinds of XML—for instance, with XML stored in a database. An SVG graphic might be automatically altered in response to a visitor-generated search or continuously updated according to data delivered by an XML news feed.

The site of a local TV news channel could use this capability to display live Metro Traffic in all its congested glory. As one traffic jam cleared and another began, the news feed would relay this information to the server, where it would be formatted as user-readable text content in XHTML and as an updated traffic map in SVG. At the same time, the data might be syndicated in RDF or RSS for sharing with other news organizations or used by SOAP to help city officials pinpoint and respond to the problem.

Although based on XML, SVG graphics are easy to create in products like Adobe Illustrator 10 (`www.adobe.com/products/illustrator/main.html`). Like Flash vector graphics, images created in SVG can fill even the largest monitors while using little bandwidth. And SVG graphics, like other standard web page components, can be manipulated via ECMAScript and the DOM. Not to mention that SVG textual content is accessible by default, and can even be selected with the cursor no matter how it's been stretched or deformed.

Still in Its Infancy

Presently, the power of SVG is somewhat limited by the need to use a plug-in (`www.adobe.com/svg/`), as with Flash. Nor does the plug-in currently work equally well across platforms and browsers. When browsers natively support SVG, its ability to add standards-based visual interactivity to all websites will be that much more enhanced.

Presently too, browser support for XML is in its infancy. Although XML powers software, databases, and web services, few browsers can usefully display raw XML files, and the creation of XML applications exceeds the capabilities of most designers and site owners.

The development community has solved the latter problem by creating XML-based languages, protocols, and products the rest of us can use "behind the screens." The W3C has solved the problem of browser support for XML by combining the familiar simplicity of HTML with the extensible power of XML in the XHTML markup standard we'll explore in Chapter 5, "Modern Markup."

Compatible by Nature

Because they share a common parent and abide by the same house rules, all XML applications are compatible with each other, making it easier for developers to manipulate one set of XML data via another and to develop new XML applications as the need arises, without fear of incompatibility.

Ubiquitous in today's professional and consumer software, widely used in web middleware and back-end development, essential to the emerging web services market, and forward compatible by design, XML solves the obsolescence problem described in Chapter 1, "99.9% of Websites Are Obsolete." XML has succeeded beyond anyone's wildest dreams because it solves everyone's worst nightmares of incompatibility and technological dead ends.

Software makers, disinclined to risk customer loss by being the "odd man out," recognize that supporting XML enables their products to work with others and remain viable in a changing market. Executives and IT professionals, unwilling to let proprietary legacy systems continue to hold their organization's precious data hostage, can solve their problem lickety-split by converting to XML. Small independent developers can compete against the largest companies by harnessing the power of XML, which rewards brains, not budgets.

In today's data-driven world, proprietary formats no longer cut it—if they ever did. XML levels the playing field and invites everyone to play. XML is a web standard, and it works.

And that is the hallmark of a good standard: that it works, gets a job done, and plays well with other standards. Call it interoperability (the W3C's word for it), or call it simple cooperation between components. Whatever you call it, XML is a vast improvement over the bad old days of proprietary web technologies. Under the spell of web standards, competitors, too, have learned to cooperate.

A New Era of Cooperation

As we might have mentioned a few hundred times, Microsoft, Netscape, and Opera finally support the same standards in their browsers. As an unexpected consequence of their *technological* cooperation, these once bitter competitors have learned to play nicely together in other, often surprising ways.

In July 2002, Microsoft submitted to the W3C's HTML Working Group "a set of HTML tests and testable assertions in support of the W3C HTML 4.01 Test Suite Development" (`http://lists.w3.org/Archives/Public/www-qa-wg/2002Jul/0103.html`). The contribution was made on behalf of Microsoft, Openwave Systems, Inc., and America Online, Inc., owners of Netscape and Mozilla. Opera Software Corporation (makers of the Opera browser) and The Web Standards Project also reviewed it.

Test Suites and Specifications

W3C test suites enable browser makers to determine if their software complies with a standard or requires more work. No test suite existed for HTML 4.01 (the markup language that is also the basis of XHTML 1.0). In the absence of such a test suite, browser makers wanting to comply with those standards had to cross their fingers and hope for the best.

Moreover, in the absence of a test suite, the makers of standards found themselves in an odd position. How can you be certain that a technology you're inventing adequately addresses the problems it's supposed to solve when you lack a practical proving ground? It's like designing a car on paper without having a machine shop to build what you've envisioned.

In the interest of standards makers as well as browser builders, a test suite was long overdue.

How Suite It Is

When Microsoft took the initiative to correct the problem created by the absence of a test suite, it chose not to act alone, instead inviting its competitors and an outside group (WaSP) to participate in the standards-based effort. Just as significantly, those competitors and that outside group jumped at the chance. The work was submitted free of patent or royalty encumbrance, with resulting or derivative works to be wholly owned by the W3C. Neither Microsoft nor its competitors attempted to make a dime for their trouble.

In the ordinary scheme of things, Microsoft is not known for considering what's best for AOL/Netscape, nor is the latter company overly concerned with helping Microsoft—and neither wastes many brain cells figuring out what's good for Opera. And these companies didn't go into business to lose money on selfless ventures. Yet here they all were, acting in concert for the good of the web, and focusing, not on some fancy new proprietary technology, but on humble HTML 4.

Ignored by the trade press, the quiet event signifies a sea change. We've come a long way from the days when browser makers focused on "our browser only" technologies at the expense of web standards and web users and in hopes of spoiling the market for their competitors. Browser makers still innovate, of course, and they still hope you'll choose their product over a competitor's. But their newfound willingness to work together shows how deeply they are committed to interoperability via web standards and how greatly the industry has changed from the days of the browser wars (1996–1999).

Don't Believe the Hype

From time to time, newspapers and trade journals seize on some shift in the browser market to declare that the browser wars have reopened. It happened in June 2002, when AOL switched its CompuServe users from an IE-based browser to a Mozilla/Netscape-based one. "Shift in Web Market Upsets Developers!" shrilled the trade journals. "Browser Wars II!" shrieked the business sections of consumer newspapers. Similar press screeches resounded a few months later, when AOL switched its Mac OS X users to a Gecko-based browser. Don't believe the hype.

In today's news economy, editors must sell papers if they want to hold onto their jobs. Crisis and conflict always outsell reasoned reportage, and tabloid instincts have little to do with the dull, pragmatic truth. Regardless of occasional shifts in market share, the browser wars are behind us, and no editor's wish can bring them back.

The web will be built on the bedrock of technologies discussed in this book and supported by all major browsers. AOL/Netscape and Microsoft will still skirmish from time to time, but competition between them has largely shifted from the realm of the browser to arenas that need not concern us (with the exception of FrontPage, discussed next).

The Web Comes of Age

Although not as miraculous (or as important) as a U.N. peace plan, the "set of HTML tests" quietly presented to W3C by Microsoft and its staunchest business foes signals a permanent shift in the way the web will move forward. When competitors cooperate in this way, it's a sign that the medium they serve has come of age.

The same thing happens in any mature industry. Record companies that hate each other will band together peaceably to present a new industry standard or to ward off perceived threats to their livelihood (such as peer-to-peer music file sharing on the Net). That Microsoft, AOL/Netscape, and Opera can work together tells us that the web has matured. What brought them together (a W3C test suite) tells us *why* the maturation has come. Our medium has grown up because of the standards discussed in this book.

We can anticipate more cooperation and increased support for standards in the years to come. We can also relax, knowing that sites built to standards will continue to work in these manufacturer's browsers today, tomorrow, or 10 years from now. Their joint actions prove they're as committed to forward compatibility as any designer or site owner could hope.

As yet another example of a browser maker's commitment to supporting standards, Netscape funds a small team of standards evangelists whose mission is to work for improved standards in the browser and on websites and who publish cross-browser solutions based on open standards, not "best viewed in Netscape" or other proprietary fixes.

Web Standards and Authoring Tools

Developed at the height of the browser wars, market-leading, professional visual editors like Macromedia Dreamweaver and Adobe GoLive initially addressed the problem of browser incompatibility by generating markup and code optimized for 3.0 and 4.0 browsers.

When browsers ran on nonstandard, invalid HTML tags, Dreamweaver and GoLive fed them what they needed. If each browser had its own incompatible Document Object Model, driven by its own proprietary scripting language, Dreamweaver and GoLive would code accordingly.

In so doing, Dreamweaver and GoLive were no more at fault than developers who authored the same kind of markup and code by hand. As explained in Chapter 2, "Designing and Building with Standards," site builders did what they had to do when standards were still being developed and browsers had yet to support them. "Feed 'em what they ask for" made sense in those days but is no longer an appropriate strategy. As browsers shored up their standards support, tools like Dreamweaver and GoLive needed to do likewise. Today they have.

The Dreamweaver Task Force

The Web Standards Project's Dreamweaver Task Force was created in 2001 to work with Macromedia's engineers in an effort to improve the standards compliance and accessibility of sites produced with Dreamweaver, the market leader among professional visual web editors. The Task Force's history can be found at www.webstandards.org/act/campaign/dwtf/.

Among the group's primary objectives as crafted by Rachel Andrew and Drew McLellan were these:

- Dreamweaver should produce valid markup "out of the box." (Valid markup uses only standard tags and attributes and contains no errors. We'll explain this further in Chapter 5.)

- Dreamweaver should allow the choice between XHTML and HTML versions, inserting a valid DTD for each choice. (A DTD, or Document Type Definition, tells the browser what kind of markup has been used to author a web page. See Chapter 5.)

- Dreamweaver should respect a document's DTD and produce markup and code in accordance with it.

- Dreamweaver should enable users to easily create web documents accessible to all.

- Dreamweaver should render CSS2 to a good level of accuracy so that pages formatted with CSS can be worked on within the Dreamweaver visual environment.

- Dreamweaver should not corrupt valid CSS layouts by inserting inline styling without the user's consent.

- Dreamweaver users should feel confident that their Dreamweaver-created pages will validate and have a high level of accessibility.

These and other objectives were met by the release in May 2002 of Dreamweaver MX. Assessing the product they had helped shape, the Task Force found that Dreamweaver MX

- Produced valid markup out of the box
- Helped users create accessible sites
- Rendered CSS2 to a reasonable level of accuracy (although CSS positioning remains somewhat problematic)
- Avoided corrupting CSS layouts
- Encouraged XHTML and CSS validation (automated testing for standards compliance)
- Respected and promoted web standards

See for Yourself

You can read the WaSP Dreamweaver Task Force's full product assessment at `www.webstandards.org/act/campaign/dwtf/mxassessed.html`.

WYSIWYG Tools Come of Age (Two Out of Three Ain't Bad)

For purposes of this chapter, suffice it to say that Dreamweaver MX goes far beyond lip service in its support for web standards and accessibility. Its capabilities and standards support are commensurate with that of today's browsers.

Although the WaSP was unable to work with Adobe, that company independently and substantially improved the standards support in its GoLive professional visual web authoring product (www.adobe.com/products/golive/main.html).

In addition to CSS and XHTML, GoLive supports the Synchronized Multimedia Integration Language (www.w3.org/AudioVideo/), the W3C standard for creating accessible multimedia presentations. Those who use either of these market-leading visual web editors can readily produce standards-compliant, accessible sites.

FrontPage: Noncompliant by Design

A third product in the category, Microsoft FrontPage, is little used by professionals but widely used by semi-professionals, possibly because it comes bundled with other Microsoft products. Professionals in the public sector might find themselves stuck using FrontPage because the budget doesn't allow for an "additional" web editor.

"We already own a web editor," the bean counters might tell you. They're wrong. FrontPage is not a visual web editor. It is an IE page editor.

Although Microsoft makes standards-compliant browsers, its FrontPage tool spews proprietary markup and code, generating sites that look and work right only in Internet Explorer. FrontPage's nonstandard output is not due to ineptitude. The bug is a feature, although not one designed for any user's benefit.

In court testimony, Microsoft's Bill Gates admitted he'd sent a memo directing that the Office software group, which includes FrontPage, stop working to make its documents interoperable with other products (that is, stop making them standards-based). Gates did not want competitive products to be able to open, save, and edit Microsoft-generated documents. As a result, if you use FrontPage to design or develop websites, you pretty much guarantee that they will only look and work right in Internet Explorer.

There is some hope. In July 2002, UsableNet announced that it had integrated its LIFT accessibility tool into Microsoft FrontPage (`www.usablenet.com/frontend/onenews.go?news_id=45`), thus encouraging FrontPage users to author accessible sites. (LIFT is also incorporated in Dreamweaver MX.) Although it's no guarantee that standards compliance is next for FrontPage, this newfound emphasis on accessibility is at least a small step in that direction.

For the time being, however, if you want to create standards-compliant, accessible sites, your best options are authoring by hand in a text editor or using Dreamweaver or GoLive. Use FrontPage only if you're prepared to edit by hand almost every tag and attribute that product generates.

The Emergence of CSS Layout

The CSS1 specification was created in 1996 to end presentational HTML, separating the way a site looked from the data it contained. By 2000, all popular browsers were finally capable of properly displaying pure CSS layouts. But designers and developers still hesitated to embrace CSS so long as a significant portion of their visitors used noncompliant 4.0 and older browsers. Something had to be done to make web standards "safe" for mainstream designers and developers. The Web Standards Project decided that guerrilla tactics were needed.

The Browser Upgrade Campaign

In February 2001, The Web Standards Project launched its Browser Upgrade campaign (`www.webstandards.org/act/campaign/buc/`). As its name suggests, the campaign was intended to foster consumer trial of newer, more standards-compliant browsers, thereby also encouraging designers to use standards instead of HTML hacks and proprietary code.

In some cases, the campaign did this by encouraging developers to *act as if* their entire audience were already using standards-compliant browsers and nothing but. A JavaScript fragment in the `<head>` of a document could test the DOM awareness of any browser hitting that page. If the browser "got" the DOM, it also got the page. If it didn't, the visitor was bounced to a page his browser could understand.

That page advised the visitor to upgrade his browser to a more recent version of IE, Netscape, Opera, or other compliant browsers, and it also told him why such an upgrade would improve his web experience.

Unlike the "Best Viewed With…" marketing campaigns of old, the WaSP's Browser Upgrade campaign was manufacturer agnostic. We didn't care whose browser you downloaded, as long as that browser complied with standards.

This brute force technique was recommended only for sites that correctly used CSS layout *and* the DOM, and only for noncommercial or nonessential sites that could afford to risk bouncing visitors in this way. Participating designers and developers were encouraged to build their own "Browser Upgrades" pages, customized to their visitors' needs; to use such techniques only on valid, standards-compliant sites; and to carefully weigh the advantages and disadvantages of taking such a step.

Browser Upgrades Used and Abused

Alas, all too often, lazy developers used the technique to bounce visitors away from sites that were not even close to complying with standards. Compounding the damage, instead of creating their own upgrade pages, these developers invariably sent them to WaSP's. As you might expect, such efforts more frequently resulted in consumer frustration than in the desired trial of compliant browsers.

Among the offenders was a site featuring pictorials of cheerleaders. Raiderettes.com [4.9], a top referrer to The Web Standards Project's Browser Upgrade campaign page, is a nice-enough looking site, but an attempt to validate its markup (http://validator.w3.org/) results in the following report:

Fatal Error: no document type declaration; will parse without validation.
I could not parse this document, because it uses a public identifier that is not in my catalog.
Raiderettes.com, like several other commercial sites, had used the WaSP's browser-bouncing code, not in the service of standards, but simply as a convenient means of rejecting browsers that could not handle its DHTML menus. Needless to say, The Web Standards Project received much mail from testosterone-maddened men who had hoped to ogle ladies, not read about CSS and ECMAScript. Nothing is uglier than the rancor of a lonely man denied his ogling time (except maybe the man himself).

4.9
Raiderettes.com, official
site of the Oakland Raider
cheerleading team
(www.raiderettes.com).
What have cheerleader
bios and pin-up shots to
do with web standards?
Read on.

A Kinder, Gentler Upgrade Path

Such failures aside, the campaign succeeded in encouraging thousands of designers and developers to give standards a try. It also raised standards awareness in the business community by seizing the attention of the trade press. And once in a while, it persuaded consumers to download compliant browsers.

Although the Browser Upgrade campaign achieved notoriety through its browser-blocking antics, it was a multilayered effort offering consumer-friendly tactics that got less press but did more good. To support the newly launched campaign and demonstrate its more consumer-friendly side, A List Apart (www.alistapart.com) simultaneously redesigned using CSS layout and valid HTML (which soon gave way to XHTML), as described in Chapter 2.

In an attempt to demonstrate the campaign's flexibility, ALA deliberately avoided excluding any visitor. Instead, the site merely hid its layout from non-compliant browsers. Readers using IE5+, Netscape 6, Opera 5+, and similarly capable browsers got content plus layout. Those using older browsers got content sans layout. Noncompliant browser users also saw a discreet "browser upgrade" message that was hidden from users of more capable browsers. Standards were in full force, yet everyone was welcome.

To pique designer interest, ALA cloaked its consumer-friendly approach in the garb of propaganda, describing its redesign manifesto-style and making much of the fact that its layout would henceforth be hidden from non-CSS-capable browsers, which the magazine indignantly consigned to Hell [4.10 and 4.11].

4.10
"To Hell with Old Browsers!" This ALA manifesto challenged designers to use CSS for layout, the DOM for code, and let markup be markup instead of forcing HTML to serve the needs of layout (www.alistapart.com/stories/tohell/).

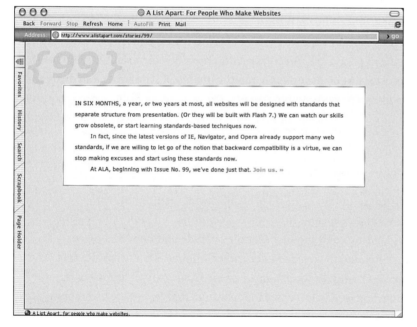

4.11
The CSS front piece to ALA No. 99 as it appeared in February 2001, concurrent with the launch of the Browser Upgrade campaign (www.alistapart.com/stories/99/).

A List Apart challenged its 70,000 weekly readers to stop making excuses and start incorporating standards on their sites. A prologue [4.11] that had been hastily written on a napkin at a web conference (and then laid out in CSS) reads like this:

> In six months, a year, or two years at most, all websites will be designed with standards that separate structure from presentation. (Or they will be built with Flash 7.) We can watch our skills grow obsolete, or start learning standards-based techniques now.
>
> In fact, since the latest versions of IE, Navigator, and Opera already support many web standards, if we are willing to let go of the notion that backward compatibility is a virtue, we can stop making excuses and start using these standards now.
>
> At ALA, beginning with Issue No. 99, we've done just that. Join us.

The Flood Begins

The editorial struck a chord. Within days, one independent site after another began converting to CSS for layout and XHTML for structure. The daily site of Todd Dominey [4.12] is representative of these CSS converts in its choice of technology, while well above average in the quality of its writing and design. A new media professional based in Atlanta, Dominey uses Flash for his multiple award-winning portfolio site [4.13], and he uses CSS and XHTML for his daily web log.

On the latter site, Dominey explains why he converted to pure web standards:

> This site uses full-blown XHTML/CSS layout techniques. No transparent gif spacers. No rows. No columns. No junk. The reason is simple—I'm a new media designer by trade and needed a place to experiment with advanced design techniques client work doesn't usually allow (rightly so, in some cases). The layout techniques are bleeding edge and will be continuously updated for newer browsers. If you are using at least Internet Explorer 5.0 (Mac and Win) or up, in addition to Mozilla, Netscape 6, and Opera, you won't have problems. Any older or beta browsers, like iCab and OmniWeb, will have problems. If all you see is gray background and blue text, you desperately need to upgrade your browser.

www.whatdoiknow.org/about.shtml

4.12
The two sides of Todd Dominey, new media designer. His smart daily site (shown here) uses XHTML for document structure and CSS for layout (www.whatdoiknow.org).

4.13
Dominey's award-winning portfolio site makes smart use of Flash (www.domineydesign.com).

Countless Converts and the Help Sites They Rode in On

Countless personal sites and web logs have gone the CSS/XHTML route in the two years since the Browser Upgrade campaign and the ALA redesign hit the design community like a double uppercut. (Well, maybe not quite like a double uppercut. We're designers, not fight fans, and our sports similes rarely stand up to scrutiny.)

To help facilitate the sudden interest in CSS layout, several personal sites published open source CSS layouts, free for the taking. Don't understand how CSS works? Unsure how to lay out pages with styles? Visit any of these sites to linger and learn or copy and paste:

- Blue Robot's Layout Reservoir [4.14]
- Eric Costello's CSS Layout Techniques (`http://glish.com/css/`)
- Owen Briggs's "Little Boxes" visual layouts page [4.15]

For those with more aggressive ambitions, Eric Meyer (author of *Eric Meyer on CSS*) offers "css/edge" [4.16], sporting cutting-edge CSS layout techniques that work only in the most compliant browsers. Such techniques by nature cannot be used in most client work, but they provide a training ground for the kind of work we'll be able to do next year.

4.14

Blue Robot's Layout Reservoir offers clean, useful CSS layouts, free for the taking (`www.bluerobot.com/web/layouts/`).

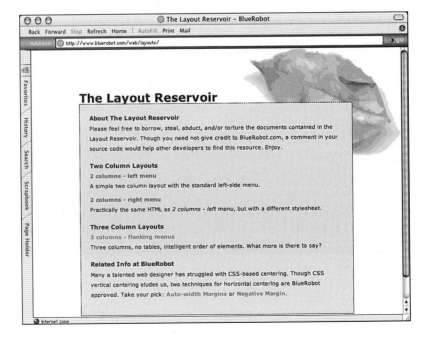

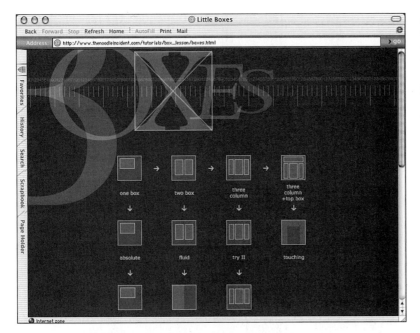

4.15
Owen Briggs's Little Boxes visual layouts page (http://www.thenoodleincident.com/tutorials/box_lesson/boxes.html). See a layout, click on it, and get the CSS that created it (yours to use and adapt on your own web projects).

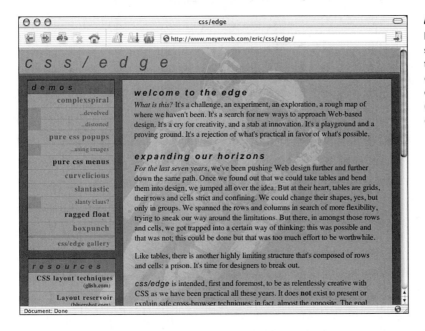

4.16
Eric Meyer's css/edge sports cutting-edge techniques that work only in the newest, most compliant browsers (www.meyerweb.com/eric/css/edge/).

Most CSS designers are content to produce sites that look right in IE5 or better and degrade acceptably (or simply show content sans layout) in Netscape 4. Mark Newhouse's Real World Style [4.17] usefully offers CSS layouts that work acceptably in Netscape 4 and other antiquated browsers. Want to say yes to CSS? Can't afford to say "to hell with old browsers?" You don't have to say anything of the kind—Real World Style points the way.

4.17

On the opposite end of the spectrum from css/edge, Mark Newhouse's Real World Style (www.realworld-style.com) offers open source CSS layouts that work reasonably well even in browsers as old and wretched as Netscape 4. (Naturally, they work well in newer, more compliant browsers, too.)

Faddishness…with a Purpose

As the CSS/XHTML combo took hold in the realm of personal and independent sites, accessibility was added to the mix via conformance with Section 508 or WAI accessibility guidelines. As of this writing, leading independent sites fall into one of two categories (as indicated by the dual productions of Todd Dominey):

- Forward-compatible, standards-based sites that use CSS for layout and XHTML for structure and comply with Section 508 or other accessibility guidelines

- Full-on Flash sites that exploit the power of ActionScript (a Macromedia scripting language based on standard ECMAScript)

It's fair to say that if your personal site does not exploit web standards or Flash, many of your peers in the design community will consider you hopelessly out of step. Such snobbery might appear faddish and trivial, and indeed it is. But by harnessing flaws in human nature, it serves a higher goal: the adoption of forward-looking techniques on mainstream sites.

Leadership Comes from Individuals

Personal and independent sites have always pushed boundaries, and their innovations have always inspired subsequent change in the mainstream. JavaScript, frames, and pop-up windows first appeared on bleeding-edge personal sites. When no one died after viewing such sites, commercial designers reasoned that it was safe to incorporate JavaScript, frames, and pop-up windows in client work. Hence, we get DHTML drop-down menus on e-commerce sites (`www.coach.com/index_noflash.asp`) and heinous pop-up and pop-under ads with our daily fix of `www.nytimes.com`. (Obviously, this hasn't always been a good thing.)

The transfer of technologies from cutting-edge sites to mainstream ones will be better this time around because this time, the cutting edge has focused on interoperable *standards and accessibility* instead of *gimmicks*. Prompted on one side by inspiring personal sites and on the other by emerging laws, the change has already begun.

The Mainstreaming of Web Standards

In 2001, the U.S. and Canada published guidelines demanding that government-related sites be developed with web standards and made accessible. The governments of Britain and New Zealand soon followed suit, as did numerous American states.

In 2002, mainstream government-related sites including Texas Parks & Wildlife (`www.tpwd.state.tx.us`) and the home page of Juneau, Alaska [**4.18**] converted to web standards including CSS layout. Texas Parks & Wildlife explained its conversion this way (`www.tpwd.state.tx.us/standards/tpwbui.htm`):

> Texas Parks & Wildlife, as a state agency, is required by Texas Administrative Code §201.12 to code web pages using the web standards set forth by the W3C. The driving force behind these requirements is the issue of accessibility. Web pages must be accessible to all users, regardless of disability or technology used to access web pages.

But if the pages do not look the same for everyone, how are they accessible?

Being accessible does not mean that everyone sees the same thing. Accessibility is about content and information. It is about making all content (text, images, and multimedia) available to the user. In order to do this according to the standards, TPW makes use of Cascading Style Sheets to separate content from presentation. Separating presentation from content will enable TPW to offer higher quality pages and dynamic, timely content.

The web coding standards set forth by the W3C make creating accessible pages possible. By using such W3C standards as Cascading Style Sheets and XHTML, Texas Parks & Wildlife has begun to create compliant web pages.

4.18

Welcome to beautiful Juneau, Alaska, home of tourism, mining, fishing, and style sheets (www.juneau.org). Juneau.org was among the first public sites to scrap old-school frames and such for CSS layout and structured XHTML markup.

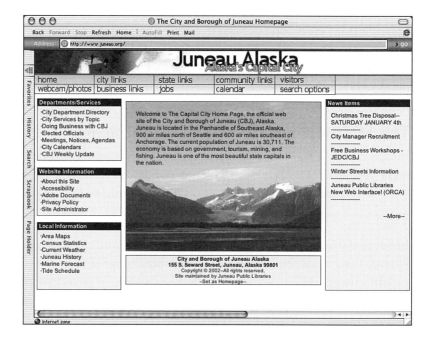

The developers of the home page for Alaska's Capital City provided a similar rationale (www.juneau.org/about/stylesheets.php):

We are converting the CBJ site from a frame structure to the Cascading Style Sheet (CSS) standard. This standard allows us greater freedom with design while increasing the accessibility of the content for our users. Using style sheets, we can make our content available to nearly all browser and computing platforms, including handheld and ADA devices, from the same page rather than maintaining "text only" or "printer friendly" duplicates of our pages. Likewise, it will allow us to avoid many of the pitfalls we encounter with our current "frame-based" layout.

…The only downside is that many older browsers are not style sheet compliant. The upside of the downside, however, is that style sheets are much kinder to non-compliant browsers than frames are to no-frames browsers. Browsers that are not style sheet compliant will display the content of a CSS web page in a "text" format. Although it is not pretty, all the information (including links and images) is displayed. In fact, using style sheets, the web designer can control the order in which the content is displayed in a non-compliant browser without compromising how the site is displayed in compliant browsers. This ability alone is a major advantage of Cascading Style Sheets. This allows web pages to be tailored to both old and new browsers. As a website designer, I would much rather have my users say my web pages "look funny" rather than saying they "don't work."

Most of the newer versions of the popular browsers are CSS-compliant. If your current browser is not style sheet compliant, please click on one of the buttons below to download a compliant browser. For older systems (with slower processors and less memory), select the Opera browser. This browser has much lower system requirements than the other two.

Commercial Sites Take the Plunge

In 2002, mainstream commercial sites also began converting to CSS and XHTML techniques their developers might once have argued against on the grounds of "backward compatibility." In July of that year, leading search engine Lycos Europe moved to XHTML markup and CSS layout, followed in December by American Lycos property HotBot. Around the same time, the super-fast AllTheWeb search engine [4.19] also converted to CSS and XHTML and added user-defined style sheets to its customization capabilities.

4.19

AllTheWeb, the search engine most likely to unseat Google (if anyone can), converted to XHTML structure and CSS layout in 2002 (www.alltheweb.com).

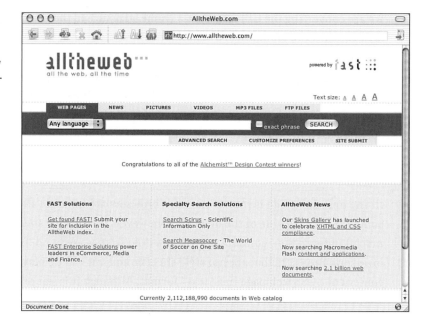

As of this writing, Google and Yahoo have yet to follow the lead of these some-what smaller competitors, but as we've just finished saying, that is the nature of change: Small independents take the risks first, and the big boys follow when they're sure it's safe.

Wired Digital Converts

In September of 2002, the popular Wired Digital site was reborn as a purely standards-compliant site: XHTML for data, CSS for presentation [4.20, 4.21]. Team leader Douglas Bowman [4.22] supervised the redesign and made standards compliance its number-one priority.

As a high-traffic, highly visible site with a well-earned reputation for under-standing and using web technology, Wired has long served as a beacon to the development community. Its conversion to web standards sent a clear signal to the industry that the time had come to put forward compatibility ahead of outmoded concerns.

4.20
Wired Digital
(www.wired.com)
converted to standards
in 2002, using XHTML
for structure and CSS
for layout.

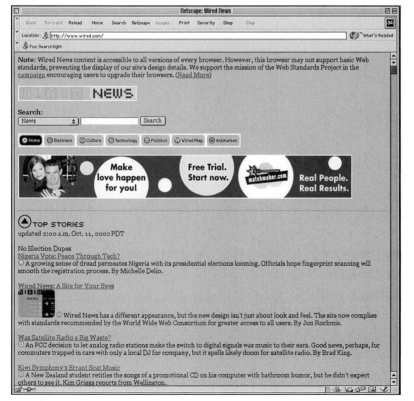

4.21
Viewed in a noncompliant
browser (in this case,
Netscape 4), Wired Digital
(www.wired.com)
provides full content
access but hides its layout,
using the same technique
deployed in the 2001 A List
Apart standards redesign,
and linking to The Web
Standards Project's
Browser Upgrades
campaign to encourage
holdouts to switch to a
modern browser.

4.22

Although many designers and developers worked on the Wired Digital redesign, its standards orientation was largely due to the work and evangelism of one man, Douglas Bowman, who thereafter left Wired to run his own company, Stop Design. The Stop Design site (www.stopdesign.com) also makes brilliant use of CSS layout and well-structured XHTML.

Poop in the Soup

Validation errors initially clouded Wired Digital's launch. Some of these errors were caused by the Vignette content management system used by Wired's in-house editorial staff. Others were due to third-party advertising content built with invalid methods and improper URL handling. My agency, Happy Cog, has faced similar obstacles, and you might have encountered the same problem yourself. After you deliver compliant templates, an outdated content management system (CMS) adds junk markup and proprietary code, thereby wrecking the site's compliance. Add poop to your soup, and it's no longer a healthy meal.

In Wired's case, these problems were quickly remedied (mainly because Bowman insisted), and within a day or two of the launch, Wired Digital was a perfectly standards-compliant, large-scale commercial site. Not every company has the technological chops to fix errors introduced by Vignette and its brethren, nor can every company afford to do so.

For the web to progress, publishing tools must become standards-compliant (see the next sidebar, "Publishing Systems and Standards"). Site owners and managers must tell CMS vendors that compliance matters, just as designers and developers once told browser makers. If enough customers do this, the vendors might be willing to upgrade their tools, and achieving standards compliance will become that much easier.

Publishing Systems and Standards

Pure XHTML/CSS validation is rarely achieved on large-scale, commercial sites, even when the initial templates validate and the client and builders are fully committed to supporting W3C specifications. Admittedly, clients and builders who care are still too rare a breed. But those who do care often find their best efforts flummoxed by outdated middleware, compromised databases, and other such roadblocks.

As we noted earlier in this chapter, independent designers and developers have no problem authoring to the W3C's CSS and XHTML specs. Some even enjoy fixing commercial sites with which they are unaffiliated, bringing such sites up to spec with a few hours' work. (For instance, Eric Meyer has done this with the KPMG site discussed in Chapter 1.)

Valid XHTML and CSS and Priority 1 accessibility are not hard to achieve. Any halfway-competent designer or developer can do it. The problem lies in the large-scale systems and third-party content that must be integrated into most big sites.

To ensure the health and interoperability of our sites, we need content management systems that encourage compliant, accessible authoring practices instead of breaking them. We need those who build such systems to recognize that compromising the front end "to force a display issue" is no longer an acceptable option. And we need clients who are willing to invest in fixing systems that "work" at the expense of forward compatibility. It will take persuasion and it will take money.

There is no shortage of persuasion. Money is another story.

In a healthy economy, companies invest in R&D, training, and long-range planning. In a sick economy, companies focus on cutting costs, eliminating personnel and processes, and keeping their doors open for the next 24 hours. Encouraging designers and developers to learn compliant authoring methods is easy; show them the benefits. Coaxing struggling companies to invest in the long-term health of their web presence is the real challenge faced by those who would wrest the web out of the Dark Ages and turn its face to the light.

Embracing Standards with Transitional Methods

Not all standards compliance demands CSS layout, and not all businesses and institutions that are eager to take advantage of the interoperability provided by web standards need take so advanced a step. Chapter 2 described an interim method of standards compliance blending old and new in a forward-compatible mix, and this method holds appeal for companies or institutions that prefer slow but steady change to evangelical conversion. It's particularly apt for organizations bogged down by a large installed base of old, noncompliant browsers.

The New York Public Library is one such institution, and in 2001, under the leadership of then-web-coordinator Carrie Bickner, The Branch Libraries (www.nypl.org/branch/) of The New York Public Library converted to XHTML 1.0 for markup and a combination of traditional table-based layouts and Cascading Style Sheets for presentation. The library also complies with U.S. Section 508 accessibility guidelines to more effectively reach and serve all its patrons.

Simultaneously with the site's conversion to standards, the library published a style guide (www.nypl.org/styleguide/), co-authored by Bickner and your present scribe, explaining the markup and design requirements for all branch libraries projects, and including a tutorial on XHTML and CSS.

Rather than confine the style guide to the library's internal site, NYPL chose to make it public, in the hope that it would help thousands of designers and developers get up to speed on XHTML and CSS and encourage other institutions to support standards. As of this writing, it appears to be succeeding on both counts.

As they initially fired the imagination of independent designers, standards now inspire institutional designers and developers in the trenches, who correctly see web standards and accessibility as the keys to fulfilling their mandate of reaching and serving all their patrons.

The W3C Gets into the Act

It was once the W3C's policy to publish but not *push* its standards. But the era of W3C passivity is ending. In 2001, the W3C formed a Quality Assurance group (http://www.w3.org/QA/) to better communicate with the design and development community and to ensure that W3C specs are usable and correctly implemented. The W3C also began publishing a series of articles intended to explain and promote its specs.

A W3C draft article (`www.w3.org/WAI/bcase/benefits.html`) on the business benefits of accessible, standards-based design includes increased market share and audience reach, streamlined efficiency (with lowered costs), reduction of legal liability, and a clear demonstration of social responsibility. The article is worth reading, printing, and sharing.

If the benefits the W3C article mentions sound familiar, you've been reading this book rather than flipping through its pages in a state of hypnotized inattention. If the benefits sound compelling, they should. Standards and accessibility expand your audience while reducing costs. If that proposition fails to interest a business owner, he or she does not live on the same planet as the rest of us.

Executive Summary

Standards like XML have changed the face of business. Support for standards has ended the browser wars and the toll they took on usability, accessibility, and long-term viability, ushering in a new era of cooperation among even the staunchest competitors. Standards like CSS and XHTML, supported in mainstream browsers and professional authoring tools, are changing site design methods for the better—not only on bleeding-edge independent and personal sites, but also on government, institutional, and commercial sites with no axe to grind beyond improved efficiency and increased outreach. Web standards are winning, and you are there.

Now let's stop exulting and get down to work. Chapter 5 gets the ball rolling and tosses it in your court. (We told you we kind of stink at sports metaphors, didn't we?)

Part II

Designing and Building

chapter five

Modern Markup

In Part I, "Houston, We Have a Problem," we described the creative and business problems engendered by old-school web design methods, outlined the benefits of designing and building with standards, and sketched a general picture of advances in the medium. The rest of this book will move from the general to the particular, and the best place to start is by taking a second look at the fundamentals of web markup.

Many designers and developers will balk at the thought. Surely those of us who've spent more than a few weeks designing professional sites know all there is to know about HTML. Don't designers and developers have newer, more powerful languages to learn in their limited free time? For instance, isn't it more important to study server-side technologies like PHP, ASP, or ColdFusion (see the sidebar, "What Is PHP") than piddle precious hours away rethinking rudiments like the HTML table or paragraph tag?

The answer is yes and no. Server-side technologies are vitally important to the creation of dynamic sites that respond to user queries.

Even traditional informational sites can benefit by storing their content in databases and fetching it as needed via PHP or similar technologies. Indeed, like the web standards this book discusses, server-side scripting languages perform a similar function of abstracting data from the interface. As standards like CSS free the designer from the need to imprison each snippet of content in semantically meaningless, bandwidth-bursting table cells, so do languages like PHP and ASP free site creators from the dunderheaded drudgery of creating each page by hand.

But those dynamically generated web pages won't be much use if they are inaccessible, incompatible with a broad range of browsers and devices, or cluttered with junk markup. If those dynamic pages don't render in some browsers and devices or take 60 seconds to load over dial-up when 10 seconds might suffice, the server-side technologies won't be doing all they can for you or your users. In short, it's not an either/or but a both. Server-side technologies and databases facilitate smarter, more powerful sites, but what those sites deliver is content that works best when it is semantically and cleanly structured. And that's where many of us (and many of the content management systems we rely on) fall short.

What Is PHP?

PHP (www.php.net) is an open source, general-purpose scripting language that is ideally suited to web development and can be embedded in XHTML. Its syntax draws upon C, Java, and Perl and is comparatively easy to learn. PHP (which stands, rather confusingly, for PHP: Hypertext Preprocessor) has many capabilities but has become vastly popular for one: When used in combination with a MySQL (www.mysql.com) database, PHP lets designers and developers easily author dynamic sites and build web applications.

PHP is a project of the Apache Software Foundation (www.apache.org) and is *free*, which is one source of its popularity. (Another is the language's wide array of profiling and debugging tools.) Open source developers and independent web designers are enamored of the language and continually create PHP-based applications they make freely available to their peers. For instance, Dean Allen's Refer (www.textism.com/tools/refer/) tracks incoming visitors who followed a third-party link to your site [5.1], and Dan Benjamin's URL Cleaner [5.2] (www.hivelogic.com/urlcleaner.php) fixes invalid web addresses created by other scripting languages like ColdFusion.

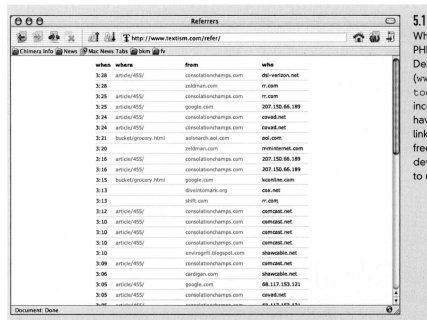

5.1

Whipped together in the PHP scripting language, Dean Allen's Refer (`www.textism.com/tools/refer/`) tracks incoming visitors who have followed third-party links to your site, and it's free to any designer or developer who wants to use it.

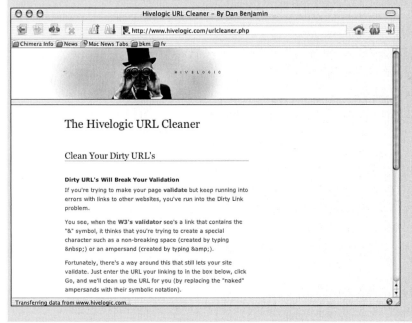

5.2

Dan Benjamin's free URL Cleaner (`www.hivelogic.com/urlcleaner.php`), created in PHP, fixes invalid web addresses.

continues

continued

PHP can run with Microsoft's server software, but it's most often used in combination with the Apache server. Apache works on both Windows and (most commonly) UNIX. Apple's UNIX-based Mac OS X operating system includes PHP and the Apache server, as do almost all Linux distributions.

Microsoft Active Server Pages, or ASP (`www.asp.net`), and Macromedia ColdFusion (`www.macromedia.com/software/coldfusion/`) are two other popular scripting languages used to deliver dynamic web content. Of these three leading server-side languages, only PHP is free. Bearing in mind that all general rules are false, ASP is frequently deployed in an all-Microsoft development environment, ColdFusion is commonly used in combination with other Macromedia development tools, including Dreamweaver and Flash—and PHP is often the choice of rebels and independents.

On the other hand, market leaders like Yahoo have recently embraced PHP (`www.theopenenterprise.com/story/TOE20021031S0001`), which suggests that the language is robust and scalable and that "free" is as appealing to large companies as small ones. Yahoo's move

to PHP and other open source tools also demonstrates the futility of trying to apply general rules to anything as vast and volatile as web development.

Each of these big three scripting languages has been used to power sites large and small. Each has its advantages, and each enjoys a large installed base of fanatic devotees. Comparisons and critiques of the three languages far exceed this book's scope. It should be noted that scripting languages often generate long URLs that include raw ampersands, an HTML/XHTML no-no. In HTML and XHTML, the ampersand character (&) is used to denote entities, such as `&#8217;`, which is Unicode for the typographically correct apostrophe. ColdFusion in particular seems to violate this long-standing standard. This can be fixed by using a ColdFusion function called `URLEncodedFormat()`. ASP has a similar function called `HTMLEncode`. In both cases, developers can (and should) avoid the problem by passing their URLs through the function before outputting them.

Java Server Pages (JSP), yet another dynamic technology, is most commonly found in large enterprise systems and is *way* beyond the scope of this book.

The Secret Shame of Rotten Markup

The more successful we've been in the field of web design and the longer we've been at it, the less likely we are to even be aware of the hidden cost of rotten markup. During our industry's first decade, designing for the web was like feeding a roomful of finicky toddlers. To build sites that worked, we dutifully learned to accommodate each browser's unique dietary requirements. Today's browsers all eat the same nutritious stuff, but many professionals haven't grasped this and are still crumbling M&Ms into the soufflé.

Bad food hardens arteries, rots teeth, and diminishes the energy of those who consume it. Bad markup is equally harmful to the short-term needs of your users and the long-term health of your content. But until recently, this fact was hidden from many of us by the high junk code tolerance of most popular browsers, as discussed in Chapter 1, "99.9% of Websites Are Obsolete."

In this chapter and those that follow, we'll investigate the forgotten nature of clean, semantic markup and learn to think structurally instead of viewing web markup as a second-rate design tool. At the same time, we'll examine XHTML, the standard language for marking up web pages, discussing its goals and benefits and developing a strategy for converting from HTML to XHTML.

By a strange coincidence, proper XHTML authoring encourages structural markup and discourages presentational hacks. In XHTML 1.0 Transitional, such hacks are "deprecated," which means you can use them if you must, but you are encouraged to achieve the same design effects in other ways (for instance, by using CSS). In XHTML 1.0 and 1.1 Strict, presentational hacks are actually forbidden: Use them and your page will no longer pass muster when you run it through the W3C's Markup Validation Service, familiarly known as "the Validator" [5.3]. (If it's not familiar to you now, it will become so as you learn to design and build with standards. See the "Validate This!" sidebar.)

5.3
The W3C's free online Validation Service (`http://validator.w3.org/`) is used by thousands of designers and developers to ensure their sites comply with web standards. Did we mention the service is free?

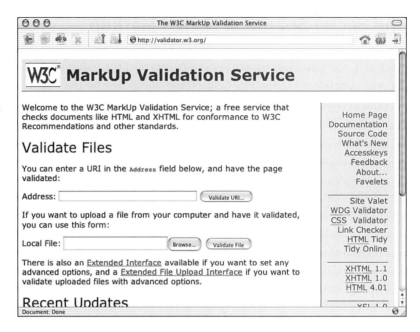

Validate This!

The W3C's Validation Service (`http://validator.w3.org/`) can test web pages built with HTML 4.01, XHTML 1.0, and XHTML 1.1 to be certain they conform to spec. Its CSS Validation Service (`http://jigsaw.w3.org/css-validator/`) does the same for your style sheets. The Web Design Group at `htmlhelp.com` maintains an equally reliable markup validation service (`http://www.htmlhelp.com/tools/validator/`). All three of these services are offered at no charge. We'll have more to say about them and about other essential (and equally free) tools throughout Part II, "Designing and Building."

Whether you choose XHTML Strict or Transitional, time and again you'll have the humbling experience of discovering that "everything you know is wrong." Line breaks (`<br>`) you've scattered like snowflakes to simulate a list; headers you've deployed "to force a display issue" instead of to convey hierarchical stature within an implied outline; transparent spacer pixel GIF images you've used to create whitespace: You'll find yourself shucking off these husks and many others.

Instead of presentational hacks, you'll begin to think structurally. You'll let markup be markup. Even in your transitional layouts that use a few presentational tables and other deprecated elements, you'll learn to do more with CSS, such as banishing complex and redundant table cell color and alignment attributes from your XHTML and replacing them with one or two rules in a global style sheet. As we learn the new language of web markup, we can also unlearn years of bad habits. So let's delve in, shall we?

A Reformulation of Say What?

According to the W3C, "XHTML (`http://www.w3.org/TR/xhtml1/`) is a reformulation of HTML in XML." In plainer if slightly less precise English, XHTML is an XML-based markup language that works and looks like HTML with a few small but significant differences. To web browsers and other user agents, XHTML works exactly the same way as HTML, although some sophisticated modern browsers might treat it a bit differently, as we'll discuss in Chapter 6, "XHTML: Restructuring the Web." To designers and developers, writing XHTML is almost the same as writing HTML but with slightly tighter house rules and one or two new elements, to be covered next.

In Chapter 4, "XML Conquers the World (And Other Web Standards Success Stories)," we described XML, a.k.a. Extensible Markup Language (`http://www.w3.org/XML/`), as a "super" markup language from which programmers can develop other custom markup languages. XHTML (Extensible Hypertext Markup Language) is one such markup language. XHTML 1.0 is the first and most backward-compatible version of XHTML, hence the most comfortable version to learn and the least troublesome to browsers and other user agents.

Additional applications and protocols based on XML are legion, and their popularity is partially due to their ability to exchange and transform data with relatively little effort and few (if any) compatibility hassles—a virtue they share with XHTML. Among these protocols are Scalable Vector Graphics (`http://www.w3.org/TR/SVG/`), Synchronized Multimedia Integration Language (`http://www.w3.org/TR/REC-smil/`), Simple Object Access Protocol (`http://www.w3.org/TR/SOAP/`), Resource Description Framework (`http://www.w3.org/RDF/`), and Platform for Privacy Preferences (`http://www.w3.org/TR/P3P/`).

Each of these protocols (and countless others) plays an important role in the emerging web, but none is as vital to designers and developers as XHTML—and none is as easy to learn.

Why "reformulate" HTML in XML or anything else? For one thing, XML is consistent where HTML is not. In XML, if you open a tag, you must close it again. In HTML, some tags never close, others always do, and still others can close or not at the developer's discretion. This inconsistency can create practical problems. For instance, some browsers might refuse to display an HTML page that leaves table cells unclosed even though HTML says it is okay not to close them. XHTML compels you to close all elements, thereby helping you avoid browser problems, save hours of testing and debugging, and stop wasting valuable neurons trying to remember which tags close and which don't.

More importantly, XML-based languages and tools are the golden coin of the web's present and the key to its future. If you author your markup in an XML-based language, your site will work better with other XML-based languages, applications, and protocols.

If XML is that important, why create an XML-based markup language that works like HTML? XML is powerful and pervasive, but you can't serve raw XML data to most web browsers and expect them to do anything intelligent with it, such as displaying a nicely formatted web page [5.4]. In essence, then, XHTML is a bridge technology, combining the power of XML (kind of) with the simplicity of HTML (mostly).

5.4

A sample XML document (http://p.moreover.com/cgi-local/page?index_xml+xml) as displayed by a modern browser (in this case, Chimera). Some browsers display XML as text, others as text plus tags. Neither approach is particularly useful. By contrast, virtually all browsers and devices know what to do with XHTML, and that makes it both useful and powerful.

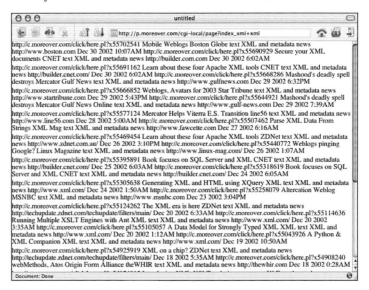

Executive Summary

Loosely speaking, XHTML is XML that acts like HTML in old and new web browsers and also works as expected in most Internet devices, from Palm Pilots to web phones to screen readers, making it portable, practical, and cost efficient.

XHTML is as easy to learn and use as HTML—a little easier for newcomers who have no bad habits to unlearn, and perhaps a little harder for old hands who embraced web design and development in the wild and wooly 1990s.

XHTML is the current markup standard (replacing HTML 4), and it's designed to return rigorous, logical document structure to web content, to work well with other web standards, such as CSS and the DOM, and to play well with other existing and future XML-based languages, applications, and protocols. We list all the benefits of XHTML after the short, but important, detour that follows.

Which XHTML Is Right for You?

In this chapter and throughout this book, we will focus on XHTML 1.0 and emphasize XHTML 1.0 Transitional, which is the most forgiving flavor of XHTML, the most compatible with existing development methods, and the easiest to learn and transition to.

Many standards geeks prefer XHTML 1.1 Strict, and there's nothing wrong with it, but it is less compatible with the past and it is properly served with a MIME type that causes some popular current browsers to misbehave. Additionally, converting old-school web pages to XHTML 1.1 Strict takes more work and requires more rethinking than converting to XHTML 1.0 Transitional. For many readers of this book, XHTML 1.0 Transitional is likely to be the best choice for the next few years.

As of this writing, a draft XHTML 2.0 specification has been presented to the development community for comment. As it is currently configured, this new spec moves closer to a semantic ideal and further from existing web development methods. By design, the present XHTML 2.0 draft is not backward compatible with HTML or XHTML 1.0. It abandons familiar conventions including the IMG element (OBJECT is to be used instead), the <BR> tag (replaced by a new LINE element), and the time-honored anchor link (in whose stead we are presently offered a technology called HLINK). These curiosities might change by the time this book hits the shelves, or they might congeal into the hard shell of reality.

Some developers have greeted the proposed XHTML 2 specification with little yelps of joy, whereas others have greeted it with incensed snorts of derision. Still others have cautiously adopted a "wait and see" policy. And many web professionals grinding away in the trenches know nothing about any of this and are still wondering what the accessibility options in Dreamweaver are for.

It remains to be seen how much of the proposed spec will make it into a final recommendation. It also remains to be seen whether developers and browser makers will rally 'round the flagpole of XHTML 2 or ignore it. Because the proposed spec is far from final and is not yet supported by any browser, its nascent existence is interesting but not yet relevant to this book or our jobs, and we once more recommend XHTML 1.0.

Finally, if the thought that the proposed XHTML 2.0 specification is not backward compatible makes you question whether XHTML is *forward* compatible, you should know that no browser or device maker has any intention of abandoning support for XHTML 1. For that matter, no browser maker intends to stop supporting HTML 4, despite our dour mutterings about badly authored HTML in Chapter 1 of this book. (In Chapter 1, we were grousing about bad markup and ill-advised scripting methods, not about any web standard—and HTML 4 is a web standard, if an outdated one.) Sites correctly authored to the HTML 4.01 specification will keep working for years to come. The same is true for sites properly authored in XHTML 1. Choosing between these two specs (HTML and XHTML) comes down to 10 key points summarized in the following list.

Top 10 Reasons to Convert to XHTML

1. XHTML is the current markup standard, replacing HTML 4.

2. XHTML is designed to work well with other XML-based markup languages, applications, and protocols—an advantage that HTML lacks.

3. XHTML is more consistent than HTML, so it's less likely to cause problems of function and display.

4. XHTML 1.0 is a bridge to future versions of XHTML. Should the XHTML 2 draft specification achieve final recommendation status, it will be easier to adapt to it (if you choose to do so) from XHTML 1.0 than from HTML.

5. Old browsers are as comfortable with XHTML as they are with HTML. There's no advantage to XHTML in this regard, but, hey, there's no disadvantage either.

6. New browsers love XHTML (particularly XHTML 1.0), and many accord it special treatment not granted to pages authored in HTML 4. This makes XHTML more predictable than HTML in many cases.

7. XHTML works as well in wireless devices, screen readers, and other specialized User Agents as it does in traditional desktop browsers, in many cases removing the need to create specialized wireless markup versions and allowing sites to reach more visitors with less work and at lower cost. We can't be positive about cause and effect, but many HTML sites are saddled with wireless versions, text-only versions, and special printer-friendly pages, while most XHTML sites are free of such encumbrances—one document serves all. (In most cases, one document serves all if it's properly styled for multiple media, and that's what CSS is for.)

8. XHTML is part of a family of web standards (also including CSS and the W3C Document Object Model) that let you control the behavior and appearance of web pages across multiple platforms, browsers, and devices.

9. Authoring in XHTML can assist you in breaking the habit of writing presentational markup, and that in turn can help you avoid accessibility problems and inconsistencies of display between different manufacturers' desktop browsers. (If you write structural XHTML and place all or most of your visual flourishes in CSS, where they belong, you'll no longer be overly concerned about differences in the way Netscape and Microsoft's browsers treat, say, empty table cells to which widths have been applied.)

10. Authoring in XHTML can get you into the habit of testing your work against Markup Validation Services, which in turn can often save testing and debugging time and help you avoid many basic accessibility errors, such as neglecting to include a usable `alt` attribute to every `<IMG>` tag. For much more on accessibility, see Chapter 14, "Accessibility Basics."

Top 5 Reasons Not to Switch to XHTML

1. You get paid by the hour.
2. You enjoy creating multiple versions of every page for every conceivable browser or device.
3. The little man in your head told you not to.
4. You're quitting the web business.
5. You don't know the rules of XHTML.

Fortunately, we can do something about Reason Number 5. See the next chapter.

chapter six

XHTML: Restructuring the Web

We might have titled this chapter, "XHTML: Simple Rules, Easy Guidelines." For one thing, the rules and guidelines discussed in this chapter are simple and easy. For another, "simple" and "easy" are to web design books what "new!" and "free!" are to supermarket packaging—namely, hackneyed but effective attention-getting devices that stimulate interest and encourage trial.

And we certainly want to stimulate interest in and encourage trial of this chapter. Why? Because after you've grasped the simple, easy ideas in this chapter, you'll rethink the way web pages work—and begin changing the way you build web pages. And we don't mean you'll write this year's tags instead of last year's tags. We mean you'll genuinely think (and work) differently. "Simple Rules, Easy Guidelines" doesn't begin to cover all that.

On the other hand, "Attain Oneness with the One True Way in a Blinding Flash of Enlightenment," another possible chapter title we kicked around, seemed a bit too thick for its pants. And *restructuring* is really what XHTML (and this chapter) is about. So, "XHTML: Restructuring the Web" it is.

In this chapter, we'll learn the ABCs of XHTML and explore the mechanics and implications of *structural* versus *presentational* markup. If you've been incorporating web standards into your design/development practice, some of this material will be familiar to you. But even old hands might feel a frisson of surprise as they unlock the hidden treasures of Chapter 6. Okay, frisson might be overstating things a bit. You might just say, "Hey, this is news to me." We'll settle for that.

Converting to XHTML: Simple Rules, Easy Guidelines

Converting from traditional HTML to XHTML 1.0 Transitional is quick and painless, as long as you observe a few simple rules and easy guidelines. (We really can't get enough of that phrase.) If you've written HTML, you can write XHTML. If you've never written HTML, you can still write XHTML. Let's zip through the (simple and easy) basics, shall we? Here are the rules of XHTML.

Open with the Proper DOCTYPE and Namespace

XHTML documents begin with elements that tell browsers how to interpret them and validation services how to test them for conformance. The first of these is the DOCTYPE (short for "document type") declaration. This handy little element informs the validation service which version of XHTML or HTML you're using. For reasons known only to a W3C committee member, the word DOCTYPE is always written in all caps.

Why a DOCTYPE?

XHTML allows designers/developers to author several different types of documents, each bound by different rules. The rules of each type are spelled out within the XHTML specifications in a long piece of text called a document type definition (DTD). Your DOCTYPE declaration informs validation services and modern browsers which DTD you followed in crafting your markup. In turn, this information tells those validation services and browsers how to handle your page.

DOCTYPE declarations are a key component of compliant web pages; your markup and CSS won't validate unless your XHTML source begins with a proper DOCTYPE. In addition, your choice of DOCTYPE affects the way most modern browsers display your site. The results might surprise you if you're not expecting them. In Chapter 11, "Working with Browsers Part I: DOCTYPE Switching and Standards Mode," we'll explain the impact of DOCTYPE in Internet Explorer and in Gecko-based browsers like Netscape, Mozilla, and Camino.

XHTML 1 offers three yummy choices of DTD and three possible DOCTYPE declarations:

- **Transitional**—The comfortable, slightly frowsy DTD whose motto is "live and let live" (see the next section, "Which DOCTYPE Is Your Type?")
- **Strict**—The whip-wielding, mysteriously aloof DTD that flogs you for using presentational markup elements or attributes
- **Frameset**—The one with the '90s haircut; also the one that lets you use frames in your design—which comes to the same thing

Which DOCTYPE Is Your Type?

Of the three flavors listed in the previous section, XHTML 1.0 Transitional is the one that's closest to the HTML we all know and love. That is to say, it's the only one that forgives presentational markup structures and deprecated elements and attributes.

The `target` attribute to the HREF link is one such bit of deprecated business. If you want linked pages to open in new windows—or even if you don't want that but your client insists—Transitional is the only XHTML DTD that lets you do so with the target attribute:

```
<p>Visit <a href="http://www.whatever.org" target=
"_blank">whatever.org</a> in a new window.</p>
```

```
<p>Visit <a href="http://www.whatever.org/" target=
"bob">whatever.org</a> in a named new window.</p>
```

To open linked pages in new windows under XHTML 1.0 Strict, you would need to write JavaScript, and you'd also need to make sure the links work in a non-JavaScript-capable environment. Whether you should open linked pages in new windows is beside the point here. The point is that XHTML 1.0 Transitional lets you do so with a minimum of fuss.

XHTML 1.0 Transitional also tolerates background colors applied to table cells and other such stuff you really ought to do with CSS instead of in your markup. If your DOCTYPE declaration states that you've written XHTML 1.0 Strict but your page includes the deprecated `bgcolor` attribute, validation services will flag it as an error, and some compliant browsers will ignore it (that is, they will not display the background color). By contrast, if you declare that you're following the XHTML 1.0 Transitional DTD, bgcolor will not be marked as an error, and browsers will honor it instead of ignoring it.

In short (well, maybe it's too late for "in short"), XHTML 1.0 Transitional is the perfect DTD for designers who are making the *transition* to modern web standards. They don't call it Transitional for nothing.

It could be argued that XHTML 1.0 Strict is the best choice for transitioning designers and developers, as it could be argued that joining the Marine Corps is a great way to shed unwanted pounds. Leaping from sloppy old HTML 4 to rigorous XHTML 1.0 Strict will put hair on the chest of your understanding that markup is for structure, not visual effects, and it might be the right decision for you. But for this chapter's (and most readers') purposes, we'll use XHTML 1.0 Transitional. Its DOCTYPE declaration appears next:

```
<!DOCTYPE html PUBLIC "-//W3C//DTD XHTML 1.0 Transitional//EN"
"http://www.w3.org/TR/xhtml1/DTD/xhtml1-transitional.dtd">
```

The frameset DOCTYPE is used for those documents that have a <frameset> element in them; in fact, you *must* use this DOCTYPE with your <frameset> documents.

The DOCTYPE declaration must be typed into the top of every XHTML document, before any other code or markup. It precedes the <head> element, the <title> element, the meta elements, and the links to style sheet and JavaScript files. It also, quite naturally, comes before your content. In short, the DOCTYPE declaration precedes everything.

(Standards-savvy readers might wonder why we haven't mentioned one element that can come before the DOCTYPE declaration: namely, the optional XML prolog. We'll get to it in a few paragraphs.)

Follow DOCTYPE with Namespace
The DOCTYPE declaration is immediately followed by an XHTML namespace declaration that enhances the old-fashioned <html> element:

```
<html xmlns="http://www.w3.org/1999/xhtml" xml:lang="en"
lang="en">
```

A namespace in XML is a collection of element types and attribute names associated with a specific DTD, and the namespace declaration allows you to identify your namespace by pointing to its online location, which in this case is www.w3.org/1999/xhtml. The two additional attributes, in reverse order of appearance, specify that your document is written in English, and that the version of XML you're using is also written in English.

With the DOCTYPE and namespace declarations in place, your XHTML Transitional 1.0 page would start out like this:

```
<!DOCTYPE html PUBLIC "-//W3C//DTD XHTML 1.0 Transitional//EN"
"http://www.w3.org/TR/xhtml1/DTD/xhtml1-transitional.dtd">
<html xmlns="http://www.w3.org/1999/xhtml" xml:lang="en"
lang="en">
```

Cut, Paste, and Go!

If you dislike trying to type markup and code out of books, feel free to view the source at zeldman.com, alistapart.com, or webstandards.org, and copy and paste to your heart's content.

Declare Your Content Type

To be correctly interpreted by browsers and to pass markup validation tests, all XHTML documents must declare the type of character encoding that was used in their creation, be it Unicode, ISO-8859-1 (also known as Latin-1), or what have you.

If you're unfamiliar with character encoding, or if ISO-8859-1 isn't ringing any bells, never fear: We'll discuss that stuff later in this chapter. (See the later section, "Character Encoding: The Dull, The Duller, and the Truly Dull.") For now, all you need to know is this: There are three ways to tell browsers what kind of character encoding you're using, but only one works reliably as of this writing, and it's not one the W3C especially recommends.

The XML Prolog (And How to Skip It)

Many XHTML pages begin with an optional XML prolog, also known as an XML declaration. When used, the XML prolog precedes the DOCTYPE and namespace declarations described earlier, and its mission in life is to specify the version of XML and declare the type of character encoding being used in the page.

The W3C recommends beginning any XML document, including XHTML documents, with an XML prolog. To specify ISO-8859-1 (Latin-1) encoding, for example, you would use the following XML prolog:

```
<?xml version="1.0" encoding="ISO-8859-1"?>
```

Nothing complicated is going on here. The tag tells the browser that XML version 1.0 is in use and that the character encoding is ISO-8859-1. About the only thing new or different about this tag is the question mark that opens and closes it.

Unfortunately, many browsers, even those from "nice" homes, can't handle their XML prolog. After imbibing this XML element, they stagger and stumble and soil themselves, bringing shame to their families and eventually losing their place in society.

Actually, the browsers go unpunished. It's your visitors who suffer when the site fails to work correctly. In some cases, your entire site might be invisible to the user. It might even crash the user's browser. In other cases, the site does not crash, but it displays incorrectly. (This is what happens when IE6/Windows encounters the prolog.)

Fortunately, there is a solution. In place of the troublesome prolog, you can specify character encoding by inserting a Content-Type element into the `<head>` of your document. To specify ISO-8859-1 encoding, type the following:

```
<meta http-equiv="Content-Type" content="text/html; charset=
ISO-8859-1" />
```

The beginning of your XHTML document would then look something like this:

```
<!DOCTYPE html PUBLIC "-//W3C//DTD XHTML 1.0 Transitional//EN"
"http://www.w3.org/TR/xhtml1/DTD/xhtml1-transitional.dtd">
<html xmlns="http://www.w3.org/1999/xhtml">
    <head>
<title>Transitional Industries: Working for Change</title>
<meta http-equiv="Content-Type" content="text/html; charset=
ISO-8859-1" />
    </head>
```

If you're working on an international site that will include a plethora of non-ASCII characters, you might author in Unicode and insert the following Content-Type element into your markup:

```
<meta http-equiv="Content-Type" content="text/html;charset=
UTF-8" />
```

Again, feel free to view source at `zeldman.com`, `alistapart.com`, or `webstandards.org` and copy and paste.

You might also want to forget all the geeky details of the preceding discussion. Many designers know nothing about these issues aside from which tags to copy and paste into the tops of their templates, and they seem to live perfectly happy and productive lives.

Aside from one even geekier topic to be touched upon with merciful brevity a few pages from now, you have now waded through the brain-addling, pocket-protector-equipped portion of this chapter. Congratulations! The rest will be cake.

Write All Tags in Lowercase

Unlike HTML, XML is case sensitive. Thus, XHTML is case sensitive. All XHTML element and attribute names must be typed in lowercase, or your document will not validate. (Validation ensures that your pages are error free. Flip back to Chapter 5, "Modern Markup," if you've forgotten about the free markup validation services offered by the W3C and the Web Design Group.)

Let's look at a typical HTML element:

```
<TITLE>Transitional Industries: Our Privacy Policy</TITLE>
```

You will recognize this as the TITLE element, and you will recognize the Privacy Policy page as the one nobody outside your legal department ever reads. Translating this element to XHTML is as simple as switching from uppercase to lowercase:

```
<title>Transitional Industries: Our Privacy Policy</title>
```

Likewise, `<P>` becomes `<p>`, `<BODY>` becomes `<body>`, and so on.

Of course, if your original HTML used lowercase element and attribute names throughout, you won't have to change them. But most of us learned to write our HTML element and attribute names in all caps, so we'll have to change them to lowercase when converting to XHTML.

Popular HTML editors like BareBones BBEdit, Optima-Systems PageSpinner, and Allaire HomeSite let you automatically convert tag and attribute names to lowercase, and the free tool HTML Tidy (see the upcoming sidebar, "Tidy Time") will do this for you as well.

Don't Worry About the Case of Attribute Values or Content

In the preceding example, notice that only the element name (`title`) converted to lowercase. "Transitional Industries: Our Privacy Policy" could stay just the way it was, initial caps and all. For that matter, the title element's content could be set in all caps (TRANSITIONAL INDUSTRIES: OUR PRIVACY POLICY) and would still be valid XHTML, although it would hurt your eyes to look at it.

Element and attribute names must be lowercased; attribute values and content need not be. All the following are perfectly valid XHTML:

```
<img src="/images/whopper.jpg" alt="Big John catches a
whopper." />
```

```
<img src="/images/WHOPPER.JPG" alt="Big John catches a
whopper." />
```

```
<img src="/images/whopper.jpg" alt="Big John catches a
Whopper and fries." />
```

Note that, depending on your server software, the filename mentioned in the `src` attribute might be case sensitive, but XHTML doesn't care. Class and ID values, on the other hand, are case sensitive.

Be careful with mixed-case attribute names. If you use a WYSIWYG tool like Macromedia Dreamweaver or an image editor like Adobe ImageReady to generate JavaScript rollovers, you will need to change the mixed-case `onMouseOver` to the lowercase `onmouseover`. Yes, really.

The following will get you into trouble:

```
onMouseOver="changeImages
```

But *this* is perfectly okay:

```
onmouseover="changeImages
```

Tidy Time

By far, the easiest method of creating valid XHTML pages is to write them from scratch. But much web design is really *re*design, and you'll often find yourself charged with updating old pages. Redesign assignments provide the perfect opportunity to migrate to XHTML, and you don't have to do so by hand. The free tool HTML Tidy [**6.1**] can quickly convert your HTML to valid XHTML.

6.1

It ain't pretty, but the price is nice. The free HTML Tidy (`http://www.w3.org/People/Raggett/tidy/`) can convert your pages from HTML to XML. Note the setting: Convert HTML to XML. That's pretty much all there is to it. There are versions of Tidy for just about every operating system. (A carbonized version for Mac OS X is shown here.)

Tidy was created by standards geek Dave Raggett and is now maintained as open source software by Source Forge (`http://tidy.sourceforge.net/`), although individuals have created some versions as a labor of love. For instance, Terry Teague (`http://www.geocities.com/terry_teague/tidy.html`) developed the Mac OS version shown in Figure 6.1.

There are online versions of Tidy as well as downloadable binaries for Windows, UNIX, various Linux distributions, Mac (OS 9 and OS X), and other platforms. Some versions work as plug-ins to enhance the capability of existing web software. For instance, BBTidy is a plug-in for BareBones Software's BBEdit (X)HTML editor.

Each version offers different capabilities and consequently includes quite different documentation. Tidy might look simple, but it is a power tool, and reading the manual can save you a lot of grief.

Quote All Attribute Values

In HTML, you needn't quote attribute values, but in XHTML, they *must* be quoted (`height="55"`, *not* `height=55`). That's pretty much all there is to say about this one. La de da. Nice weather we're having.

Okay, here's something else worth mentioning. Suppose your attribute value includes quoted material. For instance, what if your `alt` attribute value must read, "The Happy Town Reader's Theater Presents 'A Christmas Carol.'" How would you handle that? You would do it like this, of course:

```
<img src="/images/carol.jpg" alt="The Happy Town Reader's
Theater presents 'A Christmas Carol.'" />
```

If you preferred to get fancy and use the escaped character sequences for typographically correct apostrophes and single and double quotation marks, you would do that like this:

```
<img src="/images/carol.jpg" alt="The Happy Town
Reader&#8217;s Theater presents &#8216;A Christmas
Carol.&#8217;" />
```

Now that you are quoting attributes, you must separate your attributes with blanks. The following is an error:

```
<hr width="75%"size="7" />
```

Note: The W3C validator has to handle both HTML and XHTML, and its parser will not detect this error. Any parser that is designed to work with pure XML will catch it.

If, for some strange reason, you need straight quotes in an attribute value, use `&quot;`, as in the following:

```
<img src="/images/hello.jpg" alt="Mrs. O'Hara says,
&quot;Hello&quot; to us." />
```

You can use apostrophes to quote an attribute; if you need an embedded apostrophe, use `&apos;`, as in the following:

```
<img src="/images/hello.jpg" alt='Mrs. O&apos;Hara says,
"Hello" to us.' />
```

Quoting attribute values was optional in HTML, but many of us did it, so converting to XHTML often represents no work at all in that area. In an effort to trim their bandwidth, some commercial sites avoided quoting attribute values. Those sites will have to *start* quoting those values when they convert to XHTML.

HTML Tidy can quote all your attribute values automatically. In fact, it can automatically perform every conversion task mentioned in this chapter.

All Attributes Require Values

All attributes must have values; thus, the attributes in the following HTML

```
<td nowrap>
<input type="checkbox" name="shirt" value="medium" checked>
<hr noshade>
```

must be given values. The value *must* be identical to the attribute name.

```
<td nowrap="nowrap">
<hr noshade="noshade" />
<input type="checkbox" name="shirt" value="medium" checked=
"checked" />
```

We know, we know. Looks weird, feels weird, takes getting used to.

Close All Tags

In HTML, you have the option to open many tags such as `<p>` and `<li>` without closing them. The following is perfectly acceptable HTML but bad XHTML:

```
<p>This is acceptable HTML but would be invalid XHTML.
<p>I forgot to close my Paragraph tags!
<p>But HTML doesn't care. Why did they ever change these
darned rules?
```

In XHTML, every tag that opens must close:

```
<p>This is acceptable HTML and it is also valid XHTML.</p>
<p>I close my tags after opening them.</p>
<p>I am a special person and feel good about myself.</p>
```

This rule—every tag that opens must close—makes more sense than HTML's confusing and inconsistent approach, and it might help avoid trouble nobody needs. For instance, if you don't close your paragraph tags, you might run into CSS display problems in some browsers. XHTML forces you to close your tags, and in so doing, helps ensure that your page works as you intend it to.

Close "Empty" Tags, Too

In XHTML, even "empty" tags such as `<br>` and `<img>` must close themselves by including a forward slash `/>` at the end of the tag:

```
<br />
<img src="zeldman.gif" />
```

Note the slash `/>` at the end of the XHTML break tag. Then note the slash `/>` at the end of the XHTML image tag. See that a blank space precedes each instance of the slash to avoid confusing browsers that were developed prior to the XHTML standard. None of this is rocket science.

Nor does it require much (if any) work. Recent versions of BBEdit, PageSpinner, and HomeSite automatically add the required space and slash to "empty" tags if you tell these editors you're working in XHTML [**6.2**]. Visual web editing tools Dreamweaver and GoLive do likewise.

Naturally, to remain valid and accessible, the image element in the second example would also include an `alt` attribute, and an optional `title` attribute wouldn't hurt:

```
<img src="zeldman.gif" alt="Jeffrey Zeldman, author of
Designing with Web Standards." title="Jeffrey Zeldman,
debonair web designer and billionaire author of Designing
with Web Standards, now in its 400th printing." />
```

Now *that* is good XHTML.

No Double Dashes Within a Comment

Double dashes can occur only at the beginning and end of an XHTML comment. That means that these are no longer valid:

```
<!--Invalid -- and so is the classic "separator" below. -->
<!----------------------------------->
```

Either replace the inner dashes with equal signs, or put spaces between the dashes:

```
<!-- Valid - - and so is the new separator below -->
<!--===============================-->
```

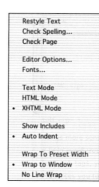

6.2
Put Optima System's PageSpinner editor into XHTML mode via the drop-down menu, and it lowercases your element names and attribute values and closes your empty tags with a space and a slash (www.optima-system.com/pagespinner/).

Encode All < and & Characters

Any less than signs (<) that aren't part of a tag must be encoded as <, and any ampersands (&) that aren't part of an entity must be encoded as &. Thus,

```
<p>She & he say that x < y when z = 3.</p>
```

must be marked up as this:

```
<p>She &amp; he say that x &lt; y when z = 3.</p>
```

The W3C validation service will let you off with warning messages on the nonencoded markup; a pure XML parser will generate a fatal error.

Note: We recommend that you always encode > as >. Even though you never *have* to encode it (with the exeception of one highly esoteric circumstance), it is there for symmetry, and your markup will be easier for others to read if you use it.

Let's review the XHTML rules we've learned.

Executive Summary: The Rules of XHTML

- Open with the proper DOCTYPE and namespace.
- Declare your content type using the META Content element.
- Write all element and attribute names in lowercase.
- Quote all attribute values.
- Assign values to all attributes.
- Close all tags.
- Close "empty" tags with a space and a slash.
- Do not put double dashes inside a comment.
- Ensure that less-than and ampersand are < and &.

Viewed as a short list in this Executive Summary, the rules of XHTML look few and simple enough—and they *are* few and simple enough. One sadly dull additional point must be made before we move on to the good stuff.

Character Encoding: The Dull, the Duller, and the Truly Dull

In reading the second rule of XHTML in the preceding section ("Declare Your Content Type"), you might have asked yourself, "Why should I declare my content type?" You might even have asked yourself, "What is a content type?" The answers to these dull questions appear next. Perhaps you're asking yourself, "Must I really read this tedious stuff?" The answer, of course, is yes. If we had to write it, you have to read it. That's only fair. Plus, you might learn something.

Unicode and Other Character Sets

The default character set for XML, XHTML, and HTML 4.0 documents is Unicode (http://www.w3.org/International/O-unicode.html), a standard defined, oddly enough, by the Unicode Consortium (www.unicode.org). Unicode is a comprehensive character set that provides a unique number for every character, "no matter what the platform, no matter what the program, no matter what the language." Unicode is thus the closest thing we have to a universal alphabet, although it is not an alphabet but a numeric mapping scheme.

Even though Unicode is the default character set for web documents, developers are free to choose other character sets that might be better suited to their needs. For instance, American and Western European websites often use ISO-8859-1 (Latin-1) encoding. You might be asking yourself what Latin-1 encoding means, or where it comes from. Okay, to be honest, you're not asking yourself any such thing, but we needed a transition, and that was the best we could do on short notice.

What Is ISO 8859?

ISO 8859 is a series of standardized multilingual single-byte coded (8 bit) graphic character sets for writing in alphabetic languages, and the first of these character sets, ISO-8859-1 (also called Latin-1), is used to map Western European characters to Unicode. ISO 8859 character sets include Latin-2 (East European), Turkish, Greek, Hebrew, and Nordic, among others.

The ISO 8859 standard was created in the mid-1980s by the European Computer Manufacturer's Association (ECMA) and endorsed by the International Standards Organization (ISO). Now you know.

Mapping Your Character Set to Unicode

Regardless of which character set you've chosen, to map it to the Unicode standard, you must declare your character encoding, as discussed in the second rule of XHTML presented earlier. (You see, there was a point to all this.) Sites can declare their character encoding in any of three ways:

- A server administrator ("systems guy") might set the encoding via the HTTP headers returned by the web server. The W3C recommends this approach, but it is rarely followed—maybe because systems guys would rather play networked games than muck around with HTTP headers. Come to think of it, who wouldn't?

- For XML documents (including XHTML), a designer/developer might use the optional XML prolog to specify the encoding. This, too, is a W3C recommendation, but until more browsers learn to handle it properly, we can't recommend it.

- In HTML or XHTML documents, a designer/developer might also specify the encoding via the "Content-Type" meta element. As opposed to the server administrator method (which fails when the server administrator forgets to do his job) and the XML prolog method (which fails when browsers choke on it), the "Content-Type" method can be counted on to work. That is the approach we recommended earlier in this chapter. Now you know why.

Congratulations! You have now read the dullest section of this book, or at least of this chapter, or anyway of this page. Let the healing begin! From hereon in, we begin the interesting work of rethinking the way we design and build websites.

Structural Healing—It's Good for Me

Developing in XHTML goes beyond converting uppercase to lowercase and adding slashes to the end of `<br>` tags. If changing "tag fashions" were all there was to it, nobody would bother, and instead of web standards, this book would be filled with delicious tofu recipes. Like tofu honey pie with blueberries. Yum! It's even better if you use cream cheese instead of tofu. And sugar—lots of sugar.

And butter and eggs—don't forget the eggs. But we digress. To benefit from XHTML, you need to think about your markup in *structural* rather than *visual* terms.

Marking Up Your Document for Sense Instead of Style

Remember: To the greatest extent possible, you want to use CSS for layout. In the world of web standards, XHTML markup is not about presentation; it's about core document structure. Well-structured documents make as much sense to a Palm Pilot or screen reader user as they do to someone who's viewing your page in a fancy-pants graphical desktop browser. Well-structured documents also make visual sense in old desktop browsers that don't support CSS or in modern browsers whose users have turned off CSS for one reason or another.

Not every site can currently abandon HTML table layouts. The W3C, inventors of CSS, did not convert to CSS layout until December 2002. Moreover, even die-hard standards purists might not always be able to entirely separate structure from presentation—at least not in XHTML 1. But that separation of structure from presentation (of data from design) is an ideal toward which we can make great strides and from which even hybrid, transitional layouts can benefit. Here are some tips to help you start to think more structurally.

Color Within the Outlines

In grammar school, most of us were forced to write essays in a standard outline format. Then we became designers, and, oh, how free we felt as we cast off the dead weight of restrictive outlines and plunged boldly into unique realms of personal expression. (Okay, so maybe our brochure and commerce sites weren't that unique or personal. But at least we didn't have to worry about outlines any more. Or did we?)

Actually, according to HTML, we should *always* have structured our textual content in organized hierarchies (outlines). We couldn't do that and deliver marketable layouts in the days before browsers supported CSS, but today we can deliver good underlying document structure without paying a design penalty.

When marking up text for the web or when converting existing text documents into web pages, think in terms of traditional outlines:

```
<h1>My Topic</h1>
<p>Introductory text</p>
<h2>Subsidiary Point</h2>
<p>Relevant text</p>
```

Avoid using deprecated HTML elements such as `<font>` tags or meaningless elements like `<br />` to simulate a logical structure where none exists. For instance, don't do this:

```
<font size="7">My Topic</font><br />
Introductory text <br /><br />
<font size="6">Subsidiary Point</font><br />
Relevant text <br />
```

Use Elements According to Their Meaning, Not Because of the Way They "Look"

Some of us have gotten into the habit of marking text as an `<h1>` when we merely want it to be large or as `<li>` when we want to stick a bullet in front of it. As discussed in the section "The Curse of Legacy Rendering" in Chapter 3, "The Trouble with Standards," browsers have traditionally imposed design attributes on HTML elements. We are all used to thinking that `<h1>` means big, `<li>` means bullet, and `<blockquote>` means, "indent this text." Most of us have scribbled our share of HTML that uses structural elements to force presentational effects.

Along the same lines, if a designer wants all headlines to be the same size, she might set all her headlines as `<h1>`, even though doing so makes no structural sense and is the kind of thing usability consultant Jakob Nielsen would call a sin if he weren't too busy worrying about link colors:

```
<h1>This is the primary headline, or would be if I had
organized my textual material in outline form.</h1>

<h1>This isn't the primary headline but I wanted it to be the
same size as the previous headline and I don't know how to use
CSS.</h1>

<h1>This isn't a headline at all! But I really wanted all the
text on this page to be the same size because it's important
to my creative vision. If I knew about CSS, I could achieve my
design without sacrificing document structure.</h1>
```

We must put our toys aside and start using elements because of what they mean, not because of the way they "look." In reality, `<h1>` can look like anything you want it to. Via CSS, `<h1>` can be small and Roman (normal weight), `<p>` text can be huge and bold, `<li>` can have no bullet (or can use a PNG, GIF, or JPEG image of a dog, cat, or the company logo), and so on.

From today on, we're going to use CSS to determine how these elements look. We can even change the way they look according to where they appear on a page or in a site. There is no longer a need, if there ever was, to use `<li>` for any reason except the one for which it was created (to indicate that the element is one in a list of several items).

CSS completely abstracts presentation from structure, allowing you to style any element as you wish. In a CSS-capable browser, all six levels of headline (h1–h6) can be made to look identical if the designer so desires:

```
h1, h2, h3, h4, h5, h6        {
        font-family: georgia, palatino, "New Century Schoolbook",
        times, serif;
        font-weight: normal;
        font-size: 2em;
        margin-top: 1em;
        margin-bottom: 0;
        }
```

Why might you do this? You might do it to enforce a branded look and feel in graphical browsers while preserving the document structure in text browsers, wireless devices, and opt-in HTML mail newsletters.

We don't mean to get ahead of ourselves by showing CSS techniques in a chapter about XHTML. We simply wanted to show that document structure and visual presentation are two distinctly different beasts, and that structural elements should be used to convey structure, not to force display.

Prefer Structural Elements to Meaningless Junk

Because we've forgotten—or never knew—that HTML and XHTML elements are intended to convey structural meaning, many of us have acquired the habit of writing markup that contains *no structure at all*. For instance, many HTML wranglers will insert a list into their page by using markup like this:

```
item <br />
another item <br />
a third item <br />
```

Consider using an ordered or unordered list instead:

```
<ul>
<li>item</li>
<li>another item</li>
<li>a third item</li>
</ul>
```

"But `<li>` gives me a bullet, and I don't want a bullet!" you might say. Refer to the previous section. CSS makes no assumptions about the way elements are supposed to look. It waits for you to tell it how you want them to look. Turning off bullets is the least of what CSS can do. It can make a list look like ordinary text in a paragraph—or like a graphical navigation bar, complete with rollover effects.

So use list elements to mark up lists. Similarly, prefer `<strong>` to `<b>`, `<em>` to `<i>`, and so on. By default, most desktop browsers will display `<strong>` as `<b>` and `<em>` as `<i>`, creating the visual effect you seek without undermining your document's structure. Although CSS makes no assumption about the display of any element, browsers make lots of assumptions, and we've never encountered a browser that displayed `<strong>` as anything other than bold (unless instructed to display it some other way by a designer's creative CSS). If you're worried that some strange browser won't display your `<strong>` as bold, you can write a CSS rule like this one:

```
strong      {
      font-weight: bold;
      font-style: normal;
      }
```

Using structural markup such as `<strong>` also protects people using text browsers and other alternative devices from downloading markup that is meaningless in their browsing environment. (What does `<b>` mean to a Braille reader?) Besides, presentation-oriented elements like `<b>` and `<i>` are likely to go the way of the Dodo bird in future versions of XHTML. Play it safe by using structural elements instead.

Visual Elements and Structure

"Web standards" abide not only in the technologies we use, but also in the way we use them. Writing markup in XHTML and using CSS to handle some or all layout chores doesn't necessarily make a site any more accessible or portable or any less of a bandwidth burster. XHTML and CSS can be misused or abused as easily as earlier web technologies were. Verbose XHTML markup wastes every bit as much of the user's time as verbose HTML ever did. Long-winded, over-wrought CSS is not an adequate replacement for presentational HTML; it's simply one bad thing taking the place of another.

The guidelines in the earlier "Structural Healing—It's Good for Me" section can help avoid overly complex, semantically meaningless interior structures (body copy and so on). But what do we do about branded visual elements, such as site-wide navigation bars, which typically include a logo? Can these elements be structural? And must they be?

The answer to the first question is yes—visual elements including navigation bars can indeed be structural. For example, as mentioned in the previous section, CSS can make an ordered or unordered list display as a full-fledged navigation bar, complete with push buttons and rollover effects.

The answer to the second question is that visual elements like navigation bars *need not be* made structural in hybrid, transitional layouts. If those layouts avoid verbosity and use good structure in their primary content areas, if their XHTML and CSS validate, and if every effort has been made to provide accessibility, then you will have achieved transitional standards compliance and will have nothing to be ashamed of. (Well, you might have something to be ashamed of, but it won't be the way your website was built.)

In the next chapter, we examine the difference between good and bad authoring (whether that bad authoring happens to use XHTML and CSS or not) and talk about how to create good, clean, compact markup in nonstructural components of hybrid, transitional layouts.

chapter seven

Tighter, Firmer Pages Guaranteed: Structure and Meta-Structure in Strict and Hybrid Markup

Whatever you do, don't skip this chapter. Reading it will improve your skills, trim unwanted fat from your web pages, and sharpen your understanding of the difference between markup and design. The ideas in this chapter are easy to follow but can make a profound difference in the performance of your sites and the facility with which you design, produce, and update them.

In this chapter, we'll show how to write logical, compact markup that can lower your bandwidth by 50% or more, restoring pep and vigor to your site's loading times while reducing server aches and stress. We'll achieve these savings by banishing presentational elements from our XHTML and learning to avoid many common practices that are frankly no good at all.

These bad practices afflict many sites on the web, especially those that incorporate some CSS into primarily table-based layouts. This is almost always done wastefully and ineptly, even when the designers are quite skilled in everything else they do. It is an equal opportunity problem, as likely to appear in hand-coded sites as in those created with the assistance of visual editing tools like Dreamweaver and GoLive.

In this chapter, we will name these common mistakes so that you can recognize and guard against them, and we will learn what to do instead. We will also make friends with the unique identifier (`id`) attribute, the "sticky note" of standards-based design, and show how it allows you to write ultra-compact XHTML, whether you're creating hybrid or pure CSS layouts.

Must Every Element Be Structural?

At the conclusion of Chapter 6, "XHTML: Restructuring the Web," we sassily asserted that it was often okay if navigational elements in transitional sites were not always structural. We'll go further out on a limb and add that *even in CSS layouts*, some components need not be structural—at least, not in the "headline, paragraph, list" sense discussed in Chapter 6.

These elements can, however, be meta-structural. That is, they can be marked up via generic structural elements and specific structural attributes that indicate the larger structural role they play within the site's design. This is not done for purposes of theory, but to gain real-world benefits including reduced bandwidth and easier site maintenance.

The Daily Report at `zeldman.com` [**7.1**] uses CSS for layout and XHTML for structure. And nearly all elements that go into its markup are structural, from lists to paragraphs to the address tag that's used to denote—you guessed it— the address.

7.1

The Daily Report at zeldman.com uses CSS for layout and XHTML for structure. The navigational graphics at the top are not structural. Or are they?

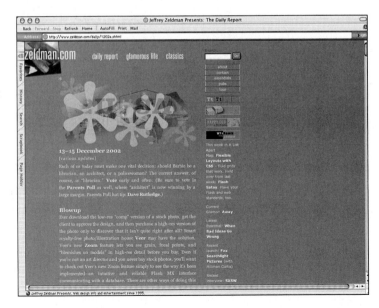

The navigational graphics at the top of the page are not structural in the sense described by Chapter 6. They are merely linked images, held in place by an XHTML block level element (a `div`) to which the site's clever designer has assigned a name by means of the unique identifier (`id`) attribute. We'll define our terms next and then go on to see how these components work together to create a meta-structure and to reduce page weight and control layout without resorting to presentational markup.

div, id, and Other Assistants

This chapter and those that follow make much reference to the `div` element and the `id` attribute. Used correctly, `div` is the Hamburger Helper of structured markup, whereas `id` is an amazing little tool that permits you to write highly compact XHTML, apply CSS wisely, and add sophisticated behavior to your site via the standard Document Object Model (DOM). The W3C, in "The Global Structure of an HTML Document," defines these elements and two other important HTML/XHTML components thusly:

> The DIV and SPAN elements, in conjunction with the id and `class` attributes, offer a generic mechanism for adding structure to documents. These elements define content to be inline (SPAN) or block-level (DIV) but impose no other presentational idioms on the content. Thus, authors may use these elements in conjunction with style sheets…to tailor HTML to their own needs and tastes (`http://www.w3.org/TR/REC-html40/struct/global.html#h-7.5.4`).

What Is This Thing Called *div*?

This is as good a place as any to explain that "div" is short for "division." When you group a bunch of links together, that's one division of a document. Content would be another, the legal disclaimer at the foot of the page would be still another, and so on.

A Generic Mechanism for Specific Structures

All HTML jockeys are familiar with common elements like the paragraph tag or `h1`, but some might be less familiar with `div`. The key to understanding the `div` element is found in the W3C's phrase, "a generic mechanism for adding structure."

In the example from zeldman.com, the primary navigational graphics are wrapped in a div because they are not part of a paragraph, list, or any other general structural element. But in a larger and more specific sense, these images *do* play a structural role, namely that of primary navigation. To underscore that role, the div that contains the images is assigned a unique id of "primenav," a name this author cunningly concocted as shorthand for "primary navigation."

You can use any name. "Gladys" or "orangebox" would be perfectly kosher within the rules of XHTML. But meta-structural names (names that explain the function performed by elements contained within) are best. You would feel pretty silly having labeled a part of your site "orangebox" when the client decides to go with blue. You would feel sillier still revising your style sheets under a deadline six months from now and trying desperately to remember whether "Gladys" was a navigational area, a sidebar, a search form, or what.

Plus, crafting structural id labels like "menu" or "content" or "searchform" helps you remember that markup is not design and that a well-structured page can be made to look any way you desire. Whether you're working with pure CSS layout or hybrid CSS/table layouts, if you cultivate the habit of assigning meta-structural names to core page components (such as the navigation, content, and search areas), you will begin weaning yourself from the habit of authoring and thinking in presentational markup.

id Versus class

The id attribute is not new to XHTML; neither is the class attribute or the div and span elements. They all date back to HTML. The id attribute assigns a unique name to an element. Each name can be used only once on a given page. (For example, if your page contains a div whose id is "content," it cannot have another div or other element with that same name.) The class attribute, by contrast, can be used over and over again on the same page (for example, five paragraphs on the page may share a class name of "small" or "footnote"). The following markup will help clarify the distinction between id and class:

```
<div id="searchform">Search form components go here.</div>
<div class="blogentry">A web log entry goes here.</div>
```

In these examples, div id="searchform" would be used to block out that area of the page containing the search form, whereas div class="blogentry" might be used to block out each entry on a web log (familiarly known as a *blog*).

There is only one search form on the page, so id is chosen for that unique instance. But a web log might have many entries, so the class attribute is used in that instance. If the web log can get by without using these divs—if it can use ordinary headline and paragraph structures instead—so much the better. The Daily Report at zeldman.com has been called a web log (although not by us), but its entries are marked up with generic h3, h4, and p elements.

The Sticky Note Theory

It might be helpful to think of the id attribute as a sticky note. We slap a sticky note on the fridge to remind us to buy milk. A sticky note stuck to the phone reminds us to call a late-paying client. Another, applied to a folder of bills, reminds us they must be paid by the 15th of the month (which also reminds us to call the late-paying client).

The id attribute is similar in that it labels a particular area of your markup, reminding you that that area will require special treatment. To perform that special treatment, you will later write one or more rules in a style sheet or some lines of code in a JavaScript file that refer to that particular id. For instance, your CSS file might have special rules that apply only to elements within the specific div whose id is "searchform". Or your style sheet might contain rules that apply only to a table whose id is "menubar". (If you've been following along, you'll guess correctly that a table assigned an id of "menubar" is a table that serves as a menu bar. In Chapters 8, "XHTML by Example: A Hybrid Layout [Part I]," and 10, "CSS in Action: A Hybrid Layout [Part II]," we'll build a working site that makes use of just such a table and id.)

When an id attribute's value is used as a magnet for a specific set of CSS rules, it is called a CSS *selector*. There are many other ways of creating selectors (see Chapter 9, "CSS Basics"), but id is particularly handy and versatile.

The Power of *id*

The id attribute is incredibly powerful. Among other tasks, it can serve in the following capacities:

- As a style sheet selector (see the preceding section), permitting us to author tight, minimal XHTML

- As a target anchor for hypertext links, replacing the outdated "name" attribute (or coexisting with it for the sake of backward compatibility)

- As a means to reference a particular element from a DOM-based script

- As the name of a declared object element
- As a tool for general purpose processing (in a W3C example, "for identifying fields when extracting data from HTML pages into a database, translating HTML documents into other formats, and so on")

Rules of *id*

An id value must begin with a letter or an underscore; it cannot begin with a digit. The W3C validation service might not catch this error, but an XML parser will. Also, if you intend to use an id with JavaScript in the form document.idname.value, you must name it as a valid JavaScript variable; that is, it must begin with a letter or an underscore, followed by letters, digits, and underscores. No blanks, and especially no hyphens, are allowed. For that matter, using underscores in class or id names is also a bad idea because of old limitations in CSS (and in some browsers).

Finally, for the deeply geeky readers in the house, note that it is possible to start an id or class name with a digit if you escape that digit—that is, if you use the proper Unicode escaped character sequence to represent that digit. But nobody ever does that.

With Great Power Comes Great Responsibility

The elements and attributes discussed here are often misused and abused, quadrupling the weight of pages instead of reducing them and removing all traces of structure instead of adding meta-structure to the generic structural elements of XHTML. After reading this chapter, you will recognize these forms of abuse and know how to avoid them.

Dare to Do Less

Now that we've discussed general-purpose XHTML elements (particularly div and id), let's look again at the example [7.1] from zeldman.com. The four large menu images are held in place by a generic div element whose unique, meta-structural label is "primenav."

```
<div id="primenav">[Linked images go here.]</div>
```

What separates this method from more familiar techniques is that the block-level element contains no presentational instructions—no width, no height, no background color, no horizontal or vertical alignment. All the things old-school layout components insist upon, our humble block-level element does without.

So how does the browser know where to stick the pictures?

Glance back at the brief discussion on CSS selectors earlier. "primenav" is used as just such a selector. In one of the site's style sheets, a CSS rule states that the particular block-level element called "primenav" has no margin and no padding—in other words, that it is not surrounded by whitespace. Because <div id="primenav"> is the first visible element listed in the site's XHTML source, CSS-compliant browsers position it at the top-left corner of the page.

The four menu images held in place by "primenav" are displayed inline, one after the other. There is no need for a table to position these images relative to each other. There is also no need to assign each image its own unique CSS positioning rule. The order in which images are listed in the XHTML is the order in which they appear on the page.

Through the logic of element order, we avoid the fussiness of table layouts and the verbosity of unenlightened style sheets (see the discussions of "classitis" and "divitis" later in this chapter), presenting the site's viewers with a reliable layout that loads fast because it contains no excess markup or CSS.

Following is the zeldman.com markup, with JavaScript elements removed, and with image and path names simplified for the sake of clarity:

```
<div id="primenav">
<a href="/"><img src="/i/home.gif" width="150" height="100"
border="0" alt="Home" /></a>
<a href="/"><img src="/i/dailyreport.gif" width="140"
height="100" border="0" alt="The Daily Report" /></a>
<a href="/glamorous/"><img src="/i/glamorouslife.gif"
width="110" height="100" border="0" alt="My Glamorous Life"
/></a>
<a href="/classics/"><img src="/i/classic.gif" width="100"
height="100" border="0" alt=" Classics, 1995-2002" /></a>
</div>
```

Note that image height and width attributes, although useful, are not strictly necessary. Note also that, thanks to CSS, the border attribute is entirely unnecessary, even though we have included it here for the sake of old browsers. Our markup *could* be as clean and simple as this:

```
<div id="primenav">
<a href="/"><img src="/i/home.gif" alt="Home" /></a>
<a href="/"><img src="/i/dailyreport.gif" alt=
"The Daily Report" /></a>
<a href="/glamorous/"><img src="/i/glamorouslife.gif" alt=
"My Glamorous Life" /></a>
<a href="/classics/"><img src="/i/classic.gif" alt=
" Classics, 1995-2002" /></a>
</div>
```

Compare and contrast the compactness and clarity of the preceding markup with the typical table layout version shown here:

```
<table border="0" cellpadding="0" cellspacing="0" width="500">
<tr>
<td valign="top" width="150" height="100" bgcolor="#339999">
<a href="/"><img src="/i/home.gif" width="150" height="100"
border="0" alt="Home" /></a>
</td>
<td valign="top" width="140" height="100" bgcolor="#339999">
<a href="/"><img src="/i/dailyreport.gif" width="140" height=
"100" border="0" alt="The Daily Report" /></a>
</td>
<td valign="top" width="110" height="100" bgcolor="#339999">
<a href="/glamorous/"><img src="/i/glamorouslife.gif" width=
"110" height="100" border="0" alt="My Glamorous Life" /></a>
</td>
<td valign="top" width="100" height="100" bgcolor="#339999">
<a href="/classics/"><img src="/i/classic.gif" width="100"
height="100" border="0" alt=" Classics, 1995-2002" /></a>
</td>
</tr>
</table>
```

There's no contest. But compact markup and meta-structural thinking are *not* limited to CSS layouts. They can power and streamline table-based layouts, too.

Hybrid Layouts and Compact Markup:
Dos and Don'ts

Fear of learning CSS layout or the inability to use it on a particular project is no reason to avoid web standards. Combine streamlined table layouts with basic CSS and structural, accessible XHTML, and you have the makings of a hybrid, transitional approach that works.

CSS is still evolving, browsers are still learning to support CSS1 and CSS2, and some layout ideas work better when their basic elements are held in place by simple XHTML tables. But table markup is not the same as stupid markup, and hybrid layouts that use a few nonstructural components are quite different from the needlessly ornate junk HTML with which most sites are still being built in 2003.

A Note of Caution

We have said that some interface components of hybrid sites might not be structural. But that does not mean that structural markup has no place on the rest of such sites; paragraphs should still be marked up as paragraphs, lists as lists, and so on. Nor is it an invitation to produce navigational menus or other components using every sloppy old trick in the book. Structural or not, every component should be produced with clear, compact markup and clean CSS. Clean markup is what this chapter is all about.

Giving Names to Bad Things

In the section that follows, we'll look at the dumb ways too many sites are built and explain why these methods are counterproductive. We'll also concoct labels for several especially unsavory techniques that are used too often. Reading this section will not only banish these bad habits from your work, but it will also help you spot these errors in the work of your colleagues and vendors.

After you've read this section of the chapter and engraved its simple lessons on your heart, when colleagues or vendors try to get away with certain kinds of foolish markup, you will call them on it with the chillingly apt descriptive labels invented in this chapter. Your colleagues and vendors will develop a newfound respect for markup, a newfound respect for you, and above all, a profound discomfort whenever you're around them.

Actually, we've named the bad authoring practices described next not to make fun of anyone, but simply to identify and banish these practices from our own work. We hope they help you, too.

Common Errors in Hybrid Markup

Consider a typical, table-based site design [7.2], complete with a menu bar [7.3] that changes state [7.4] to indicate the visitor's location as she moves from page to page. The site's logo will obviously be a graphic element, most likely a GIF image. The menu labels (EVENTS, ABOUT, CONTACT, and so on) can also be images, or they can be simple hypertext links. If hypertext is chosen, old-school web designers might litter their markup with font tags to control textual appearance (size, face, color) and outdated attributes to control the alignment, border properties, and background color of the table cells containing these menu labels. Modern designers would use CSS instead, but the results might be no better if approached the wrong way.

Even if GIF images are chosen instead of hypertext, the designer will seek a way to differentiate the appearance of the menu table from other table structures on the site. For instance, the menu table [7.3, 7.4] seems to require thin black borders, whereas other table structures on the page are border-free. In a worst-case scenario, the designer will wrap the menu table inside another table whose only purpose is to create the black outline effect. That's how we built 'em back in 1997. Today's designers might combine junk markup with overwrought CSS to differentiate the menu table from other tables on the page. This is no better than the old stuff.

Classitis: The Measles of Markup

How *do* we instruct navigational table cells to display differently from all other table cells on the page? Or command the links inside these navigation bar table cells to display differently from other links on the page? *Not* with deprecated presentational tags and attributes like bgcolor and font, as you've already gathered. We don't want this:

```
<td align="left" valign="top" bordercolor="black"
bgcolor="white">
<font family="verdana, arial" size="2"><b>
<a href="/events/">Events</a></b></font></td> etc.
```

7.2
Design comp for the i3Forum conference site. (In Chapters 8 and 10, we will build the site.)

7.3
The menu as it will appear when the visitor lands on the home page. The logo is highlighted with a white background.

7.4
When the visitor moves to the EVENTS page, the EVENTS label is highlighted.

But we also most assuredly do *not* want to apply a class to every element that requires special handling. We see far too much of this kind of stuff:

```
<td class="whitewithblackborder"><span class="menuclass"><b>
<a href="/events/">Events</a></b></span></td> etc.
```

We've even, we're sorry to say, seen bastard spawn like this:

```
<td class="whitewithblackborder"><span class=
"menuclass"><font class="menufontclass"><b>
<a href="/events/">Events</a></b></font></span></td> etc.
```

We call this style of markup *classitis*. In a site afflicted by classitis, every blessed tag breaks out in its own swollen, blotchy class. Classitis is the measles of markup, obscuring meaning as it adds needless weight to every page. The affliction dates back to the early days of semi-CSS-capable browsers and to many designers' initially childlike comprehension of how CSS works.

Alas, many have not yet outgrown that childlike misunderstanding of CSS, either because they moved on to study some other technology or because their visual editing tool applies a class to every tag it generates, and they have "learned" CSS by studying the source their tool produces. Classitis is as bad in its own way as the `<font>` tag ever was; rarely does good markup require it.

Visual Editors and Classitis

Even the best, most sophisticated visual web editors tend to cough up needless classes like so many cold germs—primarily because they *are* visual editors, not people. People can abstract from the specific to the general. When you style a paragraph in CSS, you know that you intend all paragraphs to be styled the same way. But a visual editor cannot know what you intend. If, while working in such an editor, you create five paragraphs that all use 11px Verdana, the tool might assign a class to each of these paragraphs. The latest versions of Dreamweaver and GoLive are sophisticated, powerful, and standards friendly. But you will still want to edit some of their output by hand to avoid classitis and divitis.

The Heartbreak of Divitis

In its better moments, classitis can be grafted on top of otherwise structural markup:

```
<p class="noindent">This is a bad way to design web pages.</p>
<p class="indentnomargintop">There is no need for all these
classes.</p>
<p class="indentnomargintop">Classy designers avoid this
problem.</p>
<p class="indentnomargintop">Class dismissed.</p>
```

The previous example is the kind of thing that a more sophisticated and more standards-aware visual-editing tool might generate (see sidebar, "Visual Editors and Classitis"). At other times classitis is exacerbated by a still more serious condition. We have named this condition *divitis*:

```
<div class="primarycontent"><div class="yellowbox"><div
class="heading"><span class="biggertext">Welcome</span> to
the Member page!</div><div class="bodytext">Welcome returning
members.</div><div class="warning1">If you are not a member <a
href="/gohere/" class="warning2">go here</a>!</div></div></div>
```

Here we have no structure whatsoever—only many bytes of non-structural and hence nonsensical junk markup. Visit such a website with a Palm or text browser, and you'll have no idea how the various elements relate to each other. For the fact is, they don't relate to each other. Divitis replaces the nutrition of structure with the empty calories of sugary junk.

Classitis and divitis are like the unnecessary notes an amateur musician plays—the noodling of a high school guitarist when he's supposed to be providing backup to a singer or featured soloist. Classitis and divitis are like the needless adjectives with which bad writing is strewn. They are weeds in the garden of meaning.

Prune classitis ruthlessly from your markup and you will see bloated web pages shrink to half their size. Avoid divitis and you will find yourself writing clean, compact, primarily structural markup that works as well in a text browser as it does in your favorite desktop browser. Do these things rigorously, and you will be well on your way to smarter, more compliant web pages. Like Smokey says, only you can prevent divitis.

*div*s Are Just All Right

Some of you are thinking: "Hey, Mister Fancy Pants Standards Book Fellow, you say div elements are bad, yet you yourself used a div element in the very first example in this chapter (the navigational images at zeldman.com). I have caught you in a big fat lie, you bad, bad man."

Actually, we never said div elements are bad and neither did the W3C, which after all created these elements. (If you skipped it, refer back to "div, id, and Other Assistants" earlier in this chapter.) Div is an entirely appropriate unit of markup for blocking out structural areas of your site.

Divitis kicks in only when you use div to replace perfectly good (and more appropriate) elements. If you've written a paragraph, then it's a paragraph and should be marked up as such—not as a div of the "text" class. Your highest-level headline should be <h1>, not <div class="headline">. See the difference? Sure you do.

Why a *div*?

Many designers use non-structural `div`s to replace everything from headlines to paragraphs. Most acquired the habit when they discovered that 4.0 browsers, particularly Netscape's, wrapped layout-destroying, unwanted white space around structural elements like `<h1>`, but managed not to ruin layouts that used only non-structural `div`s. (See "The Curse of Legacy Rendering," Chapter 3, "The Trouble with Standards.")

To preserve pixel-perfect layout nuances for rapidly vanishing 4.0 browser users, many designers persist in using non-structural `div` elements to the exclusion of standard paragraphs, headlines, and so on. The cost of so doing is high. The practice renders sites semantically impenetrable to an ever-growing audience of wireless, phone, alternative, and screen-reader users. And it doubles or triples the bandwidth for every site visitor, regardless of what browser or device they're using. Not worth it.

Another classic example of divitis kicks in when a designer catches the "tables are bad, CSS is good" virus (see Chapter 4, "XML Conquers the World [And Other Web Standards Success Stories"]) and righteously replaces 200 tons of table markup with 200 tons of nested `div`s. They haven't gained a thing (except a smug, self-satisfied feeling) and they may even have made their document harder to edit.

Loving the *id*

So if presentational HTML is out, and classitis and divitis are out, how *would* we apply separate design rules to our navigational area in a hybrid layout combining tables with CSS? We would do it through the wizardry of `id`. Assign a unique, meta-structural label to the table that contains the menu:

```
<table id="menu">
```

Later, when you write your style sheet, you'll create a "menu" selector and an associated set of CSS rules that tell table cells, text labels, and all else exactly how to display. If you choose to use hypertext links to construct your menu, you can do so with a minimum of fuss:

```
<td><a href="/events/">Events</a></td>
```

"Where's the rest of it?" you might ask. There isn't any "rest of it," aside from the other table cells required. By labeling the table with an `id` of "menu" (or another appropriate name of your choice) and by using "menu" as a CSS selector in the style sheet you write later in the design process, you banish all this chapter's boogie men.

No classitis. No divitis. No need for obsolete `<font>` tags. No need to apply redundant, bandwidth-gobbling presentational height, width, alignment, and background color attributes to each instance of the `<td>` element. With one digital sticky note (the `id` label "menu"), you have prepared your clean, compact markup for specific presentational processing in a separate style sheet.

CSS will control every aspect of these particular table cells' appearance, including background color (and background image, if any), border treatments (if any), whitespace (padding), horizontal and vertical alignment, and rollover effects. CSS table cell rollover effects often include changes to the background color, border color, or both. These rollover effects are well supported in most modern browsers and do no harm in browsers that don't understand them. Likewise, CSS will control the look of the link, including font, size, color, and numerous other variables.

But What About Images?

Does this combination of a unique `id`, compact XHTML, and a style sheet work as well for table-based menus that use images as it does for those that use hypertext links? Glad you asked! It works every bit as well. Author your table using only those elements it absolutely requires, do the same thing with your image elements, and make sure every image element includes a usable `alt` attribute.

In fact, you can combine transparent GIF images with CSS rules that create subtle or stupendous rollover effects without JavaScript. But that would be getting ahead of ourselves, and we hate to do that.

Because this chapter seems to foster names, we have called the `id`-driven combination of minimal XHTML and smart CSS the "clean text method" when it uses primarily hypertext menu items and the "clean image method" when it uses primarily image-driven menus. If this book were part of a sinister global conglomerate, these approaches would be copyrighted, trademarked, and patented, and merely alluding to this chapter would cost you a hefty licensing fee. But we're not like that. Feel free to use these methods and to call them by these names or by any other name you like.

One other important point deserves to be made if we're to understand how table layouts can be made more intelligent and less harmful.

Banish Redundant Table Cells

Consider the website of The Marine Center [7.5], designed and produced in 2003 for the web's oldest supplier of rare, net-collected fish and corals. Notice that the site's layout is divided into several task-oriented areas. For instance, an impulse-buyer's column at the right promotes currently available items, invites the visitor to join the site's mailing list, and provides a means of searching and browsing. The content area at the left promotes new arrivals, offers a rotating series of beauty shots, and invites the reader to peruse a monthly "Fish Tales" column.

Such layouts ordinarily enclose each component within its own table cell, much like The Gilmore site we examined in Chapter 2, "Designing and Building with Standards," [2.3, 2.4]. In a typical layout created by slicing Photoshop comps or positioning elements in a visual web editor, the large fish picture would live in its own table cell, as would each smaller fish image, as would the graphic header for "Fish Tales," and so on. Other table cells would contain transparent spacer GIF images to control the amount of vertical or horizontal whitespace between sections.

Dozens of cells would be involved, introducing dangerous dependencies. For instance, if the site's content specialists wrote too many lines of introductory copy one week, the large fish picture would be pushed lower down on the page, and its movement might create unwanted vertical gaps in the column on the right. The site would also be fairly bandwidth intensive, not because it contained images, but because it relied on complex tables with all their associated presentational attributes.

Although The Marine Center uses hybrid layout techniques, it avoids the problems commonly associated with them by restricting its use of tables to an absolute minimum. The basic table grid creates the left and right columns. Elements are inserted in these columns in order of appearance, and nuances of whitespace and alignment are handled exclusively in CSS. We'll explain the CSS methods used in Chapter 10. For this chapter's purposes, the moral is to use as few table elements as possible. When you begin to combine minimal tables with CSS, you'll see that many techniques you once thought essential are anything but.

7.5
Fish on the menu:
The Marine Center (www.
themarinecenter.com)
offers rare, net-collected
fish and corals and hybrid
standards compliance.

Outdated Methods on Parade

For reference purposes (and in case you still use some of these methods), we'll wrap up this chapter by examining outdated production methods in the order in which they first came to the web.

The Year of the Map

In the earliest days of commercial web design, image maps were used to deliver a branded navigation bar such as the one in Figure 7.3 or at the top and bottom of Figure 7.5. Early image maps consisted of five parts:

- A Photoshop (or Canvas, or other image editor-generated) file that was quite literally a picture of a user interface, saved in GIF or (later) JPEG format

- A map file containing the coordinates of each "active" region of the image, along with the URL to which each active region linked

- A CGI program, typically written in PERL and installed in a special directory of the server, whose job was to translate the user's mouse clicks into the URLs specified in the map file

- An "ISMAP" attribute that was added to the image element in the page's source code

- A hypertext anchor around the image element that pointed to the CGI program's location

The HTML typically looked something like this:

```
<A HREF="/cgi-bin/imagemap/image.map"><IMG SRC=
"/images/image.gif" ISMAP></A>
```

This was the famous server-side image map of the early mid-1990s, so named because the CGI script on the site owner's *server* did the work of translating user mouse clicks to mapped URLs. Of course, the designer did a lot of work as well. Image map design was no picnic, but it was the only way a designer could create the visual effect desired.

Server-side image maps were soon replaced by client-side image maps, so named because the translation of clicks to coordinates took place "on the client"—that is, in the visitor's browser—instead of on the server. Client-side image maps did not require a separate map file; instead, the coordinates were encrusted right in the page's HTML, where they might look something like this:

```
<map name="navigation">
<area shape="rect" coords="0,400,75,475" href="index.html">
<area shape="rect" coords="401,500, 425, 525" href=
"events.html">
...
</map>
```

Client-side image maps were easier, and so, of course, server-side image maps went by the wayside. Ain't progress grand?

The Map and Its Discontents

Image-map-using developers who wanted to keep visitors abreast of their changing location within the site's hierarchy [7.3, 7.4] had no choice but to create a separate navigational image file for each page. And beleaguered, modem-using visitors had no choice but to download a new, hefty image file for each page. If the developer were extra slick, he or she would change the *map* file for every page as well, so that the portion of the image pertaining to the current page could not be clicked.

It took a metric ton of bandwidth to achieve these effects, and since dial-up speeds in 1994–1996 were anything but peppy, users were often unhappy. The budding usability movement, taking note of this user frustration, declared that images were generally bad.

Today almost no one uses image maps. Yet, still smarting from these early experiences, some usability consultants and their followers remain hostile to images and graphic design. This is rather like despising automobiles because a Model T once scared your horse. But we're not here to dispute anyone's entrenched views (except those that misconstrue or misrepresent web standards).

No Access, No Structure

Image maps delivered a branded look and feel, but they worked only in graphical desktop browsers with images turned on, and they required of the user both physical mobility (to click the mouse) and unimpaired eyesight (to see the pictures). Image maps could be made more accessible by means of the `alt` attribute, but this generally was not done.

Most importantly for our purposes, image maps conveyed no structural mean-ing. They were simply pictures you could click if you had the right equipment (including physical human equipment). The precedent for nonstructural HTML had been set.

Slicing and Dicing

Chief among the defects of image maps was their inability to save bandwidth by caching recurring image components. Designers soon began slicing and dicing their Photoshop comps, exporting the sliced image segments in GIF and JPEG format, and using HTML tables to position the pieces. (We doubt any reader of this section of the book will require a refresher, but if you do, we once again commend your attention to Figures 2.3 and 2.4 in Chapter 2.)

The slice and dice method was not structural, but it saved considerable user and server bandwidth by storing recurring elements in the browser cache on the user's hard drive. And it could be made accessible (and often is) by means of the `alt` attribute to the image tag:

```
<a href="/events/">
<img src="/images/events.gif" alt="Events">
</a>
```

Because "slice and dice" facilitated the creation of a branded look and feel without the brutal bandwidth overhead of image maps, designers and developers naturally gravitated to this method.

The Slice Comes of Age

In the early days, we flattened our Adobe Photoshop layers, selected each "slice" by hand via the rectangular marquee tool, and copied and pasted each one to a separate, new file. We used third-party plug-ins to export a GIF version of each file. We wrote our HTML tables by hand and prayed that our manually selected "slices" would recombine seamlessly. We churned our own butter and darned our own socks.

Then several things happened.

Netscape extended the JavaScript object model it had invented in 1996 to include the ability to swap images in response to user mouse actions. The rollover was born. Some of us learned JavaScript to include rollover states in our hand-coded slice-and-dice table layouts. Others copied and pasted from then bleeding-edge sites like Project Cool. Many of us did a bit of both.

Meanwhile, Photoshop was beefing up its web capabilities, to which Adobe soon added additional shortcuts via its ImageReady application, which was originally sold separately but is now integrated with Photoshop. With ImageReady, you could drag Photoshop guides and let the program do your slicing and dicing for you. ImageReady would even write the HTML table markup, and in subsequent versions it also generated JavaScript rollovers.

Macromedia's Fireworks web image creation tool did the same thing (still does), and Macromedia and Adobe soon began offering WYSIWYG web editing tools that could spit out tables and rollovers whether you knew how to code them by hand or not.

Developers now had the best of both worlds—a visually pleasing effect with all the heavy lifting done by computers (which, unlike human beings, never tire of performing grunt work).

In Defense of Navigational Table Layouts

HTML tables (or XHTML tables) containing GIF images and JavaScript are still a norm of modern web design and development. Some standards advocates dislike them because they are nonstructural, and some usability consultants disdain them as they disdain nearly everything to do with graphic design.

But as we've tried to show in this chapter (and will show in more detail in the next three chapters), such tables remain an appropriate tool for hybrid, transitional layouts that require a branded look and feel. Their chief defect is that it takes a great deal of work to change them when a site revises its architecture or updates its look and feel. This defect penalizes designers and site owners but does not harm users.

Tables are not the only way to achieve branding effects, but they are reliable across browsing environments, can be rendered with compact and accessible markup, and often squander less bandwidth than the image-free alternatives that many designers explored in the mid-1990s.

The Redundant Verbosity of Redundantly Verbose Tables

In an attempt to save bandwidth, increase accessibility, and make sense to search engines (which cannot read images), in the mid-1990s some web designers stopped using GIF text and began simulating slice-and-dice layouts by writing their navigational labels in HTML and inserting them into table layouts. CSS was not yet supported in browsers, but proprietary HTML "extensions" were. Thus, we got junk like the example that follows, which might actually waste more bandwidth than the images it replaced:

```
<!-- Begin outermost table. This creates the black border
effects. -->
<TABLE WIDTH=80% BORDER=0 CELLSPACING=1 CELLPADDING=0>
<TR>
<TD WIDTH=100% VALIGN=TOP BGCOLOR="#000000">
<!-- Begin actual navigational content table. -->
<TABLE WIDTH=100% HEIGHT=100% BORDER=0 CELLSPACING=
1 CELLPADDING=0>
<TR>
<TD WIDTH=25% HEIGHT=50 VALIGN=TOP BGCOLOR="#FF9900">
<FONT SIZE=2><BR><BR><FONT FACE="GENEVA, ARIAL,
HELVETICA"><B>
<A HREF="item1.html">Menu Item 1</A></B></FONT><BR><BR>
</FONT></TD>
<TD WIDTH=25% HEIGHT=50 VALIGN=TOP BGCOLOR="#FF9900"><FONT
SIZE=2><BR><BR><FONT FACE="GENEVA, ARIAL, HELVETICA"><B>
<A HREF="item2.html">Menu Item 2</A></B></FONT><BR><BR>
</FONT></TD>
```

```
<TD WIDTH=25% HEIGHT=50 VALIGN=TOP BGCOLOR="#FF9900">
<FONT SIZE=2><BR><BR><FONT FACE="GENEVA, ARIAL,
HELVETICA"><B>
<A HREF="item3.html">Menu Item 3</A></B></FONT><BR><BR>
</FONT></TD>
<TD WIDTH=25% HEIGHT=50 VALIGN=TOP BGCOLOR="#FF9900">
<FONT SIZE=2><BR><BR><FONT FACE="GENEVA, ARIAL,
HELVETICA"><B>
<A HREF="item4.html">Menu Item 4</A></B></FONT><BR><BR>
</FONT></TD>
</TR>
</TABLE>
<!-- End actual navigational content table. -->
</TD>
</TR>
</TABLE>
<!-- End outermost visual effects creation table. -->
```

Such markup might stink to the clouds above, but it is still used on many big, commercial sites, including those of industry leaders—even though it is a definite step backwards in terms of markup aesthetics. (Compare and contrast with the markup we'll create in Chapters 8 and 10.) Many compound the horror by storing chunks of purely presentational markup in the records of their database. Thus, even if a lean, clean, primarily structural redesign is attempted, old junk markup, flown in from the database, will destroy it.

Organizations that have used these techniques can only emerge from the digital Stone Age with tremendous labor and at great expense. Because there is no future in continuing to produce sites of this ilk, such organizations will have to bite the bullet sooner or later. If you are working with one of those organizations, we hope this book will encourage you to bite the bullet sooner.

Bad CSS Comes to Town

In 1997, when MSIE3 began offering partial support for CSS1, those of us intrigued by the W3C design language's promise initially approached our task with the same nonstructural, redundant verbosity we had so lovingly lavished on our image-free table layouts.

Instead of linking to a single style sheet that could be cached on the visitor's hard drive, we used inline styles per the example in the next section ("Party Like It's 1997") that wasted every bit as much bandwidth as the old-school font and `bgcolor` attributes. In an effort to support "non-CSS browsers," we often stuck the font tags and other junk in anyway, effectively doubling the bandwidth our layouts wasted. And it goes without saying that we gave not the slightest consideration to document structure.

The true power of CSS to separate structure from presentation was not yet available in browsers, and more importantly was not in the minds of most professional web designers. (And in many cases, it still isn't.) Designers weren't ready to move forward to CSS because it wasn't ready for them.

To the discussion of classitis and divitis earlier, add its predecessor, which is even worse than classitis and divitis because it includes all CSS styles inline, thus entirely missing the point that CSS can save bandwidth and preserve meaning by applying global styles to structured markup across an entire site. We've dredged up the following piece of bad 1997-style CSS/XHTML to show you what it looks like and to help you avoid ever writing anything remotely like it.

Party Like It's 1997

The snippet immediately following is a perfect example of the kind of bad CSS (combined with bad markup) that many of us wrote in 1997. It is also the kind of CSS that visual web-editing tools of the time generated if you set them to author CSS at all:

```
<font color="#FFFFFF">|</font>
 
 
<a style="color:#FFFFFF;text-decoration:none;" href=
"/isapi/gosearch.asp?target=/us/default.asp" target="_top"
onmouseover="this.style.color='#FFCC00';"
onmouseout="this.style.color='#FFFFFF';">Search</a> 
```

Incredible as it might seem, this little piece of toilet debris was not unearthed from the archives of a 1997 design portfolio, nor is it student work, nor is it the tragic effort of an obscure small business site. It was lifted exactly as you see it from the Microsoft home page [**7.6**] on January 7, 2003 and had been freshly updated that very day.

7.6

Where would you like to go today? Back to 1997, to judge by the markup and CSS used on the Microsoft home page in 2003 (www.microsoft.com).

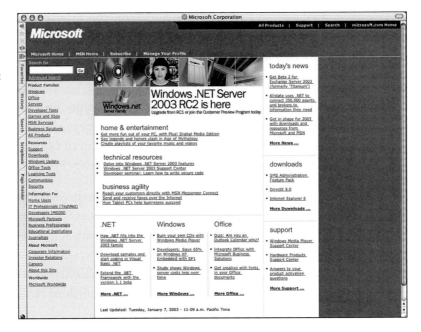

Because redundancy is as bad in books as it is in code, we'll avoid explaining what's wrong with this markup. If you don't know by now, one of us hasn't done our job.

Microsoft is a member of the W3C, a key contributor to the CSS and XHTML specs, and the maker of compliant browsers that have long outgrown their taste for wretched HTML and CSS like that used on their home page. Reread "A New Era of Cooperation" in Chapter 4 and scratch your head over this strange return to the worst markup and CSS methods of the 1990s.

Thankfully, by late 1997 or early 1998, most designers had moved on from this kind of brain-dead authoring. Unfortunately, what most of us moved on to was nearly as bad (classitis and divitis). But the clouds are lifting.

Moving On

Table layouts can be well made, lightweight, accessible, and standards-compliant. And CSS layouts can do even more: lightening your workload and the load on your server, separating structure from presentation to increase the reach and utility of your site, and giving visual designers fresh tools to unlock their creativity. In the next three chapters, we'll consolidate what we've learned so far and begin our journey into CSS by building a compact, compliant site.

XHTML by Example: A Hybrid Layout (Part I)

This chapter and the two that follow it form a tight little unit. In this chapter, we'll roll up our sleeves and apply what we've learned about XHTML thus far to mark up a real-world design project. The markup we create will be partly structural, partly transitional, and fully standards-compliant. In Chapter 9, "CSS Basics," we'll cover Cascading Style Sheets (CSS) basics for beginning and intermediate users. Finally, in Chapter 10, "CSS in Action: A Hybrid Layout (Part II), we'll learn still more about CSS while using it to complete our project. This "teaching by doing" business is not unlike learning to swim by being tossed into deep, cold water, although we prefer to think of it as picking up French by visiting Paris. For good measure, as we build this project, we'll start learning how to incorporate accessibility into our markup (and hence, into our sites).

Benefits of Transitional Methods Used in These Chapters

In this chapter, we'll begin crafting a hybrid, transitional layout combining traditional (but here, streamlined) table layout techniques with structured textual markup and accessibility enhancements. The techniques used in this project and explained in these three chapters are ideal for libraries and other public institutions, along with small companies and any other organization that seeks to do the following:

- Manage large amounts of content on a limited budget
- Support a wide range of browsers and devices
- Conserve visitors' bandwidth (and their own)
- Begin the transition to web standards with publishing methods that are reliable, cost-effective, and easy to implement

Style Sheets Instead of JavaScript

By the end of these three chapters, we will have produced a standards-compliant template for the i3Forum site [**8.1**]. The final templates created in these chapters can be viewed on the Happy Cog staging server at `http://i3.happycog.com/`. The finished site, produced by means of these templates, is located at `http://i3forum.com/`.

In this chapter, we'll nail down our markup. In Chapter 10, we'll add CSS to control the color, size, and relative positioning of elements. (We'll pause in Chapter 9 to learn CSS basics.) Among other things, the CSS we create will deliver menu rollover effects more commonly accomplished with images and JavaScript. There's nothing wrong with images or JavaScript, but by using XHTML text and CSS instead, we'll save bandwidth while making the site readily accessible to a wide variety of environments, including screen readers and text browsers, nondesktop-browsers (such as PDA and phone-based browsers), and non-CSS-capable browsers.

Basic Approach (Overview)

The i3Forum layout is designed to deliver a crisp, punchy brand identity with a minimum of fuss, and its XHTML is equally straightforward. It is composed of two XHTML tables, both centered, and both enhanced and controlled via CSS. The first table delivers the navigational menu; the second provides the content [**8.2**].

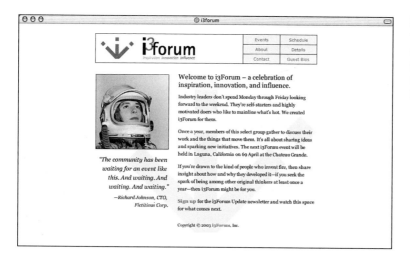

8.1
The finished template, as it will appear when the work explained in Chapters 8 through 10 has been completed.

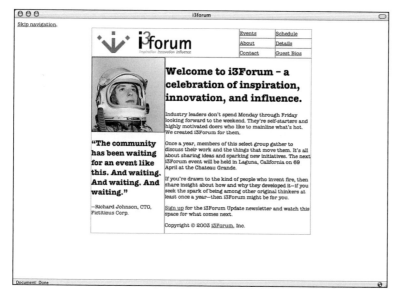

8.2
The template we'll build in this chapter, with CSS turned off and borders turned on. Note the slightly thicker line between menu and content areas, where two separate tables meet.

The XHTML for the tables will be shown in the pages that follow. But a preliminary question might already have occurred to you. Traditionally, such layouts would use a single table, with `rowspans` and `colspans` juggling the various rows and columns. If we used Adobe ImageReady to automatically slice and dice the Photoshop comp used to design the site (and to sell the design to the client), ImageReady would render the entire page in a single table. So why have we used two tables?

Separate Tables: CSS and Accessibility Advantages

If you skipped Chapter 7's ("Tighter, Firmer Pages Guaranteed: Structure and Meta-Structure in Strict and Hybrid Markup") discussion of "div, id, and Other Assistants," you might want to glance at it before going any further. Breaking our layout into two tables allows us to harness the power of the id attribute to do the following:

- Streamline the CSS we'll create in Chapter 10

- Provide certain accessibility enhancements

- Structurally label each table according to the job it does, making it easier to some day revisit the layout and replace presentational XHTML tables with divs styled via CSS

The Table Summary Element

In addition, breaking the layout into two tables allows us to add a summary attribute to each:

```
<table id="nav" summary="Navigation elements" ... etc. >
<table id="content" summary="Main content." ... etc. >
```

The summary attribute is invisible to ordinary desktop browsers like IE and Netscape. But the screen-reading software used by nonsighted visitors understands the summary attribute and will read its value aloud. In our case, the screen reader will say "Navigation elements" and "Main content." Well-designed screen readers allow users to skip the table if they don't think it will interest them. Writing table summaries thus forms a good accessibility backup strategy to accommodate users who might miss the Skip Navigation link described two paragraphs from now.

Page Structure and *id*

We've assigned an id attribute value to each table according to the structural job it does—navigation or content. Doing so now allows us to later write compact CSS rules that apply to an entire table, avoiding classitis and divitis (defined and discussed in Chapter 7).

It also allows us to provide a Skip Navigation link in the top of our markup.

The What and Why of Skip Navigation

As its name implies, the Skip Navigation link allows visitors to bypass navigation and jump directly to the content table by means of an anchor link.

The id attribute whose value is "content" provides the anchor to which we link:

```
<div class="hide"><a href="#content" title="Skip navigation."
accesskey="2">Skip navigation</a>.</div>
```

Skipping navigation is not an urgent requirement for most sighted web users, who can focus their attention on particular parts of a web page simply by glancing at those parts and ignoring other parts that don't interest them.

But nonsighted visitors who are using screen readers experience the web in a linear fashion, one link at a time. It frustrates such users to endure a constant audio stream of menu links each time they load a page of your site. Skip Navigation lets these users avoid this problem.

Skip Navigation can also help sighted readers using non-CSS-capable PDA browsers and web phones avoid tediously scrolling through a fistful of links every time they load a new page. Finally, Skip Navigation can benefit sighted users who are physically impaired, although the method is not perfect. (See the later section titled "accesskey: Good News, Bad News.")

Skip Navigation and *accesskey*

Our Skip Navigation link enables visitors who are using nonvisual or non-CSS browsers to jump directly to content in the second table, whose id attribute name (and thus whose anchor link) is "content":

```
<table id="content" ...> etc.
```

In these nonvisual or non-CSS environments, the link is readily available at the top of the page [**8.3, 8.4**]. You'll create a rule to hide the Skip Navigation link in CSS-capable browsers in Chapter 10. (If you're the impatient type, we've also included it here.)

```
.hide    {
    display: none;
    }
```

Because of this CSS rule, visitors who are using modern browsers with CSS turned on will not see the Skip Navigation link—but most of them do not need to see it because they do not require Skip Navigation functionality for the reasons discussed in "The What and Why of Skip Navigation." Screen readers that ignore CSS will merrily read the content of the div, thus informing non-sighted visitors that they can avoid the boring recitation of the other links. (Alas, some screen readers obey CSS even though their users can't see it.)

8.3

In a non-CSS browser (or a CSS-capable browser with CSS turned off), the Skip Navigation link is clearly visible at the top of the page.

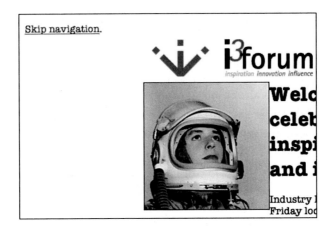

8.4

The visible Skip Navigation link in context—in our layout with CSS turned off.

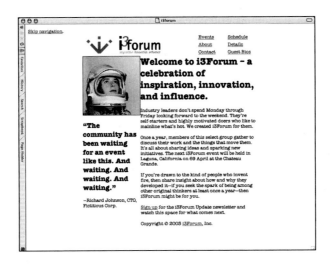

There's an exception to every assumption, of course. A person who has impaired mobility, viewing the site via a CSS-capable browser, might desire to skip the navigation area and jump directly to content. Most web users who have impaired mobility can see an entire web page at once (the exception being users who are visually *and* physically impaired). But to navigate that page, impaired users employ the keyboard or an alternative, assistive input device. Tabbing their way past unwanted navigation links could be a nuisance, or worse.

How can we help these users skip navigation if they can't see the Skip Navigation link in their browser? We've provided that option via the `accesskey` attribute, which works even when the Skip Navigation link is invisible in the browser. Alas, the method is imperfect, as discussed next.

accesskey: Good News, Bad News

The `accesskey` attribute to HTML/XHTML enables people to navigate websites via the keyboard instead of a mouse. To assign an `accesskey` to an element, you simply declare it, as in the earlier XHTML excerpt, which we reprint here with the relevant attribute and value highlighted in bold:

```
<a href="#content" title="Skip navigation." accesskey="2">Skip
navigation</a>.
```

In our markup, we've assigned the Skip Navigation link an `accesskey` of 2. Therefore, to skip navigation, the visitor simply presses 2 on her keyboard. As is often true of accessibility enhancements, the required markup is easy to write and has no effect on the site's visual design. In this case, that's both good and bad.

For how does the visitor know to press 2 on her keyboard? No widely used browser displays `accesskey` letter assignments. Neither do most little-used browsers.

accesskey and iCab

As of this writing, only iCab [8.5], a Macintosh browser, visually displays `accesskey` letter assignments. Most web users are not Macintosh users, and most Macintosh users are not iCab users. Making matters worse, iCab cannot show the `accesskey` assignment when the Skip Navigation link is hidden via CSS. As this book goes to press, iCab still does not support much of CSS1, the W3C's first CSS recommendation, published way back in 1996. In short, although iCab is an interesting browser and its commitment to supporting HTML 4 is impressive (and no, we're not being facetious: iCab's HTML 4 support is superb), iCab is not going to solve the world's `accesskey` problem.

8.5

Of all the world's browsers, only iCab for Macintosh (`http://www.icab.de/`) displays our `accesskey` of 2, cuing the user that she can skip navigation by pressing 2 on her keyboard.

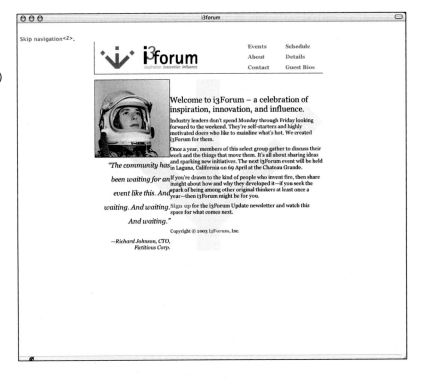

Two Utopian Possibilities for *accesskey*

Clearly, the majority of users who might benefit from `accesskey` have no way of knowing which `accesskey` letters or numbers to press; therefore, they cannot benefit from it. Because of that, including `accesskey` in your markup is somewhat idealistic.

If the W3C would recommend standard `accesskey` assignments for universal functions like "skip navigation" (and if designers and developers would follow those recommendations), users would always know which keys to press. That would be a good thing.

Alternatively, browser makers might decide to beef up their `accesskey` support by visually displaying `accesskey` values if the user decides to turn on this accessibility option in his preferences. IE for Windows provides an accessibility option allowing users to ignore font sizes on any web page. It might also add an option to Always Show Accesskey Values.

We must admit it feels rather Utopian to hope that the W3C will standardize `accesskey` shortcuts any time soon, and it also feels Utopian to hope that any major browser vendor (let alone all of them) will devote engineering time and resources to an always-visible-accesskey option. Nevertheless, we continue to use accesskey. Some users might view source to see which accesskey values are in use on a page and thereafter use the appropriate keys to navigate. We hope things become easier for these users soon.

Additional *id* Attributes

In addition to the primary id attribute names (nav and content), in our first pass at the site's markup we also assign unique id attribute names to each cell of the navigation table. Two cells should suffice to make the method clear:

```
<td width="100" height="25" id="events"><a href=
"events.html">Events</a></td>
<td width="100" height="25" id="schedule"><a href=
"schedule.html">Schedule</a></td>
```

We also assign unique id attribute values to each of the two primary divisions of the content table, namely the sidebar (id="sidebar") and primary content (id="primarycontent") areas. Next, with much data removed for clarity, is the shell of the content table; id attributes and values have been highlighted in bold:

```
<table id="content" etc.>
<tr>
<td width="200" id="sidebar">
Sidebar content goes here.
</td>
<td width="400" id="primarycontent">
Primary content goes here.
</td>
```

For good measure, we slap an id attribute name on the secondary rows of the navigation bar. Thus, the *second* row of navigation "buttons" has the following id value:

```
<tr id="nav2">
```

And, as you might expect, the *third* row of navigation "buttons" has this id value:

```
<tr id="nav3">
```

How Much Is Too Much?

The latter two id attribute names (nav2 and nav3) aren't required for this layout's purposes, but they might come in handy one day, in the event a redesign is required. Should we include them or not? Including them now adds a few bytes to our XHTML, and we might with equal merit have chosen not to do so.

If, on the final site, the navigation bar lives in a separate Server-Side Include file (or in a unique record managed by PHP, JSP, ColdFusion, or ASP), the client could easily edit that file at any point in the future, changing the entire site by adjusting a single file. If the client plans to use server-side technologies, it might be silly to include nav2 and nav3. On the other hand, if no server-side technologies are used and the menu markup is manually repeated on every page, it might be safer to go ahead and include nav2 and nav3 to avoid potential search-and-replace errors in a future redesign. And that is what we've done.

First Pass Markup: Same as Last Pass Markup

On this and the next few pages, you'll find our first pass at the site's markup from <body> to </body>. It is also our *final* pass at the site's markup. Any subsequent design adjustments were handled entirely in CSS. That is one benefit of offloading as much presentational stuff as possible to your style sheets, even in a hybrid layout like this one. To save space in this book, we've replaced the lovely body copy used in the template with generic placeholder text.

Note, too, that in this markup we've used relative image file reference links (img src="images/logo.gif") instead of absolute ones (img src="/images/logo.gif") because we're working off our desktop instead of on the staging server. The final markup will use absolute file reference links. (Absolute URLs are more reliable than relative URLs because they don't break if file locations change; for instance, if /events.html moves to /events/index.html, the absolute reference to /images/logo.gif will still work. Also, absolute URLs help avoid a CSS bug in some old browsers that misunderstand relative file references in style sheets.)

Technically speaking, the "final" markup differs slightly from the first pass markup by replacing relative file references with absolute file references. Not that most of you care, but there is always one reader who views page source to verify claims made in a book.

You might find it easier to view source *at* the source. As mentioned earlier in this chapter, the project is archived at http://i3.happycog.com/.

Navigational Markup: The First Table

What follows is the navigation section, from the body element on. To keep things interesting, we'll tell you in advance that this portion of the markup, although it validates, commits a "sin" of nonpresentational markup purity. See if you can spot the sin.

```
<body bgcolor="#ffffff">
<div class="hide"><a href="#content" title="Skip navigation."
accesskey="2">Skip navigation</a>.</div>
<table id="nav" summary="Navigation elements" width="600"
border="0" align="center" cellpadding="0" cellspacing="0">
<tr>
<td rowspan="3" id="home" width="400"><a href="/" title=
"i3Forum home page."><img src="images/logo.gif" width="400"
height="75" border="0" alt="i3forum home" /></a></td>
<td width="100" height="25" id="events"><a href="
"events.html">Events</a></td>
<td width="100" height="25" id="schedule"><a href=
"schedule.html">Schedule</a></td>
</tr>
<tr id="nav2">
<td width="100" height="25" id="about"><a href=
"about.html">About</a></td>
<td width="100" height="25" id="details"><a href=
"details.html">Details</a></td>
</tr>
<tr id="nav3">
<td width="100" height="25" id="contact"><a href=
"contact.html">Contact</a></td>
<td width="100" height="25" id="guestbios"><a href=
"guestbios.html">Guest Bios</a></td>
</tr>
</table>
```

Presentation, Semantics, Purity, and Sin

How big a standards geek are you? Did you spot the worst sin in our XHTML? The primary offense took place in the first line—namely the use of the outdated bgcolor (background color) attribute to the body element to specify, even in non-CSS browsers, that the page's background color should be white (#ffffff). Here it is again:

```
<body bgcolor="#ffffff">
```

Writing old-school markup like that could get us thrown out of the Pure Standards Academy faster than a greased meteor. After all, CSS lets us specify the body background color, and the W3C recommends that CSS, not HTML or XHTML, be used for this purpose. In the eyes of many standards fans, our use of bgcolor is a sin.

A Transitional Book for a Transitional Time

To the kind of standards geek who spends hours each week arguing about the evils of presentational markup on W3C mailing lists, what we've done here is evil and harmful. For that matter, we've also sinned by using tables as anything other than containers of tabular data, by specifying widths and heights in our table cells and by setting image margins to zero in markup. In fact, in the eyes of some, this entire chapter is sinful. Some standards geeks might not think much of this book, quite frankly. In their view, we should be telling you how to write semantic markup instead of letting you think it's okay to sometimes use tables for layout.

But the thing is, it is okay. Maybe it won't be okay some years from now, when designers use and browsers support purely semantic future versions of XHTML and rich future versions of CSS and SVG. But this is a transitional book for a transitional time. "Web standards" is not a set of immutable laws, but a path filled with options and decisions. In our view, people who insist on absolute purity in today's browser and standards environment do as much harm to the mainstream adoption of web standards as those who have never heard of or are downright hostile toward structural markup and CSS.

Making Allowances for Old Browsers

Why did we use the scarlet bgcolor attribute in spite of its shameful wickedness? The hybrid site we're producing makes no assumptions about the browsers used by its visitors. In an old, non-CSS-capable browser, if the default background color were set to any color other than white, the site's transparent GIF logo image would be afflicted by nonangelic halos caused by mismatched edge pixels. No client wants his logo to look shoddy in any browser, even if the rest of the site is just so-so in some old browsers.

One popular old browser that did not support CSS set medium gray as its default background color. Our logo is not antialiased against medium gray but against white. If we hadn't set the background color via the XHTML bgcolor attribute, our logo would look bad in such browsing environments.

In reality, you might not care what your site looks like in a 2.0 or 3.0 browser. For that matter, you might not care what it looks like in a 4.0 browser—neither might your boss or your client. The semantically impure techniques used in this chapter do not attempt to create the same visual experience in all browsers. In a non-CSS browser, our layout will not look any better than what you see in Figure **8.3**. And that's okay.

We used tables for this site and included bgcolor to show you that such compromises can be made in XHTML 1.0 Transitional and the site will still validate. We also did this to suggest that any effort to include standards in your work—even a compromised (but realistic) effort that uses some presentational markup—is worth making.

Content Markup: The Second Table

The "content" table immediately follows the navigational one and should be self explanatory to anyone who's ever written HTML or XHTML. The two things worth noting are the compactness of this markup and its use of id:

```
<table id="content" summary="Main content." width="600"
border="0" align="center" cellpadding="0" cellspacing="0">
<tr>
<td width="200" id="sidebar" valign="top">
<img src="images/astro.jpg" width="200" height="200"
border="0" alt="i3Forum. Breeding leadership." title="i3Forum.
Breeding leadership." />
<h2>Subhead</h2>
<p>Text</p>
</td>
<td width="400" id="primarycontent">
<h1>Headline</h1>
<p>Copy.</p>
<p>Copy.</p>
<p>Copy.</p>
<p>Copy.</p>
<div id="footer">
<p>Copyright &copy; 2003 <a href="/" title="i3forum
home page.">i3Forum</a>, Inc.</p>
</div>
</td>
</tr>
</table>
</body>
```

In Chapter 9, we'll explore CSS basics. Then, in Chapter 10, we'll use CSS to add visual control and panache to our hybrid site.

chapter nine

CSS Basics

In Chapter 8, "XHTML by Example: A Hybrid Layout (Part I)," we began creating a hybrid, transitional, standards-compliant site. In Chapter 10, "CSS in Action: A Hybrid Layout (Part II)," we'll finish the job with Cascading Style Sheets (CSS). But a few basics must be covered first. That's this chapter's job. In this chapter, we'll move swiftly through the rudiments of CSS grammar, cover a few not-so-basic ideas, and end by describing a CSS design method that is different from the one used by most designers and taught in most books. Even if you're familiar with CSS, you might want to stick around.

CSS Overview

The W3C rather crisply defines CSS as "a simple mechanism for adding style (for example, fonts, colors, spacing) to web documents" (www.w3.org/Style/css/). A few details omitted from that summary are worth noting:

- CSS is a standard layout language for the web—one that controls colors, typography, and the size and placement of elements and images.

- Although precise and powerful, CSS is easy to author by hand, as this chapter will show.

- CSS is bandwidth friendly: a single CSS file can control the appearance of an entire site, comprising thousands of pages and hundreds of megabytes.

- CSS has long been intended by its creators (W3C) to replace HTML table-based layouts, frames, and other presentational hacks, but as we'll see in the next chapter, it can also be highly effective in hybrid, transitional layouts.

- Pure CSS layout, combined with structural XHTML, can help designers separate presentation from structure, making sites more accessible and easier to maintain, as described in the next section, "CSS Benefits."

CSS Benefits

A Russian proverb states, "Repetition is the mother of learning." So forgive us if we wax a tad repetitive in reminding you that CSS, like other web standards, was not created for abstract purposes and was not intended for some distant future. Used well, right now, CSS provides practical benefits including (but not limited to) these:

- Conserves user bandwidth, speeding page load times, especially over dial-up.

- Reduces owner server and bandwidth overhead, thus saving money. (See the section "Outdated Markup: The Cost to Site Owners" in Chapter 1, "99.9% of Websites Are Obsolete.")

- Reduces design and development time. Producing the site shown in Chapters 8 and 10 took only a couple of hours, and part of that time we were working on Chapters 8 and 10, not the site. (These savings pertain only to time spent on development, of course: Creating content and artwork still takes as long as it takes.)

- Reduces updating and maintenance time:
  - Content folks no longer need to worry about complex tables, font tags, and other old-school layout components that can break when text is updated. Because there are no (or few) such elements, there is little or nothing to break.
  - Designers, developers, and agencies no longer need to worry about clients breaking the site.
  - Global changes can be accomplished in minutes. Text too dark? Tweak a rule or two in the CSS file and the entire site instantly reflects the change.
- Increases interoperability by adhering to W3C recommendations (web standards).
- Increases accessibility by removing some, many, or all presentational elements from markup.

CSS by the Book(s)

The *CSS Pocket Reference* (Eric Meyer: O'Reilly & Associates, Inc., 2001), as its name suggests, fits in your pocket or purse. But don't let the small size fool you. It is the clearest and most complete guide we know to the ins and outs of CSS1.

If you enjoy following along with design examples, you'll also benefit from *Eric Meyer on CSS* (Eric Meyer: New Riders, 2002), a remarkable hands-on book filled with design projects like the one discussed in Chapters 8 and 10.

Considered one of the world's leading CSS experts, Eric Meyer is a standards evangelist for Netscape Communications, the co-founder of the CSS-Discuss mailing list, and (to our infinite pleasure) one of this book's technical editors. We strongly recommend both of Eric Meyer's books. One demystifies the grammar of CSS; the other shows how to use it creatively.

Anatomy of Styles

In this section, we'll introduce you to the thighs, wings, and drumsticks of CSS. Well, anyway, we'll introduce you to the thighs and drumsticks. This book is not a full-blown CSS reference manual. A CSS reference manual could exceed the length of this book, although our favorite CSS reference is small enough to fit in your pocket—see the previous sidebar, "CSS by the Book(s)." On the other hand, how many full-blown CSS reference manuals use the word "thighs" three times in one paragraph? You're right, none of them do. Your money was well spent on this book.

Our anatomy of styles begins next. We'll learn still more about CSS by applying it in Chapter 10, and we'll keep talking (and learning) about CSS as the rest of this book unfolds.

Selectors, Declarations, Properties, and Values

A style sheet consists of one or more rules that control how selected elements should be displayed. A CSS rule consists of two parts: a *selector* and a *declaration*:

```
p      { color: red; }
```

In the preceding rule, p is the selector, whereas { color: red; }, contained within curly braces, is the declaration.

Declarations, in turn, also consist of two parts: a *property* and a *value*. In the earlier declaration, color is the property, red the value.

Choices and Options

Instead of the English word red, we might have written the hexadecimal (web color) value of #ff0000:

```
p      { color: #ff0000; }
```

We might save a few bytes by using CSS shorthand that means exactly the same thing:

```
p      { color: #f00; }
```

We could also have used RGB in either of two ways:

```
p       { color: rgb(255,0,0); }
p       { color: rgb(100%,0%,0%); }
```

Zero Is Optional, Except When It's Not

Notice that when you're using RGB percentages, the percent sign appears even when the value is zero. This is untrue in other CSS situations. For instance, when specifying a size of 0 pixels, the 0 need not be followed by px.

Many of us consider it bad form to write 0px or 0in or 0pt or 0cm. Zero is zero. Who cares what the unit of measurement is when its value is zero? But when specifying RGB percentages, the value of zero requires a percentage sign. Don't ask us; we just work here. Like the rule forbidding underscores in class and id names (see Chapter 7, "Tighter, Firmer Pages Guaranteed: Structure and Meta-Structure in Strict and Hybrid Markup"), the insistence on the percentage sign in RGB is a fact of CSS life, whose rationale, if any, has long been lost to the hoary mists of history.

We didn't mean to start our anatomy of styles by complaining about inconsistencies and exceptions, but we've fallen and we can't get up, so you'll have to bear with us as we continue to use color to explore the rudiments of CSS.

Multiple Declarations

It is bad form to specify a color without also specifying a background color, and vice-versa:

```
p       { color: #f00; background: white; }
```

A value of transparent can be used to avoid having one rule's background paint over another's:

```
p       { color: #f00; background: transparent; }
```

Notice that a rule can consist of more than one declaration and that semicolons are used to separate one declaration from the next.

Danger, Will Robinson! Transparent Backgrounds and Netscape 4

Warning: Netscape 4.x will in many cases interpret transparent as black. If you use background: inherit; instead, the color comes out chimp vomit green. This is because Netscape 4 takes unrecognized strings of characters and forces them through its hex parser even when they are clearly not valid hexadecimal values. (IE/Windows might have done the same thing prior to its 4.0 days, but don't quote us on that.)

The point is this: Because the default background color value is transparent whether you say so or not, if Netscape 4 users figure prominently in your audience, you might want to avoid declaring background color altogether. The W3C's CSS validation service will issue a warning if you do this, but a validation warning might be preferable to a hideously disfigured website. Again, this is only worth thinking about if you support a high percentage of Netscape 4.x users.

Semicolon Health

Here we go again with the inconsistencies and exceptions. The last rule in any declaration need not end in a semicolon, and some designers leave out the final semicolon in a series of declarations. (That's because, as in the English language, the semicolon functions as a separator, not a terminator.)

But most experienced CSS authors add the semicolon to the end of every declaration anyway. They do this partly for consistency's sake, but mainly to avoid headaches when adding and subtracting declarations to and from existing rules. *If every property/value pair ends in a semicolon, you don't have to worry when you move declarations from one place to another.*

Whitespace and Case Insensitivity

Most style sheets naturally contain more than one rule, and most rules contain more than one declaration. Multiple declarations are easier to keep track of and style sheets are easier to edit when we use whitespace:

```
body  {
    color: #000;
    background: #fff;
    margin: 0;
```

```
        padding: 0;
        font-family: Georgia, Palatino, serif;
    }

p   {
font-size: small;
    }
```

Whitespace, or its absence, has no effect on the way CSS displays in browsers; and unlike XHTML, CSS is not case-sensitive. Naturally, there is an exception: class and id names are case-sensitive when they're associated with an HTML document. myText and mytext are not matches in such a situation. CSS itself is case-insensitive, but the document language might not be. See http://devedge.netscape.com/viewsource/2001/css-class-id/ for details.

Alternative and Generic Values

A web designer might specify fonts for an entire site as follows:

```
body   {
        font-family: "Lucida Grande", Verdana, Lucida, Arial,
        Helvetica, sans-serif;
    }
```

Notice that multiname fonts ("Lucida Grande") must be enclosed within straight ASCII quotation marks, and that the comma follows rather than precedes the closing quotation mark, to the annoyance of literate American designers accustomed to placing the comma inside the quotation marks.

Fonts are used in the order listed. If the user's computer contains the font Lucida Grande, text will be displayed in that face. If not, Verdana will be used. If Verdana is missing, Lucida will be used. And so on. Why these fonts in this order?

Using Order to Accommodate Multiple Platforms

Order matters. Lucida Grande is found in Mac OS X. Verdana is found in all modern Windows systems, in Mac OS X, and in older Mac operating systems. If Verdana had been listed first, OS X Macs would display Verdana instead of Lucida Grande.

With the first two fonts—Lucida Grande and Verdana—the designer has met the needs of nearly all users (Windows and Macintosh users). Lucida follows for

UNIX folks, and then Arial for users of old Windows systems. Helvetica will be used in old UNIX systems. If none of the listed fonts is available, the generic sans-serif assures that whatever sans-serif font is available will be pressed into service. In the unlikely event that the user's computer contains no sans-serif fonts, the browser's default font will be used instead.

Not a Perfect Science

No one pretends that Lucida, Verdana, Arial, and Helvetica are equivalent in their beauty, elegance, x-height, or fitness for screen service (or even that all pressings of Helvetica are equally good). Our goal is not to create identical visual experiences for all users; platform, browser, monitor size, monitor resolution, monitor quality, gamma, and OS anti-aliasing settings make that quite impossible. We simply try to ensure that all visitors have the best experience their conditions permit, and that those experiences are fairly similar from one user to the next.

Grouped Selectors

When several elements share stylistic properties, you can apply one declaration to multiple selectors by ganging them together in a comma-delimited list:

```
p, td, ul, ol, ul, li, dl, dt, dd    {
     font-size: small;
   }
```

This ability comes in handy when you're coping with old browsers that don't understand CSS inheritance.

Inheritance and Its Discontents

According to CSS, properties inherit from parent to child elements. But it doesn't always happen that way. Consider the following rule:

```
body   {
      font-family: Verdana, sans-serif;
   }
```

Having come this far in Chapter 9, you know as well as we do what this rule says. The site's body element will use Verdana if that font is found on the visitor's system; otherwise, it will use a generic sans-serif font.

All Its Children

Per CSS inheritance, what's true for the highest-level element (in this case, the body element) is true for its children (such as p, td, ul, ol, ul, li, dl, dt, and dd). Without the addition of even one more rule, all body's children should display in Verdana or a generic sans-serif, as should their children and their children's children. And that's exactly what happens in most modern browsers.

But it doesn't happen in user agents created during the bloodiest years of the browser wars, when standards support was no manufacturer's priority. For instance, it doesn't happen in Netscape 4, which ignores inheritance and also ignores rules applied to the body element. (IE/Windows right up through IE6 has a related problem in which font styles are ignored in tables.) What's a mother to do?

"Be Kind to Netscape 4"

Fortunately, you can work around that old browser's failure to understand inheritance by using what we call the "Be Kind to Netscape 4" principle of redundancy:

```
body   {
    font-family: Verdana, sans-serif;
    }
p, td, ul, ol, li, dl, dt, dd     {
    font-family: Verdana, sans-serif;
    }
```

4.0 browsers might not understand inheritance, but they do understand grouped selectors. And a good Verdana will be had by all. Does this duplication of effort (the creation of a redundant rule) waste a bit of user bandwidth? Why, yes it does. But you might want to do it anyway.

By the way, Netscape 4 is not the only old browser that completely bungles inheritance. It's just the only one still used by a loyal minority.

Is Inheritance a Curse?

What if you don't want Verdana, sans-serif to inherit to every child element? What if, for instance, you want your paragraphs to display in Times? No problem. Create a more specific rule for p (highlighted in bold in the following code), and it will override the parental rule:

```
body   {
    font-family: Verdana, sans-serif;
    }
td, ul, ol, ul, li, dl, dt, dd   {
    font-family: Verdana, sans-serif;
    }
p   {
    font-family: Times, "Times New Roman", serif;
    }
```

And a good Times will be had by… Okay, we won't do that.

Contextual (Descendant) Selectors

You can avoid classitis and keep your markup neat and clean by making the style of an element dependent upon the context in which it appears. Selectors that apply rules in this way are called *contextual selectors* in CSS1 because they rely on context to apply a rule or refrain from doing so. CSS2 calls them *descendant selectors*, but their effect is the same no matter what you call them.

To italicize text that's marked <strong> and prevent it from displaying in boldface when it occurs within a list item, you would type:

```
li strong   {
    font-style: italic;
    font-weight: normal;
    }
```

What does a rule like that do?

```
<p><strong>I am bold and not italic because I do not appear in
a list item. The rule has no affect on me.</strong></p>
<ol>
<li><strong>I am italic and of Roman (normal) weight because I
occur within a list item.</strong></li>
<li>I am ordinary text in this list.</li>
</ol>
```

Or consider the following CSS:

```
strong      {
    color: red;
    }
```

```
h2     {
       color: red;
       }
h2 strong     {
       color: blue;
       }
```

and its effect on markup:

```
<p>The strongly emphasized word in this paragraph is
<strong>red</strong>.</p>
<h2>This subhead is also red.</h2>
<h2>The strongly emphasized word in this subhead is
<strong>blue</strong>.</h2>
```

You probably won't use contextual (a.k.a. descendant) selectors to slim down and italicize normally boldface text in lists. You *might* use these selectors to create sophisticated design enhancements, such as adding a background image to an ordinary XHTML element, along with sufficient whitespace (padding) to prevent the text from overlapping the image. But more likely, you would create those kinds of effects with contextual id or class selectors.

id Selectors and Contextual *id* Selectors

In modern layouts, id selectors are often used in contextual selectors:

```
#sidebar p     {
       font-style: italic;
       text-align: right;
       margin-top: 0.5em;
       }
```

The preceding style will be applied only to paragraphs that occur in an element whose id is sidebar. That element will mostly likely be a div, or a table cell, although it could also be a table or some other block-level element. It could even be an inline element, such as <em></em> or <span></span>, although such usages would be as bizarre as a rat in spats, not to mention invalid—you can't nest a <p> inside a <span>. Regardless of which element is used, it must be the only element on that page to use an id of sidebar. Flip back to Chapter 7 if you've forgotten why.

One Selector, Multiple Uses

Even though the element labeled `sidebar` will appear only once per page in the markup, the `id` selector can be used as a contextual/descendant selector as many times as needed:

```
#sidebar p    {
     font-style:  italic;
     text-align:  right;
     margin-top:  0.5em;
     }
#sidebar h2   {
     font-size:  1em;
     font-weight:  normal;
     font-style:  italic;
     margin:  0;
     line-height:  1.5;
     text-align:  right;
     }
```

Here, p elements in `sidebar` get a special treatment distinct from all other p elements on the page, and h2 elements in `sidebar` get a different, special treatment distinct from all other h2 elements on the page.

The Selector Stands Alone

The `id` selector need not be used contextually. It can stand on its own:

```
#sidebar    {
     border:  1px dotted #000;
     padding:  10px;
     }
```

According to this rule, the page element whose `id` is `sidebar` will have a dotted black (#000) border that's one pixel thick, with padding (inner whitespace) of 10 pixels all the way around.

Class Selectors

Discrimination on the basis of class is a terrible thing in life but a fine thing in style sheets. In CSS, class selectors are indicated by a dot:

```
.fancy    {
     color:  #f60;
     background:  #666;
     }
```

Any element of class `fancy` will sport orange (#f60) text on a gray (#666) background. Thus, both `<h1 class="fancy">Boy Howdy!</h1>` and `<p class="fancy">Yee haw!</p>` will share this striking color scheme.

Like `id`, classes can also be used as contextual selectors:

```
.fancy td    {
    color: #f60;
    background: #666;
  }
```

In the preceding example, table cells within some larger element whose class name is `fancy` will have orange text with a gray background. (The larger element whose name is `fancy` might be a table row or a `div`.)

Elements can also be selected based on their classes:

```
td.fancy     {
    color: #f60;
    background: #666;
  }
```

In the preceding example, table cells of class `fancy` will be orange with a gray background.

```
<td class="fancy">
```

You can assign the class of `fancy` to only one table cell or to as many as you want. Those so labeled will be orange with a gray background. Table cells that are not assigned a class of `fancy` will not be influenced by this rule. Just as significantly, a paragraph of class `fancy` will not be orange with a gray background, nor will any other element of class `fancy` be orange with a gray background. The effect is limited to table cells labeled `fancy` because of the way we wrote the rule (using the `td` element to select the `fancy` class).

Combining Selectors to Create Sophisticated Design Effects

Class, `id`, and contextual selectors can be combined to create subtle or striking visual effects. In The Marine Center site designed by Happy Cog, the brand-appropriate image of a fish (lister2.gif) replaces the boring black dot found in ordinary unordered lists [9.1].

9.1

Contextual, class, and id selectors can be combined to create visual effects. On The Marine Center site (http:// marine.happycog.com/) the boring black dot found in most unordered lists is replaced by the more brand-appropriate image of a fish.

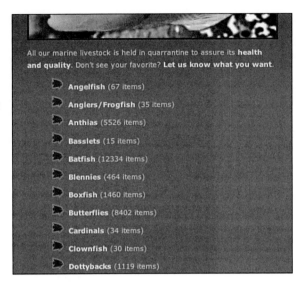

Following is the CSS rule that tells unordered lists of class inventory to display an image instead of a boring old dot (and to show a disc in old browsers that aren't capable of displaying the image):

```
ul.inventory {
    list-style: disc url(/images/common/lister2.gif) inside;
}
```

And here, abbreviated to fit on this page, is the markup it rides in on:

```
<ul class="inventory">
<li><a href="/angelfish">Angelfish</a> (67 items)</li>
<li><a href="/anglers">Anglers/Frogfish</a> (35 items)</li>
<li><a href="/anthias">Anthias</a> (5526 items)</li>
<li><a href="/basslets">Basslets</a> (15 items)</li>
</ul>
```

IE/Windows and Opera/Windows users get an extra (unintended) treat: The site displays ordinary dots first and then fills in the fish images. The effect is of Flash or JavaScript-like animation, but it is purely accidental and simply a result of the order in which IE and Opera for Windows load and display web page components. In other browsers, users simply see the fish.

If you've been following along, you'll understand that an unordered list of a different class will not show the fish image, nor will the fish image appear if the class is applied to anything other than an unordered list.

Branded fish images also appear in the site's "impulse buy" column [9.2], thanks to an inline element (span) of class cartier:

```
.cartier    {
    padding-left: 5px;
    background: transparent url(/images/common/cartfish.gif)
no-repeat top left;
    }
```

9.2
Branded fish also appear in the site's "buy now" elements. No `<img>` tags were harmed (or used) in the creation of these effects. See the text for an explanation of how it was done.

You can study additional techniques by viewing source on the staging server at http://marine.happycog.com/, where the site's original templates are stored [9.3].

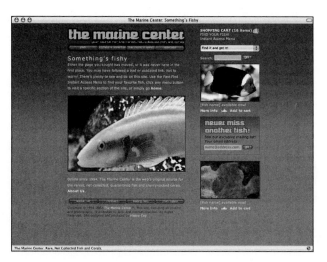

9.3
Between the fish photos and the CSS-generated fish images, no one could miss what this site is about. Even the "404 not found" error page keeps the visitor in a fishy frame of mind.

Moving Ahead

We will learn more about CSS grammar in the next chapter, but at this point, we must pause to consider a query: Where do we stick our CSS? Does it get tucked into the XHTML somewhere? Is it a separate file, or what? (Hint: Keep reading.)

External, Embedded, and Inline Styles

Style sheets can be applied to a web page in any of three ways: external, embedded, or inline. We'll start with the best first.

External Style Sheets

An *external style sheet* (CSS file) is a text document that lives separately from the XHTML pages it controls. An XHTML page uses that CSS file by referring to it via a link in the head of the document or by importing it into the style element (also in the head of the document). A style sheet link looks like this:

```
<link rel="StyleSheet" href="/styles/mystylesheet.css"
type="text/css" media="all" />
```

The @import directive, used to import a style sheet, looks like this:

```
<style type="text/css" media="all">
@import "/styles/mystylesheet.css";
</style>
```

or this:

```
<style type="text/css" media="all">
@import url("/styles/mystylesheet.css");
</style>
```

Greatest Power, Lowest Cost

Whether linked or imported, external style sheets provide the greatest power at the lowest cost. After an external style sheet has been downloaded to the user's cache, it remains active and can control the design of one, dozens, hundreds, or even hundreds of thousands of pages on the site without requiring an additional download. That's mighty handy.

Linking and Importing as Browser Selectors

Virtually all CSS-capable browsers support the link method, including old browsers whose CSS support is less than stellar. By contrast, the @import method works only in 5.0 and later browsers. Thus, designers can use @import to hide style sheets from 4.0 browsers.

This does not necessarily mean hiding all CSS from old browsers, as was discussed in Chapters 2, "Designing and Building with Standards," and 4, "XML Conquers the World (And Other Web Standards Success Stories)." Indeed, just the opposite is true: The fact that some browsers "get" @import and others don't enables us to serve them all. How does that work?

Because more than one style sheet can be used on a site, designers can place basic styles in a linked style sheet and sophisticated styles in an imported sheet. The linked, basic style sheet, visible to all browsers that even pretend to understand CSS, provides basic design elements such as fonts used, and text, background, and link colors. The imported sheet, whose styles are visible only to more compliant browsers, contains additional CSS rules that new browsers understand and old browsers would bungle.

Your XHTML might look something like this:

```
<!DOCTYPE html PUBLIC "-//W3C//DTD XHTML 1.0 Transitional//EN"
    "http://www.w3.org/TR/xhtml1/DTD/xhtml1-transitional.dtd">
<html xmlns="http://www.w3.org/1999/xhtml">
  <head>
<title>Your Title Here</title>
<link rel="StyleSheet" href="/css/basic.css" type=
"text/css" media="all" />
<style type="text/css" media="all">
@import "/css/sophisto.css";
</style>
<meta http-equiv="Content-Type" content=
"text/html; charset=ISO-8859-1" />
</head>
```

By taking this layered approach, you can support all users without blocking your content from anyone—and without the agony of browser detection. (The technique will be discussed in greater detail in the later section, "From Embedded to External Styles: The Two-Sheet Method.")

These benefits of greatly lowered user and server bandwidth, plus the ability to support variously capable browsers, are available only when you use external style sheets. When we finish designing the i3Forum site in Chapter 10, we will use external style sheets to reap these benefits. We're no dummies. (They have their own book series, anyway.)

Embedded Style Sheets

Instead of linking to or importing one or more separate style sheet files, a designer can embed the style sheet rules in the head of an XHTML 1 page, using the style element as shown (and highlighted in bold) next:

```
<!DOCTYPE html PUBLIC "-//W3C//DTD XHTML 1.0 Transitional//EN"
    "http://www.w3.org/TR/xhtml1/DTD/xhtml1-transitional.dtd">
<html xmlns="http://www.w3.org/1999/xhtml">
  <head>
<title>i3forum</title>
<style type="text/css">
<!--
body    {
    background: white;
    color: black;
    }
-->
</style>
<meta http-equiv="Content-type" content="text/html; charset=
iso-8859-1" />
</head>
```

Unlike linked or imported styles, embedded styles offer no bandwidth benefit because the user must load a new embedded style sheet each time she opens a new page. Even if the embedded style sheet is the same on every page, the user still has to download it. You might wonder, then, why a designer would ever use an embedded style sheet. Here are a few reasons:

- The site consists of only one page. We didn't say it was likely—we just said it was possible.

- The designer's audience lives in a time warp and is using IE3 to visit the site. IE3 was the first browser to begin supporting bits and pieces of CSS. It did not support external style sheets. Okay, come to think of it, that's not a very likely reason either.

- The designer has used external style sheets to control the entire site, but he needs to create additional rules for just one page. That is an excellent reason to create an embedded style sheet. In fact, it is the only way to achieve certain visual effects. When we design the i3Forum style sheet in the next chapter (trust us, we're nearly there), we will add an embedded style to each page of the site to control the "you are there" highlighting of menu items as the visitor clicks from page to page.

- The designer is still creating the style sheet and needs to immediately see the effect of changes made to it. This is the other excellent reason to create an embedded style sheet.

When you're designing a site (be it hybrid or pure CSS), it makes perfect sense to embed the style sheet in the `<head>` of the page you're working on. Then, when your design is just the way you like it, you can copy the styles to an external CSS file and delete the embedded style from your markup.

During the process outlined in the next chapter, we used an embedded style sheet because it offered the quickest and easiest means of doing our work. (Change a rule, reload the page in a browser, and see if you get what you expected.) When our CSS worked as we wanted it to, we removed it from the `<head>`, saved it as an external CSS file within a /css/ subdirectory on the server, and linked to it to save oodles of user bandwidth on the finished site.

Inline Styles

CSS can be applied to an individual element by using the style attribute to that element, as in the examples that follow:

```
<h1 style="font-family: verdana, arial, sans-serif; ">
Headline</h1>
<img style="margin-top: 25px;">
```

As you might expect, inline styles save no bandwidth—indeed, they add bandwidth to every page that uses them and are generally as wasteful as `<font>` tags in that regard. They are most often used for scummy skullduggery or clueless, helpless, mindless, paddle-armed animal fumbling of the sort shown in the section "Party Like It's 1997" in Chapter 7.

Web pages should never be styled primarily with inline CSS. It's as absurd as painting your house with a tube of White-Out. But used with respect and discretion, inline CSS can be a helpful tool. Inline styles are the touch-up paint of CSS, and they have saved many a dented digital fender.

The "Best-Case Scenario" Design Method

In the old days, when we created layouts almost entirely with presentational markup, we would test our work in the oldest, crummiest browser on our hard drive. To make it look right in that old browser, we'd build deeply nested tables; use nonstructural divs in place of structural elements like h1, h2, li, and p; and do all the other things we don't want to do any more. When the site looked right in the bad old browser, we would test it in a new browser, where it also quite likely looked good—but at a terrible cost to bandwidth and semantics. Many web designers still follow this practice of designing for the worst browser they can get their hands on. But the cost is too high; the method is no longer productive.

Instead, write your CSS in an embedded style sheet and preview your work in a browser you trust, such as Mozilla, Chimera, Netscape 7, IE6/Windows, IE5/Mac, or Opera 7 (to name a few good ones). In this way, you'll create accessible, low-bandwidth, compliant pages that let markup be markup and that use CSS correctly.

When you're satisfied with what you've designed, test the page in other good, compliant browsers. It should look the same in all of them. If it doesn't, you have more work to do. One of your CSS rules might be incorrectly written, yet your favorite browser understood what you intended, as a friend sometimes understands you when you talk with your mouth full.

From Embedded to External Styles: The Two-Sheet Method

When your site looks and works right in all the compliant browsers at your disposal, it's still not time to open your worst old browser. Instead, copy your CSS rules to a new file called basic.css, upload the file to the /css/ directory on your server, delete the embedded style sheet from your page, and link to it from the head of your document:

```
<link rel="StyleSheet" href="/css/basic.css"
type="text/css" media="all" />
```

Empty your caches, quit and restart your browsers, and test again to make certain you haven't accidentally deleted rules when moving from embedded to external CSS.

Testing In and Supporting Noncompliant Browsers

If you're still happy, now is the time to open any noncompliant browsers you want to support. There's a slight chance the site might look okay in your worst browser. If it doesn't, create a new, empty document, call it sophisto.css, and begin transferring those CSS rules whose sophistication you suspect of tripping up the bad old browser. As you copy suspiciously sophisticated rules to sophisto.css, delete them from basic.css. (The names, of course, can be anything. We like basic and sophisto, but any clear names will do.)

Upload sophisto.css to your /css/ subdirectory and link to this second external style sheet by means of @import:

```
<style type="text/css"
media="all">@import "/css/sophisto.css";</style>
```

Empty your bad browser's cache, reload the page, and see if the display is now acceptable. It might be. If it's not, you need to move a few more rules from basic.css to sophisto.css. Eventually your site will look the way it should in compliant browsers and will still be reasonably attractive in the old, prestandards relics.

For example, The Fox Searchlight site (www.foxsearchlight.com), designed by Hillman Curtis in collaboration with Happy Cog, uses the Two-Sheet method to present most of the site's look and feel to all browsers, while hiding tricky styles from 4.0 browsers that can't handle them. In a 4.0 browser, the site is less tight, but it looks okay and is usable. As the Best-Case Scenario design method saved us from coding to the limitations of the least common denominator, so the Two-Sheet CSS method saves us from excluding the least common denominator. (Take a look at foxsearchlight.com and compare it in multiple browsers.)

Relative and Absolute File References

When creating the initial CSS, we use relative image file references because we're working on our desktop, not on a staging server. The final style sheet we create in Chapter 10 will use absolute (not relative) file references to avoid bugs in old browsers that misunderstand relative links in CSS.

The fact that old browsers bungle relative links in CSS files is another good reason to turn the accepted wisdom on its head and preview your work in good, rather than bad, browsers. Using the old method ("test in your worst browser first"), if you designed your pages offline and consequently used relative file references, the browser would botch those references, images would fail to appear, and you might spend hours trying to figure out what was "wrong" with your style sheet, when in fact nothing was wrong with it.

Benefits of the Best-Case Scenario and Two-Sheet Methods

Using the Best-Case Scenario design method saves us from coding to the limitations of the least common denominator. We can create a commercial, well-branded, hybrid layout without writing reams of garbage markup.

Using the Two-Sheet CSS method saves us from excluding the least common denominator, or sticking users of least common denominator browsers with nothing to look at. We give these users the best visual experience we can under their limited circumstances, we don't lecture them about the crappiness of their browser, and we don't hate them for forcing us to deform our CSS and XHTML (because we haven't done anything of the kind).

This is not semantic markup, it's not pure CSS layout, it's not the vanguard of web standards, and it's far from the only way to design a modern site. But it is a good way to bring the benefits of standards to a market in transition. As Klaatu said to the people of the earth, "It may not be perfect, but it's a system, and it works."

The Two-Sheet method is not limited to hybrid design. It can be just as effective at delivering pure CSS layouts to variously capable generations of browsers. In either case, the goal is the same: to create an enjoyable and well-branded experience for each visitor, to the greatest extent that her browser or device permits.

We are now ready to use the CSS we've learned (and more CSS) to complete the layout for the site we began in Chapter 8. In Chapter 10, we'll do exactly that. Please join us.

chapter ten

CSS in Action: A Hybrid Layout (Part II)

In Chapter 8, "XHTML by Example: A Hybrid Layout (Part I)," we created hybrid markup for the i3Forum site, combining structural elements like <h1>, <h2>, and <p> with nonstructural components (XHTML tables used to lay out the basic grid), and we used table summaries, accesskey, and Skip Navigation to make the site more accessible in nontraditional browsing environments.

In this chapter, we'll complete our production task by using CSS to achieve design effects that support the brand and make the site more attractive without relying on GIF text, JavaScript rollovers, spacer pixel GIF images, deeply nested table cell constructions, or other staples of old-school web design.

Figure 10.1 shows the home page template as it appears after our first pass at writing a style sheet. As with all design, using CSS is an iterative process. In this chapter, we'll complete our CSS in two passes. The first pass handles 90% of what's needed; the second fixes errors and adds finishing touches.

10.1

The template as it appears after our first pass at CSS. Elements, sizes, fonts, and colors are in place, but backgrounds don't quite fill the right-side menu "buttons." A bit more work is needed.

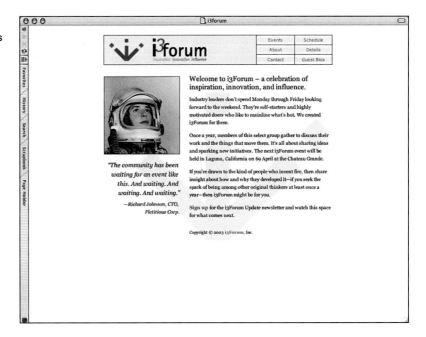

Preparing Images

Although the site was designed in Photoshop, it's not your typical slice-and-dice job. Figure **10.2** shows the six images used to create the entire site. Three are for foreground use: the astronaut photo, the "best of breed" dog photo, and the transparent logo GIF used at the top-left corner of the menu bar.

The remaining three images are backgrounds. Arrow.gif is a screened image derived from the logo that will be placed in the background as a watermark. Bgpat.gif [**10.3**], consisting of single-colored pixels alternating with single transparent pixels, will be used to create background color effects in the menu bar. Nopat.gif, a plain-white background, will replace bgpat.gif in CSS rollover effects and might also be used to indicate the visitor's position within the site's hierarchy via an embedded style added to each page at the end of the project (see the following sidebar, "The Needless Image").

The Needless Image

Strictly speaking, one of our six images is not needed in this execution. Nopat.gif, the plain-white background image [10.2], is superfluous. A CSS rule specifying background: white would have the same effect (and later in this chapter we'll use a rule like that instead of nopat.gif).

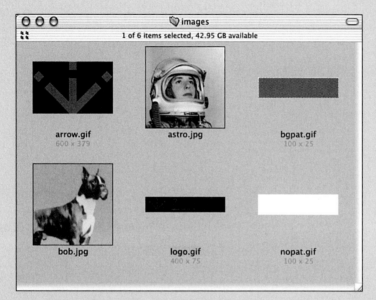

10.2
Just six images were used in this site, three of them as backgrounds. Photoshop's/ImageReady's "slice-and-dice" features are not needed.

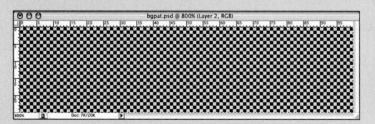

10.3
The alternating pixel background GIF image enlarged 800% and with a black background, inserted for this book's purposes, standing in for the transparent pixels.

For our nav bar, however, we've gone ahead and used this background anyway, so you can see how a CSS background image swap is achieved. In an execution involving swapped watermarked or textured backgrounds, you need two images; therefore, you would need to write the kind of CSS rules shown in this part of the chapter.

Establishing Basic Parameters

Our images are in place, and with our original comp to guide us, we can begin using CSS to establish basic design parameters. We know that the site's background will be white, that its text will be set in several sizes of Georgia (or an alternative serif), that a screened watermark based on the logo will hug the bottom of the content area, and that certain whitespace values must be enforced without using spacer GIF images or additional table junk. Let's make it happen.

Overall Styles, More About Shorthand and Margins

In our first rule, we establish basic page colors and upper and lower margins:

```
body   {
        color: #000;
        background: #fff;
        margin: 25px 0;
        padding: 0;
        }
```

Per this rule, all text will be black (#000) on a white (#fff) background. The colors are described in CSS shorthand, as explained in Chapter 9, "CSS Basics." (#000 is shorthand for #000000; #fff is the same as #ffffff.) Shorthand can only be used to replace paired characters; #fc0 is the same as #ffcc00. Shorthand cannot be used in the absence of paired characters. There is no shorthand for a nonwebsafe color like #f93C7a, for example.

Shorthand and Clock Faces

The first rule also establishes a top and bottom margin of 25px and left and right margins of 0. It is a shorthand version of this:

```
    margin: 25px 0 25px 0;
```

The preceding, in turn, is a shorthand version of this:

```
    margin-top: 25px;
    margin-right: 0;
    margin-bottom: 25px;
    margin-left: 0;
```

In CSS, values are assigned in the order of the main numbers on a clock: 12 o'clock (the top margin), 3 o'clock (the right margin), 6 o'clock (the bottom margin), and 9 o'clock (the left margin). If we wanted our page to have a top margin of 25px, a right margin of 5px, a bottom margin of 10px, and a left margin of 30% of the entire width, our rule would read like this:

```
margin: 25px 5px 10px 30%;
```

When the vertical margins are the same at the top and bottom (as they are in this site—namely, 25px) and when the horizontal margins are the same at left and right (as they are in this site—namely 0), we can save a few bytes of user bandwidth by typing this:

```
margin: 25px 0;
```

As mentioned in Chapter 9, the 0 value does not require a unit of measurement. 0px is the same as 0cm, 0in, or 0bazillionmiles. (There is no "bazillion miles" unit of measurement in CSS, but if there were, we wouldn't need to use it when the value is zero.)

Finally, our rule sets padding to 0 to accommodate Opera, which uses padding rather than margins to enforce page gutters.

Hide and Block

In our next step, with two simple rules, we accomplish several useful things:

```
.hide   {
        display: none;
        }

img {
        display: block;
        border: 0;
        }
```

The first rule creates a class called hide that can be used to make elements or objects invisible in CSS-capable browsers. As explained in Chapter 8, we're using this CSS feature to hide our Skip Navigation link in modern browsers while making it readily available to users of text browsers, screen readers, and PDA- and phone-based browsers that do not support CSS. (As of this writing, some PDA-based browsers partially support CSS, but they do about as poor a job as 3.0 and 4.0 desktop browsers did. Hopefully, many of these implementations will have improved by the time you read this book.)

The Image Rule

The second rule is more useful and less problematic. First, `display: block;` states that every image on the page will be rendered as a block-level element instead of inline. If you're unfamiliar with these terms, here are two easy examples. Paragraphs are block-level elements; the deprecated `<i>` (italic) tag is an inline element. Block-level elements exist in their own "box" and are followed by an implied carriage return. Inline elements are part of the flow, with no carriage return and no clear-cut "box."

By telling the browser to treat images as block-level elements, we avoid having to write `<br>` or `<br clear="all">` or similar junk before and after our images, and we also avoid having to stick those images in their own table cells to preserve our layout's spacing requirements. (You'll learn more about that in Chapter 11, "Working with Browsers Part I: DOCTYPE Switching and Standards Mode." If you can't wait, you might also read "Images, Tables, and Mysterious Gaps" at `http://devedge.netscape.com/viewsource/2002/img-table/`.)

This seems so simple that many of you will skip over it without thinking about it, but explicitly assigning `block` or `inline` status to an element is an incredibly powerful tool. Ordinary links, by being made block-level elements via CSS, can turn into buttons, for example. In a later rule, using an additional selector, we will be able to add specific vertical whitespace to images that live in a particular part of the layout, thus achieving with a few lines of CSS what would otherwise require a markup mess of slicing, dicing, table cell nesting, and spacer GIF images.

Read it again. We're telling you how to achieve layouts that look like 50 table cells and a dozen sliced images but are just a few lines of markup and a few CSS rules. Okay. Point made.

Next, the `border: 0;` declaration turns off image borders, so we don't have to write `border="0"` in our markup. (If we care about the way the site looks in non-CSS browsers, we *will* have to write `border="0"` in our markup anyway. We did so, and explained why we did so, back in Chapter 8.)

Coloring the Links (Introducing Pseudo-Classes)

In presentational HTML, we controlled link colors via attributes to the `body` element such as `vlink="#CC3300"`. In modern web design, we can leave our `body` naked and unadorned and use CSS instead. To sweeten the deal, CSS adds a "hover" state to the familiar link, visited, and active states we learned to love in the 1990s. CSS also allows us to do more than merely change link colors.

CSS calls these anchor (link) states *pseudo-class selectors*. In the CSS way of thinking, a "real" class is one that you specify explicitly with a `class=` attribute. A pseudo-class is one that depends on user activity or browser state (`:hover`, `:visited`). There are also pseudo-elements (`:before` and `:after`). In any case, with the four rules that follow, we control link colors and more [**10.4, 10.5**].

```
a:link {
      font-weight : bold;
      text-decoration : none;
      color: #c30;
      background: transparent;
      }
a:visited {
      font-weight : bold;
      text-decoration : none;
      color: #c30;
      background: transparent;
      }
a:hover {
      font-weight : bold;
      text-decoration : underline;
      color: #f60;
      background: transparent;
      }
a:active {
      font-weight : bold;
      text-decoration : none;
      color: #f90;
      background: transparent;
      }
```

> Sign up for the i3Forum Update newsletter and watch this space for what comes next.

10.4
The link color is dark red, bold, and without an underline, per the CSS a:link rule.

> Sign up for the i3Forum Update newsletter and watch this space for what comes next.

10.5
When the visitor's mouse hovers over the link, its text color "lights up" in orange, and an underline appears, per the CSS a:hover rule.

More About Links and Pseudo-Class Selectors

In the previous four rules, the only thing that might be new to you is the text-decoration property. When its value is none, there is no underline. When its value is underline—you guessed it—the link is underlined, just like all links were back in the mid-1990s. When its value is overline, a line appears *over* the text instead of under it. You can combine overline and underline like so:

```
text-decoration: underline overline;
```

What would that look like? It would look like the linked text was in a box with a top and bottom but no sides. We know two web designers—one of them being us—who have used that effect at least once. Two additional points are worth noting before we leave the land of lovely links.

Use LVHA or Be SOL

Mark you this, oh brothers and sisters: Some browsers will ignore one or more anchor element pseudo-class rules unless they are listed in the order shown earlier, namely link, visited, hover, active (LVHA). Change that order at your peril. A popular mnemonic to remember the order is "LoVe—HA!" (There are some bitter people out there.) If you want to understand why the order matters, http://www.meyerweb.com/eric/css/link-specificity.html explains it in some detail.

Pseudo-Shenanigans in IE/Windows

Note that even in its latest, greatest incarnation (at least as of this writing) Internet Explorer for Windows has trouble with the hover and active pseudo-classes. Hover states tend to get stuck. Use your Back button in IE/Windows, and you will very likely find that the last link you moused over is still in its hover state. For that matter, you will very likely find that the link you clicked to move forward is still in its active state. You will probably not like this one bit.

Because the active color also gets stuck, if you apply background images to the a:active pseudo-class, IE/Windows will get them wrong. If your audience includes IE/Windows users (and whose audience does not?) you might decide to avoid a:active altogether. Or you might choose, as we have, not to do anything especially creative or challenging with it.

Whether this freezing of link states is a bug or a useful feature depends on whom you ask. Two hundred million IE/Windows users are probably accustomed to it by now, and many might believe the web is supposed to work this way.

Sketching in Other Common Elements

In the code block that follows, we see our good friend, the "Be Kind to Netscape 4" rule (Chapter 9) being used to tell the browser that the entire site should use Georgia or an alternative serif face [**10.6**].

```
p, td, li, ul, ol, h1, h2, h3, h4, h5, h6    {
            font-family: Georgia, "New Century Schoolbook",
Times, serif;
            }
```

> Welcome to i3Forum – a celebration of inspiration, innovation, and influence.
>
> Industry leaders don't spend Monday through Friday looking forward to the weekend. They're self-starters and highly motivated doers who like to mainline what's hot. We created i3Forum for them.
>
> Once a year, members of this select group gather to discuss their work and the things that move them. It's all about sharing ideas and sparking new initiatives. The next i3Forum event will be held in Laguna, California on 69 April at the Chateau Grande.
>
> If you're drawn to the kind of people who invent fire, then share insight about how and why they developed it—if you seek the spark of being among other original thinkers at least once a year—then i3Forum might be for you.
>
> Sign up for the i3Forum Update newsletter and watch this space for what comes next.

10.6

Fonts are specified by a single rule applied to multiple selectors (p, td, li, ul, ol, h1, h2, h3, h4, h5, h6). Sizes and white-space are controlled by means of additional rules and selectors.

Georgia, a Microsoft screen font designed by Type Directors Club (TDC) Medal winner Matthew Carter to be legible even at small sizes, is found on nearly all Windows and Macintosh systems. New Century Schoolbook is found on most UNIX systems; Times has been found on Paleolithic computing systems; and when all else fails, there's our other good friend, the generic serif.

In the following rule, we let the browser know that headlines should be slightly larger than the user's default font size. When no base font size has been specified, the browser will consider the user's default font size to be 1em. (It doesn't matter if the user's default font size is 12px or 48px. It's still 1em.) To make the headline a bit larger than the user's default, we'll set it at 1.15em. We'll also insist that the headline be of normal (not bold) weight:

```
h1    {
      font-size: 1.15em;
      font-weight: normal;
      }
```

There is no need to tell the browser that h1 should be set in Georgia. We did that in the previous rule.

Now we use the `html` selector to add more detail to our p style. All elements on the page except `html` itself are descendants of `html`. We could as easily have written p instead of `html` p, but we wanted you to feel your money was well spent on this book. Here is the rule, followed by explanations:

```
html p    {
          margin-top: 0;
          margin-bottom: 1em;
          text-align: left;
          font-size:  0.85em;
          line-height: 1.5;
          }
```

In the preceding rule, we establish that paragraphs have no whitespace at the top (thus enabling them to snugly hug the bottoms of headlines and subheads), 1em of whitespace at their bottoms (thus preventing them from bumping into each other), and are somewhat smaller (0.85em) than the user's default font size (using the same reasoning applied to the h1 earlier, but in the opposite direction).

More About Font Sizes

It is tricky to specify relative font sizes as we've done in the previous rule. Specifically, it is tricky to specify that fonts should be slightly smaller than the user's default because the user might have set a small default. If he *has* set a small default, your small text might be too small for his liking.

For example, if the user has specified 11px Verdana as his default font, your small text might be 9px or 10px tall—hardly a comfortable size for reading long passages of text. The user so afflicted can easily adjust the layout by using his browser's font size widget, but some users might find it annoying to do so, and a few might not know they can resize text.

In most systems as they come from the factory, default font sizes are as huge as the least attractive part of a horse, and a size like 0.85em should look darn good. If the user is visually impaired and has set her size much larger than the default, the font will still look good to her, and she will see that it is slightly smaller than normal. But if a Windows user chooses "small" as his default browsing size, or if a Mac user sets her browser to 12px/72ppi, our text might look too small, causing the user to weep piteously or (more likely) exit the site in frustration and haste.

Alternatively, we might have chosen a pixel value for our text size:

```
font-size: 13px;
```

We could have done this and created the leading as well using CSS shorthand:

```
font: 13px/1.5 Georgia,"New Century Schoolbook", Times, serif;
```

Unlike relative sizes based on em, pixel-based sizes are 99.9% dependable across all browsers and platforms. And if a pixel-based size is too small for a given user, he or she can adjust it via Text Zoom or Page Zoom in every modern browser on earth but one. Unfortunately that one browser is IE/Windows, currently the web's most used browser.

It's especially ironic because Text Zoom was invented in a Microsoft browser (IE5/Mac) in early 2000. But this incredibly useful feature *still* has not made its way to the Windows side.

This means that if you use pixels to safely control font sizes, you risk making your text inaccessible to visually impaired IE/Windows users. But if you try to avoid that problem by using ems, as we've done on the site we're building in this chapter, you will frustrate visitors who've shrunk their default font size preference to compensate for the fact that the factory-installed default is way too big for most humans.

In short, no matter what you do, you are going to frustrate somebody. We once designed a site setting no font sizes at all. We figured all users would finally be happy. Instead, that site provoked hundreds of angry letters complaining that the text was "too big." For more about the joys and sorrows of font size, see Chapter 13, "Working with Browsers Part III: Typography."

The Wonder of Line-Height

Look again at the line-height declaration in the rule currently being discussed:

```
line-height: 1.5;
```

Line-height is CSS-speak for leading. Line-height of 1.5 is the same as leading of 150%. The line-height could be marked 1.5em, but that is not necessary.

Before CSS, we could only simulate leading by making nonstructural use of the paragraph tag (see the discussion of Suck.com in Chapter 1, "99.9% of Websites Are Obsolete"); by using <pre>; or by sticking spacer pixel GIF images between every line of text, forcing that text into table cells of absolute widths, and praying that the invisible spacer pixel images downloaded seamlessly. If they didn't, the visitor would see broken GIF placeholder images instead of lovely leading.

But why even think about it? CSS solves this problem forever.

The Heartache of Left-Align

Finally, if you can find your way back to the previous rule, you might wonder why we've specified text-align: left. The answer is simple. If we don't do that, IE6/Windows might center the text due to a bug. IE5/Windows did not suffer from this defect, nor do any other browsers. The behavior appears to be random. Many elements not overtly left-aligned in CSS will correctly show up left-aligned anyway in IE6/Windows. But some won't. And you never know which ones will do what. Use left-align and you avoid this bug.

Setting Up the Footer

By now, you're hip to the CSS lingo and will be able to understand the little rule that follows…

```
#footer p    {
     font-size: 11px;
     margin-top: 25px;
     }
```

…without our having to tell you that it uses the unique id of footer as a selector and that any paragraph inside footer will be set in a font size of 11px and graced with 25px of whitespace at its top.

We also don't have to remind you that the browser knows which font to use because it was established by an earlier rule on the page.

Laying Out the Page Divisions

Our next set of rules establishes basic page divisions. We have put them close to each other in our CSS file to make editing and redesign easier, and we've preceded them with a comment to remind us—or to explain to a colleague who might subsequently have to modify our style sheet—what the set of rules is for. If you're familiar with commenting in HTML, it's the same deal here, but with a slightly different convention based on C programming.

Following the comment, we have a rule that establishes that the primary content area will have 25px of whitespace at its left and top [**10.7**], and another that places a nonrepeating graphic background image (arrow.gif) at the bottom and in the center of the table whose id is content [**10.8**].

10.7
Vertical spacing between the navigation area and body content and horizontal whitespace between the sidebar photo area and the body text are both handled by a single rule applied to the primary content selector. No spacer GIF images or table cell hacks are needed.

10.8
A screened-back arrow image derived from the logo anchors the content area and serves as its watermark thanks to a background declaration applied to the content selector. Because the selector encompasses the entire table, the arrow is able to span the two table cells (sidebar and primary content). Simple as the effect is, achieving it via old-school methods would be difficult if not impossible.

To achieve this effect by means of the deprecated background image attribute to the table cell tag would be difficult if not impossible. For one thing, the background image would have to span two table cells. Therefore, we would need to slice our background image in pieces, assign each piece to a different table cell, and hope all the pieces lined up.

Then, too, the deprecated background image tag in HTML tiles by default, and there is no way to prevent it from tiling. We would have to make two transparent images exactly as tall as the table cells that contain them and pray that the user would not resize the text, thus throwing the table cell heights out of alignment.

We would also have to insist that every page be the same height, which would limit how much text our client could add to or subtract from each page. Our client might not appreciate that.

With CSS, we never have to think about such stupid stuff again. The rules take far less time to read and understand than the paragraphs we just wrote to describe them:

```css
/* Basic page divisions */
#primarycontent    {
      padding-left: 25px;
      padding-top: 25px;
      }
#content {
      background: transparent url(images/arrow.gif)center
      ➥bottom no-repeat;
      }
```

Next, we establish rules for the sidebar:

```css
/* Sidebar display attributes */
#sidebar p    {
      font-style: italic;
      text-align: right;
      margin-top: 0.5em;
      }
#sidebar img    {
      margin: 30px 0 15px 0;
      }
#sidebar h2    {
      font-size: 1em;
      font-weight: normal;
      font-style: italic;
      margin: 0;
      line-height: 1.5;
      text-align: right;
      }
```

The first rule says that paragraphs within the element whose unique id is sidebar will be right-aligned and italic and have an upper margin (whitespace) of half their font size height (0.5em). If it looks familiar, it's because we snuck it into Chapter 9's discussion of `id` selectors in CSS.

The second rule says that images within the element whose unique `id` is `sidebar` will have an upper margin of 30px, a lower margin of 15px, and no extra whitespace at left or right [**10.9**]. We alluded to this rule earlier in the chapter in the section "The Image Rule." Now it has arrived.

10.9
Carefully chosen vertical whitespace values above and below the sidebar photograph are achieved by applying upper and lower margin values to #sidebar img. Images within the `div` labeled `sidebar` will obey these whitespace values; images elsewhere on the site will not.

It's rules like this that make life worth living because they free us from the necessity of using multiple empty table cells and spacer GIF images to create whitespace. (Can you imagine any other visual medium forcing designers to jump through their own eardrums simply to create whitespace? That's how the web was, but we don't have to build it that way any more.)

The third rule in this section makes h2 headlines look like magazine pull quotes (especially in smooth text environments like Windows Cleartype and Mac OS X Quartz) instead of HTML headlines [**10.10**]. It specifies that h2 text within `sidebar` will be of modest size (1em), normal weight, italic, and right-aligned, and that it will have the same line-height value (1.5) as other text on the page.

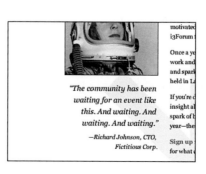

10.10
Sidebar pull quotes, marked up as second-level headlines (h2), nevertheless look like magazine pull quotes, not like HTML headlines.

Navigation Elements: First Pass

Up to now, we've been doing all right. Every rule we've written displays as
expected in the standards-friendly, best-case-scenario browser we use to test
our work. Getting the navigation bar just right will be trickier. In our first pass,
shown next, we nail certain desired features and just miss on others:

```
/* Navigation bar components */
table#nav    {
    border-bottom: 1px solid #000;
    border-left: 1px solid #000;
    }
```

This rule tells the table whose id is nav to create a 1px solid black border effect
at its bottom and left (but not at the top or right).

```
table#nav td    {
    font: 11px verdana, arial, sans-serif;
    text-align: center;
    vertical-align: middle;
    border-right: 1px solid #000;
    border-top: 1px solid #000;
    }
```

You don't need us to explain that this rule specifies 11px Verdana as the
preferred menu text font and fills out the border elements that the previous
rule neglected (namely, at the right and top). If we had told the table to create
a border effect around all four sides, then the table cells would have added an
extra pixel of border at the top and right, bringing shame to our family and
sadness to all viewers.

The preceding rule also tells text to be horizontally centered in each table cell
and vertically aligned in the middle of the table cell, much like the old-school
td valign="middle" presentational hack we all know and love. (This seemed
like the right thing to do, but in our second pass, we had to remove it.)

```
table#nav td a    {
    font-weight: normal;
    text-decoration: none;
    display: block;
    margin: 0;
    padding: 0;
    }
```

In the preceding rule, you recognize that we're telling links how to behave, and you also recognize that we're doing so with a sophisticated chain of contextual selectors. The multipart selector means "apply the following rule only to links within table cells, and only if they are found in the table whose unique identifier is nav."

As we hinted in the "The Image Rule" discussion, we're also using the CSS `display: block` declaration to turn the humble XHTML links into block-level elements that completely fill their table cells. (At least, we *hope* they will completely fill their table cells.)

```css
#nav td a:link, #nav td a:visited {
    background: transparent url(images/bgpat.gif)repeat;
    display: block;
    margin: 0;
    }
#nav td a:hover {
    color: #000;
    background: white url(images/nopat.gif)repeat;
    }
```

The final two rules use contextual and `id` selectors to control the link, visited, and hover pseudo-classes, filling the first two classes with our alternating-pixel background color image [refer to **10.3**] and using a plain-white background image for the hover/rollover state. (See the following sidebar, "Needless Images II: This Time It's Personal.")

Needless Images II: This Time It's Personal

Remember our earlier sidebar about "the needless image," where we said the plain-white background really isn't needed for this execution? Well, the plain-white background really isn't needed for this execution.

Instead of this…

```css
#nav td a:hover {
    color: #000;
    background: white url(images/nopat.gif)repeat;
    }
```

continues

continued

…we might have written the following rule:

```
#nav td a:hover {
     color: #000;
     background-image: none;
     }
```

Removing the image from hovered link states (`background-image: none;`) would create the same rollover effect of a plain-white background with one less image to worry about and a bit less bandwidth consumed. A bit later in this chapter, when we create the "you are here" effects for individual pages, we'll do so without relying on the plain-white background GIF.

Nevertheless, because swapped CSS background image swaps are cool and because you might want to harness their power on your own projects, we've used them to create our navigation bar rollover effects in this chapter.

A glance back at Figure **10.1** shows you everything we've gotten right and wrong in our first pass at styling the site. Everything we wanted to achieve we have, except for the navigation bar. The logo is okay; the background color is completely filled in [**10.11**], and on-hover rollover effects [**10.12**] work as expected.

10.11
CSS rollover effects in action, accomplished by means of link, visited, and hover pseudo-classes applied to table cells within the table whose id is nav. Here we see the default state of a menu graphic.

10.12
CSS rollover effects, part two: When the visitor's cursor hovers over a menu graphic, the background turns white. Look, Ma, no JavaScript! (Not that there's anything wrong with it.)

But the default (link, visited) background pattern [10.1] fills only *part* of each right-side menu item, and we intended to fill the entire space. We feel inadequate, vulnerable, and slightly ashamed. In a first attempt at a "final" CSS solution, we will solve this problem but create new ones.

Navigation Bar CSS: First Try at Second Pass

In a first try at a second pass, we specify sizes on our link effects:

```
#nav td a:link, #nav td a:visited {
    background: transparent url(images/bgpat.gif)repeat;
    display: block;
    margin: 0;
    width: 100px;
    height: 25px;
    }
```

As expected, this causes the right-side buttons to be filled in completely, but it louses up our logo, whose background is also now a mere 100 × 25 pixels [10.13]. 100 × 25 is the right value for the little buttons, but it's wrong for the logo (which is 400 × 75).

10.13
One step forward, two steps back: Specifying sizes on nav pseudo-classes fills in their backgrounds completely but louses up the logo's background. It also obliterates the vertical alignment we established earlier. Text now hugs the top of each cell.

Somehow, the changes we've made also kill the vertical alignment we established earlier. Elements *are* vertically aligned within their cells, but their content is not. As Figure **10.13** makes plain, "button" text now hugs the top of each table cell instead of being vertically aligned in the middle. This top-hugging presentation is the same in all CSS-compliant browsers tested. It is not a bug, but unexpected behavior that falls out of the CSS layout model.

Fortunately, when creating the markup way back in Chapter 8, we gave each cell of the table a unique identifier. Home is the id for the cell that contains our logo. Can we use home to create an additional set of rules that override the rules used to fill in the 100 × 25 buttons? You bet we can:

```
td#home a:link, td#home a:visited {
     background: transparent url(images/bgpat.gif) repeat;
     width: 400px;
     height: 75px;
     }
td#home a:hover {
     background: white url(images/nopat.gif) repeat;
     width: 400px;
     height: 75px;
     }
```

These new rules fill in the logo just right, and the site is nearly perfect. But the loss of the behavior we expected with vertical-align: middle is still unacceptable. We'll fix it in the final pass.

Navigation Bar CSS: Final Pass

In the final pass, we get everything we wanted:

```
/* Navigation bar components */
table#nav    {
     border-bottom: 1px solid #000;
     border-left: 1px solid #000;
     }
table#nav td    {
     font: 11px verdana, arial, sans-serif;
     text-align: center;
     border-right: 1px solid #000;
     border-top: 1px solid #000;
     }
table#nav td a    {
     font-weight: normal;
     text-decoration: none;
     display: block;
     margin: 0;
     padding: 0;
     }
#nav td a:link, #nav td a:visited {
     background: transparent url(/images/bgpat.gif) repeat;
     display: block;
     margin: 0;
     width: 100px;
```

```
        line-height: 25px;
        }
#nav td a:hover {
        color: #f60;
        background: white url(/images/nopat.gif) repeat;
        }
td#home a:link img, td#home a:visited img {
        color: #c30;
        background: transparent url(/images/bgpat.gif) repeat;
        width: 400px;
        height: 75px;
        }
td#home a:hover img {
        color: #f60;
        background: white url(/images/nopat.gif) repeat;
        width: 400px;
        height: 75px;
        }
```

What changed? We removed the vertical-align: middle instruction altogether. Then we deleted the line that said buttons were 25px tall and replaced it with this:

```
        line-height: 25px;
```

Line-height filled in the 25px just as height had done, but it also correctly positioned the text in the vertical middle of each button. It would take a CSS genius to explain why this method worked better than the other. The main thing is, it worked.

Final Steps: External Styles and the "You Are Here" Effect

To wrap the site and ship it to the client, two more steps are needed. First, we must move our embedded styles to an external CSS file and delete the embedded style sheet, as explained in Chapter 9. Then we must create a "you are here" effect [**10.14**, **10.15**] to help the visitor maintain awareness of which page she's on. Remember: We're not changing the markup. We want to create this effect using CSS, *without* applying additional classes to our navigation bar.

10.14
The "you are here" effect on the Events page template.

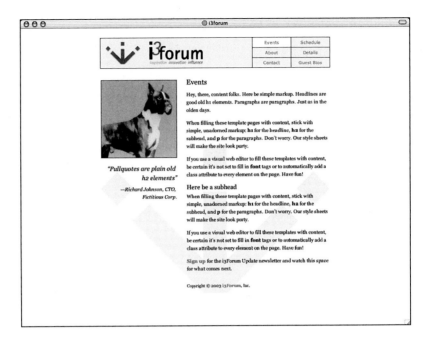

10.15
The "you are here" effect on the About page template.

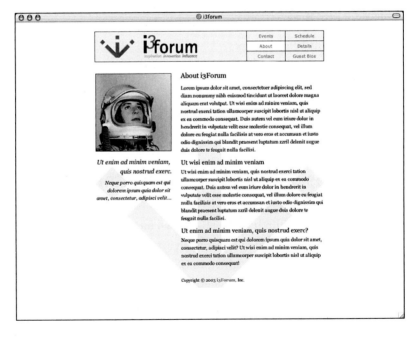

The "you are here" effect is quite easy to do. Now that we've removed embedded styles, every template page gets its CSS data by linking to an external style sheet like so:

```
<!DOCTYPE html PUBLIC "-//W3C//DTD XHTML 1.0 Transitional//EN"
    "http://www.w3.org/TR/xhtml1/DTD/xhtml1-transitional.dtd">
<html xmlns="http://www.w3.org/1999/xhtml">
  <head>
 <title>i3forum</title>
<link rel="StyleSheet" href="/css/i3.css" type="text/css"
media="all" />
```

All we need to do is use the style element to add an embedded style sheet to each page. That embedded style sheet will contain just one rule: a rule that inverts the ordinary presentation of the "menu button" for that page. It's easier to show you than to explain it.

On the Events page, the embedded rule reads as follows, with the important selector highlighted in bold:

```
<style type="text/css" media="screen">
td#events a:link, td#events a:visited {
      color: #c30;
       background: #fff;
       }
</style>
```

Notice that we're using background: #fff; instead of nopat.gif to create the plain-white background highlighting, as promised in the earlier sidebar, "Needless Images II: This Time It's Personal."

On the About page, the embedded rule reads like so:

```
<style type="text/css" media="screen">
td#about a:link, td#about a:visited {
      color: #c30;
      background: #fff;
      }
</style>
```

Each page of the site contains a rule like this; therefore, every page tells the visitor "you are here" without changing one line of markup. You might ask, "Why not change the markup from page to page? Why not create a `thispage` class for the 'you are here' indicator and use it to override the menu style for that link?" That could certainly be done, and often it is.

But leaving the navigation markup untouched from page to page makes it possible to insert the same data over and over via server-side includes— a handy approach for small- to mid-sized sites like the one we're producing.

At `www.zeldman.com`, we use this technique to modify a pure CSS nav bar's "you are here" indicator on a page-by-page basis while using SSI to insert the same XHTML data on every page. But that's another site and another story, and we've come to the end of another chapter. In the next chapter, we'll plumb new CSS depths, learn about browser bugs and workarounds, discover some things browsers do right (but we might not want), and discuss stubborn elements that seem to resist every effort to use web standards.

chapter eleven

Working with Browsers Part I: DOCTYPE Switching and Standards Mode

How do today's browsers "know" when you've created a forward-compatible site? How can they display your standards-based site correctly when they must also do a decent job of supporting antiquated sites built with outdated methods?

The answer is that most modern browsers use our old friend the DOCTYPE, whose acquaintance we made in Chapter 6, "XHTML: Restructuring the Web," to toggle between Standards mode (where your site works as W3C specs say it should) and backward-compatible Quirks mode (so named because old-school sites are authored to the *quirks* of variously incompatible browsers). If you want to control how your site looks and behaves, this chapter is for you.

To keep things interesting, Standards mode in Gecko browsers like Mozilla and Netscape works slightly differently from Standards mode in Internet Explorer, and these slight differences can have a profound and unexpected influence on your layout. To smooth over potential problems (and to make things even more interesting), later Gecko browsers such as Mozilla 1.01+ and Netscape 7 add a *third* mode that works more like IE's Standards mode. (Making life still more exciting, Opera 7 has implemented DOCTYPE switching as well, although how it works is anyone's guess as this book goes to press.)

Gecko browsers call this third, IE-like mode "Almost Standards." The name is not meant to insult IE's Standards mode—at least, we don't *think* it's meant to do that—but to indicate that in the view of Gecko's standards experts, the visual behavior most of us expect from our browsers differs from the letter of the law laid down by CSS specifications.

This chapter explains how the various modes work and provides a simple method of ensuring that your site looks the way you want it to despite differences in the way good browsers interpret CSS and other specs. If you've converted a transitional (tables plus CSS) site to XHTML, discovered that after doing so some browsers treat your layout differently, and wondered why the browsers changed your layout and what you can do to change it back, this chapter has your name all over it.

"The Saga of DOCTYPE Switching" that follows explains why most browsers needed a toggle to alternate between Standards and Quirks modes, and how they came to choose the humble DOCTYPE as the switch. If you're the kind of person who likes to know where things come from and why they are as they are, read on. If you prefer to bypass the background data and get right to the tips and techniques, kindly skip the next couple of sections and proceed directly to "Controlling Browser Performance: The DOCTYPE Switch."

The Saga of DOCTYPE Switching

In the late 1990s, as leading browser makers recognized that complete and accurate support for web standards was important to their customers who designed and built websites, they asked themselves how they could fashion new browsers that supported standards correctly without ruining old, noncompliant sites in the process.

After all, existing versions of Netscape and Explorer had persuaded legions of designers to learn their particular quirks, including proprietary extensions to HTML, partial and incorrect CSS implementations, and manufacturer-specific scripting languages. Microsoft and Netscape were willing to do a much better job of supporting standards, but not if it meant breaking billions of dollars worth of existing sites. For a browser maker, that would be suicide.

An example might help explain the browser makers' dilemma.

In the mid-1990s, when early versions of Internet Explorer began to partially support CSS1, they naturally got a few things wrong, such as the box model (explained in Chapter 12, "Working with Browsers Part II: Box Models, Bugs, and Workarounds"). First drafts are always rough, and Microsoft is to be commended for beginning to support CSS at the dawn of 1997.

But commendable or not, Microsoft's early misinterpretation of the CSS box model posed a problem. Tens of thousands of designers had already "learned" the incorrect box model used by IE4.x and IE5.x and had tailored their CSS to display appropriately in those versions of IE. If later versions of IE, let alone other manufacturers' browsers, supported the box model more accurately, existing designs would surely fall apart, to the displeasure of client, builder, and user alike. What to do?

A Switch to Turn Standards On or Off

Even before Netscape and Microsoft agreed to build browsers that supported standards more accurately and completely, an unsung hero had solved the problem of gently handling sites built with noncompliant methods. That hero was user interface technologist Todd Fahrner, a contributor to the W3C's CSS and HTML working groups and cofounder of The Web Standards project. You will find Fahrner's name scattered about the pages of this book, and you will also find it in this book's index if the indexers have done their job.

In early 1998, on an obscure W3C mailing list (all W3C mailing lists are fairly obscure, of course, but the adjective lends a certain mystique to our story), Fahrner proposed that browser makers incorporate a switching mechanism capable of toggling standards-compliant rendering on or off. He suggested that the presence or absence of a DOCTYPE be used as the on/off switch.

If a web page's markup began with a DOCTYPE, Fahrner reasoned, the odds were high that its author knew about and had made an attempt to comply with standards. Browsers should parse such a web page according to W3C specs. By contrast, a DOCTYPE-free page could not pass W3C validation tests (http://validator.w3.org/) and would most certainly have been built using old-school methods. Browsers should treat it accordingly; that is, they should display that web page the way older, noncompliant browsers handled such pages.

One problem remained: There were no standards-compatible browsers. The world would have to wait two years to see if DOCTYPE switching held the key to forward *and backward* compatibility. (But you don't even have to wait two minutes. Read the next paragraph.)

Throwing the Switch

In March 2000, Microsoft released IE5 Macintosh Edition, whose Tasman rendering engine, created by Microsoft engineer and W3C standards geek Tantek Çelik, provided substantially accurate and mostly complete support for standards, including CSS1, XHTML, and the DOM. IE5/Macintosh included Text Zoom to enhance accessibility, and it was the first browser to use DOCTYPE switching to toggle between Quirks and Standards modes.

Busily creating their own innovations and preparing to release their own standards-compliant browser family, the engineers who were working on Gecko-based browsers knew two good things (DOCTYPE switching and Text Zoom) when they saw them. Gecko browsers including Netscape 6, Mozilla, and Chimera, released soon after IE5/Mac, included DOCTYPE switching and Text Zoom, along with the rigorous and detailed standards support made possible by the Gecko/Mozilla rendering engine (`http://www.mozilla.org/newlayout/`).

When IE6/Windows joined its standards-compliant peers, it likewise supported DOCTYPE switching and added a DOM property that could show whether or not Standards mode was switched on for a given web document (`http://msdn.microsoft.com/workshop/author/dhtml/reference/properties/compatmode.asp`).

No Toggle for Opera

Prior to version 7.0, the Opera Software's Opera browser did not play by these rules; it always attempted to render pages in standards-compliant mode, no matter how the pages might have been authored. Versions of the Opera browser prior to 7.0 also did not support the W3C DOM; therefore, compliant sites that use DOM-based scripting do not work correctly in older Opera browsers. Fortunately, Opera users are a self-selecting group that tends to download improved Opera versions as soon as they are released. And, as mentioned earlier, Opera 7.0 now has DOCTYPE switching, although the company has not yet documented how it works. (Does it work like IE's DOCTYPE switching? Like Mozilla/Netscape's? Or some third way? We will all have to wait and see.)

Controlling Browser Performance:
The DOCTYPE Switch

As explained earlier, most modern browsers use the presence or absence of certain DOCTYPEs to toggle between rigorous standards compliance and fault-tolerant, backward-compatible displays. Browser implementations and details differ, but the gist of DOCTYPE switching follows the outline Todd Fahrner sketched back in 1998, when standards-compliant browsers were barely a gleam in developers' eyes. Here's a simplified overview of how it works:

- An XHTML DOCTYPE that includes a full URI (a complete web address) tells IE and Gecko browsers to render your page in Standards mode, treating your CSS and XHTML per W3C specs. Some complete HTML 4 DOCTYPES also trigger Standards mode, as discussed a few pages from now. In Standards mode, the browser assumes that you know what you're doing.

- Using an incomplete or outdated DOCTYPE—or no DOCTYPE at all— throws these same browsers into Quirks mode, where they assume (probably correctly) that you've written old-fashioned, invalid markup and browser-specific, nonstandard code. In this setting, browsers attempt to parse your page in backward-compatible fashion, rendering your CSS as it might have looked in IE4/5 and reverting to a proprietary, browser-specific DOM.

To control which tack the browser takes, simply include or omit a complete DOCTYPE. It's that easy. *Almost*.

Three Modes for Sister Sara

For reasons we'll explain later in this chapter, newer Gecko browsers toggle between *three* modes: Quirks (as described earlier), Almost Standards (equivalent to Standards mode in IE), and Standards (slightly different from IE's Standards mode in one or two key particulars). Also, some DOCTYPEs that trigger Standards mode in early Gecko browsers instead trigger Almost Standards mode in later Gecko browsers.

To the uninitiated, this might appear deeply and painfully confusing, but a few pages from now, you will find it cruelly and brutally confusing. Nonetheless, there are legitimate reasons for it, and, just as importantly, there are also good, easy workarounds that help ensure correct display not only in browsers that use various methods of DOCTYPE switching, but also in browsers like Opera 5/6 that don't use DOCTYPE switching at all. Hang in there and read on. Together we *will* get through this.

Before we probe the fine points of browser differences, let's study what browsers have in common.

Complete and Incomplete DOCTYPEs

Browsers that use DOCTYPE switching look for *complete* DOCTYPEs. That is to say, they look for DOCTYPEs that include a complete web address such as http://www.w3.org/TR/xhtml1/DTD/xhtml1-strict.dtd. The following DOCTYPE triggers Standards mode in any modern browser that employs DOCTYPE switching:

```
<!DOCTYPE html PUBLIC "-//W3C//DTD XHTML 1.0 Strict//EN"
        "http://www.w3.org/TR/xhtml1/DTD/xhtml1-strict.dtd">
```

Yes, this is a Strict DOCTYPE, and yes, we've been promoting the use of XHTML 1.0 Transitional so far. We use Strict here because it makes our point without a heap of caveats, which we'll get to soon enough. Our point right now is that a complete DOCTYPE like the preceding one will trigger Standards mode.

Alas, many of us write—and many of our authoring programs insert by default— incomplete DOCTYPEs that trigger backward-compatible Quirks mode instead of the desired Standards mode. For instance, many authoring tools insert DOCTYPEs like the following, which they derive from the W3C's own site:

```
<!DOCTYPE html PUBLIC "-//W3C//DTD XHTML 1.0 Strict//EN"
        "DTD/xhtml1-strict.dtd">
```

How does this string of geeky text differ from the one that preceded it?

If you look closely at the last part of the previous DOCTYPE ("DTD/xhtml1-strict.dtd"), you'll see that it is a relative link rather than a complete URI. In fact, it is a relative link to a DTD document on W3C's website. Unless you've copied the W3C's DTD and placed it on your own server in the directory indicated—and nobody does that—the relative link points to nothing at all. Because the DTD resides on W3C's site but not yours, the URI is considered incomplete, and the browser displays your site in Quirks mode.

(Do current browsers actually try to locate and load the DTD? No, they simply recognize the incomplete DOCTYPE from their database and go into Quirks mode. Does this mean that pages at w3.org that use this relative URI DOCTYPE will also be rendered in Quirks mode? It seems like it would mean exactly that. Although the irony is delicious to contemplate, we don't know for sure, and in any case, it's not our problem or yours.)

Now let's look again at the complete version that will trigger the desired Standards mode:

```
<!DOCTYPE html PUBLIC "-//W3C//DTD XHTML 1.0 Strict//EN"
    "http://www.w3.org/TR/xhtml1/DTD/xhtml1-strict.dtd">
```

Notice that it includes a complete URI at the end of the tag. You could copy and paste that URI into the address bar of any web browser, and if you did so, you would be able to read the XHTML 1.0 Strict DTD in all of its incomprehensibly geeky glory. Because the URI at the tail end of this DOCTYPE indicates a valid location on the web, DOCTYPE-switching browsers consider this DOCTYPE to be full and complete and render your page in Standards mode.

In an additional wrinkle, please note that Internet Explorer switches into Standards mode in the presence of any XHTML DOCTYPE, whether or not that DOCTYPE includes a full URI. However, an XHTML DOCTYPE that does not include a full URI is technically invalid. Thus, in the discussion that follows, we will encourage you to use a full URI in your DOCTYPE. (After all, why switch into Standards mode if your web page is not valid?)

Prolog Quirks in IE6/Windows

There's an exception to every rule. Even with a complete XHTML DOCTYPE, IE6/Windows will kick back into Quirks mode if you include the optional XML prolog. No, really. That is why we advised you to skip the prolog way back in Chapter 6. You see? We've got your back.

A Complete Listing of Complete XHTML DOCTYPEs

Accurate as of this writing, listed next are the complete XHTML DOCTYPEs that trigger Standards or Almost Standards modes in DOCTYPE-switching browsers. What is Almost Standards mode? Patience. We'll get to that soon.

XHTML 1.0 DTD

XHTML 1.0 Strict—Triggers full-on Standards mode in all browsers that support DOCTYPE switching. Has no effect in Opera pre-7.0 or in versions of IE/Windows before 6.0.

```
<!DOCTYPE html PUBLIC "-//W3C//DTD XHTML 1.0 Strict//EN"
    "http://www.w3.org/TR/xhtml1/DTD/xhtml1-strict.dtd">
```

XHTML 1.0 Transitional—Triggers full-on Standards mode in compliant IE browsers (IE6+/Windows, IE5+/Macintosh). Triggers full-on Standards mode in first-generation Gecko browsers (Mozilla 1.0, Netscape 6) and Almost Standards mode in updated Gecko browsers (Mozilla 1.01, Netscape 7+, Chimera 0.6+). Has no effect in Opera pre-7.0 or in versions of IE/Windows before 6.0.

```
<!DOCTYPE html PUBLIC "-//W3C//DTD XHTML 1.0 Transitional//EN"
    "http://www.w3.org/TR/xhtml1/DTD/xhtml1-
    ➥transitional.dtd">
```

XHTML 1.0 Frameset—Triggers full-on Standards mode in compliant IE browsers (IE6+/Windows, IE5+/Macintosh). Triggers full-on Standards mode in first-generation Gecko browsers (Mozilla 1.0, Netscape 6) and Almost Standards mode in updated Gecko browsers (Mozilla 1.01, Netscape 7+, Chimera 0.6+). Has no effect in Opera pre-7.0 or in versions of IE/Windows before 6.0. DOCTYPE switching might affect the way frames are rendered, but if it does so, no browser maker seems to have documented these variants.

```
<!DOCTYPE html PUBLIC "-//W3C//DTD XHTML 1.0 Frameset//EN"
    "http://www.w3.org/TR/xhtml1/DTD/xhtml1-frameset.dtd">
```

XHTML 1.1 DTD

XHTML 1.1 (Strict by definition)—Triggers full-on Standards mode in all browsers that support DOCTYPE switching. Has no effect in Opera pre-7.0 or in versions of IE/Windows before 6.0.

```
<!DOCTYPE html PUBLIC "-//W3C//DTD XHTML 1.1//EN"
    "http://www.w3.org/TR/xhtml11/DTD/xhtml11.dtd">
```

Save Your Pretty Fingers

If you dislike trying to type stuff like this out of a book (and who can claim to enjoy it?), feel free to copy and paste from A List Apart's "Fix Your Site with the Right DOCTYPE" (http://www.alistapart.com/stories/doctype/).

Executive Summary: XHTML DOCTYPE Triggers in IE and Gecko

Let's review what we've learned so far:

- Any complete XHTML 1 or 1.1 DOCTYPE triggers Standards mode in compliant versions of Internet Explorer (IE5+/Macintosh, IE6+/Windows) and in early Gecko browsers (Netscape 6, Mozilla 1.0).

- A complete, Strict XHTML DOCTYPE has the same effect in all the preceding browsers and in later Gecko browsers (Mozilla 1.01+, Netscape 7, Chimera 0.6+).

- A complete XHTML 1.0 Transitional or Frameset DOCTYPE triggers Almost Standards mode in later Gecko browsers.

- Incomplete DOCTYPEs that have relative or missing URIs trigger Quirks mode in all browsers that support DOCTYPE switching. They also generate CSS validation errors, but they do *not* generate XHTML validation errors because of a bug in the W3C's XHTML validation service or a difference between its XHTML and CSS validation services, depending on whom you ask. Okay, forget we said anything except that incomplete DOCTYPEs trigger Quirks mode and CSS validation errors.

- Many authoring tools insert incomplete DOCTYPEs by default, thus triggering Quirks mode and generating CSS validation errors.

This author and individual members of The Web Standards Project have contacted makers of popular authoring tools to alert them to the need to insert complete DOCTYPEs by default. We've also requested that W3C publish an easy-to-find listing of complete DOCTYPEs on its website at www.w3.org. Meanwhile, to ensure that your site triggers Standards mode, you might need to manually edit the DOCTYPE that your authoring tool generates when you create a new XHTML page.

DOCTYPE Switching: The Devil Is in the Details

DOCTYPE switching is not limited to XHTML. As mentioned earlier, some complete HTML DOCTYPEs also trigger Standards mode. For instance, IE toggles into Standards mode (and recent Gecko-based browsers toggle into Almost Standards mode) in the presence of a complete HTML 4.01 Strict DOCTYPE:

```
<!DOCTYPE HTML PUBLIC "-//W3C//DTD HTML 4.01//EN"
        "http://www.w3.org/TR/html4/strict.dtd">
```

But in both IE and Gecko-based browsers, a complete HTML 4.0 DOCTYPE triggers backward-compatible Quirks mode instead. What a difference a 0.1 makes. If these inconsistencies suggest that you are better off authoring your site in XHTML than HTML, hey, we've been saying that all along.

For details on additional DOCTYPES that trigger Standards, Quirks, and Almost Standards mode in recent Gecko browsers, see "Gecko's 'Almost Standards' Mode" at `http://devedge.netscape.com/viewsource/2002/almost-standards/`. If you find the level of detail overwhelming, stop reading the article and pretend you never saw it. As the next discussion will soon make clear, most of us need not worry about these complexities as long as we author in XHTML 1.0 Transitional or Strict and employ a few simple CSS workarounds described in the following section.

Celebrate Browser Diversity! (Or at Least Learn to Live with It)

Gecko's Standards mode differs from IE's in a few details, and this difference can be disagreeable if you're not expecting it. The difference is especially visible and can be especially disagreeable in hybrid (CSS plus table) layouts when viewed in first-generation Gecko browsers.

After converting from HTML 4.01 Transitional to XHTML 1.0 Transitional, making no changes to their markup except those described in "Converting to XHTML: Simple Rules, Easy Guidelines" (Chapter 6), designers will expect their layout to look just the way it always has. After all, they're only changing a few markup tags; they're not altering the design. Nevertheless, their layout might look unexpectedly different in early Gecko browsers such as Netscape 6.0 and Mozilla 1.0. If the designers have converted to XHTML Strict, the layout will look different in all Gecko browsers, old and new. There is a standards-based reason for the change—and there is also an easy way to change it back.

The Image Gap Issue in Gecko

Figure **11.1** shows The Daily Report at `www.zeldman.com` as it looked for several years, when the site was laid out with transitional techniques combining CSS and tables.

After converting from HTML 4.01 Transitional to XHTML 1.0 Transitional (and changing from a complete HTML 4.01 DOCTYPE to a complete XHTML 1.0 Transitional DOCTYPE), the site looked the same as it always had in Internet Explorer for Windows and Macintosh. But in Gecko browsers, mysterious, unwanted gaps appeared between images in the table that controlled the site's navigation menu [**11.2, 11.3**].

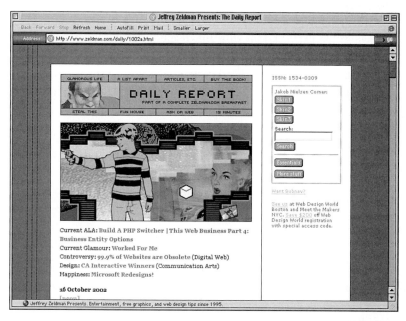

11.1

This old hybrid table/ CSS layout at `www.zeldman.com` used a complete DOCTYPE to trigger Standards mode. After converting from HTML to XHTML, it looked the same as it always had in Internet Explorer (`www.zeldman.com/ daily/1002a.html`).

11.2

In early Gecko-based browsers, before apply- ing the CSS solution described in this chapter, the site's navigation table suffered from mysterious, unwanted gaps.

11.3

The same figure is enlarged here to more clearly display the gaps. Early Gecko browsers were not *wrong* to display the table this way, but their rendering was unexpected and undesired.

11.4

Two quick CSS rules removed the unwanted gaps in Gecko, and all was right with the world. In Almost Standards mode used by later Gecko browsers, the gaps are not present, and no CSS workarounds are needed. But we recommend using them anyway, for reasons explained next.

One (or Two) Rules to Bind Them All: Use CSS to Turn Off Gaps

There was a perfectly valid reason for this unexpected behavior (see the sidebar, "Baselines and Vertical Whitespace in Gecko's Standards Mode"). But before bogging down in theory, let us explain how we restored the navigation bar back to its desired state [11.4] in Gecko as well as IE browsers. All it took was two lines of CSS:

```
img {display: block;}
.inline {display: inline;}
```

The first rule closed the gaps by instructing all browsers to treat images as block-level rather than inline elements. (If you've forgotten the difference between block-level and inline elements, refer back to "Hide and Block" in Chapter 10, "CSS in Action: A Hybrid Layout [Part II].) But what if we wanted some of our images to display inline? The second rule (.inline) created a class allowing us to do just that. Images that must display inline will be marked up like so:

```
<img class="inline" ... etc. />
```

There are other ways of doing the same thing. For instance, some designers might prefer to write a rule specifying that when a table cell contains only one image, that image should be displayed as a block-level element:

```
td img {display: block;}
```

With this simple, single rule, navigation menus that typically contain one image per table cell will display block-level and gap-free, whereas other images on the site will display inline. The advantage to this alternative method is that it uses one rule instead of two, saving a bit of bandwidth, and it removes the need to add classes to some images, saving a bit more.

Each method works better for some layouts than others. The method you choose depends on your design. Hint to CSS novices: Try one method. If it fails, try the other. You might even come up with a third method of your own.

The Birth of Almost Standards Mode

Creating simple CSS rules like those presented earlier takes no time at all. Incorporating them into your design practice frees you from the need to worry about browser differences. Nevertheless, when the image gap issue first reared its head and when it seemed to occur only after converting from HTML to

XHTML, some designers leaped to the conclusion that XHTML was at fault, whereas others wrongly determined that Netscape 6 and other Gecko browsers were broken or buggy. In fact, Gecko's addition of whitespace to unstyled images was a feature, not a bug (see the sidebar, "Baselines and Vertical Whitespace in Gecko's Standards Mode"). However, it was not a feature that designers initially understood, and it was certainly not one they had requested.

To better serve transitioning designers, Gecko/Netscape engineers created an Almost Standards mode that behaves like IE's Standards mode. That is to say, in Almost Standards mode, no unexpected gaps arise. Because the unexpected behavior primarily occurs in transitional layouts, the engineers determined that XHTML Transitional DOCTYPEs would invoke Gecko's Almost Standards mode, whereas *Strict* DOCTYPEs would continue to trigger Gecko's more rigorous Standards mode. (After all, if you're writing Strict, nonpresentational markup, you are probably not sticking images in table cells.)

Baselines and Vertical Whitespace in Gecko's Standards Mode

As described in the earlier section "The Image Gap Issue in Gecko," IE and Gecko browsers differ in their Standards mode treatment of image elements in relation to the implied grid of a web page. In true Standards mode, Gecko considers images to be inline unless you have specified in your style sheet that they are block level. All inline elements, such as text, live on a baseline to make room for the descending shapes of lowercase letters such as y, g, and j. That baseline's size and placement depends on the size and font family of the containing element—for instance, on the size and family of text in a paragraph that contains the inline image.

Figure 11.5 shows text and an inline image sitting on a baseline. In Gecko's Standards mode, there will always be whitespace below inline images to make room for the containing block's type descenders, whether the block actually contains text or not. For a more detailed and readable explanation, see Eric Meyer's "Images, Tables, and Mysterious Gaps," at Netscape DevEdge, written before the creation of Almost Standards mode, but not made irrelevant by it (`http://devedge.netscape.com/viewsource/ 2002/img-table/`).

continues

continued

11.5

All text lives on a baseline that makes room for type descenders. In Gecko's Standards mode, all inline elements, including images, share the baseline with their containing element (in this case, a one-sentence paragraph).

Mind your baselines.

(descender space)

Limitations of Almost Standards Mode

If all Gecko users routinely upgraded to the latest browser versions, Almost Standards mode would solve the image gap problem in transitional layouts. Many Gecko users *do* upgrade religiously, but some—CompuServe users, for instance—do not. (CompuServe users upgrade when their service provider sends a new installation disk.) Therefore, it makes sense to routinely write CSS rules like the ones described earlier in "One (or Two) Rules to Bind Them All: Use CSS to Turn Off Gaps." Doing so could also curb unexpected results in present and future non-IE and non-Gecko browsers, which might be as rigorous in their handling of images and other inline elements as Gecko is in Standards mode. In addition, it will wean you from presentational markup and the normative browser behaviors associated with it and help you do more "CSS thinking."

From "Vive la Difference" to "@#$! This $#@$."

Correct behavior, however unexpected, is one thing. Bugs and errors are something else again. In Chapter 12, we'll study common browser bugs and learn how to work around them. We'll also learn vital aspects of CSS layout. Be there or be (broken box model) square.

chapter twelve

Working with Browsers Part II: Box Models, Bugs, and Workarounds

"Create once, publish everywhere" is the Grail of standards-based design and development. We don't learn proper XHTML authoring to win a gold star. We do it so that our sites will work in desktop browsers, text browsers, screen readers, and hand-held devices—today, tomorrow, and 10 years from now. Likewise, we don't use CSS exclusively for short-term rewards like reducing bandwidth to save on this month's server costs. We do it primarily to ensure that our sites will look the same in Netscape 14.0 as they do today and that unneeded presentational markup won't impede user experience in non-CSS environments.

Standards-compliant user agents move forward compatibility from the realm of wishful thinking to the forefront of rational, sustainable design strategies. If the web were still viewed mainly in Netscape and Microsoft's 4.0 browsers, forward compatibility would be unattainable by all but the most rudimentary sites. If the leading user agents that succeeded 4.0 browsers had continued to promote proprietary technologies at the expense of baseline standards, the web's future as an open platform would be open to doubt.

Thankfully, all leading and many niche browsers released within the past few years can justifiably be called "standards-compliant." But some are more compliant than others. Coping with compliance hiccups is what this chapter is all about.

The Box Model and Its Discontents

With the publication of CSS1 in 1996, the W3C proposed that any object on a web page inhabits a box whose properties designers can control by creating rules. It doesn't matter if the object is a paragraph, list, headline, image, or generic block-level element such as `<div id="navigation">`. If it can be inserted into a web page via markup, it lives in a box.

Figure 12.1 illustrates the four areas of the CSS box: content, padding, border, and margin. Content (dark gray in our diagram) is the innermost area, followed by padding (light gray), border (black), and margin (white). These areas should be familiar to you. In Chapter 10, "CSS in Action: A Hybrid Layout (Part II)," while creating a hybrid layout for the i3Forum site, we specified border, padding, and margin values for various page elements. We also assigned size values to the content area when we wrote rules like the one that follows. (Content values are highlighted in bold.)

```
td#home a:link img, td#home a:visited img {
    color: #c30;
    background: transparent url(/images/bgpat.gif) repeat;
    width: 400px;
    height: 75px;
    }
```

In this rule, the width of the content area is 400 pixels and its height is 75 pixels. Notice that we didn't write this:

```
content: 400px;
```

We also didn't write anything like this:

```
content-width: 400px;
content-height: 75px;
```

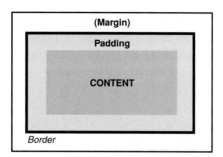

The four areas of the generic CSS box: content, padding, border, and margin. (The outer edge of the margin was artificially darkened for your viewing pleasure.)

There are no such rules in CSS. Border, margins, and padding are assigned their values by name; the content area is not. In beginning to learn and use CSS, you might understandably assume that width: 400px applies to the entire box (excluding the margin). After all, that is how page layout programs work, it is how designers think, and it is how users understand layouts. If you create a CSS layout containing two divs side by side and assign each a width of 50% of the visitor's browser window, you might expect the two to retain that value as you add padding and borders. But that is not how CSS works.

Likewise, if you were a browser maker implementing CSS at the dawn of standards history, you might incorrectly apply width: 400px to the entire box (excluding the margin) instead of limiting it to the content area as the specification dictates. It would be pretty easy to make a mistake like that, especially if you were implementing CSS1 while the specification was still oven-hot and fresh. Hold that thought; we'll return to it in a few paragraphs.

In fact, the CSS box model is more sophisticated—and in some ways more troublesome—than what common sense, graphic design norms, and early (incorrect) browser implementations would lead you to expect.

How the Box Model Works

According to CSS, each of the four areas (content, padding, border, and margin) can be assigned values, and these values are additive. To determine the overall width of the box, add the content, padding, and border values together [12.2]. If the content width is 400px, the padding is 50px on each side, and the border is 2px per edge, the overall width would be 504px (400 content + 2 left border + 50 left padding + 50 right padding + 2 right border = 504 total).

12.2
The box model in action. Values for content, padding, and border are added together to make up the total width of the box.

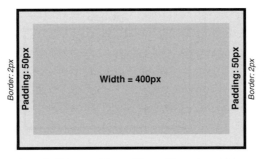

Overall width: 2px + 50px + 400px + 50px + 2px = 504px

CSS doesn't care how you choose to play chef or which kinds of values you choose to mix and match. For instance, you might specify that the content width is 67% of the visitor's browser window width at the time the page is viewed, the padding is 5em, and the border is 1px. The overall size would then be… uh, pretty hard to figure out, and it would depend on the width of the visitor's browser window and the default (1em) size of text.

There is more to the box model than what we've explained so far. For one thing, upper and lower margins of vertically adjacent elements collapse upon each other. (Brew a double espresso or something stronger and peruse `http://www.w3.org/TR/REC-CSS2/box.html`.) For another thing, size values are meaningless when the box is empty. If you specify that an empty box should take up 100% of the height and width of the page, it will actually take up 0% because there is nothing inside the box. This is different from the way HTML frames work, and it is also different from the way table layouts sometimes work in 4.0 browsers. If you try to achieve color effects by filling two adjoining block-level elements with background colors (but no actual data), the technique works in frames and might work in table layouts viewed in 4.0 browsers, but it will not work in CSS. In that sense, paradoxically, you cannot separate presentation from structure; for where there is no data, there will be no presentation. (If a tree does not fall, there is no forest.)

How the Box Model Breaks

If you've been paying attention, you will already have a clue about the way the box model breaks in early CSS implementations such as the one in IE 4 through IE5.5/Windows. In these browsers and in IE/Mac prior to 5.0, width and height values intended only for the content area are instead applied to the entire box (excluding margins).

Figure **12.3** shows the broken box model in action. To revisit the previous example, in IE4–5.5/Windows, if content width is 400px, padding is 50px per side, and border is 2px, the overall width will still be 400px instead of the correct 504px—and the content area will be squeezed down to 296px (400 − 50 − 50 − 2 − 2). The higher the padding and border values, the farther your layout will depart from your intentions and the tighter your content area will be squeezed.

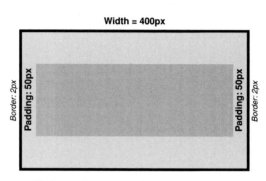

12.3
The broken box model in Internet Explorer 4.0 through 5.5/Windows: 400 + 2 + 50 + 50 + 2 = 400. Bad arithmetic—but maybe good thinking.

The broken Box model in IE. Overall width: 400px.

Hundreds of millions of people still use IE5.x/Windows as of this writing, and tens of thousands of designers have learned the incorrect IE5.x/Windows box model and used it in their designs, resulting in broken layouts in browsers that interpret the box model correctly, such as IE6/Windows, IE5/Macintosh, Netscape 6, Netscape 7, Mozilla, Chimera, Kmeleon, Safari, Opera 5, Opera 6, and Opera 7.

Conversely, designers who understand the box model and author to the actual specs will produce the desired results in the browsers we've just mentioned, but will get ugly or unusable layouts in IE5.5/Windows and earlier, used, as we might have mentioned, by hundreds of millions of people.

There is a solution—in fact, there are several—and the most-used solution came, of all places, from a Microsoft engineer. But before we compensate for the broken box model, let us take a moment to consider its virtues.

In Defense of the Broken Box Model
The box model in IE4/5.x/Windows (and also in all versions of IE/Macintosh prior to 5.0) is unquestionably broken and wrong per the CSS specification, but it is not stupid. In some ways, this box model is easier to use and more practical

than the actual specification spelled out in CSS. The CSS box model works well when used to create layouts based on absolute pixel values, but its complexity can make it cumbersome, unintuitive, and even counterproductive when you try to create percentage-based ("liquid") layouts that reflow to fit the visitor's monitor.

Consider a simple, two-celled design whose left and right column widths add up to 100% of the width of the visitor's monitor. It is trivial to create such layouts using HTML tables but difficult to do it with CSS. To fashion a two-column liquid layout in CSS, a human being would normally create two `divs` and use the CSS `float` property to position one beside the other:

```
#nav    {
    width: 35%;
    height: 100%;
    background: #666;
    color: #fff;
    margin: 0;
    padding: 0;
    }

#maintext    {
    width: 65%;
    height: 100%;
    color: #000;
    background: #fff;
    margin: 0;
    padding: 0;
    float: right;
    }
```

Here we have two page divisions: one for navigation and the other for main text. As its name makes clear, `float: right` tells the main text column to float to the right of the navigation column. The navigation column is told to take up 35% of the visitor's browser window width. The main text area gets the remaining 65%. Between them, the two page divisions should take up 100% of the window (35 + 65 = 100).

Figure **12.4** shows that the approach works as long as padding and borders are not used. Borders are optional and depend on the design, but padding is essential to prevent ugly and illegible wall-to-wall text such as that seen in this illustration. When a designer adds padding and borders to a basic, side-by-side layout like this, the page falls apart. In some browsers, elements overlap [**12.5**]. In others, because the numbers now add up to more than 100%, the layout becomes too wide to be viewed in the monitor, and the reader must scroll horizontally. No matter how large of a monitor is used, the layout will always be too wide for it.

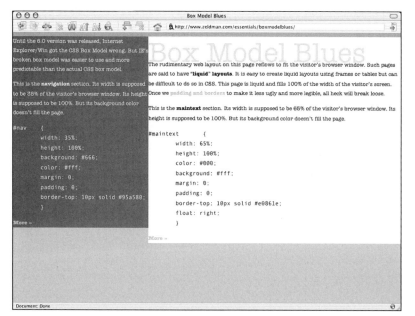

12.4
CSS makes it harder to achieve flexible, percentage-based layouts that reflow to fit the visitor's monitor. This layout positions two liquid divs side by side (`http://www.zeldman.com/essentials/boxmodelblues/`).

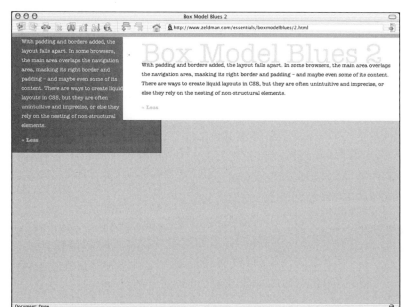

12.5
When we add padding and borders, the layout falls apart. In some browsers (as seen here), elements overlap. In other browsers, the page becomes too wide for the screen.

Things work better if you set your padding and widths in percentages, all of which will scale to fit the visitor's browser window. But accurately mixing percentages with length-based padding is essentially impossible. To correct this problem, CSS3 contains a proposed "box-sizing" property to let designers decide which sizing model they want to use for a given element. If the CSS box model worked like the incorrect implementation in old versions of IE/Windows, we would not need a box-sizing property. And, of course, as of today, we don't have such a property in our browsers.

In the absence of a box-sizing property, designers often cheat by defining divs with no padding, inserting subelements into those containing divs, and assigning margins to those subelements to simulate the desired "padding" effect. The problem with this solution is that it generates extraneous markup elements that are not structural; they're just there to fix layout problems. (The "brave four hundred" element in Chapter 16, "A CSS Redesign," can be considered such a subelement because its only purpose is to fix a formatting issue.) Add too many of these, and your clean markup will start to resemble the divitis we warned about in Chapter 7, "Tighter, Firmer Pages Guaranteed: Structure and Meta-Structure in Strict and Hybrid Markup."

Admittedly, these concerns are rather purist. Aside from a few extra bytes of bandwidth, what is the harm in creating and nesting nonstructural elements to force layout issues? Practically speaking, there is no huge harm in it. But it is a kludge, and it's the same old mentality that got us into trouble in the first place. ("Design busted? Write some extra code!") With standards, that kind of thinking should be going the way of the Dodo bird. But the complexity and at the same time the limitations of CSS1/2 layout sometimes force us to do the very thing they were created to help us avoid.

Under the broken IE4/5/Windows box model, you could create liquid layouts that combined length and percentage values without nesting needless divs or turning your brain inside out. We're not saying IE4/5/Windows was the epitome of standards compliance because it surely was not. All we're saying is that the incorrect box model had its points.

There is a divitis-free way to create combination length/percentage liquid layouts in CSS, but it is not the way any human being would think of doing the job, and it is an inexact science at best. The trick is to create only one div, to use the page as the other, and to negotiate between them via float. Because it is impossible to calculate the exact overall dimensions, the numbers must be guessed at and fudged, and they will never add up to exactly 100%.

When A List Apart magazine converted from HTML tables to CSS layout in February 2001, it took three designers, including this author, to figure out how to do it. The two others were experts Fahrner (who contributed to the CSS specifications) and Çelik (who contributed to the CSS specifications and built the Tasman rendering engine in IE5/Mac). The original, table-based design [12.6] was essentially a two-column layout with a liquid content area and a right-hand sidebar whose width was cast in stone. Between the three of us, we managed to achieve roughly the same effect in CSS [12.7] using the nonintuitive method sketched in the preceding paragraph. The overall width is kludged with values that never add up to exactly 100%. It should not be that hard to create a two-column layout combining liquid and fixed elements.

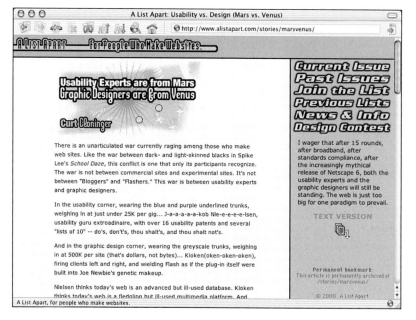

12.6

A List Apart magazine (www.alistapart.com) was originally laid out with table cells that reflowed to fit the visitor's monitor.

12.7
It required three CSS designers (two of them acknowledged experts) to figure out how to achieve a similar look and feel with style sheets during the site's CSS redesign in February 2001.

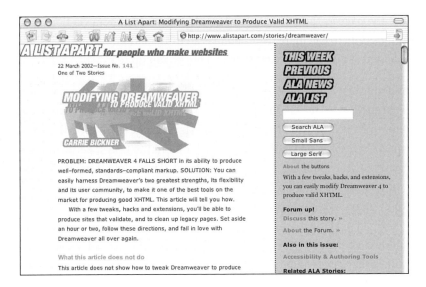

Admittedly, this is easier today because designers now have the example of A List Apart and other CSS sites as models whose techniques they can copy and modify. Let it be noted that CSS 2.1 solves some of these problems, and proposals in CSS3 solve more of them. Let it also be noted that as of this writing, browsers mainly support CSS1 with bits and pieces of CSS2. The complexity of the CSS1 box model remains a sticking point for those who want to create certain kinds of liquid layouts, and it is counterintuitive to the way designers think.

In a 2002 interview, DOM expert Peter-Paul Koch put it this way:

> "Logically, a box is measured from border to border. Take a physical box, any box. Put something in it that is distinctly smaller than the box. Ask anyone to measure the width of the box. He'll measure the distance between the sides of the box (the 'borders'). No one will think of measuring the content of the box. Web designers who create boxes for holding content care about the *visible* width of the box, about the distance from border to border. The borders, and not the content, are the visual cues for the user of the site. Nobody is interested in the width of the content."
> http://www.netdiver.net/interviews/peterpaulkoch.php

Overly complex or not, the spec we have is the spec we must use. Browser makers are not asked to improve that spec but to implement it correctly and completely, and all leading and most niche browsers now do so. How, then, are we to create layouts that work as well in browsers that misunderstand the box model as they do in those that get it right?

The Box Model Hack: Making CSS Safe for Democracy

Tantek Çelik, whose name has already appeared prominently in this chapter, has provided one widely used solution to the problem posed by incorrect box model implementations. His Box Model Hack takes advantage of a CSS parsing bug in IE5.x/Windows to apply a false width that IE5.x/Windows likes and then overwrite it with the actual value [**12.8**]. In the example that follows, taken from `http://www.tantek.com/CSS/Examples/boxmodelhack.html`, the correct value for the content area is 300px, but IE/Windows misunderstands it by subtracting 100px worth of padding and borders.

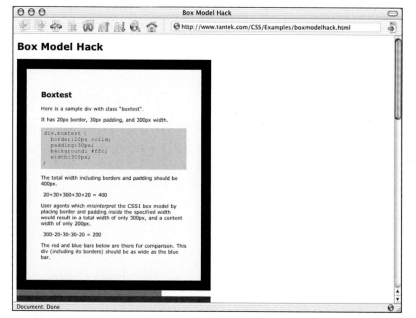

12.8

Tantek Çelik's Box Model Hack solves the box model problem and is useful in fixing other browser issues as well (`http://www.tantek.com/CSS/Examples/boxmodelhack.html`.)

First, here's the uncorrected CSS rule as you might write it for all conformant browsers:

```
div.boxtest {
  border:20px solid;
  padding:30px;
  background: #ffc;
  width:300px;
}
```

Browsers that understand CSS correctly will create a box whose total width is 400px (20 + 30 + 300 + 30 + 20 = 400). But outdated versions of IE/Windows will subtract the padding and border values from the content area's 300px, resulting in a box that is 300px wide and a content area that is 200px wide (300 − 20 − 30 − 30 − 20 = 200). So we feed them a false value of 400px (the actual overall size we desire) and then confuse them with two lines containing CSS selectors that IE4/5/Windows does not understand. (The two lines that IE does not grok are marked in bold.)

```
div.content {
    width:400px;
    voice-family: "\"}\"";
    voice-family:inherit;
    width:300px;
}
```

We finish by providing the true value, which is 300px. IE5.x/Windows stops reading when it encounters the voice-family rules it does not understand. More compliant browsers keep reading and use the true value.

Opera browsers (at least prior to Opera 7) present an additional problem, in that they understand the CSS2 selectors and the box model but suffer from the same parsing bug as IE/Windows. Thus, Opera browsers, too, might use the false values, and this is not what we want. Tantek solves this problem by creating an additional "Be Kind to Opera" rule:

```
html>body .content {
    width:300px;
}
```

Opera might miss the true value in the previous rule, but it honors the true value in the additional rule because it is of greater specificity, and in CSS, the more specific rule always outweighs the less specific rule (just as a rule of #menu p outweighs the rule of p).

Since its introduction in late 2000, the Box Model Hack has been used on thousands of sites to facilitate CSS layout by feeding outdated browsers the incorrect values that their broken box model requires, while providing accurate values to more conformant user agents. It is more cumbersome to explain (and to read about on this page) than it is to work with. We use it constantly.

Note that the Box Model Hack is not needed when padding and borders are set to zero. Depending on your design sensibility and the requirements of a given project, it also might not be needed when padding values are minimal, the design is fairly "loose," and you don't care if the box size varies by a few pixels between one browser and another. (For some designs, you can also cheat by choosing values that deliberately add up to less than 100%.)

Browser Hide and Seek

The Box Model Hack (also called the Tantek method) relies on a parsing bug to trick outdated versions of IE/Windows into correctly supporting the box model. As discussed in the section "External Style Sheets" in Chapter 9, "CSS Basics," the `@import` method of linking to a style sheet fools 4.0 and older browsers into disregarding that style sheet. In these and other methods, we are using standards to support standards. That might sound Orwellian, but all it means is that we are allowing limited browsers to gracefully ignore what they cannot understand. And we are doing this not through old-school methods like browser sniffing and code forks, but by letting basic standards do what they do best. For more methods of hiding various elements from differently capable browsers, see `http://w3development.de/css/hide_css_from_browsers/summary/`.

The Whitespace Bug in IE/Windows

Lest we weary you with too much theory, let's turn to a simpler issue with a less complex solution—namely, the whitespace bug in IE/Windows. Figure **12.9** shows the havoc the whitespace bug can wreak in hybrid layouts (compare with Figure **11.4** in Chapter 11, "Working with Browsers Part I: DOCTYPE Switching and Standards Mode"), but it is equally damaging to pure CSS layouts.

12.9
Another day, another display problem. This time, the source is a whitespace bug in IE/Windows. The image has been enlarged to show details. Compare and contrast with Figure 11.4 (Chapter 11), which shows the intended display.

Each of the two markup snippets that follow is functionally equivalent. However, because of the snippets' varying use (or nonuse) of whitespace, they will display differently in a browser that wrongly attempts to parse whitespace in XHTML. Thus:

```
<td><img src="foo.gif" /></td>
```

…will display differently from this:

```
<td>
 <img src="foo.gif" />
</td>
```

The second example—the one with whitespace in its markup—might result in unwanted visual gaps on your web page, as in Figure 12.9. The same is true for the following example. The next markup (with no whitespace)…

```
<td><a href="#foo"><img src="foo.gif" /></a></td>
```

…might look different in your browser from the functionally identical

```
<td>
 <a href="#foo">
  <img src="foo.gif" />
 </a>
</td>
```

Why does this happen? The whitespace bug was a known problem in Netscape Navigator dating back to Version 3.0 (if not earlier). When Microsoft decided to build a competing browser, its engineers emulated much of Netscape's behavior—including, unfortunately, a few of its bugs. As of this writing, IE/Windows browsers right up through IE6 continue to emulate this old Netscape bug. The solution? Remove the whitespace from your markup.

The whitespace bug can be as tough on CSS layouts as it is on hybrid CSS/table layouts. Consider the following list, taken from a January, 2003 version of zeldman.com:

```
<div id="secondarynav">
<ul>
<li id="secondarytop"><a href="/about/" title="History, FAQ,
bio, etc.">about</a></li>
<li id="contact"><a href="/contact/" title="Write to us."
>contact</a></li>
```

```
<li id="essentials"><a href="/essentials/" title="Vital info."
>essentials</a></li>
<li id="pubs"><a href="/pubs/" title="Books and articles."
>pubs</a></li>
<li id="tour"><a href="/tour/" title="Personal appearances."
>tour</a></li>
</ul>
    ...</div>
```

CSS (provided a few paragraphs from now) transforms the list into user-clickable "buttons," as shown in Figure 12.10. But in IE/Windows, the whitespace in the markup throws the buttons' spacing and positioning out of whack. To work around this IE/Windows bug, it is necessary to remove the whitespace like so:

```
<div id="secondarynav"><ul><li id="secondarytop"><a
href="/about/" title="History, FAQ, bio, etc.">about
</a></li><li id="contact"><a href="/contact/" title="Write to
us.">contact</a></li><li id="essentials"><a href="/essentials/"
title="Vital info.">essentials</a></li><li id="pubs"><a
href="/pubs/" title="Books and articles.">pubs</a></li><li
id="tour"><a href="/tour/" title="Personal
appearances.">tour</a></li></ul> ...</div>
```

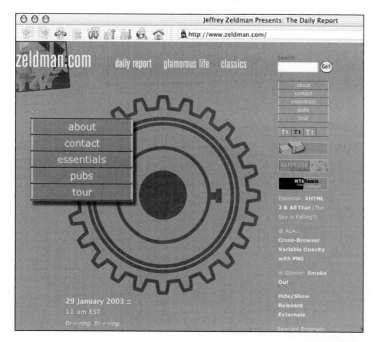

12.10

Applying CSS rules to an unordered list creates the visual effect of navigation "buttons" (enlarged, inset). The list's markup must be compacted to avoid the whitespace bug in IE/Windows (www.zeldman.com).

This is harder to read and edit than the normal version that uses whitespace, but we have no choice if we want our site to display correctly in an extremely popular browser. In removing whitespace, we also shave our file size by a byte or two, which provides some consolation for the entire hassle. The CSS that creates these menu button effects is reprinted next and can be viewed in situ at `http://www.zeldman.com/c/sophisto.css`.

```
#secondarynav ul {
     list-style: none;
     padding: 0;
     margin: 0;
     border: 0;
     }

#secondarynav li    {
     text-align: center;
     border-bottom: 1px solid #066;
     width: 100px;
     margin: 0;
     padding: 0 1px 1px 1px;
     font: 10px/12px verdana, arial, sans-serif;
     color: #cff;
     background: #399;
     }

#secondarytop    {
     border-top: 1px solid #066;
     }

#secondarynav li a {
     display: block;
     width: 96px;
     font-weight: normal;
     padding: 1px;
     border-left: 2px solid #6cc;
     border-right: 2px solid #6cc;
     background-color: #399;
     color: #cff;
     text-decoration: none;
     }

#secondarynav li a:hover {
     font-weight: normal;
     border-left: 2px solid #9cc;
```

```
    border-right: 2px solid #9cc;
    background-color: #5aa;
    color: #fff;
    text-decoration: none;
    }
```

We will use nearly identical markup and rules for our CSS redesign in Chapter 16. For more ways that CSS can be used to turn structured lists into graphical navigation elements, see Mark Newhouse's "CSS Design: Taming Lists" (http://www.alistapart.com/stories/taminglists/).

The "Float" Bug in IE6/Windows

Earlier in this chapter we explained how the CSS "float" property allows one element to sit alongside another. For instance, the rule that follows would cause a div with the unique id of "maintext" to float to the left of a sidebar or other right-hand element:

```
#maintext    {
    float: left;
    }
```

You'd better hope that the text in "maintext" is short and to the point. IE6/Windows has an unfortunate bug whereby long passages of text contained in a floating div are artificially truncated, preventing the reader from seeing the complete text while also causing the scrollbar to disappear. To see the complete text or restore the browser's scrollbar, the reader must (get this) refresh the page or press F11 twice in quick succession. Do your site's visitors routinely press F11 twice in succession upon loading any new web page? Neither do ours.

The problem affects an unknown (and hopefully small) percentage of IE6 users, but that's like saying it affects only a small percentage of the Chinese. The bug was first spotted and reported in 2001, while IE6/Windows was still in beta, and Microsoft's engineers have tried to fix it. However, as this book goes to press in 2003, the bug remains.

Microsoft's engineers might be unable to reproduce the bug in their labs or track down its cause, but the independent design community seems to have discovered the source of the problem, as well as a workaround. Read on.

Stuck on Old Values

Apparently, IE6 has trouble calculating the heights of block-level elements. Eddie Traversa of http://dhtmlnirvana.com/ found that IE6/Windows caches the values it calculates on one page of a site and then incorrectly applies those values to other pages. For instance, if the "maintext" div happened to be 300px tall on the first page of your site and 1400px tall on the following page, IE6 might display only the first 300px. Manually reloading each page "fixes" this bug by clearing the cache of the stuck initial value—until the reader clicks through to a new page and begins a new cycle of stuck values and unreadable text.

Fixed with a Script

The first step is acknowledging that you have a problem. The second is diagnosing that problem's exact nature. In the third step, programmer Aaron Boodman of Youngpup.net wrote a tiny JavaScript function that, in the presence of IE/Windows, iterates an existing property of the floated block, causing the page to reflow and display correctly. Here is Aaron's entire script:

```
if (document.all && window.attachEvent)
➥window.attachEvent("onload", fixWinIE);
function fixWinIE() {
        if (document.body.scrollHeight
            ➥< document.all.content.offsetHeight) {
                document.all.content.style.display = 'block';
        }
}
```

If you prefer, feel free to copy and paste these few lines of JavaScript from the beginning of http://www.alistapart.com/tightmen.js. These lines might allow you, too, to create CSS layouts that use float fearlessly. In your own version, replace references to .content with the name of your floated div. For instance, if your page contains floated content in a div whose id name is "maintext," your code should read as follows:

```
if (document.all && window.attachEvent) window.attachEvent
➥("onload", fixWinIE);
function fixWinIE() {
        if (document.body.scrollHeight <
            ➥document.all.maintext.offsetHeight) {
                document.all.maintext.style.display='block';
        }
}
```

Another way to do it is to avoid the whole thing by using CSS absolute position-ing to emulate float—a technique we will use in Chapter 16.

Flash and QuickTime: Objects of Desire?

Many of us embed multimedia objects such as Flash and QuickTime movies in our sites. There is no standards-compliant way of doing so that works reliably across multiple browsers and platforms. To understand how this can be, we must tell a tale of hubris and vengeance as floridly melodramatic as anything in Shakespeare or Italian opera. Well, okay, not quite that melodramatic, but close.

Embeddable Objects: A Tale of Hubris and Revenge

When the creators of the original Mosaic and Netscape browsers first seized on the brilliant idea of allowing designers to include images in web pages, they "extended" HTML by creating an `<img>` tag specifically for their browsers. The W3C did not approve. It advised web authors to use the `object` element instead. But millions of websites later, the `<img>` tag was still going strong—and support for the W3C's `<object>` element was nonexistent.

Then came the FutureSplash plug-in (later rechristened Flash) along with other multimedia elements such as Real and QuickTime movies. Again, the W3C suggested that the `<object>` tag be used to embed such content in web pages. But Netscape invented the `<embed>` tag instead—and as competitive browsers came onto the scene, they too supported Netscape's `<embed>` tag.

In the view of Netscape and Microsoft, their customers expected the web to function as a rich multimedia space, and it was up to browser makers to fulfill that desire through innovation—not coincidentally gaining market share in the process.

In the view of the W3C, browser makers were creating their own tags and ignor-ing perfectly good (standard) specifications. And what was the point of creating useful, open specifications if W3C member companies paid them no heed? In the years to come, the W3C would wreak a bloody double vengeance on those who had ignored its beautiful standards.

(Okay, okay, they wouldn't wreak a bloody double vengeance or anything of the kind. They simply did what their charter told them to do and what they felt certain was right. Namely, they established markup standards that made sense. But it's a lot more fun to tell it the way we're telling it. Indulge us.)

The Double Vengeance of W3C

The W3C's first act of revenge was to avoid including the <embed> tag in any official HTML specification, in spite of the fact that hundreds of thousands of designers were using it on millions of sites. <embed> was not included in HTML 3.2. It was not added to HTML 4 or to HTML 4.01, whose sole purpose was to include commonly used tags that had been left out of HTML 4. And because XHTML 1 was based on HTML 4.01, <embed> was not part of XHTML, either. Therefore, any site that used <embed> could not—and still cannot—validate as HTML or XHTML.

That is correct. You read that right. Millions of sites that embed multimedia cannot validate against a W3C spec because the W3C never deigned to recognize the <embed> element.

As if the wound still smarts, and yet more vengeance is desired, the W3C has banished the humble <img> element from its initial XHTML 2.0 specification (see "Which XHTML Is Right for You?" in Chapter 5, "Modern Markup"). You want pictures? Use <object>. You want Flash? Use <object>. You want QuickTime? Use <object>. So says the W3C.

The trouble is, support for <object> is sketchy in some modern browsers and nonexistent in older ones. And designers are not going to stop using Flash or embedding other kinds of multimedia content simply because the W3C objects (sorry!) to the tags they use. When a designer believes in and uses web standards but needs to embed rich content, what can she do?

Twice-Cooked Satay: Embedding Multimedia While Supporting Standards

In November 2002, Drew McLellan of Dreamweaverfever.com and The Web Standards Project conducted an experiment. In an article for A List Apart magazine, Drew discarded the bloated, invalid markup universally used to embed Flash content in web pages, replacing it with lean, compliant XHTML (http://www.alistapart.com/stories/flashsatay/). He threw away the invalid `<embed>` element altogether and replaced cumbersome IE-style markup such as this:

```
classid="clsid:D27CDB6E-AE6D-11cf-96B8-444553540000"
```

with compliant markup like this:

```
type="application/x-shockwave-flash"
```

The HTML that Flash generates when you publish a movie typically looks like this:

```
<object classid="clsid:D27CDB6E-AE6D-11cf-96B8-444553540000"
    codebase="http://download.macromedia.com
    /pub/shockwave/cabs/flash/swflash.cab#version=6,0,0,0"
      width="400" height="300" id="movie" align="">
      <param name="movie" value="movie.swf">
    <embed src="movie.swf" quality="high" width="400"
      height="300" name="movie" align=""
      ➥type="application/x-shockwave-flash"
    pluginspage="http://www.macromedia.com/go/
    ➥getflashplayer">
</object>
```

The HTML is obese and invalid, but it works for any browser in which the Flash plug-in has been installed. Drew honed it down to the following lean, clean, and valid XHTML:

```
<object type="application/x-shockwave-flash" data="movie.swf"
    width="400" height="300">
      <param name="movie" value="movie.swf" />
</object>
```

Not only is Drew's version lean, clean, and valid, but it also actually plays Flash movies in Netscape and IE browsers. Alas, these movies do not stream in IE/Windows, due to who knows what bug. The lack of streaming is not a terrible problem if your Flash content is limited to a few K. It *is* a major problem if your Flash files are large.

Drew solved the IE/Windows streaming problem by using one small Flash movie to load a larger movie. It seemed that a standards-compliant way of embedding multimedia had at last been found. After testing Drew's Flash Satay method in every available browser and platform, A List Apart published the article.

A Fly in the Ointment: Object Failures

Regretfully, after the article was published, another problem was discovered. Instead of the embedded Flash content, some visitors saw a blank text area [**12.11, 12.12**]. This happened mainly in IE/Windows browsers (5, 5.5, and 6), although most IE/Windows users were able to view the Flash content as expected. Similar problems were reported with Konqueror and Mozilla in Linux. As with the IE6 float bug described earlier in this chapter, the object bug affected an unknown percentage of users.

How many users were affected? Hundreds? Thousands? Millions? It was enough that the discussion forum (`http://www.alistapart.com/stories/flashsatay/discuss/`) associated with the article was soon filled with bug reports.

According to a published comparison of object implementations in browsers (`http://www.student.oulu.fi/~sairwas/object-test/results/`), IE/Windows and other user agents that sometimes inexplicably failed to display the Flash movie are supposed to understand and correctly handle the `<object>` element. IE/Windows has similar problems when `<object>` is used to embed an image, as XHTML 2 recommends. Drew's `<object>` method seems to work for most users, but most might not be enough. Because `<object>` is supposed to work and because it *does* work in nearly all browsers most of the time, some designers use the `<object>` method. But for others, the need to embed rich media content still remains incompatible with the goal of standards compliance.

Cheating with JavaScript *document.write*

In an effort to embed Flash content and still achieve XHTML validation, some designers have used JavaScript browser detection and `document.write` to sneak the invalid `<embed>` tags past the W3C validation testing service:

```
<!-- used to create valid xhtml with embed tag -->
<script type="text/javascript">
//<![CDATA[
if (navigator.mimeTypes && navigator.mimeTypes["application/
➥x-shockwave-flash"]){
document.write('<embed src="/media/yourflashmovie.swf" ...
```

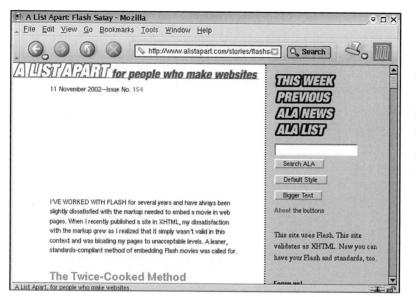

12.11
The Satay method uses 100% valid markup to embed Flash content, but it can fail mysteriously in some browsers, as it does here in Mozilla (SuSE Linux 8.0), even with Flash installed [12.12] (`http://www.alistapart.com/stories/flashsatay/`).

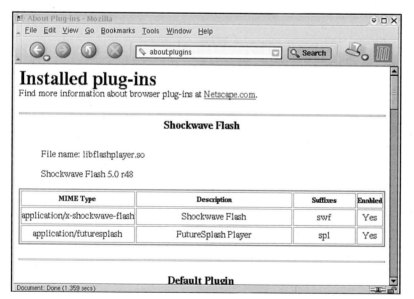

12.12
Flash 5 is installed and markup is valid, yet the Flash file does not play for this particular user.

This technique works; the Flash displays correctly in all JavaScript-capable browsers (unless the user has bought into the "JavaScript is the bogeyman of security risks" hype and turned off JavaScript), and the W3C validation service is fooled into thinking that your page's markup is kosher.

But as we said at the beginning of this chapter, we don't strive for XHTML validation to win a gold star. Tricking the validation service is not the same thing as achieving compliance.

In the highly unlikely circumstance that your client (or boss) demands standards compliance along with reliably embedded multimedia, the JavaScript method will allow you to seem to fulfill both requirements. But we recommend being honest with your client or boss, explaining the problems described earlier in the simplest language possible, and accepting that—for now at least—those parts of your site that use embedded rich media will not validate.

As a glance at any newspaper will remind you, we live in an imperfect world where noble ideals clash daily with harsh realities. Inability to achieve XHTML compliance while embedding Flash or QuickTime content is the least of anyone's worries. As browser handling of `<object>` improves, we will eventually be able to use it fearlessly to insert multimedia content into perfectly compliant sites.

A Workaday, Workaround World

Workarounds help us begin fulfilling the promise of standards ("create once, publish everywhere") in spite of the fact that no browser is perfect and some are less perfect than others. In so doing, workarounds free us to improve our sites' content, design, and usability, instead of wasting costly hours on proprietary, dead-end technologies.

But not everyone approves of workarounds, however practical or beneficial. In the view of some, if browsers don't fully or correctly support a given W3C spec, it is too bad for that browser's users—or the standard should simply be avoided. The problems with this perspective are many, including these:

- If you limit yourself to specifications that are completely and accurately supported by all browsers, guess what? You can't create a web page. Even HTML 3.2 is not universally and accurately supported in its entirety.

- Getting standards right takes time—and time is tight in competitive markets. Commercial pressures sometimes force engineers to release products before nailing every nuance of a particular specification. Occasionally they must release software knowing it is flawed. (Netscape 6.0 and IE 6.0 both contained bugs of which their engineers were aware,

such as the IE6 float bug mentioned earlier in this chapter.) If we are
too purity conscious to use workarounds, our site's visitors will suffer
needlessly.

- Specifications are occasionally vague in places, and some specs change
  after being published. Take CSS2—please. As mentioned a few pages ago,
  CSS2 was revised to CSS2.1 in 2002 because the original version contained
  a few obscure or nonworkable ideas. When goal posts move, teams
  fumble. Likewise, in the original CSS1 specification, the scaling factor
  between adjacent font size keywords was 1.5. Netscape 4, of all browsers,
  implemented keyword scaling exactly the way W3C said browser makers
  should. And guess what? Small fonts were too small, and big fonts were
  too big. The spec changed later.

- Most of us must compensate for the flaws of older user agents, particularly
  if those flawed agents are still widely used—as IE5.x/Windows, with its
  incorrectly implemented CSS Box model, is.

Readers who fear that by recommending workarounds, we are leading them into
a morally questionable universe, should note that all workarounds shared in
this chapter are perfectly compliant. We are not writing proprietary code or
junk markup to work around browser limitations. We are using standards to
support standards. For instance, in the Box Model Hack, we are using CSS2
selectors to ensure that browsers with broken box models get our CSS1 layout
requirements right. We are removing needless whitespace from our markup
and striving to create text that is legible and accessible to all.

There is nothing wrong with these techniques, and much right with them; they
allow us to use standards today instead of turning our eyes to a distant horizon
filled with perfect browsing software. As browsers improve, and as old browsers
fall into disuse, fewer workarounds will be needed, although we might continue
to use them to ensure that our sites are as backward compatible as they are
forward looking. In the next chapter, we'll conclude our brief survey of browser
joys and sorrows by examining one of the most basic aspects of design—namely,
the control of typography.

chapter thirteen

Working with Browsers Part III: Typography

Along with positioning and color, typography is a basic and essential tool of design. Print designers spend years studying the history and application of type. They learn to distinguish between faces that, to the uninitiated, look almost identical, such as Arial versus Helvetica. When these traditionally educated designers come to the web, with its limited and contradictory typographic toolsets, they have often been less well equipped to navigate its tight and rocky shoals than those from a nontraditional design background.

Size Matters

Windows, UNIX, and Macintosh come with different installed fonts, at different default resolutions, and often with different default rendering styles—from pixellated to gently antialiased (as in Mac OS 9) to type so smooth that it borders on Photoshop text (as in Mac OS X Jaguar by default, and Windows XP with Cleartype—but only if the user turns on the Cleartype option). The old `<font size=3>` thus means something different among operating systems, not only in size but also in appearance. Sadly, most CSS font-sizing methods also result in different sizes from one operating system to the next, despite efforts by leading browser makers to reduce or eliminate cross-browser problems by establishing a standard default font size.

User Control

In addition to differences between platforms, outdated methods, and CSS renderings, the web differs from print in that the user is supposed to retain some control over what she sees. Accommodating the user is as tricky with standards as it is with old-school methods, due to problems discussed in this chapter. (And oh, boy, will we discuss these problems in this chapter.) It is also difficult for traditionally trained designers to accept the premise of user control. Sadder still, CSS methods (ems, percentages, font size keywords) that are intended to deliver user control suffer from cross-browser and cross-platform problems. For one brief shining moment, these problems were resolved by the goodwill of browser makers, as they agreed to uniformly support a cross-platform standard size. But new browsers are unwittingly undoing that good work, making it tougher to balance design requirements with the user's need for control.

In this chapter, we will discuss the history and problems of web typography and study two methods of setting text via web standards. Both methods work well but neither one is perfect. We will also look at methods that are even less perfect because they're more fraught with problems. Thirteen is an unlucky number; designers who care about branding and design but who also want to do right by all users face tough and occasionally unfortunate choices, as this chapter will explain. We'll cover the techniques, their benefits, and their occasionally unhappy risks and tradeoffs. As always, you will decide which tradeoffs work best for your audience.

Old-School Horrors

Tim Berners-Lee, the inventor of the web and the founder of the W3C, viewed his creation as a medium for the easy exchange of text documents; therefore, he included no typographic control in the structured language of HTML. As described in the section "Jumping Through Hoops" in Chapter 2, "Designing and Building with Standards," web designers initially used `<tt>`, `<pre>`, `<blockquote>`, and semantically meaningless paragraph tags to vary typefaces, achieve positioning effects, and simulate leading. They next began using GIF or

Flash images of text, a practice that continues to this day [13.1], often at the hands of skilled designers who have difficulty accepting the limitations of CSS and XHTML and the tradeoffs that are inherent in balancing user versus designer needs.

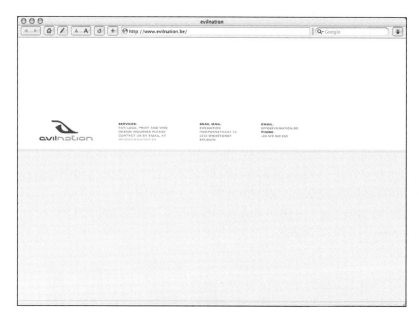

13.1
Every "word" on this page (http://www.evilnation.be/) is a Flash vector, not real text, hence not searchable, accessible, or amenable to copying and pasting. Skilled designers who care about typography often have difficulty accepting the limitations of XHTML and CSS and the tradeoffs of user control.

By 1995, with commercial sites springing up right and left and designers hacking HTML to ribbons, something had to be done to provide at least a few basic typographic tools. Netscape gave us the `<font>` tag whose attribute was size. You could specify numbers (`<font size=2>`) or relative numbers based on the user's default (`<font size=+1>`). Designers quickly abandoned paragraph tags and other structural elements and controlled their layouts by combining `<font size...>` with `<br>` tags. Not to be outdone, Microsoft gave us `<font face...>`.

Most readers of this book will remember those days and will also recall the problems—chiefly, those of platform difference. Windows assumed a default base size of 16px at 96ppi (pixels per inch). Macintosh, closely tied to print design, assumed a size of 12px at 72ppi based on the PostScript standard. Font sizes that looked dandy on one platform looked too big or too small on the other.

"Stupid Windows," said the Mac-based designers.

"Stupid Macintosh," said the Windows-based designers.

Points of Difference

Next came early CSS implementations such as that of IE3, thrusting the cross-platform problem into even greater relief. Points (pts) are a unit of print, not of the screen, but designers are familiar with points, and many chose to specify their web text using this unit. In the Windows world, 7pt type was 9px tall, which is the lowest threshold of legibility. On the Mac, 7pt type was 7px tall, making it illegible, and as useless as a beard on a baby.

In 1997, Microsoft.com chose 7pt type [**13.2**] to ballyhoo the CSS prowess of their new IE3 browser for Windows and Macintosh. This was like inviting folks to a movie premiere and de-focusing the projector before screening. The type was equally illegible in IE4.x and in Netscape 4 on the Macintosh, not because of browser problems, but because of platform differences. Todd Fahrner, soon to be the father of DOCTYPE switching (see Chapter 11, "Working with Browsers Part I: DOCTYPE Switching and Standards Mode"), posted Figure **13.2** on his personal site, annotating it to show that points were a useless unit of CSS in terms of screen design (although they are fine for print style sheets).

13.2

In this mid-1990s screen shot, Todd Fahrner documented problems of CSS misuse including screen type specified in points (`http://style.cleverchimp.com/font_size/points/font_wars.GIF`). Such type was often illegible on the Macintosh due to platform differences.

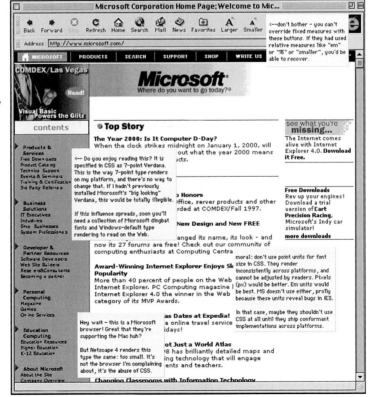

Fahrner also pointed (sorry) out that text set in points and pixels could not (at the time) be resized via the browser's built-in font size adjustment widget. This was not because CSS1 considered points and pixels fixed units. (CSS1 did not define *any* sizing method as being nonresizable.) It was simply a decision made by the first browser makers to begin supporting CSS. The user *could* reset type set in ems and percentages, but IE3, IE4, and Netscape 4 all suffered from horrendous bugs where type set in ems or percentages was concerned. Fahrner would soon propose a solution to at least some of these problems.

At the time the screen shot shown in Figure **13.2** was posted, the only size unit that worked the same way across browsers and platforms was the nonresizable pixel. Five years later, the only reliable unit is still the pixel, and it is still non-resizable in IE/Windows.

A Standard Size at Last—But for How Long?

In an effort to transcend platform differences, the makers of Netscape and Microsoft's browsers and Mozilla put their heads together in late 1999 and decided to standardize on a default font size setting of 16px/96ppi across platforms. By putting all platforms on the same page, as it were, browser makers and users could avoid the problems of cross-platform size differences and cruelly useless, illegible text.

The 16px/96ppi Font Size Standard

On a W3C mailing list in 1998, the plucky Todd Fahrner puckishly proposed standardizing on a 16px default per Windows usage. His recommendation was adopted by all leading browser makers in the year 2000. Although Fahrner's concerns were practical in nature (he wanted to ensure that type could be read online), in the quotation that follows, he refers to something that might strike you as bizarre.

The framers of CSS were bound to a pet abstraction wherein the "average" length of a web user's arm was essential to defining the size of a pixel. No, really. Anyway, in advancing his idea about a standardized cross-platform font size, Fahrner was careful to cover the all-important arm length issue along with more pedestrian matters like usability. He wrote:

continues

continued

Since before Mosaic, the default font size value in all major browsers has been set at 12pt. I propose redefining the default as 16px.... The current default of 12pt rasterizes very differently across platforms. On Macs, it rasterizes into 12px (logical res fixed at 72ppi). On Wintel PCs, it rasterizes by default into 16px (logical res defaults to 96ppi). ...All scalable font-size values... operate relative to this inconsistent base rasterization. For a designer, this means that the only way to suggest a [consistent cross-platform] font size is to use CSS pixel units, which are not user-scalable, and are thus not optimally user-friendly/portable...

The appropriate corrective measure... is for Mac (and X11?) browsers to break with tradition and ship with the default value of "medium" text set at 16px, instead of 12pt. This should of course remain subject to user adjustment, but a consistent initial value will at least make the use of scalable font-size values less problematic for designers, as any variance from the default will be due to express user preference rather than capricious legacy OS differences.

If designers tend to believe that 16px is too large as a base, why suggest it as the default?

One reason is pure expediency. The Mac is a smallish minority platform, though very strongly represented in the web design field. (I use a Mac!) It is unrealistic to expect that Windows/X11 browsers will change their defaults to match the Mac's rather quaint limitation to 72ppi logical resolution.

The 1996 CSS1 standard suggests a 1/90" value for a "reference pixel," extrapolated from a visual angle of 0.0227 degrees visual angle at arm's length. [User agents] are expected to scale pixels appropriately if the physical resolution is known to vary significantly from this value. A 1/90" reference pixel would suggest a rasterization of 12pt into 15px, rather than 16. 15 is, of course, much closer to 16 than to 12, however. Because no OS/UA currently assumes a 90ppi logical resolution (nor implements pixel-scaling) ... the reference pixel value should be amended to 1/96". It's simple to preserve the suggested 0.0227 degrees visual angle by giving the reference user a longer arm's length.

Designers think that 16px is too large simply because they are used to the 12px base size of their Macs. Readability is 9/10ths familiarity.

http://lists.w3.org/Archives/
Public/www-style/1998Dec/0030.html

Two years later, the first generation of significantly standards-compliant browsers embraced Fahrner's recommendation. In Internet Explorer, Netscape, and Mozilla, on both the Windows and Macintosh platforms, the default text size became 16px/96ppi, and increased legibility was enjoyed throughout the globe (except when users quickly changed it back).

Fahrner's efforts eventually led the W3C to agree to a standard reference pixel size related to the 16px/96ppi concept, as seen in the CSS 2.1 working draft. In the excerpt that follows, you'll note that the W3C remains quite concerned about the average length of a reader's arm. We should be grateful they're only talking about the length of an *arm*:

> It is recommended that the reference pixel be the visual angle of one pixel on a device with a pixel density of 96dpi and a distance from the reader of an arm's length. For a nominal arm's length of 28 inches, the visual angle is therefore about 0.0213 degrees.
> —CSS 2.1 Working Draft,
> http://www.w3.org/TR/CSS21/syndata.html#length-units

While the standard reference pixel would seem to clear the way for a W3C standard user default size, the two are not officially related. The W3C has spoken to the first issue, but not to the second.

Netscape 6+, Mozilla, IE5+/Macintosh, and IE/Windows offered all users the same default font size setting. As long as the user did not change her preferences, points, ems, percentages, and font size keywords would work the same way across platforms, and no user would be needlessly hurt because of a designer or developer's ignorance about platform differences. There were still bugs and inheritance problems in some browsers' implementation of percentages and ems (more about those problems a few pages later), but the primary hurdle had been cleared.

Alas, browser makers don't explain why they do what they do, and web users don't study design issues (and why would they?). The benefit of a standard size evaporated as users changed preferences and designers missed the point— literally.

Good Works Undone with a Click

An unknown percentage of Macintosh users, disgusted by text sizes they perceived (not incorrectly) to be huge and ugly, immediately switched their browsers back to the old 12px/72ppi setting, thus defeating the attempt at standardization and placing themselves once again in the position of being unable to read the text on many sites. On the web, the user is supposed to be in charge, and that remains true even if he doesn't realize what is in his best interest.

When these "switch back to 12px" fans happen to be designers, they might produce sites that look great on the Macintosh but appear to suffer from a glandular condition in the dominant Windows space. Many Macintosh-based designers misguidedly use 12px/72ppi, and their work (or their audience) suffers as a result.

Of course, many Windows users also find the 16px default too big for their liking and consequently set their browser to view all websites at a text setting below the norm. When Mac and Windows users do these things, it has no effect on sites that use pixels to specify type sizes, but it does cause problems for sites that use ems, percentages, and (to a lesser extent) CSS font size keywords. We will examine these dilemmas as this chapter unfolds.

Sniffing Oblivion: The Wrong Reaction to the Change in Browsers

Users who switched to smaller-than-standard type were simply making themselves more comfortable. They were not the only ones to miss the point of a standard size, nor should they have been expected to understand it. Many web professionals also missed the point, in part because Netscape and Microsoft did not publicize it.

In particular, the Browser Quirks Brigade, who had come to believe that browsers would always differ greatly in appearance and behavior and that the way to solve these differences was to combine browser detection with code forks and tag soup, quickly did what they had been trained to do.

Prior to 2000, instead of using pixels to ensure that text rendered at the same size on virtually any browser or platform, these developers had used points. Because points were (a) meaningless in terms of the screen and (b) implemented in vastly different ways between the two dominant computing platforms, these developers had created multiple, point-driven style sheets, using platform detection to serve one point-driven style sheet to Windows users, another to Macintosh users. Often, it got far more complicated than that, but we haven't had our breakfast yet.

The Snake Swallows Its Tail: Conditional CSS

With the release in 2000 of standards-compliant browsers that supported the same default font size and resolution across platforms, web designers had the opportunity to abandon browser detection and point-driven, conditional CSS. Instead, the Browser Quirks Brigade updated their scripts and banged out additional conditional CSS files. "Additional conditional" sounds funny, doesn't it? The results were anything but.

Instead of working as they were supposed to, these extended scripts and conditional files often defeated their own purpose, resulting in illegible or bizarrely formatted pages, as described in Part I, "Houston, We Have a Problem." The scripts and the ill-conceived style sheets they served often seemed to behave like a malfunctioning robot waiter.

> **Browsers**: We'll all take the chicken dinner.
>
> **Waiter**: Okay, that's two burgers and one vegetarian meal.
>
> **Browsers**: No, chicken. We all want chicken, please.
>
> **Waiter**: Hold on a second [spoken to a particular browser], I know what *you* want, little man. You want ice cream with your burger!
>
> **Browsers**: Chicken, chicken, we all want chicken.
>
> **Waiter**: You like ice cream, boy? Sure, who doesn't like ice cream?
>
> **Browsers**: [Beginning to weep] Chicken.
>
> **Waiter**: And whipped cream! There you go, have a nice day, pay as you exit.

Most of the developers who created these little nightmares of nonusability were not stupid. Often, they were highly skilled, highly experienced, and (let's be honest) highly paid professionals. Their clients forked over big bucks for needlessly complicated sites that never worked right and that required constant, expensive maintenance to continue failing in ever more complex ways at increasingly higher costs. It doesn't sound like what any sane being would desire, but it was (and often still is) the norm.

Eventually, coffers empty, budgets evaporate, and owner and visitors are stuck with an obsolete site as described in Chapter 1. With the shadow of doom upon them, in an effort to forestall the inevitable, some developers will slap a "Best viewed with…" banner on their front page. This is like popping a Surgeon General's warning on a pack of cigarettes and expecting it to turn into a jar of vitamins.

We can prevent such chaos when we understand that browsers support common standards and that the best solution is often the simplest. (That is, send all browsers the same style sheet and avoid pts except for print.) Lucky are you, who bought this book; unlucky are those who still believe that every browser is supposed to act differently, and that with a sufficiently swollen budget and a Ph.D. in tail swallowing, the nonproblem of platform difference can be "solved" through Escher-like convolutions. Gosh, that was quite a sentence. (Must. Delete. Overwrought. Sentence. Before. Manuscript.)

Chimera and Safari: Great Performance, Shame About the Size

As this book nears publication, emerging browsers for Macintosh OS X, although excellent and even inspiring in many ways, are unfortunately undoing the good work of 2000 where standard font sizes are concerned. The Gecko-based Chimera (Navigator) browser and Apple's KHTML-based Safari are both in beta as of this writing, but they are widely distributed and have already won many fans. Both betas offer solid support for CSS and other standards, and Chimera's is especially meritorious because it combines the standards compliance of Mozilla/Gecko with the silken text rendering and advanced user features of OS X. By the time you read this, Chimera may have changed its name to Camino due to a legal issue (`http://www.mozilla.org/projects/camino/`). We'll continue to refer to the browser as Chimera because that is how it's known as this book goes to press.

Alas, neither Chimera nor Safari currently ships with the 16px font size default. Both come set at 14px, which is neither the standard setting nor the pre-2000 Macintosh default. The manufacturers seem to be hedging their bets, giving Mac users fonts that fall shy of the standard but are hopefully not too small to render text legibly. Like Goldilocks, they seem to have decided that 14px porridge is "just right."

This might be what Macintosh users want, but it is a slippery slope. Indeed, the preference panels [13.3, 13.4] of both browsers make it tough to switch to 16px, which is not offered as one of the defaults, although the number can be entered manually if the user knows and is inclined to do so. Some users do change their browsers' default font sizes and faces, but few indeed base these changes on an arcane and preternatural awareness of standards. Thus, in both of these OS X browsers, at their default settings, unless a web page's text has been specified in pixel values, Mac users will once more have to put up with undersized text whose lower range might be illegible to them.

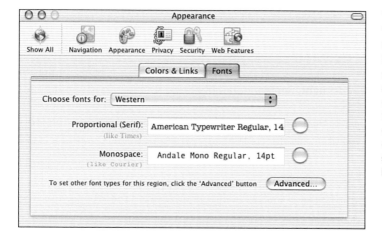

13.3

The Gecko-based Chimera (Navigator) browser for OS X offers superb standards compliance, but unfortunately does not ship with the 16px size default. Nor does its Preference pane offer an obvious way to switch to 16px (if users knew to do so).

13.4

The surprisingly standards-savvy Apple Safari beta browser also ships with a nonstandard size, and its Preference pane is as unlikely as Chimera's to lead users to choose the 16px standard setting. In both OS X browsers, at their default settings, Mac users will once more have to put up with undersized text.

The Effect of Nonstandard Sizes on Accessible Text Treatments

Figures **13.5** through **13.10** show the i3Forum site we created in Chapters 8, "XHTML by Example: A Hybrid Layout (Part I)," 9, "CSS Basics," and 10, "CSS in Action: A Hybrid Layout (Part II)," using ems to enable users to resize text in any browser, even the maddeningly stubborn IE6/Windows. You will notice that there are variations in page height because each browser comes with differing depths of user interface chrome, and there is a waste of vertical space in the free version of Opera [**13.8**] because it includes paid advertising banners to subsidize the cost of development.

In spite of these differences, you can readily see that text is the same size in Netscape 7/Macintosh (**13.5**), IE5/Macintosh (**13.6**), IE6/Windows (**13.7**), and Opera 7/Windows (**13.8**). This suggests that browser and platform detection, as well as conditional CSS serving different point sizes for different platforms, is a load of phlegm no designer should pursue and no client should pay for.

You can also see that text is noticeably smaller in Chimera/Camino (**13.9**) and Safari (**13.10**) than the others. Indeed, the text is downright dinky, a problem that shows up more clearly in serif faces like the one used here (Georgia) than in sans-serifs, which tend to stay crisp in milk and legible even at small sizes. In short, some Chimera and Safari users might find the site hard to read. They can easily resize the type via Text Zoom, and in so doing solve the problem. But not every user knows about Text Zoom, and some might find the initially small size annoying.

We can only hope that the brilliant and standards-aware engineers behind Chimera and the equally gifted team behind Safari will see the wisdom of supporting the common 16px/96ppi default font size and will do so in an upgrade. (By the time you read this, Safari may have switched to the 16px/96ppi defult.) In using relative em-based sizes, we were doing what accessibility advocates have long advised, but it doesn't work well unless all browsers support the same default font size. It also doesn't work well in other circumstances, as you are about to see.

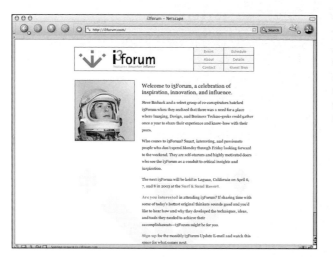

13.5
The i3Forum site we created in Chapters 8 through 10 uses ems to control font sizes. Here we see it in Netscape 7 on the Macintosh platform (www.i3forum.com).

13.6
Here it is again, in IE5/Mac. Although the page appears slightly deeper due to differences in browser chrome, the text size is the same.

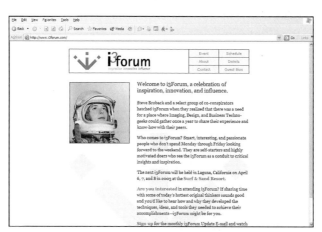

13.7
When we switch to Windows XP and IE6, text size remains the same.

13.8

Likewise, when viewed in Opera 7, text size holds steady. The benefit of the default font size setting used by all these browsers should be clear. Text is both legible and resizable in all these browsers.

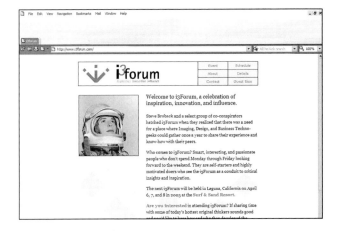

13.9

Alas, in the otherwise outstanding Chimera (Navigator) browser, text looks dinky and might be hard to read. Users can resize text easily, but they shouldn't have to bother—and a few users might not know how to do so.

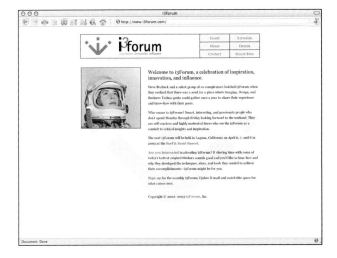

13.10

Like Chimera, Apple's Safari beta renders text smaller than the default size. We can only hope the engineers that are behind Safari and Chimera will see the wisdom of supporting the 16px/96ppi default.

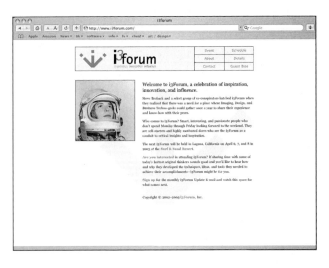

The Heartbreak of Ems

Accessibility advocates and the creators of CSS have long agreed that ems are the way to go. Sadly, they are often the way to go to hell. Listen to all the lectures, read all the books and articles, and you will come away feeling dirty and ashamed if you use anything other than ems to specify your type sizes. But the beautiful theory of ems breaks down in coarse practice—and not only in browsers that fail to support the common default font size.

On a minor note, there is the problem of old browsers. Netscape 4 ignores em and ex units that are applied to text, although it bizarrely respects these units when they are used for line height. IE3 treats em units as pixels. Thus, 2em is mistranslated as 2 pixels tall. Almost no one uses IE3 any more, but still.

Likewise, older browsers often bungle inheritance on nested elements sized with em units. Because fewer and fewer people are stuck with Netscape 4, we won't waste your time going into the details of that browser's mishandling of relatively sized nested elements. Just know that if you need to support outdated browsers and if you use em units (especially on nested elements), you are letting yourself and your users in for a world of pain [**13.11**].

Text as 0.8em.	Text as 0.8em.	Text as 0.8em.
Text as 0.8em with base 100%	Text as 0.8em with base 100%	Text as 0.8em with base 100%
Text as keyword small.	Text as keyword small.	Text as keyword small.
Text as keyword small, ALA style.	Text as keyword small, ALA style.	Text as keyword small, ALA style.

13.11
What's in an em? Not cross-platform, cross-browser size consistency, that's for sure (`http://www.thenoodleincident.com/tutorials/box_lesson/font/`).

User Choices and Em Units

A more common problem with em units is that users often downsize their default font size settings as noted several times in this chapter. Mac users switch back to 12px/72ppi; Windows folks set their browsers' View: Text Size menu to "small" rather than "medium." Such changes make any text sized below 1em smaller than it is supposed to be and might make it too small to be read. In 2002, CSS/DHTML expert Owen Briggs tested every available text sizing method across a vast range of browsers and platforms to find out what worked and what failed. 264 screen shots later, despite hoping to prove that ems were always viable, he had actually discovered the opposite [**13.11**].

Ems work well as long as you never spec your text below the user's default size. Ems work well as long as users never adjust their preferences. But most designers and many clients favor smaller type and many designs require them. Many users consider the 16px default size uncomfortable for normal reading and change their preference settings accordingly. When em units are used to design sites, the designer's and user's shrinkage efforts compound on one another, resulting in text that might be hard to read or even entirely illegible.

When you set small type with em units (or percentages), you run afoul of a universe of unknowable, uncontrollable user preference settings. What looks elegant on your monitor might be mouse type on your users'. If you commit this act in the name of accessibility, you're kidding yourself.

In the i3Forum site, we tried to minimize the potential damage by sticking to sizes that were only slightly smaller than 1em. But the user's mileage might vary.

Alternatively (`http://www.alistapart.com/stories/dao/`), client and aesthetics permitting, you can design all your sites using only normal or over-sized type set with em units. This will avoid size-based accessibility problems. But very few designs work with a default size of 16px and higher—and some users will complain that your site is ugly because the text is "too big." If the moral seems to be that you can't please everybody, the additional moral is that you are even less likely to please everybody when you use em units to specify your text size.

Some standards evangelists and some accessibility advocates will choose to disbelieve what we've said, just as some people choose to believe that the 1969 moon landing was a hoax. Was it T.S. Eliot or Woody Allen who said, "Too much reality is not what the people want."? Whoever said it first, he was right.

So what *do* the people want? They might want the two methods described in the remainder of this chapter, which seem to work better than any we have considered so far, although even the methods we are about to discuss have their problems.

Pixels Prove Pixels Work

Alone among all CSS values, with a few exceptions to be discussed next, the humble and much-maligned pixel (px) unit works in browsers old and new, compliant and noncompliant, on any platform you care to name. 13px is 13px whether viewed in Windows, Mac OS, or Linux/UNIX. Set your text in pixels, and it will look the same in Gecko/Mac OS X, [**13.12**], IE6/Windows [**13.13**], and Opera 7/Windows [**13.14**].

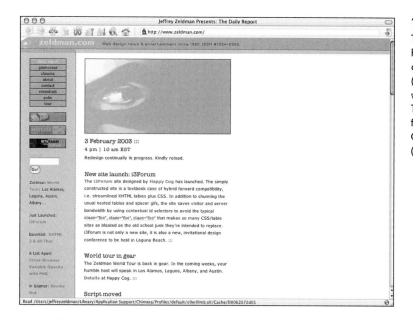

13.12
The beginnings of a February 2003 redesign of zeldman.com (`http://www.zeldman.com/`). Text is set in pixels; therefore, it is the same size in Chimera for Mac OS X (shown here)...

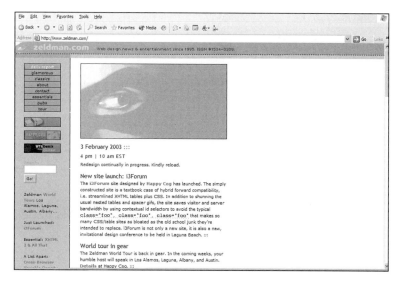

13.13
...as it is in IE6 for Windows XP. Not only that...

13.14
...it even looks the same
in Opera 7/Windows,
despite some theorists'
claims that Opera always
abstracts pixel values.

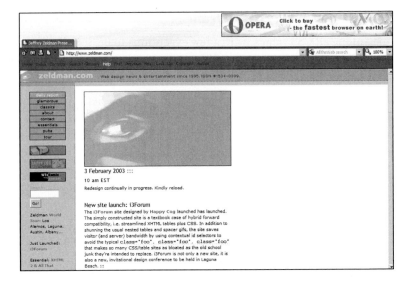

The benefits are not limited to fonts. Images are created in pixels. If our product shot is 200px × 200px and we use CSS to specify a left margin of 100px, we know that the size relationship of picture to margin will be 2:1, and we also know that all users will see this size relationship. At Happy Cog, we refer to the ability to create these size-based relationships as *pixelism*. Size-based relationships are a component not only of grid-based designs but also of rules-based designs, which we will discuss in Chapter 16, "A CSS Redesign."

For crisp layouts, pixels are a natural. If we say that our headline text is 25px tall, that our left margin is 100px, and that our body text is 11px, all users will see the same thing, although the real-world *size* of what they see will depend on their PC's resolution and their monitor's dimensions.

The Smallest Unit: It's Absolutely Relative

At a resolution of 1200×870, a single pixel looks hefty on a 22" monitor and petite on a 17" one. CSS considers the pixel a *relative* unit because monitors and resolutions vary. This is true. It is also true that 10px is 10px, from one corner of a screen to any other corner of that screen, and from one screen to the next. The pixel is always the smallest unit of a given screen, making it the atom of new media design. Most designers and most users thus think of the pixel as an *absolute* unit. Unlike most other units, the pixel is familiar to all web users regardless of their level of sophistication. They know the pixel from years of watching TV.

If the CSS standard views pixels abstractly (remember that "average length of the web user's arm" business), the makers of most browsers do not. They understand the pixel unit the way the rest of us understand it: as the smallest dot on the screen.

Thus, virtually all browsers, from the superb to the barely passable, support pixels the same way, and if you use px to specify your font sizes, you (and your users) will see what you expect in nearly every browser and on nearly every platform. As with any rule, there are exceptions: one sophisticated and vaguely troubling, and the other dumb and negligible.

When Pixels Fail in Opera

Some versions of the Opera browser consistently deliver smaller sizes than those specified. For example, if you specify 11px text, Opera 5 for Macintosh shows something closer to 10px.

Håkon (pronounced *How-come* or *Hokum*) Lie (pronounced *Lee*) is Opera's chief technical officer. He is also the father of CSS, to whom most designers with a lick of sense are grateful. Håkon Lie is also said to be the scientist who argued that CSS should define pixels abstractly (the arm length stuff) rather than the simple way the rest of us understand them (as the "smallest dot on the screen"). We might perhaps be less grateful for that—and relieved that most browser makers have chosen to understand pixels the way most humans do.

Some have argued that Opera's subsize handling of pixel values is based on the "average arm length" abstraction—as opposed to, say, calling it a bug in the Macintosh version of Opera that Opera doesn't seem to care about fixing. These intellectuals might be right, but we notice that Opera 7/Windows treats pixels the same way that other browsers do [13.14].

Given that Opera 7 now supports DOCTYPE switching, our intellectual readers might wonder if Opera 7 treats pixels the way other browsers treat them only when in Quirks mode, while continuing to treat pixels abstractly in Standards mode. These intellectual readers are over-thinking the issue. Figure 13.14 shows Opera 7 treating pixels the way the rest of us understand them; the page in question is valid XHTML 1.0 Transitional with CSS layout. Thus, we are strongly inclined to believe that Opera is determined to render pixels the way other browsers do, regardless of theoretical quibbles.

In short, when you use pixels to specify type sizes, most Opera users will see what you want them to see, although some folks who are using older versions of Opera might see something a bit smaller.

When Pixels Fail in Netscape 4 Point Something or Other

There is another exception to the fail-safe reliability of pixels. Some versions of Netscape 4 get pixel values wrong. In one or two incremental upgrades on one or two platforms, the old warhorse sometimes forgets how to interpret pixel units, as Grandfather sometimes forgets our names. Don't ask us which versions of Netscape 4 get pixels wrong. Is it 4.73 for Linux/UNIX? Is it 4.79 for Windows 98? We neither know nor care. *Most* versions of Netscape 4 get pixels right, even if they get practically everything else wrong.

This rare Netscape 4 pixel snafu has no basis in abstract theoretical concerns. It is simply a bug—one that users can avoid by upgrading to the next incremental version of the ancient relic, or preferably to a Netscape browser released in this century. Some users won't do it. One of them might be your boss or your client. If beating them about the head and shoulders with the nearest heavy object fails to enlighten them as to the benefits of a standards-compliant browser, start looking for a new job. (After beating your boss about the head and shoulders, you'll have to look for a new job anyway. What were you thinking?)

The Trouble with Pixels

The trouble with pixels has been discussed elsewhere in this book and mainly comes down to this: In IE/Windows, users cannot resize text set in pixels. If you've used 9px type for your site's body text, many visitors will click their browser's Back button faster than you can say *squint*. Even 11px type might be too small for some, depending on the font chosen (11px Verdana gets fewer complaints than 11px Times, for instance), the monitor size and resolution, the visitor's eyesight, the degree of foreground/background contrast, and the presence or absence of distracting backgrounds. To a person who has less than 20/20 vision, the problem might be annoying. To one who is seriously visually impaired, it might be far worse than that.

There is also the occasional CAD engineer who likes to surf the web on his 4,000×3,000 32" workstation monitor and pepper web design mailing lists with angry letters about flyspeck-sized text. If he actually wished to solve his problem, he could use a browser that supported Text Zoom or Page Zoom. If he preferred to use IE/Windows, he could switch on its option to ignore font sizes (described a few paragraphs later). He could even write a user style sheet like this one:

```
html, body {font-size: 1em !important;}
```

But he might rather complain about his problem than solve it in any of these ways.

As a designer, you are responsible for your users' problems, even bizarre problems like those of the man who views the web at an abnormally high resolution. The trouble with pixels is, like every other method of font sizing available to us, they inevitably upset one or more users.

No Size Fits Some

As this book goes to press, Text Zoom is three years old. Text Zoom solves the problem with pixels. Microsoft's Mac browser engineering team invented Text Zoom. You would think by now that Text Zoom would be part of IE/Windows. You would be wrong. We have lobbied for it. We have begged for it. We are now convinced that the world will expire in flames of apocalyptic destruction before Microsoft brings Text Zoom and other IE5/Macintosh user advances to its flagship Windows browser.

What IE/Windows offers instead [**13.15**, **13.16**] is an option to "ignore font sizes specified on web pages." Buried deep in Internet Options, General tab, Accessibility, this little-known feature allows the visually impaired (or those who use super high-resolution monitors) to view all web text at a size that suits them. At least, it allows those visually impaired users who can *find* the feature to view all web text at a size that suits them.

The feature is commendable, as far as it goes. But this all-or-nothing approach is not the same as Text Zoom (in IE5+/Macintosh, Netscape, Mozilla, Chimera, Kmeleon, and Safari since the Millennium) or Page Zoom (in Opera since the beginning of time).

Text size relationships convey meaning that gets lost when users can no longer see font sizes. The loss is acceptable if the designer has taken pains to write structural markup. But nonstructural markup currently dominates web production, as we know. With divitis and classitis as described throughout this book, text relationships are lost when sizes are turned off by this brute force method. Text Zoom and Page Zoom maintain size relationships that help readers make sense of content even if the content was poorly authored. IE/Windows is a fine browser, MSIE6 especially so. But hiding font sizes is no substitute for allowing users to enlarge or reduce text as needed.

13.15
Buried in IE/Windows is an option to ignore font sizes specified in web pages. The user must first navigate to the Internet Options, General tab and click on Accessibility (shown here).

13.16
The user must then choose Ignore Font Sizes Specified on Web Pages, click OK, and exit the dialog box.

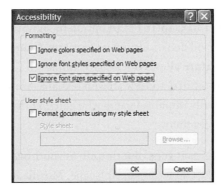

Given the current dominance of IE/Windows and its unwillingness to let its users scale text set in pixels, you will be tempted to give up on the reliable, cross-platform pixel. But you might not need to do so. In Chapter 15, "Working with DOM-Based Scripts," we'll explore a technique that allows designers to use pixels without punishing visually impaired IE/Windows users.

Meanwhile, we offer another possible approach that is accessibly resizable in any browser (even in IE/Windows) and that avoids most, although not all, of the problems associated with ems and percentages.

The Font Size Keyword Method

Little known and scarcely ever used, CSS1 (and later, CSS2) offered seven font size keywords intended to control text sizes without the absolutism of pixels or the inheritance, cross-platform, and user option hazards of ems and percentages. The seven keywords appear next, and their meaning will be obvious to anyone who has ever bought a tee shirt (`http://www.w3.org/TR/CSS2/fonts.html#value-def-absolute-size`):

```
xx-small
x-small
small
medium
large
x-large
xx-large
```

Why Keywords Beat Ems and Percentages

As mentioned earlier in "The Heartbreak of Ems," when you use ems or percentages, there is always the danger that their values will multiply, resulting in text that is too small or too large. By contrast, keyword values do not compound even when the elements nest. If `<body>` is `small`, `<div>` is `small`, and `<p>` is `small`, and p lives inside `div`, which lives inside `body`, the three small values do not compound (as ems and percentages do), and the result is still legible. Moreover, the result is still `small` (not `x-small` or `xx-small`). Ems and percentages compound. Keyword values do not compound.

In addition, at least in Gecko and modern IE browsers, `xx-small` can never be smaller than 9px, which means it can never be illegible. Text might be hard for some users to read, of course, but that is not the same thing as illegibility.

Like ems, keywords are based on the user's default font size. Unlike ems, keywords never descend below the threshold of adequate resolution. If the user's default size happened to be 10px (unlikely, but possible), `x-small` would be 9px and `xx-small` would also be 9px. Obviously, in such a case, you would lose the size difference between `x-small` and `xx-small`. But you wouldn't lose your readers.

Sounds perfect, doesn't it? We get to specify sizes without smacking up against IE/Windows' inability to resize pixels, and also without inflicting illegibly teeny type on any visitor. Font size keywords seem to balance accessibility with the designer's need for control. So what could go wrong? One word: browsers.

Initial Problems with Keyword Implementations

The seven font size keywords might have been implemented correctly and uniformly, but they were not. Unfortunately, the keywords were ineptly or incorrectly implemented in the first browsers that attempted to support them—although, in one case, they were correctly implemented with results so bad, they actually caused a subsequent version of the CSS standard to change.

Whereas Netscape 4 largely ignored CSS keywords, Netscape 4.5 and higher and IE3 rendered them at illegible sizes. For instance, Netscape 4.5 and IE3 rendered xx-small at six pixels—three pixels below the threshold of legibility.

In Netscape's case, the engineers were following an early recommendation of the W3C, which was that each size should be 1.5 times larger than the size below it. If small was 10 pixels, then medium—one size larger—would be 15 pixels. x-small would have to be 6.6667 pixels (10/1.5), and as for xx-small... don't ask. The W3C changed its recommendation to a gentler scaling value of 1.2 after the original 1.5 scaling value proved to be unworkable and unsound. One thing that proved it unworkable and unsound was Netscape 4's accurate rendition of the spec as written.

Netscape 4.5 had done the right thing and followed W3C recommendations to the letter. For this, it was soundly chastised. It was one of the few times that Netscape 4.x got a web standard right. (Two other times come to mind, with equally sorry consequences. Netscape 4 refused to let class or ID names contain underscores, and it also refused to let class or ID names start with numerical digits. This was entirely correct behavior under CSS1, and once again Netscape 4 was lambasted for doing the right thing.) Netscape got smacked when it flubbed standards and whacked when it got them right. You've got to feel at least a bit sorry for those Netscape 4 engineers.

The Keyword Flub in IE/Windows

Meanwhile, IE4/Windows, IE5/Windows, and even IE5.5/Windows got keywords wrong in a different way. In these browsers, there is a logical disconnection between the keyword and the way it is rendered. Small is medium, `medium` is larger than normal, and so on. How the heck did something that weird happen?

The engineers who developed IE for Windows were trying to do the right thing. Remember the seven `<font size>` tags of Netscape, mentioned in the beginning of this chapter? Sure you do: `<font size=1>`, `<font size=4>`, and so on. The IE developers mapped the seven CSS keywords directly to the seven Netscape font sizes. In many ways, it was a logical thing to do. Let's give the team some credit for trying to support keywords in a way that would make sense to designers who had cut their teeth on Netscape font size hacks.

The problem, of course, is that the sizes do not map to the keywords. In old-school browsers, `<font size=3>` is the default or `medium` size that the user has specified in her preferences. In Netscape's extended HTML markup, `<font size=3>` is assumed unless you specify another size. Logically, a default size should map to the `medium` CSS keyword. Unfortunately, in the original IE/Windows scheme, `<font size=3>` maps to `small` instead of `medium` because `small` is the third size up from the bottom of the list.

Progress Happens, but Usage Eludes

Eventually, IE5/Macintosh, Netscape 6+, Mozilla, and IE6 got font size keywords right. But by the time that happened, millions were using IE5 and Netscape 4, which got keywords wrong. If designers used CSS keywords as intended, the display would be off in IE4-5/Windows (and, less importantly, it would also be off in Netscape 4). If designers deliberately misused keywords to make the display look right in IE4-5/Windows, the display would be off in all other browsers and in later versions of IE/Windows. What could designers do? What most of us did was consider CSS font size keywords to be just another option that didn't work.

The Keyword Comes of Age: The Fahrner Method

Once more it was Todd Fahrner (who by all rights should collect royalties from every web designer on the planet) who came up with a solution. And it was the Box Model Hack described in Chapter 12, "Working with Browsers Part II: Box Models, Bugs, and Workarounds," and created by Tantek Çelik (of whom gold statues will one day grace city parks) that made that solution possible. You can read the evolution and details of Todd's method in A List Apart's "Size Matters" (`http://www.alistapart.com/stories/sizematters/`), and you can peruse the Happy Cog variation on Todd's method in the colophon at `http://www.happycog.com/thinking/colophon.html`.

The method works like this:

- Hide styles from 4.0 browsers by using the @import directive (Chapter 9). Because 4.0 browsers don't understand @import, they ignore the imported style sheet containing CSS rules they would only bungle. Let 4.0 browser users see text in the size they choose as their default, or if necessary, serve them pixel values in a linked external style sheet.

- Use the Box Model Hack to serve false font size keyword values to IE5.x/Windows and correct values to more compliant browsers, just as we used it to serve false and true margin, padding, and content area values to differently enabled browsers in Chapter 12.

- Add a CSS rule with greater specificity to protect Opera from one of its bugs. (See the "Be Kind to Opera" rule in Chapter 12's discussion of the Box Model Hack.)

The Method in Action

Following is a simple example. We want our paragraph text to be small (one step below medium). Compliant browsers will give us that value if we ask for it. IE5/Windows must be tricked. If we tell IE to give us x-small, it will give us what more compliant browsers know to be small. Here's the rule:

```
p    {
font-size:    x-small;
              /* false value for WinIE4/5 */
    voice-family:  "\"}\"";
              /* trick WinIE4/5 into thinking the rule is over
*/
    voice-family: inherit;
              /* recover from trick */
    font-size:    small;
              /* intended value for better browsers */
    }
```

As we did in Chapter 12, we now add a "be nice to Opera" rule. Because this rule's selector has greater specificity than the previous rule's selector, Opera pays attention to it and is saved from using the false value intended for IE4/5/Windows only:

```
html>p    {
    font-size:    small;
              /* be nice to Opera */
    }
```

As long as this is done in an imported style sheet, Netscape 4 won't see it and won't become confused by it. If you need to apply the size to multiple selectors, you can do it easily. To see how, view the style sheet at `http://www.happycog.com/c/sophisto.css`; feel free to adapt it to your own needs.

Flies in the Ointment

The previous method works quite well, but font size keywords still suffer from a problem that is identical to one that plagues ems and which we have already talked about when discussing em units: Namely, anything that is below the user's default font size choice might be too small to be comfortably read. This is especially true for our same old three horsemen of typographic apocalypse:

- Windows users who set their browsers' View, Text Size menu to `small` instead of `medium`
- Mac users who switch back to the comfort of 12px/72ppi (or any other value below 16px)
- Users of new browsers like Chimera and Safari that fail to support the big, ugly, but useful cross-platform 16px/96ppi default size

Font size keywords, when approached with @import and the Tantek hack, protect users from the worst damage ems can wreak in that they ensure that no font is ever smaller than 9px. But if the user has established a tiny default size, `medium` will be tiny, as will anything below it.

Usable Type: The Quest Continues

Thirteen years into the web's maturation as a medium, there is no way to set type that reliably and consistently delivers both the control designers require and the freedom users need to change a design's initial size values. There *would* be a way if IE/Windows permitted users to resize text set in pixels, as IE5/Macintosh, Mozilla, Netscape, Navigator, and Kmeleon have done for three years and Opera has done forever. But Moby (the techno guy, not the white whale) will grow hair before Microsoft brings this technology it invented to its Windows client.

This is not a standards problem. Text zoom falls outside the parameters of CSS or any other web standard. There is no specification and no law that says users must be able to scale text on web pages. Common sense says that, but common sense is not a standard.

Do not infer that this is a problem for standards-based designers alone. Those who avoid even thinking about web standards fare even worse and deliver even less predictable results.

Do not envy those who design exclusively in Flash. They also suffer from problems of monitor resolution and face tougher accessibility challenges than the rest of us do. Moreover, even the ability to enlarge Flash content via user-selectable contextual menus does not guarantee legibility, particularly when Flash content is contained in framesets whose borders might hide enlarged areas from view.

So what can you do? Sometimes you will want to use pixels and provide a DOM-driven text size widget to work around IE/Windows's limitations. At other times, you may want to apply the Fahrner method to create accessible font size keywords, which can be resized in any browser. *You pays your money and you takes your choice.* This has been Chapter 13. Now, in the words of Clint Eastwood, "Do you feel lucky?"

chapter fourteen

Accessibility Basics

Accessibility and standards have much in common. They are both about ensuring that our work will be useable and available to the largest possible number of readers, visitors, and customers. Accessibility is so closely linked to the other standards discussed in this book that in the 1990s, the W3C launched a Web Accessibility Initiative (WAI) to advise web builders on strategies for achieving it (http://www.w3.org/WAI/GL/).

WAI offers three standardized levels of access, from the readily achieved (Priority 1), to one that requires slightly more work (Priority 2), to a master level (Priority 3). The point of the three levels is that accessibility, like the other forms of standards compliance discussed in this book, is a *continuum* rather than an "all or nothing" affair. Even if we are unready to convert to CSS layout, we can forward-proof our sites and comply with standards using the hybrid methods shown in Chapters 8, "XHTML by Example: A Hybrid Layout (Part I)," 9, "CSS Basics," and 10, "CSS in Action: A Hybrid Layout (Part II)." So too, with a small and reasonable effort, any of us—even those who are new to accessibility—can attain Priority 1 conformance or something close to it. In so doing, we'll begin making our sites available to those whom we had previously locked out.

Many nations have laws proscribing denial of access to the disabled, and many nations have applied those laws to new media via web accessibility edicts like U.S. Section 508. Some of these national laws adhere closely to WAI Priority 1. Others pick and choose randomly from the access buffet. Some nations' laws would confuse even the members of WAI, who have spent years studying the problems of access. Some laws are vague, and some straightforwardly practical. Many laws go ignored by the very bodies that created them. No wonder designers and developers are confused.

In this chapter, we will cut through confusion, dismiss cobweb-coated myths that befuddle many otherwise sophisticated professionals, and provide a practical overview of common sense, *applied* accessibility. We'll also discuss tools that can help you incorporate accessibility into your design practice and point out the limitations of those tools.

No single chapter could cover the field of accessibility in its entirety; to claim otherwise would insult not only accessibility experts but more importantly those whose needs they serve. Indeed, few books really get at the heart of the thing we will cover all too briefly in this chapter, and some inadvertently contribute to designers' confusion about and hostility toward access. Two books, however, do focus on accessibility in a designer-friendly way, and we commend them to your attention.

Access by the Books

Many well-intended accessibility books preach fire and brimstone. The smell of sulfur does not inspire designers. All too frequently, these books contain only visually ugly—or completely unrealistic—examples of accessible sites, along with impractical advice such as "never specify type sizes." Some in the field are hostile to design. Others have no experience in developing commercial sites. Designers might come away from these books believing that accessibility is irrelevant.

Other books are well researched and fueled by passionate insight. These are worth the devotee's time. But they are not recommended for the general web professional because they are pitched at readers who live with one or more disabilities. In serving that readership, these books spend much time presenting alternate input methods and assessing the merits and demerits of alternative user agents. Nondisabled designers are likely to feel alienated if not unconsciously fearful that somehow they too will be afflicted. Fear of blindness, paralysis, and other disabilities partly fuels some designers' discomfort with the very concept of accessibility, and such books will not help designers shirk that prejudice.

We recommend the following:

- ***Building Accessible Web Sites*, by Joe Clark (New Riders: 2002)**

  Not merely the best and most complete book yet penned on the subject of web accessibility, Joe Clark's *Building Accessible Web Sites* is also among the most compellingly written web design books ever: witty, opinionated, and truthful. In our strange line of work, we see most new design books and many new computer books. Few are complete, fewer still are entirely lucid, and with very few indeed do we feel that we are in the hands of a master communicator. We devoured Clark's book from cover to cover as if it were the latest James Ellroy novel or a recently unearthed Raymond Chandler. Then we read it again. Not only will you learn everything you need to know from this book, but you can actually read it for pleasure.

  Building Accessible Web Sites covers it all, from the basics of writing usable `alt` attributes to the complexities of captioning rich media. Joe Clark, whom the *Atlantic Monthly* called "the king of closed captions," has spent 20 years in the field of media access, and it shows. He is uniquely positioned to guide the reader clearly and confidently from the big picture to the smallest detail—offering phased accessibility strategies that fit any budgetary or time constraint, and straight talk that clarifies regulations and debunks myths. Moreover, Clark cares as much about design aesthetics as access, and he shows how the two are compatible. As with *Eric Meyer on CSS* (see Chapter 9), we recommend this book unreservedly.

- ***Constructing Accessible Web Sites*, various authors (Glasshaus: 2002)**

  Written by multiple subject matter experts including Jim Thatcher, Shawn Layton Henry, Paul Bohman, and Michael Burks, this task-focused book is like a wonderful compendium of best-of-breed magazine articles, each of which covers in thoroughly researched and practical detail a particular aspect of the access puzzle. Among other subjects covered, *Constructing Accessible Web Sites* includes vital material on the limitations of push-button accessibility testing software, discusses feasible methods of implementing accessibility across large enterprises, and provides detailed tips on accessible Flash MX authoring.

Although it lacks the Clark book's advantage of a single, authorial voice, the choir that *Constructing Accessible Web Sites* offers instead is compelling in its own right. Both books demand space on the shelf of anyone who designs, builds, owns, or manages websites. Among other benefits, reading these two books will help overturn many mistaken and sadly widespread ideas such as those we are about to discuss.

Widespread Confusion

Presented with the notion of accessibility, many otherwise savvy designers, developers, and site owners tend to spout meaningless aphorisms about serving their customers. Informed of accessibility laws such as U.S. Section 508 of the Workforce Investment Act, they often subside into what we can only characterize as mental incontinence.

The Genius Puts His Foot in It

On more than one stage, lecturing to a professional audience, we have heard a highly respected fellow web designer respond to a spectator's accessibility question with nonsense like this: "We create cutting-edge branding work for the elite consumers our client is trying to reach. That accessibility stuff—that's a very small part of our market, and… uh… our client doesn't mind losing those few people. I mean, hey, our client makes high-definition wide-screen TVs. Blind folks aren't buying those this year (chuckle, chuckle)."

Actually, blind people might buy those TVs for a sighted partner or family member if the site allowed them to read the specifications and use the online ordering forms. Moreover, the overwhelming majority of visually impaired web users are not entirely blind or even close to it. Most who require access enhancements range from people with low vision to the color blind to the slightly myopic, and any of these might desire and be willing to purchase a high-quality, big picture television set.

The "Blind Billionaire"

Moreover, web crawlers are, in effect, blind users. At a recent conference we attended, a speaker pointed out that the Google search engine is the biggest blind user on the web, and this "user" gives out recommendations in the form of search results to a metric ton of customers every minute of every day.

Looked at (sorry) another way, Google's aggregate readership makes the search engine much like a blind billionaire. How many sites would willingly say no to potential clients who have a few billion dollars to spend? Considered a third way, if you count all the disabled folks in America alone, it's something like the combined populations of the greater metro areas of Los Angeles and New York City. Would it be smart to exclude everyone living in and around those cities from your site?

Access Is Not Limited to the Visually Impaired

But access is not limited to the visually impaired. Motor impaired (partly or completely paralyzed) consumers might want to buy a nice television and might also prefer shopping online to hassling with a trip to a brick and mortar store. Many access enhancements are targeted to that group rather than to the cane-and-tin-cup crowd that invariably springs to mind when the ill-informed contemplate accessibility. Access enhancements also help nondisabled consumers who are attempting to buy that spiffy TV while viewing the site on a Palm Pilot or a web-enabled phone.

In short, the designer or developer or site owner who says "Blind people don't buy our products" is missing the point and the boat. He himself is blind to the true nature of the audience he needlessly rejects—including millions of nondisabled visitors who might have found his site via a search engine if the site had only made an effort to conform to access guidelines. Sadly, he is not unique in misunderstanding what access entails and whom it serves.

A Cloud of Fuzzy Ideas

Over the years, we have heard many misguided utterances flow from the lips of otherwise extremely clued-in web professionals, including these:

"Dude, I'm a designer. I make stuff that looks good. How am I supposed to make stuff that looks good to a bunch of blind people?" (The answer: Nearly all access enhancements have no effect on visual design. They take place in the markup, under the hood of your site's shiny surface. Dude, your stuff can look great *and* be totally accessible [14.1].)

14.1

This site (`http://www.spazowham.com/`) complies with U.S. Section 508 accessibility guidelines. Can you tell by looking? Of course you can't. And that's the point.

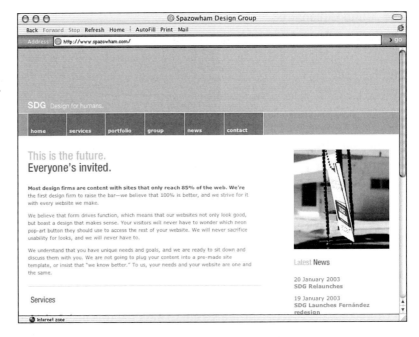

"That's our client's problem. If they don't include it in the RFP (Request for Proposal), we don't have to worry about it," said a lead developer at one of the largest and most famous of global web agencies shortly before it went bankrupt and its remnants were bought by a small company in Central Asia. By the way, he was wrong about accessibility being his client's problem.

"Section 508? That's for the government. We're not government employees." We heard this one from a design agency whose client was legally mandated to provide access.

"One of our committee members is looking that over. We're supposed to get a white paper about it some time or other." A senior project manager at a U.S. government facility shared this insight with us one year after Section 508 became the law of the land.

"Well, we're a Dreamweaver shop," a designer informed us, "so that whole accessibility thing is handled in the new upgrade, right?" (Yes and no. Dreamweaver MX provides numerous access enhancements, but you have to know how to use them. Merely opening Dreamweaver does not guarantee an accessible site.)

The Law and the Layout

The volume of confusion was already high when the passage of Section 508 of the U.S. Workforce Investment Act cranked it up to 11. (Note: We write from an American perspective and use American examples in this section, but the same principles apply no matter where you are and no matter what your local laws might be.)

Section 508 requires that many sites accommodate people with disabilities ranging from limited mobility to a vast range of visual impairments, and it spells out what accessible means. (Hint: Adding `alt` attributes to your images is not enough.) Faced with such a task, many web professionals conclude that accessibility means text-only pages or unattractive, "low-end" design. This isn't so.

Images, CSS, table layouts, JavaScript, and other staples of contemporary web design are entirely compatible with 508 compliance; they simply require a little extra care. As this chapter progresses, we'll examine some of what accessibility and Section 508 compliance specifically entails, and we'll explore how you can use intelligent judgment and available tools to make your sites comply beautifully.

Section 508 Explained

Section 508 [**14.2**] is part of the Rehabilitation Act of 1973, which is intended to end discrimination against people who have disabilities. Enacted by the U.S. Congress on August 7, 1998, Public Law 105-220 (Rehabilitation Act Amendments of 1998 [http://www.usworkforce.org/wialaw.txt]) significantly expanded 508's technology access requirements. The law covers computers, FAX machines, copiers, telephones, transaction machines and kiosks, and other equipment used for transmitting, receiving, or storing information. It also covers many websites.

Section 508 became U.S. law on June 21, 2001. It directly affects Federal departments and agencies, as well as web designers who produce work for them. The law also applies to government-funded projects and to any states that choose to adopt it. Many have done so. American readers can check their state's status online at http://www.resna.org/taproject/policy/initiatives/508/508Stateactions.htm.

14.2
The official site of Section 508 complies with its own guidelines (www.section508.gov). This is not always the case for government sites and was not originally the case for section508.gov. Note the ALA-influenced type size switchers at top right, intended to compensate for browsers that don't let users resize text. See Chapter 15, "Working with DOM-Based Scripts," for more about style switchers.

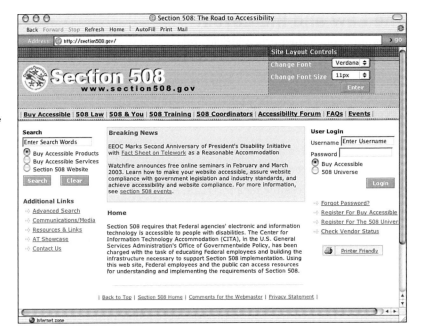

In a nutshell, Section 508 applies to the following:

- Federal departments and agencies (including the U.S. Postal service)
- Deliverables from contractors who serve them
- Activities sponsored or funded by the Federal government
- Activities sponsored by states that have adopted the regulation

"Equal or Equivalent Access to Everyone"

Section 508 requires all websites under its jurisdiction to provide "equal or equivalent access to everyone," including the visually impaired, the hearing impaired, the physically disabled, and people who have photosensitive epilepsy.

Problems faced by these web users might surprise you. For example, small, nonresizable text can prevent people who have limited vision from reading your content. (See the discussion of the pixel problem in IE/Windows in Chapter 13, "Working with Browsers Part III: Typography.") Tiny navigation buttons that have small "hit" areas can thwart those who have impaired motor skills. Blinking or flashing pages can trigger life-threatening seizures in people who have epilepsy. (This is probably *not* what David Siegel had in mind when he wrote *Creating Killer Web Sites* [New Riders, 1997].) The list goes on. The law explains many common access problems and suggests, but does not dictate, possible solutions.

Section 508 does not forbid the use of CSS, JavaScript, images, or table layouts. Nor does it prevent you from incorporating rich media such as Flash and QuickTime, as long as you follow certain guidelines discussed later in this chapter. Naturally, most 508-compliant (like most standards-compliant) sites will look spiffier in new browsers than old. That's no problem under the law because web users can freely upgrade simply by downloading, and most popular browsers are available at no charge.

Conformance with accessibility guidelines, along with standards compliance, not only makes your site more available to millions who are living with disabilities, but it also helps you reach millions more, including consumers who use PDAs, web-enabled cell phones, "off-brand" browsers, and kiosks—and attract still more via search engines.

More visitors. More readers. More users. More members. More customers. It all sounds pretty good. So why are designers, developers, and site owners confused about or hostile to Section 508 and similar accessibility regulations? Primarily, they are confused or hostile because myths about access have long soiled the pool. Let us try to clear away some of these mistaken notions.

Accessibility Myths Debunked

The myths that follow are but a few of many that rattle the heads of otherwise clear-thinking web professionals. Our rebuttals are likewise limited in scope due to chapter constraints.

Myth: Accessibility Forces You to Create Two Versions of Your Site

Not true. If you design with web standards and follow certain guidelines, your site should be as accessible to screen readers, Lynx, PDAs, and old browsers as it is to modern, compliant browsers. Standards and accessibility converge in agreeing that one web document should serve all readers and users.

If you design exclusively in Macromedia Director/Shockwave, then, yes, to conform to WAI Priority 1 or Section 508 guidelines, you need to create a separate version. If access is part of your brief, design with standards, and save

Shockwave for assignments where it's more appropriate. Note that an upcoming version of Macromedia Director will enable developers to create far more accessible Shockwave files. Whether those files will fully meet WAI or other access guidelines remains to be seen.

Myth: A Text-Only Version Satisfies the Requirement for Equal or Equivalent Access

Not true. Adaptive technology has come a long way, and most anything on a conventional web page can be made fully or at least partially accessible, with no visible alteration to your layout. (Remember: The work takes place under the hood.) Shuttling off disabled visitors to a text-only site assumes that the color blind can't see at all, or that those who have limited mobility have no use for images. It also assumes that these users have no interest in shopping on your commerce site or participating in an online discussion forum. In short, the outdated text-only approach helps no one. Not only that, creating and maintaining text-only pages costs more than simply adding access tags and attributes to your site.

Myth: Accessibility Costs Too Much

Not true. What is the cost of creating a Skip Navigation link or of writing a table summary, as described in Chapter 8? What is the cost of typing a brief alt text for each image on your page? Such tasks can be accomplished in minutes. You might charge by the hour, but unless you charge millions per hour, the cost of adding most access features required by WAI Priority 1 or U.S. Section 508 is negligible—especially if so doing protects you from antidiscrimination lawsuits. And *those* can cost plenty.

Higher-level conformance entailing specialized work will, of course, cost more than these simple tasks. For instance, it costs significantly more to author closed captions for Real or QuickTime videos or to caption live streaming media news feeds in real time. But few sites deliver the kind of content that requires such specialized work. As we said at this chapter's outset, access is a continuum; complying with its basic guidelines costs next to nothing.

With large sites whose content is updated by nondevelopment (editorial) personnel, adding access to new pages is often as simple as updating the content management system to prompt for required attributes. On a dynamic site, it might be as easy as reworking the templates that generate pages on the fly. Adding access attributes to forms, structural summaries to table layouts, and making other, similar adjustments to global templates can be a one-time cost that pays off by welcoming new customers and waving garlic before the occasional vampires of the legal profession.

We're Too Busy Wasting Thousands to Spend a Few Bucks Wisely

We have this friend. He is always buying CDs he has no time to listen to and DVDs he has no time to watch. He rents a studio in case he feels like painting even though he hasn't painted in two years. He gets all the cable channels although he never watches TV because he is always going out to clubs. The only downside to his thrilling consumer lifestyle is a throbbing around his lower-left molar. He's had a toothache for two months but "can't afford" to see a dentist.

You might say that our friend's priorities are out of whack, but his attitude is no different from that of many companies.

Those who complain about the cost of accessibility (and who also typically complain about the cost of web standards) are invariably the same people who waste thousands on browser detection, conditional scripts, conditional CSS, and even conditional HTML as described in Chapter 13. They think nothing of squandering cash money sending 10 different style sheets to 10 different browsers, all of which would be better served by a single CSS file. But cough up a few dollars on accessibility? "It costs too much," they claim.

As recently as February 2003, MSN.com [14.3] actually went to the trouble of sending Opera 7 different HTML and CSS than it sent to Opera 5 or 6. Did these conditional files improve the display in Opera? Actually, they made it worse (http://deb.opera.com/howcome/2003/2/msn/). And needless to say, the site was not entirely accessible, according to a text-only-browser test [14.4] and to Watchfire's Bobby, a free online accessibility validation service: http://bobby.cast.org/bobby/bobbyServlet?URL=http%3A//www.msn.com/&gl=wcag1-aaa.

Microsoft is not the only organization that wastes untold riches on outdated workarounds that exponentially increase the cost of web publishing while providing absolutely no benefit to anyone. Nor are they the only company to fling fistfuls of lucre at largely imaginary technical problems while pinching pennies on accessibility.

14.3
Can you tell by looking
that this site is inaccessible
(www.msn.com)?
You could if you were
disabled, as shown in
Figure 14.4.

14.4
The text browser, Lynx,
reveals some of MSN's
accessibility problems,
including Search forms
with no place to enter
text, blind (so to speak)
"Click here!" links, and
useless image map
references.

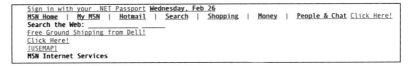

Many companies that claim they cannot afford to implement even the most
basic levels of accessibility nevertheless seem to have plenty of dough for back-
end development, streaming media, and (often needlessly) complex JavaScript.
If these expenses are considered part of doing business, the far tinier cost of
providing access must be regarded in the same way.

Myth: Accessibility Forces You to Create Primitive, Low-End Designs

Not true. Images, table layouts, CSS, JavaScript, server-side technologies like
PHP, and other staples of contemporary web design are perfectly compatible
with WAI Priority 1 and U.S. Section 508 compliance; they simply require care
and judgment. You can also use plug-in-based technologies like Flash and

QuickTime, as long as you follow the guidelines that pertain to them (discussed later in this chapter). All sites produced by Happy Cog in the past two years employ DOM-based scripts, CSS or hybrid layouts, GIF and JPEG images, et cetera ad infinitum, yet they all pass online access validation tests quite handily.

Important: As we'll soon see, passing online access validation tests does not guarantee that your site is truly accessible or compliant. There are limits to the kinds of tests that software can perform; human judgment must temper and evaluate all such tests. On the other hand, failing WAI Priority 1 or U.S. Section 508 tests is a pretty good sign that your site does not comply.

Myth: According to Section 508, Sites Must Look the Same in All Browsers and User Agents

Not true. How could they? Naturally, most 508-compliant sites will look better in new browsers than old. That's no problem under the law because web users can freely upgrade simply by downloading. Content must be accessible in Lynx, and to screen readers, PDAs, and other user agents. Visual design cannot be present in many of these environments, and need not look the same from one graphical browser to the next. Old-school methods intended to make sites look the same in all browsers and on all platforms are one reason the web has so many inaccessible, invalid, hard-to-maintain sites.

Myth: Accessibility Is "Just for Disabled People"

Not true. Certainly, conformance can improve (or in some cases, provide for the first time) access for people who have major disabilities. But it will also help the following:

- Anyone who uses Palm Pilots, web-enabled cell phones, and other non-traditional browsing devices—a growing market segment
- People who have temporary impairments and disabilities (for example, broken wrists)
- People who have minor, correctable vision problems, including aging baby boomers (a huge segment of the population)
- Those who are temporarily accessing sites away from their customary environment—for instance, via kiosks or feature-limited browsers in airports and other public places

- Site owners who want to reach any of these people rather than sending them to a competitor's site

- Site owners who want to benefit from search engines, the biggest "blind users" of them all (see "The 'Blind Billionaire'," earlier)

Myth: Dreamweaver MX/Watchfire's Bobby/*Insert Tool Name Here* Solves All Compliance Problems

Not true. These tools help, but they cannot take the place of human judgment. Watchfire's Bobby accessibility validation service [14.5], the Cynthia Says™ Portal (http://www.contentquality.com), or UseableNet's LIFT (http://www.usablenet.com/) can help you test for WAI or Section 508 conformance problems. Elements of LIFT that are present in Dreamweaver MX can also help you test and can encourage you to author more accessibly. But these tests and tools are not miracle cures or push-button solutions. Think of them as aids that can help you formulate best practices and identify specific problem areas on each project you develop.

14.5

Watchfire's Bobby (http:// bobby.watchfire.com/), a free accessibility validation service that is available online, can help you whip your pages into conformance with WAI or Section 508 guidelines. But like all such software, Bobby has limitations, and you must evaluate its reports with judgment and common sense.

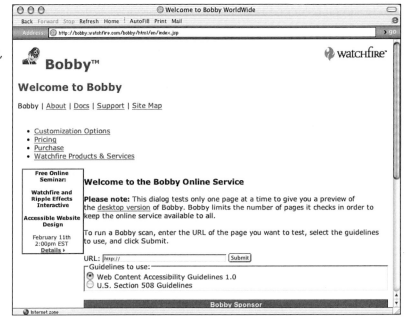

Myth: Designers Can Freely Ignore Accessibility Laws if Their Clients Tell Them To

That remains to be seen. We know of no cases where web designers have been held liable for creating inaccessible sites—*yet*. But the U.S. Justice Department has gone after architects who violate the Americans with Disabilities Act, whether the client told them to "build it that way" or not. Web designers might someday face similar penalties. It's our job to educate clients (or bosses), not blame them when we knowingly do the wrong thing.

Accessibility Tips, Element by Element

The following guidelines offer approaches to bringing commonly used web page elements into conformance with WAI (or governmental) accessibility guidelines.

Images

Leaving out `alt` text will cause users of Lynx, screen readers, and other non-mainstream browsers and devices to hear or see [IMAGE] [IMAGE] [IMAGE] [IMAGE] [IMAGE] [IMAGE] or something equally unhelpful. For a visual example, flip back to Chapter 2, "Designing and Building with Standards," Figure 2.5. Lack of `alt` texts will also be flagged as a WAI access error and an XHTML validation error. Use the `alt` attribute to the `img` element (http://www.w3.org/WAI/GL/WCAG20/checkpoints.html) to describe the *purpose* of each image.

Your Friend, the *null alt* Attribute

For meaningless images, such as spacer GIFs (not that *you're* still using spacer GIF images), use `alt=""`, also known as the `null alt` attribute, or `null alt` text. Do not compound users' problems with literal `alt` text for meaningless images like `alt="pixel spacer gif"` or `alt="table cell background color gradient"`. Use the `null alt` attribute for images that are intended to create purely visual (nonmeaningful, nonsemantic) design effects.

Use *alt* Attributes That Convey Meaning to Your Visitors

Use `alt` attributes that convey meaning to your visitors, rather than meaning to you and your colleagues. For instance, on a logo that also works as a link back to the home page, use `alt="Smith Company home page"` instead of `alt="smith_logo_rev3"` or `alt="Smith Company logo"`. To a visually disabled user, it is of scant interest to be told that an image she can't see is a "logo." The fact that clicking the image will take her back to the home page is far more significant. If you feel you must, you can hedge your bets by writing something like this:

```
alt="Smith Company home page [logo]"
```

Resist "helpful" software that generates `alt` attributes for you; this software will most likely generate useless `alt` texts derived directly from filenames:

```
alt="smith_logo_32x32"
```

In short, never send a robot to do a human being's job. In fact...

Don't Trust Software to Do a Human Being's Job

Don't assume that your `alt` attributes work if your page passes Bobby's WAI or Section 508 accessibility tests. A page that uses `alt="mickeymouse"` for every image (or `alt=""` for every image) could pass these tests just fine. No software can tell if your `alt` texts are appropriate. And frankly, we wouldn't want to live in a world where software *could* make these kinds of judgments. If you don't know what we're talking about, watch *2001*, *Blade Runner*, *The Matrix*, *Minority Report*, or *The Music Man*. Okay, *The Music Man* has absolutely nothing to do with it, but wasn't Robert Preston great in that role? Come on, he was really great. Kids, ask your parents about it.

The *alt* ToolTip Fandango

Some leading browsers misguidedly display `alt` attributes as ToolTips when the visitor's mouse cursor hovers over the image. Although millions of web users are accustomed to it by now, it is a horrible idea for many reasons. Chiefly, `alt` text is an accessibility tool, not a nifty ToolTip gimmick. (The `title` attribute is fine for nifty ToolTip gimmicks.) W3C explicitly states that `alt` text should be visible only when images cannot be viewed:

> The alt attribute specifies alternate text that is rendered when the image cannot be displayed... User agents must render alternate text when they cannot support images, they cannot support a certain image type, or when they are configured not to display images.
>
>   http://www.w3.org/TR/REC-html40/struct/objects.html#h-13.2

No browser should display redundant `alt` text that describes what the sighted visitor can already plainly see. But IE/Windows, for instance, does just that [14.6], and Netscape/Windows did it first. This is not your problem, unless it misleads you into writing "creative" `alt` text that fails to do its primary job of explaining images to those people who can't see them.

14.6
The positioning of the eBay logo suggests that it is a clickable Home button, but it is not (`www.ebay.com`). Its `alt` attribute ("eBay logo") is appropriate but feels redundant in browsers like IE/Windows that display `alt` text as a ToolTip, even though they should not do so.

No *alt* for Background Images

Access novices often ask if they need to write `alt` text for CSS (or HTML) background images. It is a logical and reasonable question, to which the answer is simply, no. In fact, you couldn't do so if you tried. There are no `alt` attributes in CSS. (For example, there is no `alt` attribute for a background image in a `<body>` tag.)

If a background image conveys important meaning that is not provided by the page's text—for instance, if the page's sole text reads, "He was honest," and the CSS background image is a portrait of Abraham Lincoln—you might try including the words "President Abraham Lincoln" inside a `title` attribute to the `body` element, or a `table summary` attribute if tables were used. Or you might with slightly less reasonableness insert the explanatory text within a `noscript` tag on the assumption that those who cannot see images are not in a JavaScript-capable environment.

Better still, you might ditch the whole idea. A picture of Lincoln with the words, "He was honest"? What kind of web page is that?

Apple's QuickTime and Other Streaming Video Media

Where a plug-in is required, include one clear link to the required item.

If you use an image to link to a required plug-in, make sure it has appropriate `alt` text.

To enhance the accessibility of QuickTime (or REAL) video, use a captioning tool or a web standard like SMIL to provide descriptive text and captions equivalent to audio tracks. See A List Apart's "SMIL When You Play That" (http://www.alistapart.com/stories/smil/) for a designer-friendly overview of SMIL, and read Joe Clark's book to learn what is involved in QuickTime captioning.

Captioning video requires expertise, time, and money. It especially takes expertise. And time. And money. And expertise. If your client is paying for streaming video, be sure captioning is part of the production budget and timeline.

WGBH Boston does excellent work delivering accessible QuickTime and Flash (http://main.wgbh.org/wgbh/access/). Joe Clark has commended the accessible video work of BMW Films (http://www.BMWFilms.com/). These sites might inspire you.

Macromedia Flash 4/5

Macromedia Flash 4 and 5 provide limited accessibility options, such as the ability to create audio tracks that describe navigational buttons. If you cannot upgrade to Flash MX, use these options and provide HTML alternatives. If at all possible, use Flash MX instead.

Macromedia Flash MX

Released in April of 2002, Macromedia Flash MX offers greatly improved accessibility features, including screen reader compatibility, although most of these enhancements work only in a Windows environment, as Flash MX communicates with Microsoft Active Accessibility.

Screen readers, sometimes incorrectly referred to as "voice browsers" or "text readers," are browsers that speak web text aloud. Currently, the access improvements in Flash MX can be understood by the two leading screen readers, namely JAWS by Freedom Scientific [14.7] and Window-Eyes by GW Micro (http://www.gwmicro.com/press/flash.htm).

14.7
Freedom Scientific's JAWS, a screen reader, works in tandem with Windows browsers to help the visually impaired access web content and navigate accessibly authored Flash MX sites (`http://www.freedomscientific.com/fs_products/software_jaws.asp`). As a plus, Freedom Scientific's site complies with WAI Priority 1 and U.S. Section 508, which is not always the case for such companies.

Flash MX meets several requirements set forth in U.S. Section 508, including the following:

- Content magnification
- Mouse-free navigation
- Sound synchronization
- Support for custom color palettes

Flash MX addresses key U.S. Section 508 issues including these:

- Ability to create text equivalents
- Ability to minimize harm caused by poor authoring of animated events
- Ability to create accessible versions of buttons, forms, and labels
- As in XHTML, ability to specify tab order to help non-mouse users navigate

In Flash MX, tab order is specified via ActionScript, Macromedia's version of ECMAScript. See the later section, "Keeping Tabs: Our Good Friend, the `tabindex` Attribute," for details on specifying tab order in XHTML.

None of these enhancements will work if you don't learn how to use them and make them part of your Flash authoring process. Nor are all of these enhancements particularly easy to understand and implement. And some aspects of basic accessibility continue to elude Flash MX.

For tips on accessible Flash authoring, see A List Apart's Issue No. 143 on Flash MX (http://www.alistapart.com/issues/143/), which surveys these Flash access enhancements and their limitations in articles by Joe Clark and designer Andrew Kirkpatrick of the CPB/WGBH National Center for Accessible Media—and if you haven't rushed out for them already, please pick up the two books recommended at the beginning of this chapter.

Additional Flash Compliance Tips

Where a plug-in is required, include one clear link to the required item.

If you use an image to link to a required plug-in, make sure it has appropriate alt text.

If you use JavaScript to detect the presence or absence of Flash, have a backup plan—that is, one clear link to the required item—for those who don't or can't use JavaScript. Also, if you use JavaScript to detect the presence or absence of Flash, for the love of Heaven, make sure you know what you're doing. The medium is littered with the corpses of broken browser and plug-in detection scripts and the bodies of web users caught in the crossfire.

Understand that despite your best, most sincere efforts, some people will not be able to access your Flash content.

Color

If you use color to denote information (such as clickability), reinforce it with other methods (for instance, bolding or underlining links). If you've turned off underlining via CSS, consider making links bolder than normal text. If you do this, avoid using bold on nonlinked text, lest you hopelessly confuse the color-blind user as to which bold text is hyperlinked and which bold text is simply bold. If the difference between linked and ordinary text is obvious even to a color-blind person (if text is black and links are white to use the most extreme example), bolding or other differentiation schemes will not be necessary.

Avoid referring to color in your text. "Visit the Yellow Box for Help" is useless direction for those who can't see (or can't see color).

Use care when creating harmonious color schemes, whose differences might not be apparent to those who have certain types of color blindness. Joe Clark devotes many readable and essential pages to this subject's details. His book is available at fine stores everywhere. You know what to do.

You will also want to visit `http://www.vischeck.com/`, which lets you see how your web pages appear to people with various types of color blindness.

CSS

Test your pages with and without style sheets to be certain they are readable either way. Don't worry about changes to graphic design with styles turned off, unless those changes render the site unusable.

Structured Markup Conveys Meaning When CSS Goes Away

If you author with well-structured XHTML, your page will work better even when styles are switched off or unavailable [**14.8**, **14.9**]. Readers "get" structured markup with or without CSS, just as they get it when using IE/ Windows' "all or nothing" font size access feature as described in Chapter 13. As we keep saying throughout the book, emphasize structure and avoid divitis. Markup like that shown next won't make much sense when CSS is unavailable to the user:

```
<div class="header">Headline</div>
<div class="copy">Text</div>
<div class="copy">Text</div>
<div class="copy">Text</div>
```

14.8
The author's personal site in a compliant browser, with CSS turned on (`www.zeldman.com`). We know, we know, you saw it back in Chapter 13. Patience.

14.9
When CSS is turned off, the relationship of subhead to paragraph remains clear because the site has been authored using simple, structural XHTML.

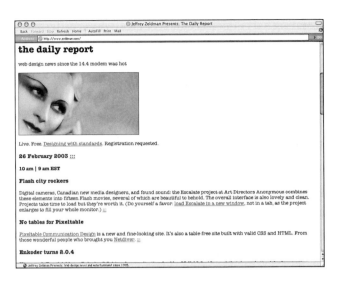

Don't Trust What You See in One Browser Alone

Write valid CSS and test it in multiple browsers. Don't write invalid CSS that happens to work in a particular browser. Bad CSS might make a page illegible. Not every web user knows how to turn off CSS, let alone how to override your CSS with user style sheets, and not every browser supports user style sheets at this time.

Take Care When Sizing Text

Don't assume you've done the right thing if you use ems instead of px (see Chapter 13). Avoid pixel-based, nonresizable text (once more, see Chapter 13) *or* use DOM- or back-end-driven style switchers that let users change text sizes even when their browser refuses to grant them that right. DOM-based style switchers will be explained in Chapter 15.

Don't, We Repeat, Don't Trust Access Validation Test Results

Don't assume that your CSS is "safe" simply because your page passes Bobby's accessibility tests. A page that uses illegible 7px type might pass these tests.

Rollovers and Other Scripted Behaviors

Code to ensure that links work even when JavaScript is turned off. Test by turning off JavaScript in your browser.

Provide Alternatives for Non-Mouse Users

Folks who have impaired mobility can and do use JavaScript-capable browsers but might be unable to click or perform other mouse maneuvers. Provide alternate code for these users:

```
<input type="button" onclick="setActiveStyleSheet('default');
➥return false;" onkeypress="setActiveStyleSheet('default');
➥return false;" />
```

In the preceding example, onkeypress is the non-mouse user equivalent to onclick. The two lines of code coexist peacefully. The alternate code is invisible to the mouse user. Yes, coding the same function two ways adds a few bytes to your page's overall weight. In this case, the fractional increase in bandwidth pays off by welcoming disabled users instead of punishing them for being disabled.

Use *noscript* to Provide for Those Who Can't Use JavaScript

The Daily Report at zeldman.com uses JavaScript on a form element to provide access to previous pages. Next, with some elements removed for the sake of clarity, are the rudiments of the simple code. You will notice that both onclick and onkeypress are used to take the visitor to the URL of a previous page:

```
<form action="foo"><input type="button" value=
➥"Previous Reports" onclick="window.location=
➥'http://www.zeldman.com/daily/0103c.shtml';" onkeypress=
➥"window.location='http://www.zeldman.com/daily/0103c.shtml';"
➥/>
...
</form>
```

This is fine for those who use JavaScript-capable browsers *and* who don't turn off JavaScript for religious reasons. But what of people who can't use JavaScript? A simple link within a noscript element takes care of their needs:

```
<noscript>
<p><a href="/daily/0103c.shtml">Previous Reports</a></p>
</noscript>
```

Following is the code with all its pieces:

```
<form action="foo"><input type="button" class="butt" value=
➥"Previous Reports" onclick="window.location=
➥'http://www.zeldman.com/daily/0103c.shtml';" onkeypress=
➥"window.location='http://www.zeldman.com/daily/0103c.shtml';"
➥onmouseover="window.status='Previous Daily Reports.';
➥return true;" onmouseout="window.status='';return true;" />
<noscript>
<p class="vs15"><a href="/daily/0103c.shtml">
➥Previous Reports</a></p>
</noscript>
</form>
```

Those who are totally unfamiliar with JavaScript might find the preceding code a bit daunting, especially when printed in a book. But it is pure baby food, as any experienced coder will tell you. *Any* designer could write this code. Yet in spite of its rudimentary nature, this code accommodates "typical" web users, the physically impaired, the blind, nontraditional device users, and the nondisabled paranoid types who use JavaScript-capable browsers but turn off JavaScript.

Avoid or at Least *Massage* Generated Scripts

Avoid using Dreamweaver- or GoLive-generated scripts, which make browser and platform assumptions. At the very least, test pages so authored in off-brand browsers and with JavaScript turned off.

Learn More

The interaction between scripted behaviors and accessibility can be quite complex, and a full discussion is beyond the scope of this chapter. For more information on working with JavaScript, read Apple Internet Developer: "Working with JavaScript" (http://developer.apple.com/internet/ javascript/) and resources like webreference.com and scottandrew.com along with those discussed in Chapter 15.

Forms

At the outset of this chapter, we highly recommended two books. *Building Accessible Web Sites* devotes an entire chapter to the ins and outs of creating accessible online forms. *Constructing Accessible Web Sites* also devotes an entire chapter to the ins and outs of creating accessible online forms. From this coincidence, you might be tempted to conclude that the creation of accessible online forms can be somewhat involved. You would be correct.

Don't panic. Most tasks involved are simple and straightforward, such as associating form fields with appropriate labels (for instance, associating the text area in a Search form with a "Search" label). It's just that there are a lot of little tasks like that, and discussing them all exceeds this chapter's scope.

After you've built what you hope are accessible forms, test your work in Lynx (`http://lynx.browser.org/`) or Jaws. Macintosh fans will need Virtual PC (`http://www.connectix.com/products/vpc6m.html`) or a real PC to run Jaws. Linux folks, a free screen reader is included in the SuSE Linux 7.0 distribution (`http://www.hicom.net/~oedipus/vicug/SuSE_blinux.html`), or you can pick up Speakup (`http://www.linux-speakup.org/speakup.html`).

Image Maps

Avoid image maps if you can, and you generally can. When required, use client-side image maps with `alt` text and provide redundant text links. Just say no to old-fashioned, server-side image maps.

Table Layouts

Don't sweat this. Write simple table summaries as explained in Chapter 8, and use CSS to avoid the need for deeply nested tables, spacer GIF images, and other such junk, as explained in Chapters 8 through 10.

That's really it. Despite what you might have heard to the contrary, the use of simple table layouts is not a major access hazard, is not illegal under WAI or Section 508 guidelines, and will not condemn your soul to eternal torment. If CSS layout is an option, go for it. If not, learn to love yourself and try not to worry so much.

Tables Used for Data

Identify table headers and use appropriate markup to associate data cells and header cells for tables that have two or more logical levels of row and column headers. In a table that lists members of the cast of *The Music Man*, a typical table header might be ***Actor***, and table cells associated with it would include *Robert Preston*, *Shirley Jones*, *Buddy Hackett*, *Hermione Gingold*, and so on.

A sighted person who is using a graphical browser will see the connection between *Actor* and the column of names directly below it. But screen reader users require additional markup that connects the table header to its associated data cells.

View source at `http://www.w3.org/WAI/wcag-curric/sam45-0.htm` to see how the WAI group clarifies the connection between headers and their associated data cells [14.10].

14.10

It's ugly, but it gets you there: An example page from the W3C's Web Accessibility Initiative shows one method of associating headers with data cells in complex tables (`http://www.w3.org/WAI/wcag-curric/sam45-0.htm`).

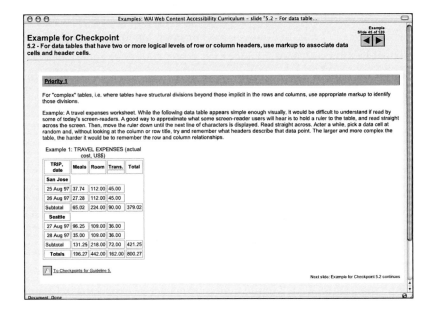

Frames, Applets

Just say no.

Flashing or Blinking Elements

Just say no. Not just no, hell no. You might not have used a `<blink>` or `<marquee>` tag since you were knee-high to a FrontPage template (if ever), but keep in mind that the ban on flashing and blinking elements applies to Flash and QuickTime content as well.

Tools of the Trade

If you use a visual editor to create web pages, several tools and plug-ins can simplify conformance with access guidelines:

- **SSB Insight LE and GoLive**

  This free SSB Insight LE plug-in for Adobe GoLive automatically identifies many (but not all) accessibility violations.
  http://www.adobe.com/products/golive/ssb.html

- **UseableNet LIFT and Dreamweaver**

  Mentioned earlier in this chapter, UsableNet's $249 LIFT for Macromedia Dreamweaver 4 offers numerous features in addition to assisting with conformance. LIFT automatically identifies many (though not all) accessibility violations. There are also standalone versions of LIFT, and two recent versions incorporate the usability guidelines recommended by the Nielsen Norman Group.
  http://www.usablenet.com/lift_dw/lift_dw.html

- **Dreamweaver MX**

  Many of LIFT's capabilities have been incorporated in Dreamweaver MX, including a built-in 508 validation checker, a 508 Reference Guide, and tools for adding accessibility features to images, tables, and frames. Remember: No tool catches all problems or offers a fail-safe substitute for your judgment and experience. Like a hammer and nails, tools only help those who know how to use them. Like eggs, milk, and flour... okay, never mind, you get the picture.

- **Microsoft FrontPage Gets LIFT**

  UsableNet announced on July 9, 2002 that it had integrated its LIFT product into Microsoft FrontPage, the widely distributed authoring tool:
  http://www.usablenet.com/frontend/onenews.go?news_id=45

  LIFT won't stop FrontPage from generating proprietary, nonstandard markup, but as in Dreamweaver MX, the inclusion of LIFT will enable FrontPage users to check for access problems and guide them toward including accessibility features in images, tables, frames, and so on.

Working with Bobby

Whether you use the products mentioned earlier or mark up and code your sites by hand, Watchfire's Bobby Accessibility Validator should be your next stop:

```
http://bobby.watchfire.com/bobby/html/en/index.jsp
```

With the touch of a button, Bobby can test any page for access conformance, although the nuances require judgment and analysis. Both WAI and Section 508 rely on a manual checklist to ensure compliance. Unlike the W3C's markup and CSS validation services, Bobby's validation tests cannot provide you with an unconditionally clean bill of health or a list of mistakes to be fixed. Instead, you must *interpret* Bobby's output. That's where things get tricky. But it's also where they become educational and where you get to earn your paycheck as a knowledgeable designer, developer, or related web specialist.

Understanding Checklists

"*If* the Section 508 issues listed below do not apply to your page, *then* it qualifies as Bobby Section 508 Approved," says Bobby after its free online version (or powerful binary version available for purchase) is finished assessing your page. Bobby will never say, "Dude, you've totally nailed it. This page is absolutely 100% compliant with WAI Priority 1 guidelines" or Section 508 or any other published access specification.

Bobby can't say that. Bobby is software. Software relies on algorithms to test for the presence of common problems. And, as we keep saying, many problems evade a machine's understanding.

We don't have time to describe every situation you might encounter when testing your site for access conformance, but this example will show you how to understand and apply the kinds of checklists that Bobby generates. In an encounter with Bobby, a hybrid (tables plus CSS) version of zeldman.com passed the software's Section 508 test, but true approval was contingent on interpreting a checklist that Bobby generated.

Bobby's checklist included this item: "Consider specifying a logical tab order among form controls, links, and objects."

Keeping Tabs: Our Good Friend, the *tabindex* Attribute

The XHTML `tabindex` attribute specifies the tabbing navigation order among form controls. If you don't create a logical tab order, people who rely on tabbing (instead of the mouse) will simply tab from link to link in the order that links appear in your XHTML source. This might not be the most useful way to guide them through your site, particularly if your body text contains numerous links or long-winded navigation that occurs early in markup.

Like Skip Navigation and `accesskey` (discussed in Chapter 8), `tabindex` spares screen reader users from the worst aspects of serial navigation, enabling them to quickly skip to content that interests them. Whereas Skip Navigation leapfrogs long lists of links, and `accesskey` provides command key access (at least theoretically) to various page components, `tabindex` provides shortcut serial access to various parts of the page—not unlike a DVD's chapter index, which lets movie fans skip ahead to the car chase or back to the love scene.

On commercial sites, after creating a tab order as described next, you would test on real users. On personal or nonprofit sites, you might not have that luxury. When user testing is not an option, construct a user scenario, create a tabbing order based on that scenario, and wait to hear from your site's visitors who use `tabindex` whether you guessed right or not.

Arriving at a Tabbing Order

Figure 14.11 shows the old hybrid site and indicates the tabbing order prior to our use of `tabindex`. When users pressed the Tab key, they moved dully from one link to the next in the order in which the links occurred in markup. This was the expected (and excruciating) default behavior. Figure 14.12 shows the revised order made possible by `tabindex`, wherein each stroke of the tab key shuttles the user to a place they might actually want to go. The numbers shown have been superimposed over the screen shots to indicate tab order; they do not appear on the actual site.

Before we discuss the required markup (which is so basic a beginner can write it), it's worth looking at the tab order we chose and why. We're not sure our decisions were the best that could be made, but they illustrate the kind of process you might go through yourself as you plan a deliberate tab order for your sites.

14.11

The hybrid Zeldman site prior to revising the tabbing order via tabindex: As visitors hit the Tab key, they move dully from one link to the next in the order in which links occur in markup (`www.zeldman.com`). The shown numbers are not part of the site's imagery. They have been superimposed to illustrate the default tab order sequence.

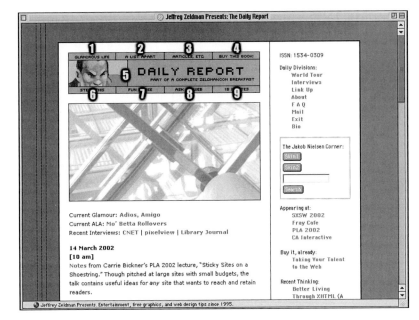

14.12

After we revised the tab order, a press of the Tab key takes the visitor to a site component they might actually want to use. The numbers have been superimposed to illustrate the changed tab order sequence. The site's visual layout looks the same as it always did. Those who don't tab won't know that anything has changed.

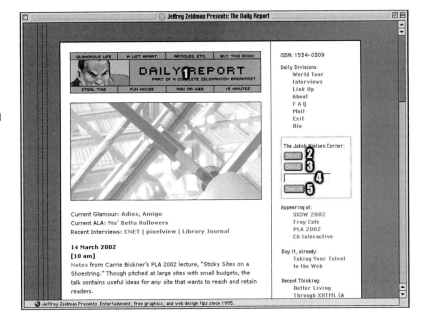

After mentally placing ourselves in a non-mouse user's position and considering which links we would want to click through and in what order, we arrived at the following tab order mapping:

1. The first click snaps visitors to the page header/Home button so that they can reload the page if desired, confirm their location in web space, and—above all—return to the home page if they happen to be anywhere else on the site.

2. The second tab takes visitors to a button that lets them choose the default type size and style sheet. The mechanics of the DOM-driven style switcher will be explained in the next chapter. Its purpose is to enhance accessibility by allowing visitors to change type size or type family (or both), although it can also be used more creatively to completely alter a site's look and feel.

3. The third tab shifts to a companion button that lets visitors choose a font size that might be more legible for the visually impaired, for Windows users who set their default text size to "smaller" (see Chapter 13) and so on.

4. The fourth tab brings the Search form input field into focus. By specifying the Search form early in visitors' link flow, we save them the heartbreak of tabbing past dozens of unwanted links.

5. The fifth tab moves to the Search button, enabling a visitor to execute searches that they initiated in the previous step.

6. The sixth tab, below the field of the screen shot, shifts visitors to the Previous Reports button at the bottom of the page (described earlier in "Use noscript to Provide for Those Who Can't Use JavaScript"). The Previous Reports button enables visitors to load older pages in reverse chronological order.

7. The seventh tab, also below the field of the screen shot, shuttles visitors to a Top of the Page button that saves them the trouble of scrolling. It is particularly useful for those who cannot scroll with the mouse.

After those seven pit stops, normal tabbing resumes, allowing readers to navigate the page's remaining links in the order they appear.

Building and Testing

Changing the tab order was easy. We merely assigned a `tabindex` value to any item we wanted to prioritize. For instance, next is a simplified version of the XHTML for our default font size button before retooling for enhanced access:

```
<form action="send">
    <input type="button" />
</form>
```

And here is the same button after retooling. (The only changed element is highlighted in bold.)

```
<form action="send">
    <input type="button" tabindex="2" />
</form>
```

The next item in the sequence was marked `tabindex="3"`; the one after that was `tabindex="4"`, and so on. Quantum physics it's not.

Since conducting this exercise, we've twice redesigned zeldman.com using pure CSS layout and structured XHTML. Nevertheless, you can still view the results of our tab order makeover by tabbing through and viewing source at `http://www.zeldman.com/daily/1002a.html`.

Most access chores are equally easy to conceptualize and mark up. Typical tasks Bobby might suggest include creating keyboard shortcuts for form elements and testing to see if the page is still readable and usable when style sheets are turned off. As you learn more about access, you will not need Bobby to suggest these things, and as you implement accessibility enhancements, Bobby will suggest fewer and fewer of them.

Annoyingly, Bobby often offers irrelevant suggestions. For instance, even if your site uses tables for layout only, Bobby responds to the presence of tables with this comment: "If this is a data table (not used for layout only), identify headers for the table rows and columns." Likewise, Bobby says of any site presented to it, "If you use color to convey information, make sure the information is also represented another way."

These utterances get old fast. They are like the random mutterings of an unfortunate soul in the grips of a psychotic episode. For this reason, some accessibility experts shun Bobby and other such tools and base their work solely on their own knowledge. But for the nonexperts among us, as long as we are willing to put up with Bobby's quirks, it can be a great help. The Cynthia Says access testing tool (`http://www.contentquality.com`), which made its debut as this book was going to press, runs more tests than Bobby and may be more pleasant to work with.

In deference to that Russian proverb about the educational benefits of repetition, we'll close this section by once again reminding you that even if Bobby gives you a clean bill of health, your site might still be inaccessible. Ignore the irrelevant checklist items but study the relevant ones, use your judgment and common sense, and read those accessibility books.

One Page, Two Designs

After a tab order facelift, our site looked the same as it always had. But in a sense, the site now had two user interface designs: one for traditional graphical browser users who navigate via the mouse, the other for those who tab in graphical or nongraphical browsers. The two designs coexisted peacefully, requiring no special "accessible" page versions and creating no change to the visual design most visitors see. (On the other hand, if our color scheme had rendered text illegible for visually impaired visitors, we would have fixed it, perhaps changing the overall design in the process.)

Planning for Access: How You Benefit

Although many sites are not legally required to provide access today, they might have to do so tomorrow. One thing we all know about laws is that they continually change. Another thing we know is that we are all subject to laws, whether we like them or not. Applying these enhancements to your site, even if you are not required to do so under today's laws, might protect you from expensive retooling should the laws change next year, and might also protect you from the cost (and bad public relations publicity) of antidiscrimination lawsuits.

Access Serves You

Having trotted out the rationale behind many site owners' sudden interest in accessibility, let us hastily add that fear of lawsuits is the wrong reason to incorporate access into your design practice. These enhancements open any site to new visitors—and whose site could not use more visitors? Those locked out of other sites will be inclined to feel quite loyal to yours if you welcome them into it by making these adjustments to your markup. If other online stores block disabled visitors and nontraditional device users and *your* store welcomes them, guess who will be selling to those customers, and guess who won't be?

And don't forget, the more accessible your site is to disabled visitors and nontraditional Internet device users, the more available its content will also be to Google, AlltheWeb, and all the other crawler-driven search engines and directories that send visitors your way. Conversely, the less accessible your site, the less traffic it will draw from Google and its brothers. zeldman.com, A List Apart, and most sites designed by Happy Cog over the past few years tend to rank high in search engine results, not because we're doing anything fancy, but because these sites are built with access-enhanced structural markup.

Gosh, we were trying to attain higher moral ground, and we still seem to have offered purely self-interested reasons for implementing accessibility. Here are two more:

Implementing access enhancements can deepen your understanding of "design." Considering things like tab order can take you beyond a vision of design as the decoration of surface appearance ("look and feel") and into the realms of user flow, contingency design, and general usability. These are issues that web designers, information architects, and usability specialists think about anyway. Accessibility is just another aspect of considering how to best build our sites to meet diverse human needs.

Implementing access and honing a conformance strategy can sharpen your development skills and provide fresh perspectives you might never have considered otherwise. Learning the ways of WAI and the particulars of 508 (or any other legally defined access standard) will increase your value as a professional web designer, position your web agency as smarter and more clued-in than its competitors, and help your sites reach more people than ever before. That is what every site owner wants and what every designer or developer strives for. Practicing accessibility will help your visitors reach their goals, yes; but it will also help you reach your own.

chapter fifteen

Working with DOM-Based Scripts

In the beginning, Netscape created JavaScript, and it was good. Then Microsoft begat JScript, and it was different. Vast armies clashed by night and the flames of DHTML threatened to engulf all. Salvation arrived with the birth of a standard Document Object Model (DOM), whose first manifestation was called DOM Level 1 (`http://www.w3.org/TR/1998/REC-DOM-Level-1-19981001/`). And it was very good indeed. For the first time, the W3C DOM gave designers and builders a standard means of accessing the data, scripts, and presentation layers with which their sites were composed.

In the years since, the W3C has continued to update its DOM specs, and, at the urging of The Web Standards Project (WaSP), browsers have come to support at least *most* of the DOM Level 1 specification, although they sometimes differ in the ways they support it. (To find out how much DOM your favorite browser upholds, visit `http://www.w3.org/2003/02/06-dom-support.html`.) In this chapter, we will meet the DOM and explore some of the ways it can help us accomplish useful tasks, such as showing or hiding content in response to visitor actions, providing customization and accessibility options, and creating dynamic menus. None of this will be too difficult or technical, we promise.

Meet the DOM

Just what *is* the DOM? According to the World Wide Web Consortium (W3C) (http://www.w3.org/DOM/), the DOM is a browser-independent, platform-neutral, language-neutral interface that allows "programs and scripts to dynamically access and update the content, structure, and style of documents. The document can be further processed, and the results of that processing can be incorporated back into the presented page."

In simple English, the DOM makes other standard components of your page (style sheets, markup elements, and scripts) accessible to manipulation. If your web page were a movie, XHTML would be the screenwriter, CSS would be the art director, scripting languages would be the special effects, and the DOM would be the director who oversees the entire production.

As a bonus, instead of taxing the server and clogging the pipes with HTTP requests, DOM-driven interactivity takes place on the client side (that is, on the visitor's hard drive). It works even if the Internet connection is terminated.

A Standard Way to Make Web Pages Behave Like Applications

Although such usage exceeds the scope of this book, the most exciting aspect of DOM-driven interactivity is that it can mimic the behavior of conventional software. For instance, the visitor can change the sort order of tabular data by clicking on the header, just as she might do in an Excel spreadsheet or in the Macintosh Finder (the application that lets Macintosh users sort, copy, move, rename, delete, or in other ways process various files and folders on their desktops) [15.1, 15.2, 15.3].

On conventional web pages, such activity requires client/server negotiations, back-end scripting, data pushing, and the generation and loading of a fresh HTML "results" page each time the sort order is changed. But with the DOM, all activity takes place whether the user is connected to the server or not. Years after the page shown in Figures 15.1 through 15.3 was downloaded, its data could still be sorted without requiring a live connection and without the distraction of page replacement.

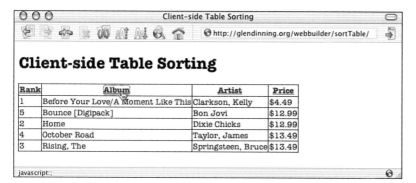

15.1
The DOM enables web pages to behave like desktop applications. In this demo by Porter Glendinning, data is sorted by album title when the user clicks the Album header (`http://glendinning.org/webbuilder/sortTable/`).

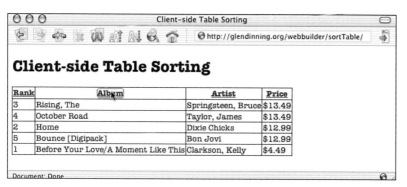

15.2
Clicking the header again reverses the sort order. The changed order is immediately visible on the original page. A separate "results" page is not needed.

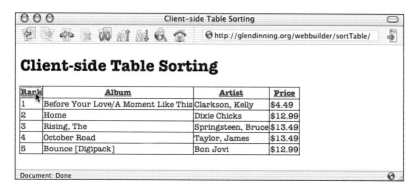

15.3
Clicking the Rank header re-sorts the list in numerical order, still without loading a new page and without requiring server/client processing or contact. View or download additional DOM demos at `http://glendinning.org/webbuilder/`.

Similarly, a potential catalog purchase can be deleted from a shopping cart without notifying the server until the customer decides to buy something or to search for additional products. Likewise, translations from one language to another can be provided at a click of the mouse [15.4, 15.5, 15.6]. The DOM handles these tasks by manipulating data in response to user actions. It can do this because every standard element of a web page is accessible to it in any

DOM-compliant user agent. (Put another way, the DOM manipulates standard web elements in the same way that ActionScript manipulates Flash file components.)

15.4
In this demo by David Eisenberg, Spanish-to-English translation is as close as a mouse click (`http://www.alistapart.com/stories/domtricks3/`).

La primera **fuente** para **conseguir** el sistema Linux es **la propia red** Internet, y es donde **estarán** siempre las **últimas** versiones y las aplicaciones **más actualizadas** en muchos **servidores** de FTP anónimo. Otra **vía** muy frecuente, de **interés** para **principiantes** y **para quienes** no **deseen** o **no puedan permitirse** copiar **tanta cantidad** de información **a traves de** la red, es **mediante** las versiones comercializadas en CDROM.

Show full translation

Click any bold word or phrase to see its meaning.

15.5
English speakers who have some knowledge of Spanish might choose to see translations for only those words or phrases that are unfamiliar to them.

La primera **fuente** para **conseguir** el sistema Linux es **la propia red** Internet, y es donde **estarán** siempre las **últimas** versiones y las aplicaciones **más actualizadas** en muchos **servidores** de FTP anónimo. Otra **vía** muy frecuente, de **interés** para **principiantes** y **para quienes** no **deseen** o **no puedan permitirse** copiar **tanta cantidad** de información **a traves de** la red, es **mediante** las versiones comercializadas en CDROM.

Show full translation

tanta cantidad
    such a quantity

15.6
The Spanish-challenged might choose Show Full Translation instead. All activity takes place on the client, without requiring a live connection, and with no need to load a separate "results" page.

La primera **fuente** para **conseguir** el sistema Linux es **la propia red** Internet, y es donde **estarán** siempre las **últimas** versiones y las aplicaciones **más actualizadas** en muchos **servidores** de FTP anónimo. Otra **vía** muy frecuente, de **interés** para **principiantes** y **para quienes** no **deseen** o **no puedan permitirse** copiar **tanta cantidad** de información **a traves de** la red, es **mediante** las versiones comercializadas en CDROM.

Show full translation

The primary source for obtaining the Linux system is the Internet itself, and it is where the latest versions and most current applications will be on many anonymous FTP servers. Another method, very frequently of interest to beginners or for those who don't want or might not be allowed to copy such a quantity of information over the net, is by means of commercial versions on CDROM.

Click any bold word or phrase at the left to see its meaning.

Although these demos are modest, their implications are profound. For years, programmers who wanted to create front-end applications had to use Java or Flash. Those tools are still available, of course, but browser support for the DOM empowers developers to create rich, powerful, web-based applications built entirely from the standards discussed in this book.

In this chapter, we'll focus on simple DOM-driven tasks that are commensurate with the needs of content and commerce sites. But DOM-driven development, combining XML, XHTML, CSS, and ECMAScript, seems poised to shape the future of the web.

So Where Does It Work?

Albeit with some differences (see the later section titled "Deep DOM Details"), the W3C DOM is supported by all of the following browsers:

- Netscape 6 and higher
- Mozilla 0.9 and higher
- Chimera/Navigator 0.6 and higher
- IE5/Windows and higher (naturally including IE6 and higher)
- IE5/Macintosh and higher
- Opera 7 (and to a limited extent, earlier versions theoretically dating back to Opera 4—but with so many parts missing in those earlier versions that they are not worth considering; fortunately, most Opera users upgrade often)
- Kmeleon (but with a few parts missing or a bit "off")
- Safari (based on KHTML, so it has a few parts missing or a bit "off")
- Konqueror (with some omissions; you cannot yet change the value of a text node, although if you don't know what that means, you're not going to try doing so anyway, so don't sweat it)

Missing in (Inter)action: Non-DOM Environments

What is missing from the previous list? IE4 (Macintosh and Windows) is missing from it. But almost no one uses IE4 any more, making its lack of DOM support pretty much of a nonissue. The iCab browser discussed in Chapter 8, "XHTML by Example: A Hybrid Layout (Part I)," is also missing from the list. That's likely not a major concern, either. Because iCab users lack access to the proprietary script-based interactivity found on nearly all websites, they are unlikely to be shocked by lack of access to *your* site's DOM-based interactivity.

Netscape 4 is also missing from the list. That might present a genuine problem for some. However, a few pages from now we'll share a simple DOM-sniffing technique that allows you to serve alternate content to Netscape 4 or almost any other browser that responds to JavaScript but does not understand the DOM.

What else is missing from the list? Handheld devices and web phones do not yet support the DOM, and text browsers like Lynx never will. In many cases, you can compensate for those user agents' lack of DOM support the same way you've always compensated for non-JavaScript environments. (You *have* always compensated for non-JavaScript environments, haven't you?)

To support non-DOM-capable devices, do the following:

- Use <noscript> elements that provide alternative access (a hypertext link instead of a fancy button, for instance).

- Test in Lynx, as described in the discussion of accessibility and JavaScript in Chapter 14, "Accessibility Basics."

- Serve genuine links with return false rather than bogus javascript: "links" that lead nowhere, such as <a href="javascript:" ...>. For instance, the code that follows is used to activate a style switcher at zeldman.com. It begins with a genuine link (/about/switch/), and its onclick trigger ends in return false:

```
<a href="/about/switch/"
➥onclick="setActiveStyleSheet('default'); return false;"
➥onkeypress="setActiveStyleSheet('default'); return false;"
➥accesskey="w">
<img src="/i/file.gif" width="25" height="16"
➥alt="Default style (white)." title="Default style (white)." />
</a>
```

Browsers that understand the DOM will ignore the link and invoke the function. Non-DOM and non-JavaScript-capable user agents will follow the link to a page [15.7] that explains the switcher and reassures users that nothing is wrong. (Other elements in the code excerpt include our old friends accesskey and onkeypress, which are both used to make the page more accessible, as described in Chapters 8 and 14, respectively.)

15.7
Beginning a JavaScript event with a genuine link and ending it with `return false` enables your site to serve DOM-capable browsers while accounting for the needs of alternative device users and non-DOM browser users (`http://www.zeldman.com/about/switch/`).

The Curse of Quasi-Semi-Demi-Hemi-Conformance

More problematic than what is missing from the list of DOM-conformant user agents is what is included on it. For instance, Opera 4, 5, and 6 think they understand the DOM even though they do not, and the user agent strings with which they identify themselves make it impossible to code around the problem via browser detection. We're not huge fans of browser detection to begin with; when we deem it necessary to send browsers down alternate paths, we prefer to test for capabilities instead of user agent strings. Alas, Opera 5/6's hallucinatory belief that it "gets" the DOM can prevent these methods, too, from working. We'll get down and dirty with the nitty-gritty details a few paragraphs from now ("Please, DOM, Don't Hurt 'Em"). But outdated Opera versions are not our only problem.

Deep DOM Details

Although all modern browsers support the DOM, they don't all support it in exactly the same way, which is a minor headache for designers using the techniques shown in this chapter, but a major migraine for coders harnessing the DOM to build complex, web-based applications. Fortunately for such developers, Peter-Paul Koch's DOM Compatibility Overview keeps detailed track of these DOM differences (`http://www.xs4all.nl/~ppk/js/index.html?version5.html`). If the page should move during one of its frequent updates, simply navigate to `http://www.xs4all.nl/~ppk/`.

The tireless Mr. Koch additionally maintains the free W3C DOM Mailing List, whose members include sophisticated script jockeys from around the globe (`http://www.xs4all.nl/~ppk/js/list.html`). The "W3C" in the group's name does not imply W3C ownership or endorsement. It is used to distinguish between the W3C DOM and any other—for instance, to make clear that it is not a mailing list for coders who are interested in discussing the Microsoft IE 4.0/Windows DOM.

DOM Fun with Dick and Jane

In addition to the resources discussed in the preceding paragraphs, the splendid Mr. Koch has penned an introduction to the DOM (`http://www.xs4all.nl/~ppk/js/dom1.html`). Read the introduction, and you will no longer feel shame when encountering buzzwords and phrases like "node" and "tree structure." You still might not know what they mean, but they will begin to take on a fuzzy familiarity—like Midwestern place names to a New Yorker.

David Eisenberg's DOM series at A List Apart provides another fine way to get comfortable with the DOM (`http://www.alistapart.com/stories/dom/`). After a friendly introductory article and tutorial, Eisenberg explains how to show and hide components (`http://www.alistapart.com/stories/dom2/`), create dynamic menus (`http://www.alistapart.com/stories/domtricks2/`), and update page content (`http://www.alistapart.com/stories/domtricks3/`), as in Figures **15.4** through **15.6**.

Please, DOM, Don't Hurt 'Em

DOM-based scripts won't do a bit of good for browsers that entirely lack support for the W3C DOM standard. Netscape 4 is our chief problem here. The solution is to sniff for DOM compliance, and in its absence, to serve alternate content or an alternate web page.

That we sometimes need to do so is regrettable. The goal of standards is to serve the same content to all user agents. In the case of HTML and XHTML, we can do exactly that. Where CSS is concerned, in Chapter 9, "CSS Basics," we saw how the Two-Sheet method enables us to send the same files to all user agents, while using the `@import` directive to protect old browsers from styles they can't handle. And in Chapters 12, "Working with Browsers Part II: Box Models, Bugs, and Workarounds," and 13, "Working with Browsers Part III: Typography," we learned how the Box Model Hack can exploit parsing bugs in IE5/Windows and outdated versions of Opera to serve the same styles to all without generating errors in browsers like IE5/Windows that get font sizes and the box model wrong.

In each of these cases, we've managed to serve the same files to all comers, albeit with the occasional stripe of tar to patch compliance potholes; however, we cannot smooth over lack of DOM support in the same way. Although IE5/Windows bungles the box model, it is still a CSS browser that can parse a CSS file. But Netscape 4 is in no way a DOM-compliant browser—and in fairness to the manufacturer, the W3C was still hammering out the DOM specification at the time Netscape 4 was released. Unless you are Nostradamus, you can't support what doesn't yet exist.

We can no more expect a non-DOM-compliant browser to make use of a DOM-driven script than we can demand that a chicken make use of a calculator. What we *can* do is test for knowledge of the DOM, and, in its absence, send the browser to an alternate page (or, better still, insert alternate content as needed via Server Side Includes [SSI], Active Server Pages [ASP], or any of the other middleware solutions).

How It Works

Dori Smith (`www.dori.com`) of WaSP invented the DOM sniff in early 2001 as a means of implementing that group's Browser Upgrade Campaign (discussed in Chapter 4, "XML Conquers the World [And Other Web Standards Success Stories]"). But it can be used for *any* purpose, in most cases replacing complicated browser detection scripts that are nearly impossible to keep up-to-date.

The way the DOM sniff works is simple. After you create a valid page, insert the following script in the `<head>` of your document or somewhere in a linked JavaScript (.js) file:

```
if (!document.getElementById) {
    window.location =
        "http://www.somesite.com/somepage/"
}
```

where *somesite*.com represents your website and /*somepage*/ represents an alternate page whose content Netscape 4 (or any other non-DOM-capable browser) can handle. This alternate page might use JavaScript to emulate the behavior of the "standard" page, or it might more usefully contain script-free content that *any* browser can handle.

The alternate page might not even do that. Instead, it might advise the user to download Netscape 7 or a similarly compliant browser. This "upgrade now" approach is outdated and will not please Netscape 4 users who are *unable* to upgrade because of stupid corporate policies. That was the legitimate gripe against WaSP's Browser Upgrade Campaign of 2001. Even today, it is still a semi-legit beef, although the number of organizations that inflict this ancient, nonstandards-compliant relic on their employees thankfully continues to shrink.

However, if rich DOM-based applications are an important part of your site, or even its *raison d'être*, you have no choice other than to recommend that the visitor return with a DOM-compliant browser. On such a site, the DOM sniff protects users from content their browser can't handle while offering them the option to come back and enjoy the content after a free download.

Simplifying Dynamic Sites: Smoking or Nonsmoking

If you already create dynamic or conditional pages, and if page components vary by user agent, you can use the DOM sniff to serve appropriate chunks of content to non-DOM browsers, and it can also vastly simplify your content management. Instead of sending one type of content to Internet Explorer 5 for Windows, another to Internet Explorer 5 for Macintosh, yet another to Internet Explorer 6, another to Netscape 6, and so on and so on ad infinitum, you can simply serve two kinds of content: DOM and non-DOM.

Code Variants

In a global .js file, the code would look as it does previously. When you're inserting the script on an individual page, naturally, you would type it between `<head>` and `</head>`. In XHTML 1 Transitional documents, the script would read as follows:

```
<script type="text/javascript" language="javascript">
<!-- //
if (!document.getElementById) {
    window.location =
        " http://www.somesite.com/somepage/"
}
    // -->
</script>
```

In XHTML Strict documents, you would either use a global .js file or insert this:

```
<script type="text/javascript">
// <![CDATA[
if (!document.getElementById) {
    window.location =
        " http://www.somesite.com/somepage/"
}
    // ]]>
</script>
```

Why It Works

The DOM sniff is binary, a toggle, no more complicated than an on-off switch. Because getElementById is a DOM method, conformant browsers skip right past it. By contrast, browsers that do not recognize getElementById are not DOM-compliant and will obey the redirect, thus being taken to a page whose content they can understand.

JavaScript redirects disable the Back button, and this is not friendly. But you *do not* need to follow the DOM sniff with window.location. You can follow the DOM sniff with any command you determine to be in your users' best interest.

Why It Rocks

There is no need to create, test, and continually update and maintain a long, complex browser detection script. We are no longer testing for user agent strings. We are testing instead for awareness of a W3C spec. Pretty neat. Pretty simple. And pretty cost effective, too.

Where It Breaks: The Not So Grand Old Opera

As suggested earlier in this chapter, the DOM sniff breaks with old versions of the Opera browser that *think* they understand the DOM. Instead of following the "else" path hewn for nonconformant user agents, these old versions of Opera blip by getElementById and then choke on a page they cannot properly parse.

How can we solve for this equation? We can't resort to old-fangled browser detection because Opera by default identifies itself as Internet Explorer. If we are using the DOM sniff to lead Netscape 4 users to an alternate page, one thing we might do on our "standard" page is include a note linking to that alternate page and inviting "Opera folks" to visit that page instead. Such a solution is as graceful as a Mack truck, and the comparison is unfair to Mack trucks. It intrudes on the consciousness of *all* visitors, disrupting user experience with awkward browser awareness and making your site appear unprofessional. Not only that, a "click here, Opera folks" notice might wrongly prompt Opera 7 users into leaving a DOM-based page their browser can actually handle.

So what do we do? In this writer's opinion, we do nothing. If our DOM-driven site fails in Opera 6, we trust the user to figure out that maybe now would be a good time to upgrade to Opera 7 or later. And now, enough sadness! Let's take this baby for a test drive and see how she does on the open road. (Our driving metaphors are nearly as bad as our sports metaphors, we fear.)

Showing and Hiding

For many reasons, you might want to cloak some of your page's content when the page loads, revealing it in response to a visitor's actions [15.8, 15.9, 15.10, 15.11]. The DOM makes it easy to show and hide content.

At zeldman.com, a sidebar to the left of the main content area contains many links to third-party sites. These links might initially overwhelm the visitor, so they are hidden from view when the page loads [15.8]. The click of a simple hyperlink reveals them [15.9] at the visitor's discretion. Another click hides them again.

The technique requires only a few components. In the site's JavaScript file (http://www.zeldman.com/j/nu.js), a simple function that makes use of our old friend, getElementByID, creates the ability to toggle display:

```
// toggle visibility
function toggle( targetId ){
  if (document.getElementById){
        target = document.getElementById( targetId );
            if (target.style.display == "none"){
                target.style.display = "";
            } else {
                target.style.display = "none";
            }
    }
}
```

An include file (http://www.zeldman.com/includes/outside2.html) contains the third-party links and the markup and code to toggle their display status.

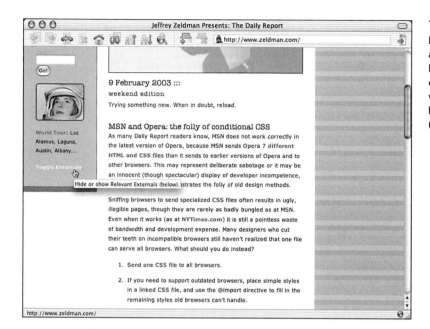

15.8
DOM-based showing
and hiding at its most
basic. The page's sidebar
contains a list of links
whose display is initially
hidden from view
(`www.zeldman.com`).

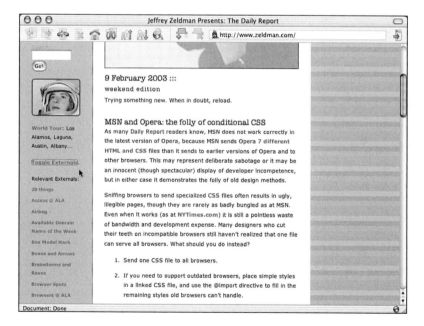

15.9
When Toggle Externals is
clicked, the list is revealed.

First comes a paragraph that initiates the toggle function, associates it with a named variable (outside2), provides basic instructional text (Toggle Externals), and supplements it with a title attribute to the anchor link:

```
<p><a href="/" onclick="toggle('outside2');return false;"
➥title="Hide or show Relevant Externals (below).">Toggle
➥Externals</a>.</p>
```

The definition list immediately following this paragraph bears the id attribute value (outside2) that the function is looking for and includes an inline CSS rule ("display: none;") that hides the list until its display status is toggled:

```
<dl id="outside2" style="display:none;">
<dt>Relevant Externals:</dt>
<dd><a href="http://www.somesite.com/"
➥title="Description.">Site name</a></dd>
etc.
```

We have used inline CSS ("display: none;"), but we did not have to do so. The site's external style sheet could as easily have included a rule stating that content whose id was "outside2" would have its display switched off by default. Such a rule would have looked like this:

```
#outside2    {
     display: none;
     }
```

If that rule were part of an external style sheet, the markup for the definition list would simply read as follows:

```
<dl id="outside2">
<dt>Relevant Externals:</dt>
<dd><a href="http://www.somesite.com/"
➥title="Description.">Site name</a></dd>
etc.
```

If you want an element to be invisible but to still take up space in your layout, use visibility: hidden instead.

Combining Show/Hide with Other Techniques

The example we've just seen is showing and hiding at its most basic. The technique can be amended to do whatever you want. On the Happy Cog Projects page [15.10], the visitor is initially treated to a series of nine neat icons, each representing a project. When an icon is pressed [15.11], text pertaining to that project is revealed. As a bonus, the icon "lights up" on rollover.

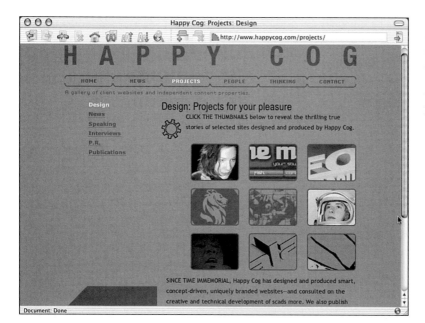

15.10
DOM-based showing and hiding can be combined easily with other effects (http://www.happycog.com/projects/).

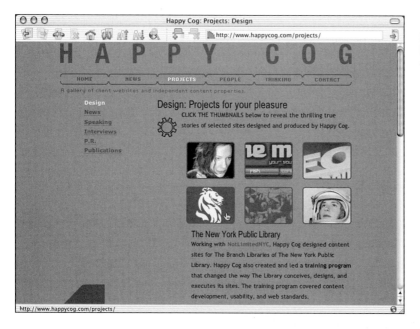

15.11
Here, showing and hiding is combined with traditional rollover effects.

We use the same "show/hide" function that we wrote for zeldman.com again in Happy Cog's primary JavaScript file (http://www.happycog.com/j/h.js). The markup at http://www.happycog.com/ is a bit more ornate, but conceptually it is as simple as what we had before. For instance, in the top row of icons, we use the function to toggle the visibility of text within an element whose id is chcopy. Here is the markup and JavaScript with an additional function not yet shown:

```
<a href="/projects/" onclick="toggle('chcopy');return false;">
<img src="/i/p/ch.gif" width="100" height="75" border="0"
➡alt="Charlotte Gray." /></a>
```

Here it is again, this time with the additional JavaScript, an ordinary rollover on the image whose name is ch, included and marked in bold:

```
<a href="/projects/" onclick="toggle('chcopy');return false;"
   onmouseover="changeImages('ch', '/i/p/cho.gif'); return
➡true;"
   onmouseout="changeImages('ch', '/i/p/ch.gif'); return
➡true;">
<img name="ch" src="/i/p/ch.gif" width="100" height="75"
➡border="0" alt="Charlotte Gray." /></a>
```

Farther down on the page, we come to the hidden content, whose markup and code you should now be able to easily understand:

```
<div id="chcopy" style="display:none">
<h2>Title of this section.</h2>
<p>The first paragraph goes here.</p>
<p>More text goes here, followed by an opportunity for the
reader to invoke the toggle function once again, thereby
hiding the content he has just read: [<a href="/projects/"
onclick="toggle('chcopy');return false;">Close text</a>.]</p>
</div>
```

Are you limited to combining show/hide with rollovers? Heck, no. You can combine showing and hiding with rollovers, pop-ups, sliding menus, and giant screaming chimps if you consider it in your visitors' interest to do so. And if you do consider it in your visitors' interest, we would be interested in meeting your visitors.

Dynamic Menus (Drop-Down and Expandable)

DHTML menus have at least four kinds of stink on them:

- Developers recall the overlarge marketing promises, undersized perform-ance, and woeful incompatibilities of proprietary 1998 "DHTML."

- Committees incapable of basing site architecture on anything other than the egos of their members have given us multilayered menus that frustrate us instead of guiding us to the content we seek.

- Undertested "DHTML" menus that fail in our browsers have prevented us all from using one site or another.

- WYSIWYG-generated DHTML menus have all too frequently "solved" the cross-browser, cross-platform problem by means of bloated, nonstruc-tural markup and gaseous, browser-specific scripts that double or triple page weight (thereby increasing page *wait*).

Between shortsighted proprietary methods, non-user-oriented architecture, insufficient testing, and sheer bloat, DHTML is widely perceived as outdated and faintly embarrassing. Like Cousin Elmer's GIF animations, DHTML is seen as one of the web's pointless annoyances; and an aroma redolent of sickness on ships hovers over the entire category.

But the DOM corrects many of these problems by working across conformant browsers and by using compact, structural markup and valid CSS to achieve its ends. Here's one of our favorites: David Lindquist's "Using Lists for DHTML Menus" (http://www.gazingus.org/dhtml/?id=109) employs unordered lists to create compact DHTML drop-down [15.12] and expandable menus [15.13, 15.14]. Demos are accompanied by downloadable CSS and JavaScript files that you can use as-is or customize to suit your site. (Sorry, not even web standards can help with the committee-driven site architecture problem.)

15.12
It looks like any other drop-down menu; however, instead of proprietary code and bloated, nonstructural markup, this one uses appro-priate list markup, valid CSS, and JavaScript (http://www.gazingus.org/html/menuDropdown.html). Download the Source files to use on your site.

15.13

An expandable menu sports clickable plus and minus icons (http://www.gazingus.org/html/menuExpandable2.html).

15.14

The menu expands as the user clicks. Once more, structural markup, valid CSS, and a bit of JavaScript work together via the DOM to offer more than the sum of the parts. Again, you can download the Source files for your own sites' use.

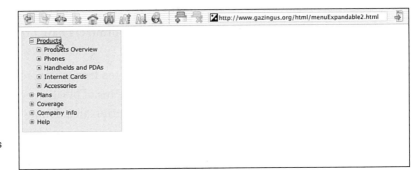

Style Switchers: Aiding Access, Offering Choice

In Chapter 13, we discussed the impossibility of delivering web type without alienating at least some of your potential visitors, and lamented that 13 years into the web's evolution as a medium, pixels are still the most reliable method of sizing type—and the most troublesome for IE/Windows users. What if you could offer your visitors a choice of user-selectable type approaches? What if you could even change your layout while you were at it?

According to CSS, you can. CSS allows you to associate any web page not only with a default (persistent) style sheet, but also with *alternate* CSS files. In the interest of enhancing accessibility, these alternate style sheets might offer much larger type or a higher-contrast color scheme [**15.15, 15.16**]. Or they could completely change the site's appearance for purposes of what was once called "user customization."

The W3C recommends that browsers provide a means of allowing users to choose any of these alternate styles, and Gecko-based browsers like Mozilla and Netscape 7 do just that. But as of this writing, no other browsers offer this function. The creative and accessibility benefits of alternate style sheets might have remained beyond reach forever. But in 2001, Paul Sowden solved the problem by taking advantage of the fact that alternate style sheets, like any other page component, are accessible to the DOM.

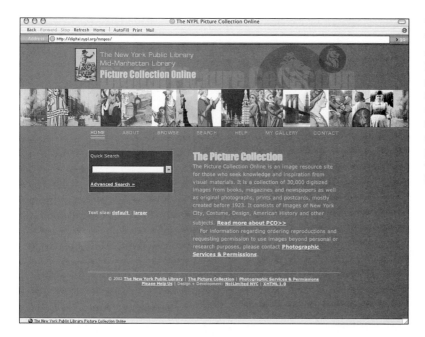

15.15
The Picture Collection Online is one of The New York Public Library's many image resource sites (http://digital.nypl.org/mmpco/). It uses a style switcher to avoid potential problems for users who suffer from visual impairments.

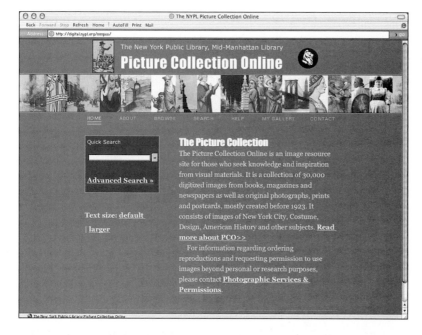

15.16
When the user chooses Larger, not only does the font size bump up, but contrast is increased, and a lovely (but potentially confusing, for low-vision people) layered background is hidden.

In A List Apart's "Alternative Style: Working with Alternate Style Sheets" (http://www.alistapart.com/stories/alternate/), Sowden wrote a JavaScript file (http://www.alistapart.com/stories/alternate/styleswitcher.js) that enabled site visitors to load alternate styles at the click of a link, a form element, or any other interactive widget. After explaining how to use his script on your site, Sowden released the code as open source. Thousands of designers and developers have since used the code on commercial, public sector, and private sites to solve accessibility problems [15.15, 15.16], explore creative effects, or both [15.17, 15.18, 15.19]. Read the ALA article, download the code, and play!

More DOM to Come?

This chapter provides merely a teasing taste of what the DOM can do and how it is being used in sometimes simple, sometimes sophisticated ways on commercial, personal, and public sector sites. You can use the DOM to create rich web applications, deliver creative effects, enhance accessibility, and more. At present, we know of no easy-to-understand book or website on the subject. A fine book could surely be written showing designers how to do amazing things with the DOM, and we trust that New Riders will bring it to you. Meanwhile, keep watching the skies.

15.17
Eric Meyer's personal and CSS-educational site uses an ALA style switcher along with handspun additions (www.meyerweb.com). Here we see the site using its alternate "natural" style sheet. (Notice the photographic background and the decorative effects at the top, right.)

15.18
Here it is again, using a basic style sheet—no photographic background, no decorative flourishes at the top right—with element positioning flipped. (The navigation has moved from right to left.)

15.19
Here, the user has switched back to the "natural" style sheet but increased the type size from 11px to 16px in "advanced" mode.

chapter sixteen

A CSS Redesign

In this chapter, we'll take much of what we've learned about markup, CSS, accessibility, and the DOM and put it to work in a site redesign that separates structure from presentation. We'll define and meet goals that serve our site's users and might benefit yours as well. For good measure, once we're pleased with the site's look and feel, we'll create a user-selectable *alternative* layout powered by CSS and the DOM.

Although the visual design of the site shown in this chapter is nothing special, the construction methods are important, for they are the techniques that we'll use to create many sites soon, and nearly all sites eventually. Previous chapters have discussed bits and pieces of the standards puzzle or told how to create hybrid sites that combine classic and modern methods. This chapter will bring you closer to the typical design practices of tomorrow's web.

This chapter will explore techniques used to create CSS layouts—from the basics of establishing page sections to ideas that are far from basic, such as creating menu buttons out of structured lists and generating JavaScript-like image rollover effects without JavaScript and without even using the XHTML img element. In addition to covering specific techniques, we will discuss ways of thinking, such as rules-based versus grid-based design.

Defining Goals

In this redesign project, undertaken specifically for this book, we will retool the look, feel, structure, and basic functionality of zeldman.com, the author's personal site. Whether you capture the attention of thousands of readers or simply work to please yourself and a family member or two, a personal site is invaluable, especially when you're experimenting with CSS and other standards you might not be entirely ready to use in client or in-house development.

A personal site can also help you realize that you are not alone as a designer or practitioner. By creating such a site, you will join a thriving community of standards-oriented designers and developers who are surprisingly eager to help one another. Many times, when stymied by a troublesome problem of CSS, markup, or JavaScript, we've shared our bafflement at zeldman.com. Soon afterward, readers have sent email messages containing the seeds of a solution to the question posed on our site. Likewise, after reading other people's sites, we've often been moved to send them a suggestion about the issues that puzzled them.

We are not unique. This happens to anyone who writes about web design or development issues on his personal site. Try it; you'll like it.

Brand Character

Launched in May 1995, zeldman.com offers tutorials, news, and insights about web design along with anything else that interests us. The brand character is irreverent, passionate, and inquisitive; the design sensibility is clean, minimalist, and quirkily stylish. Our redesign must preserve these attributes.

Top 10 Goals

Additional requirements of the redesign are less brand specific. They might be as relevant to your site as to ours. Listed next are our top 10 goals for this project:

1. The site must be as usable in nongraphical environments as it is in the best and latest browsers by Netscape, Microsoft, Opera, and others. Its content and basic functions must be available to any browser or device; its layout should work in any reasonably CSS-savvy browser.

2. Markup must validate against the XHTML 1.0 Transitional spec and must avoid presentational elements. We are separating structure from presentation, which means no nonsemantic spans and divs when p or h1 would serve. It means no spacer GIF images, no tables except those used to present tabular data, no outdated or invalid attributes like bgcolor or marginheight, no misuse of <blockquote> to achieve formatting, and no cheating with <br /> tags when a structural element can create the desired visual effect while also conveying meaning. (If these goals confuse you, reread Chapter 7, "Tighter, Firmer Pages Guaranteed: Structure and Meta-Structure in Strict and Hybrid Markup.")

3. CSS must validate and should be as compact and as logically arranged as possible (see Chapters 9, "CSS Basics," and 10, "CSS in Action: A Hybrid Layout [Part II]").

4. To help meet our goal of delivering content and basic functions in almost any conceivable browsing environment, the site should strive to be seamlessly *accessible*. Too often, the desire to attain accessibility falls by the wayside except as a string of empty words. To avoid such a fate, we will test our work against an accepted accessibility standard. We've chosen U.S. Section 508 (Chapter 14, "Accessibility Basics"), but any standard would do. The point is to choose a set of guidelines and then adhere to them. (Imagine that.)

5. The site must deliver a recognizably branded look and feel without squandering visitor or server bandwidth on bloated markup, excessively complex scripts, or needless images. The site must not waste resources, but it must possess style. It need not blow the visitor away (excessive fripperies lie far outside the brand character), but it should feel like a place. It should also feel like the recognizable evolution of a *familiar* place rather than a radical departure from previous incarnations.

6. The site should offer visual interactivity (some of it playful) so that it feels like a living thing.

7. Wherever possible, equivalents to dynamic elements should be provided for the benefit of those who are using text browsers or other nontraditional devices. (This is just another way of saying that you shouldn't use interactivity as an excuse for poor accessibility.)

8. The site should provide user customization options without losing its brand character in the process.

9. Text should be easy and pleasurable to read and should be made the focus of the site, which is a reading, rather than a shopping/clicking/button-pushing site. Thoughtful handling of text is important to any site, but it is absolutely essential to one that is read like a daily newspaper.

10. Navigation should be clear, intuitive, and obvious. It can and probably should have some visual panache, but it must also work in nonvisual environments. Visitors who access the web in linear fashion (for instance, via screen readers) should be able to skip right past it. If the navigation can be achieved using structural elements, such as the components of an unordered list, so much the better.

There are additional goals as well, but those will do.

By all rights, these requirements should be part of any web design practice and of most site design projects. They ought to be commonplace and unremarkable. Most of the requirements should go without saying, just as it goes without saying that a grocery store's produce should be edible and free from disease, or that automobiles should be capable of controlled movement, or that clothing should protect the body from the vagaries of weather and the inappropriate scrutiny of strangers. Yet because of the odd way our industry has grown up, these goals are far from commonplace and they actually needed to be stated.

Method and Madness

At the end of this chapter, we will have produced a default CSS layout [16.1] and an alternate version [16.2] that the visitor can select by clicking a user interface widget. Designing the alternate version is mainly a matter of saving the original CSS file under a new name and editing its values. Colors change, as do a few fonts, and a nonscrolling image is positioned at the bottom of the screen, but essentially it will take little additional work to create the alternate style. How many alternate styles can you serve on one site? As many as you like.

16.1
Here we see the completed site's front page in its default (white) look and feel (www.zeldman.com).

16.2
Here's the site again with an alternate look and feel, an orange flavor that will likely look pretty darned murky in the pages of this black-and-white book but feels nice on the web.

Both designs look simple, and they *are* simple, but it would take an entire book to completely explain the thinking behind each and every rule used in the two style sheets. Our discussion will focus on the highlights (and on a few interesting or important tangents) rather than tediously listing and describing every CSS rule and every XHTML or accessibility nuance. Such a listing would also be somewhat redundant because Chapters 7 through 14 have covered many of the CSS, XHTML, and accessibility enhancement techniques that are used in this pure CSS redesign.

Little Topsy and How She Grew

The revised look and feel discussed in this chapter evolved over a period of days and made use of some components from a previous CSS incarnation that had also evolved over time, occasionally changing in response to reader feedback. This was not your father's project management style.

In designing commercial sites, we all study brand character, dream up user scenarios to guide navigational and architectural decisions, and collaborate with various specialists to determine site flow and technical and business requirements. We then spend weeks designing and refining in Photoshop, Illustrator, or FreeHand.

Revisions follow presentations. Dates are met or missed, scope expands and contracts, tears fall, and hearty Anglo-Saxonisms echo from den to dale (or more accurately, from cubicle to cubicle). Next comes coding and testing and recoding and retesting on staging servers, until we hope that our most obvious mistakes have been recognized and fixed. Months later, the project finally makes its live debut.

Evolving the Whole from Its Parts

The methodology discussed previously is typical of use- and brand-driven site design assignments. But for this project, we were having none of it. Instead, with no overarching plan and no comps to guide us, we began tentatively sketching individual site components, designing on a modular rather than a global level. (First, design the doorknob. It will lead you to the design of the door. Eventually, without quite knowing how you got there, you will have designed a house. We swiped the idea of modular design from interface expert Jeffrey Veen, who has long been a proponent of it.)

We made one decision up front: The layout would consist of three primary areas. Having come to that conclusion, we ceased all attempts at a master plan.

Instead of the whole, we focused on bits and pieces. What should the navigation widget look like? How will paragraphs sit in relation to subheads? If we link to third-party sites, should those links be visible the moment the site loads, or should the visitor have the option to turn them on and off?

We did most of our designing in code, not in Photoshop. And we did it in public, changing the site in fits and starts as readers watched. Some thought we had lost our minds. Others enjoyed peeking over our shoulder. Some complained about one piece or another, and their gripes gave rise to new ideas. In this way, we discovered, rather than planned and executed, much of what is discussed in this chapter. In a sense, all design works that way, but most of the fumbling is hidden from our users and our clients, who see only the results, never the struggle. For purposes of delivering a coherent chapter, we will pretend we always knew what we were doing and omit interim steps and bad ideas along the way.

Visit www.zeldman.com to be certain you are viewing the latest and most correct versions of markup, CSS, and code. You can view style sheets at http://www.zeldman.com/c/wh.css and http://www.zeldman.com/c/or.css. Like any living site, zeldman.com is a work perpetually in process, and some design aspects might have changed by the time you read this book.

Enough talk. Let's rock.

Establishing Basic Parameters

We've decided that our template will contain three main areas [**16.3**]:

- A brand bar at the top will double as a Home button and might also contain the primary navigation. We will call this area "new menu."

- A sidebar at the left will contain secondary navigation, Search, user interface widgets, blurbs, and links. "Secondary nav" seems like an okay label for this area.

- The primary content area, as one might expect, will hold the site's primary content (which we hope will be more interesting than this sentence). Let's get super creative and name this area "primary content."

16.3
The template will be divided into three main areas.

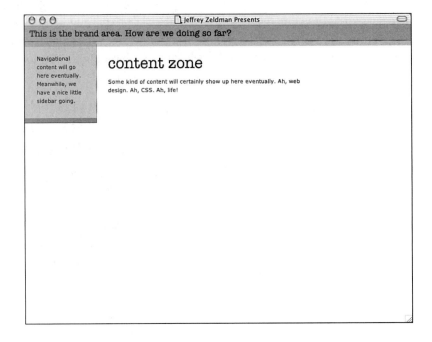

In our XHTML page, following the DOCTYPE, namespace, and meta data, our first, tentative strokes look like this:

```
<div id="newmenu"></div>
<div id="secondarynav"></div>
<div id="primarycontent"></div>
```

Each of these three main areas will eventually flow with the sap of content. But first, each must be styled. In our default (white) style sheet, we establish general layout parameters, grouping them together toward the top. Let's begin with the new menu area, which is visible at the top of Figure **16.3** and stretches all the way from left to right:

```
/* Establish general layout parameters */
#newmenu    {
    background: #e0861e;
    color: #000;
    border: 0;
    border-bottom: 1px dotted #000;
    margin: 0;
    padding: 0;
    text-align: left;
    height: 31px;
    }
```

After reading Chapters 9 and 10 and boning up on the box model in Chapter 12, "Working with Browsers Part II: Box Models, Bugs, and Workarounds," you know how to interpret these rules, but we'll summarize: The area is 31px tall, its background is painted a non-web-safe orange (#e0861e), its content is deliberately aligned left to avoid a bug in some versions of Internet Explorer, and its bottom sports a dotted border effect. We don't need to compensate for box model incompatibilities because margins, padding, and borders are all set to zero. The 1px dotted border at the bottom might eat into the area above by exactly one pixel in IE5/Windows because of that browser's confusion about the way margins, padding, and borders interact with one another in the CSS box model. But no one will notice, and it isn't worth worrying about.

Installing the Sidebar

The secondary navigation or Sidebar area [**16.4**] comes next:

```
#secondarynav    {
     /* float: left; */
     position: absolute;
     left: 0;
     margin: 0;
     padding: 0 25px 25px 25px;
     background: #bdcdbd url(/i/2003/sbbot4.gif) repeat-x
     ➥bottom left;
     border: 0;
     border-top: 10px solid #95a580;
     border-right: 1px dotted #000;
     border-bottom: 1px dotted #000;
     width: 151px;   /* False value for IE4-5.x/Win */
     voice-family: "\"}\"";
     voice-family:inherit;
     width: 100px;    /* Actual value for conformant browsers
*/
     }
html>#secondarynav {
     width: 100px; /* Be nice to Opera */
     }
```

16.4

Hey, look at me! I'm a Sidebar! The strip of color at the top is created with a CSS border property. The slightly darker strip at the bottom is a GIF image created in Photoshop.

Navigational content will go here eventually. Meanwhile, we have a nice little sidebar going.

This is a lot to look at, especially on a printed page, but you are familiar with most of it by now. The area is 151px wide overall (100px content, with left and right margins of 25px, and one additional pixel for the dotted border at the right). We're using the Box Model Hack (Chapter 12) to feed IE5/Windows the values it likes, and a "Be Nice to Opera" rule to save the Opera browser from one of its parsing bugs. But there *is* a lot going on here, so let's look closer at some of it, starting with the positioning part.

The Positioning Part

The positioning part of the rule looks like this:

```
#secondarynav    {
     /* float: left; */
     position: absolute;
     left: 0;
```

Lines that accomplish the positioning are highlighted in bold; `/* float: left; */` is merely a comment on what these two lines of CSS are achieving, or, if you prefer, on what they are emulating. (CSS comments are written in the same fashion as the C programming language.) The first rule takes the sidebar out of the normal flow of the document (`position: absolute;`); the second (`left: 0;`) sticks it all the way to the left, under the menu area.

Could we have done this a different way? Oh, you betcha. In fact, in an earlier version, we did it the following way, with the point of difference highlighted in bold:

```
#secondarynav    {
    float: left;
    margin: 0;
    padding: 0 25px 25px 25px;
    background: #bdcdbd url(/i/2003/sbbot4.gif) repeat-x
    ➥bottom left;
    border: 0;
    border-top: 10px solid #95a580;
    border-right: 1px dotted #000;
    border-bottom: 1px dotted #000;
    width: 151px;   /* False value for IE4-5.x/Win */
    voice-family: "\"}\"";
    voice-family:inherit;
    width: 100px;      /* Actual value for browsers that get
                        ➥CSS */
}
```

Notice that the area is told to float: left. This causes it to float to the left. You were expecting, maybe, Shakespeare? To the wrong place hast thou sojourned, gentle reader. Okay, enough of that—and on to the reason we ended up choosing absolute positioning instead of float.

The Trouble with *float*, Part 999

Unfortunately, as discussed in Chapter 10, some popular browsers have trouble with float, including the inability to actually float, or the tendency to miscalculate the height of floated areas as the visitor links from page to page, thus chopping off bits and pieces of your content. You can compensate for the latter problem via JavaScript, but doing so might whisk you into a fresh hell of creepy, crawly browser bugs we'll let someone else write about in another book.

Also, when you float an area, you risk breaking the layout if the visitor's monitor is set smaller than the overall width of the page. Using absolute positioning to *emulate* float seems to solve this problem in most cases. CSS layouts are based on float, and patchy support for it remains a real problem. It's as if cars worked swell except for the steering part. But for each bug there is a workaround, and float emulation via absolute positioning was ours. (Actually, Drew McLellan of DreamweaverFever.com and The Web Standards Project's Dreamweaver Task Force recommended the workaround.)

Filenaming Conventions

In our mania to save bandwidth, we strive to use short names for directories: /i/ instead of /images/; /j/ instead of /javascript/; and /c/ instead of /css/ or /styles/.

We take the same approach to filenames. For instance, the image used to fill in the bottom of the sidebar in "Creating Color Bars," is titled sbbot.gif rather than sidebar_bottom.gif. The fewer characters we use, the fewer bytes we waste. We're not 100% consistent in this practice, but we try.

Likewise, in "A Home Button with CSS Rollover Effects," instead of using logo_banner.gif for the default state of a logo banner image and logo_banner_over.gif for the hover or "over" state of that image, we use lb.gif and lbo.gif, respectively. Where numbers appear in these filenames, they indicate versions; thus lbo2.gif is a second draft. (The "o" in lbo2.gif is the letter "o" for "over." It is not a zero.)

Creating Color Bars

Still studying the rules that give rise to the sidebar, notice that we're painting a warm gray-green background color (#bdcdbd) and positioning a solid 10px #95a580 (medium gray-green) color block at the top via the CSS border-top property, which can be used to create a color block as tall as you would like:

```
border-top: 10px solid #95a580;
```

We want a matching 10px solid block of color at the bottom of the area, but we've already used up our border-bottom property to create the 1px dotted border effect. We can't have two border-bottom properties. (There is a CSS way around that, but as far as we know, it only works in IE5/Macintosh.)

But we can do something else. We can create an appropriately sized colored rectangle in Photoshop. We can name it sbbot (for sidebar bottom), save a GIF copy (sbbot4.gif), and use it as a background that will be positioned at the bottom left and will only repeat horizontally (repeat-x), not vertically (repeat-y). And that, friends, is exactly what we've done here:

```
background: #bdcdbd url(/i/2003/sbbot4.gif) repeat-x bottom
➥left;
```

We now have an appropriately colored and sized sidebar with a thin dotted border and 10px-tall color stripes at its top and bottom [**16.4**]. (We're getting a ton of mileage out of Figure **16.4**, but getting a ton of mileage out of an ounce of components is part of what good web design is about.)

The Color Matching Problem

Interestingly, it is impossible to get the lower color bar—the one created in Photoshop—to match the upper bar created via the CSS border property, even when you copy and paste the CSS border-top color (#95a580) directly into Photoshop's color picker. Thanks to conflicting technologies, color matching simply isn't possible on the web. Here are some issues that prevent it:

- All browsers adjust gamma before they display pages. You might have calibrated your monitor. You might even have set it to sRGB (http:// www.w3.org/Graphics/Color/sRGB.html), a standard default color space for the Internet. But browsers aren't smart enough to know you've done that. They will tweak your gamma anyway. And each browser changes the gamma differently from the way every other browser does it.

- 16-bit systems can't accurately reproduce *any* color other than black or white. On 16-bit systems, web browsers miscalculate CSS colors in one direction and image colors in the opposite direction, as explained by David Lehn and Hadley Stern (http://hotwired.lycos.com/ webmonkey/00/37/index2a.html?tw=design).

We chose to view the color-matching dilemma as a creative opportunity and selected a *different* color for the bottom bar—a darker color that felt more like the "bottom."

A Space for Content

Creating the primary content area (the big whitespace in Figure **16.3**) is straightforward enough:

```
#primarycontent    {
     border: 0;
     border-top: 10px solid #bdcdbd;
     padding: 0;
     margin: 0;
     margin-left: 150px;
     width: auto;
     }
```

Once again, we've used CSS to create a 10px tall stripe of color (`border-top:` `10px solid #bdcdbd;`). In spite of our lack of a comp or a plan, the site is starting to acquire consistent design elements. We've also turned off all other borders, established a left margin that tells the content area to begin where the sidebar ends (`margin-left: 150px;`), and turned off all other margins as well as all padding. And we've told our primary content area to fill all available horizontal space, from its left edge to the edge of the browser window, via one neat little rule (`width: auto;`).

A Box Inside Another Box

If we wanted wall-to-wall text that reflowed to fit any browser window width, we would be finished laying out the basic parameters and could break out the wholesome beverages and small, salty snacks. But we don't want that (we want beverages and snacks, but we don't want wall-to-wall text), and our readers don't want that. Text that is easy and pleasurable to read is, after all, item number nine in our top 10 goals for the redesign.

One way to make text easier to read, as any book or magazine designer knows, is to set it in a column that is neither too wide nor too narrow. 400px strikes us as the right width for this layout's text column. And it is narrow enough that its width when combined with the width of the sidebar should fit comfortably in all but the tiniest monitors.

You might think that we can simply edit `primarycontent`, adjusting it to be 400px wide, but that won't do. When we try, one browser shoves the content all the way to the right of the page, while another perversely sticks it in front of the sidebar. We will have to create a 400px wide content holder and place it inside the primary content area. The CSS for that content holder looks like this:

```
#bravefourhundred    {
     margin: 0;
     border: 0;
     padding: 15px 25px;
     width: 450px; /* False value for IE4-5.x/Win */
     voice-family: "\"}\"";
     voice-family:inherit;
     width: 400px; /* Actual value for conformant browsers */
     }
html>#bravefourhundred {
     width: 400px; /* Be nice to Opera */
     }
```

Knowing how to interpret the preceding rules, you recognize the actual value (400px), the Tantek hack that tricks old versions of IE into displaying the correct width, and the "Be nice to Opera" rule that follows. Let's move on to the markup, where our "brave four hundred" content holder is inserted like so:

```
<div id="primarycontent">
      <div id="bravefourhundred">
      Content will go here.
      </div>
</div>
```

Let us pause and refresh. (Now where did we leave those salty snacks?)

Rules-Based Design

We have now laid the groundwork in CSS and in markup for a layout that will work in any browser released in this century, and content that will work in any user agent, period.

As we begin to fill our template with for-instance text and images, we add rules that control the presentation of selected markup elements and also control the way they will interact with one another. Although our activity seems humble and simple—and it *is*—what we are actually doing is evolving from a comp-driven mindset to a new and more web-like kind of design. In short, we are moving toward rules-based design.

We won't cover every little rule in the style sheet (as mentioned earlier, you can explore it on your own at http://www.zeldman.com/c/wh.css), but let's look at one of them as a way of easing into an explanation of rules-based design:

```
p {
      margin-top: 0;
      margin-bottom: 1em;
      font: 11px/1.5 Verdana, Trebuchet, Lucida, Arial,
            ➥sans-serif;
      }
```

The key elements here are a top margin of 0 and a bottom margin of 1em (that is, roughly speaking, one carriage return based on the size of the text). If we failed to specify this margin-bottom value, browsers would be left to guess at our intentions, and they might leave no vertical space between paragraphs.

But the goal is not merely to avoid unexpected behavior in web browsers. The goal is to establish rules that will control the look and feel on a modular level. Rules-based design is a technique for creating modular design. In setting the top margin to 0, we allow subheads to sit snugly on top of paragraphs (especially if we set subhead margin-bottom values to 0, which we do in a subsequent rule). In setting the margin-bottom value to 1em, we differentiate the space between paragraphs from the space between subheads and paragraphs.

It is a small thing, but CSS layout is filled with such tiny decisions, and they make the difference between design that feels pleasing and controlled and layouts whose random quality signifies a lack of care. Best of all, this feeling of control can be achieved without resorting to convoluted presentational markup and its associated bandwidth costs.

Establishing many small rules of this kind also often frees us from the need to fill our markup with class attributes. For instance, the humble paragraph rule shown earlier frees us from the need to write this:

```
<p class="notopmargin">
```

Of such small steps are giant leaps of bandwidth conservation achieved. Gosh, that sounded pretty, didn't it? As we establish rules for various page elements, we include instructions as to how those elements will interact with one another. For instance, we could create a rule that not only wraps a 1px black border around images but also inserts 10px of whitespace below every image. Using id selectors, we can establish one kind of border and spacing for images that occur in Area A of a layout and an entirely different border and spacing treatment for images that occur in Area B. CSS2 even lets us vary an element's positioning depending on which other elements precede it:

```
p+p    {
       text-indent: 2em;
       margin-top: -1em;
       }
```

This rule says that if a paragraph is preceded by another paragraph (p+p), the first line of the second paragraph will be indented by 2em, and normal margin-bottom rules will be suspended, to emulate the kind of paragraph treatment you most often find in books [16.5]. We can create rules for almost any contingency:

```
img+h3    {
       margin-top: 15px;
       }
```

16.5
Print-style paragraph indentation can be achieved without resorting to class selectors.

This rule tells browsers to leave 15px of whitespace above any h3 heading that is immediately preceded by an image—such as, for instance, an ever-changing h3 heading directly beneath an ever-changing photograph at the top of a news site. Not every browser supports this kind of CSS selector yet, but those that don't understand it simply ignore it, and no harm is done. Most rules-based design can be accomplished without resorting to CSS2 selectors that some browsers don't yet understand. Rules-based design is the sum total of many such small and interrelated rules.

Let's consider a few more highlights of the redesign.

A Home Button with CSS Rollover Effects

Early in the day, we established a 31px tall "new menu" area. After tinkering with the navigation (discussed later in this chapter), we found that it could be contained entirely in the sidebar. So what should we do with the so-called "new menu" area? We'll use it to hold a branded Home button [**16.6**].

![zeldman.com Web design news & entertainment since 1995. ISSN #1534-0309.]

16.6
Behold one of two similar images that will be used to create a branded Home button with CSS rollover effects.

The Home button will change in response to user mouse activity, and, as in Chapter 10, the rollover effect will be accomplished with CSS, not with JavaScript. As in that chapter, images will be inserted via the CSS background property instead of a conventional <img> tag.

In Photoshop, we create two similar images, one of which is shown in Figure 16.6. In the default image, the logo text is off-white (#fdf8f2). When the visitor hovers over the logo, the logo text shifts to pure white (#fff). The effect is too subtle to reproduce in this book, which is why we show one figure instead of two. The background of both GIF images is transparent so that the CSS background color of #newmenu will show through. (Remember: If we tried to match the color in Photoshop, it would be off.)

In our markup, inside the new menu area, we insert a div with the unique identifier "bannerlogoban:"

```
<div id="bannerlogoban"><div>
```

We style it like this:

```
        /*  Image-free logo banner with rollover  */
#bannerlogoban {
        margin: 0;
        padding: 0;
        border: 0;
        width: 600px;
        height: 31px;
        background: url(/i/2003/parts/lbo2.gif) no-repeat;
        }
```

The width is 600px to match the actual width of the image. The height is 31px to match the height of the image and the height of the containing element ("new menu"). The background image rule *preloads the image in its hover state* (lbo2.gif) so there will be no delay when the CSS "rollover" is triggered by the user's mouse movement.

Fahrner Image Replacement (FIR)

Now we have a logo/Home button in its hover state, but it isn't clickable and it doesn't do anything. We actually want the page to show the non-hover state until the visitor's mouse cursor hovers over the image. The next step is kind of mind-bending and is based on a concept pioneered by the oft-mentioned Todd Fahrner. First we create a class called `alt` whose sole purpose is to be invisible in CSS environments:

```
.alt {
     display: none;
     }
```

Next we create a second set of rules, to be applied to an anchor link to the root, or home page:

```
#logoban {
     display: block;
     padding: 0;
     border: 0;
     margin: 0;
     background: url(/i/2003/parts/lb2.gif) no-repeat;
     width: 600px;
     height: 31px;
     }
a#logoban:hover {
     background: url(/i/2003/parts/lb02.gif) no-repeat;
     }
```

The first rule loads the background image (`lb2.gif`) in its non-hover state. The second tells the browser to show the hover version when the mouse, well, hovers over it.

Now let's construct the required markup, from the inside out. First we create some text that will show up in non-CSS environments:

```
Zeldman.com. Web design news and entertainment since 1995.
ISSN #1534-0309.
```

Next we wrap that text in a span element of the `alt` class to hide it from CSS-capable browsers:

```
<span class="alt">Zeldman.com. Web design news and
entertainment since 1995. ISSN #1534-0309.</span>
```

The text will be visible to screen readers and Palm Pilots but invisible in CSS-capable desktop browsers. In the next step, we wrap that text in an anchor link back to the home page, apply our `id` of "logoban" to the link, and throw in a `title` attribute for good measure:

```
<a id="logoban" href="/" title="Zeldman.com. Web design news
and entertainment since 1995."><span class="alt">Zeldman.com.
Web design news and entertainment since 1995. ISSN
#1534-0309.</span></a>
```

At this point we have a working link. In CSS-capable environments, it displays as an image with a rollover effect. In non-CSS environments, it is simply linked text. Now we wrap the whole kaboodle inside the "bannerlogoban" rule we created at the beginning of this section:

```
<div id="bannerlogoban"><a id="logoban" href="/"
title="Zeldman.com. Web design news and entertainment since
1995."><span class="alt">Zeldman.com. Web design news and
entertainment since 1995. ISSN #1534-0309.</span></a></div>
```

Whew! It's a lot of markup, but it's smaller in terms of bytes served than an `image` element, a JavaScript preload, a JavaScript mouseover script, and the JavaScript `onmouseover` and `onmouseout` event handlers that would ordinarily be stuck inside the `image` element. (Plus, it's cool.)

Here is the whole enchilada as it appears on the page, including the "new menu" parent element:

```
<div id="newmenu"><div id="bannerlogoban"><a id="logoban"
href="/" title="Zeldman.com. Web design news and entertainment
since 1995."><span class="alt">Zeldman.com. Web design news
and entertainment since 1995. ISSN #1534-
0309.</span></a></div></div>
```

Arguably, we could have saved a step and shaved a `div` by adding the rules of "bannerlogoban" to "newmenu" and then leaving off the "bannerlogoban" `div`. But we might want to add something to the right (or, less likely, the left) of the Home button one day, and we can only do that if we ensure that the module is self contained.

Additional Uses of Fahrner Image Replacement (FIR)

Fahrner's "Look, Ma, no IMG tags" technique can be used many ways. For instance, you could use it to insert an ultra-wide image in the center of a liquid layout. As the visitor widened her browser window, more of the image would be revealed. Back at the ranch (that is, elsewhere in our zeldman.com CSS redesign), we use the technique to create the appearance of three banners, with rollover effects not only on the images, but also on their borders [**16.7**].

16.7
The Fahrner method is re-used elsewhere on the site to create the illusion of three banners, with rollover effects on images, and separate rollover effects on borders.

The initial CSS was exactly like that shown in the preceding example, except for the addition of rules that created borders. But not all current browsers were built to handle this kind of CSS gamesmanship. Opera 6 had one problem. Netscape 7 had another. Fixing those problems created a different problem in IE5/Macintosh. From deep in the rice paddies, we wired for reinforcements. Putting it less poetically, we asked for help working around some of these bugs and differences, and the oft-mentioned Porter Glendinning obliged. Between that gentleman, Mr. Fahrner, and ourselves, we created the CSS torture chamber that follows:

```
/*  Banners without img elements, thanks Todd and Porter  */
#banner1, #banner2, #banner3 {
     margin: 10px 0 0 0;
     padding: 0;
     width: 100px;
     height: 25px;
     }


#banner1    {
  /* Opera uses this background for the rollover effect. */
     background: url(/i/bans/hc100bano.gif) no-repeat 1px;
     }


#banner2    {
  /* Opera uses this background for the rollover effect. */
     background: url(/i/bans/ala100bano.gif) no-repeat 1px;
     }
```

continues

```
#banner3    {
  /* Opera uses this background for the rollover effect. */
     background: url(/i/bans/zeldmix2.gif) no-repeat 1px;
     }


#hcban, #alban, #wtban {
     display: block;
     padding: 0;
     border: 1px solid #000;
     background: url(/i/bans/hc100ban.gif) no-repeat 1px;  /*
start hiding from macie\*/
     background-position: 0px; /* stop hiding */
     width: 100px;
     height: 25px;
     voice-family: "\"}\"";    /* Need we explain? */
     voice-family: inherit;
     width: 98px;
     height: 23px; /* Actual values to overlap borders */
     }

html>body #hcban, html>body #alban, html>body #wtban {
     width: 98px;
     height: 23px; /* Be nice to Opera */
     }

#alban {
     background-image: url(/i/bans/ala100ban.gif);
     }

#wtban {
     background-image: url(/i/bans/zeldmix.gif);
     }

a#hcban:hover {
     background-image: url(/i/bans/hc100bano.gif);
     border: 1px solid #ffc;
     }

a#alban:hover {
     background-image: url(/i/bans/ala100bano.gif);
     border: 1px solid #ffc;
     }
```

```
a#wtban:hover {
      background-image: url(/i/bans/zeldmix2.gif);
      border: 1px solid #ffc;
      }

.alt {
      display: none;
      }
```

And here is the markup it rides in on:

```
<div id="banner2"><a id="alban"
href="http://www.alistapart.com/" target="eljefe"
title="A List Apart, for people who make websites.">
<span class="alt">A List Apart</span></a></div>

<div id="banner1"><a id="hcban" href="http://www.happycog.com/"
target="eljefe" title="Happy Cog Studios. Web design and
consulting."><span class="alt">Happy Cog Studios</span></a>
</div>

<div id="banner3"><a id="wtban" href=
"http://w3mix.web-graphics.com/" target="eljefe"
title="Remix the W3C."><span class="alt">WThRemix</span></a>
</div>
```

Visually, this method works in any browser released in this century. More importantly, it delivers content to any browser or Internet device, old or new. (If the style sheet is linked, the technique will fail in the JAWS screen reader, which absurdly reads aloud only what is visible in a browser after rendering the CSS. But if you *import* your style sheet, the text will no longer be hidden from JAWS.)

Having come out on the other side of the exercise, from our point of view, it makes little sense to create border effects this way. You can get the same result with far less bandwidth by simply changing the border colors in Photoshop. But it was worth doing to learn if it could be done. As with all CSS discussed in this chapter, feel free to visit the actual style sheet, copy and paste, and then adapt it as you see fit.

A CSS/XHTML Navigation Bar

Consider the sidebar we left naked and aching back in Figure 16.4. Let us now fill it. For instance, let us fill it with navigation so that our visitors can find their way around the site. Conceptually speaking, a nav bar is merely a list of links. Let's honor that notion by typing our links as a standard-issue, unordered list:

```
<ul>
<li id="secondarytop"><a href="/" title="The Daily Report. Web
design news and info.">daily report</a></li>
<li id="glam"><a href="/glamorous/" title="My Glamorous Life:
Episodes and recollections.">glamorous</a></li>
<li id="classics"><a href="/classics/" title="Entertainments,
1995&#8211;2002.">classics</a></li>
<li id="about"><a href="/about/" title="History, FAQ, and
suchlike.">about</a></li>
<li id="contact"><a href="/contact/" title="Write to us.">
contact</a></li>
<li id="essentials"><a href="/essentials/" title="Info for web
designers.">essentials</a></li>
<li id="pubs"><a href="/pubs/" title="Zeldman&#8217;s books
and articles.">pubs</a></li>
<li id="tour"><a href="/tour/" title="We may be coming to your
town: personal appearances.">tour</a></li>
</ul>
```

That is how any sensible person would format an unordered list. Alas, to avoid the whitespace bug discussed in Chapter 12, we must remove the whitespace, like so:

```
<ul><li id="secondarytop"><a href="/" title="The Daily Report.
Web design news and info.">daily report</a></li><li
id="glam"><a href="/glamorous/" title="My Glamorous Life:
Episodes and recollections.">glamorous</a></li><li
id="classics"><a href="/classics/" title="Entertainments,
1995&#8211;2002.">classics</a></li><li id="about"><a
href="/about/" title="History, FAQ, and suchlike.">about</a>
</li><li id="contact"><a href="/contact/" title="Write to
us.">contact</a></li><li id="essentials"><a href="/essentials/"
title="Info for web designers.">essentials</a></li><li
id="pubs"><a href="/pubs/" title="Zeldman&#8217;s books and
articles.">pubs</a></li><li id="tour"><a href="/tour/"
title="We may be coming to your town: personal
appearances.">tour</a></li></ul>
```

It's pretty darned hard to read, now, isn't it? But we have no choice if we care how the site looks in Internet Explorer for Windows—and we care a heck of a lot about that, of course.

Adding the Style

We've banged out a list. Now we transform it:

```
    /*  Create buttons   */
#secondarynav ul {
    list-style: none;
    padding: 0;
    margin: 15px 0;
    border: 0;
    }


#secondarynav li    {
    text-align: center;
    border-bottom: 1px solid #000;
    width: 100px;
    margin: 0;
    padding: 0;
    font: 10px/15px Verdana, Lucida, Arial, sans-serif;
    color: #000;
    background: #e0861e;
    }

#secondarytop, #tertiarytop    {
    border-top: 1px solid #000;
    }

#secondarynav li a {
    display: block;
    font-weight: normal;
    padding: 0;
    border-left: 1px solid #000;
    border-right: 1px solid #000;
    background: #e0861e;
    color: #000;
    text-decoration: none;
    width: 100px;    /* False value for IE4-5.x/Win. */
    voice-family: "\"}\"";
    voice-family:inherit;
    width: 98px;    /* You get it. Good value for compliant
                    ➥browsers. */
    }
```

continues

```
html>#secondarynav li a {
      width: 98px;    /* Be nice to Opera */
      }

#secondarynav li a:hover {
      font-weight: normal;
      border-left: 1px solid #000;
      border-right: 1px solid #000;
      background: #c90;
      color: #fff;
      text-decoration: none;
      }
```

When you finish mopping up the beverage you sprayed all over this book and yourself, we'll walk calmly through each of these rules that turn an ordinary list into a bride's most cherished memory. (That came out wrong, but never mind.) The point is that we will now consider each of the rules that goes into the menu button treatment.

```
#secondarynav ul {
      list-style: none;
      padding: 0;
      margin: 15px 0;
      border: 0;
      }
```

The preceding rule is self explanatory. Just kidding. Actually, in this rule, we're telling the list not to display bullets (list-style: none;). We're also setting padding, borders, and left and right margins to o and giving the whole thing 15px of whitespace at the top and bottom. Next:

```
#secondarynav li     {
      text-align: center;
      border-bottom: 1px solid #000;
      width: 100px;
      margin: 0;
      padding: 0;
      font: 10px/15px Verdana, Lucida, Arial, sans-serif;
      color: #000;
      background: #e0861e;
      }
```

Having styled the parent (ul) in the previous step, we now grant the child— the list item—the loving care it deserves. Text is aligned center, width is nailed down (and there are no padding or horizontal border values to mess up that width in browsers that misunderstand the box model), and each list item is told to generate a solid black line at its bottom. When that line is added to others described later, the effect of a box, or of a button's outline, will be created.

Finally, note the line-height value, which is the second value listed after font (15px). (Font: 10px/15px is CSS shorthand. It means the same thing as font-size: 10px; line-height: 15px. But you knew that.) With this rule, we are telling each list item, or "button," to stand 15 proud pixels tall and to place the text in the vertical middle (because that's how line-height works). For such a simple-looking rule, it sure does a lot.

```
#secondarytop, #tertiarytop     {
    border-top: 1px solid #000;
    }
```

The preceding rule sticks a black border at the top of an element with the unique id of secondarytop or tertiarytop. We are only concerned with secondarytop here. If you glance back at the markup—oh, heck, we'll make it easy and reprint it here.

```
<ul><li id="secondarytop"><a href="/" title="The Daily Report.
Web design news and info.">daily report</a></li>
```

You can see that the first list item has an id of secondarytop. Therefore, in addition to the rules that style every list item in the sidebar, this bad boy is beholden to an additional rule that tells it to don a black line (1px border) at its top. In other words, the first "button" will have a top and bottom. It's kind of obvious when you think about it. If we applied a top and bottom border to every list item, we would have one line banging up against the other, and that would be bad. This, on the other hand, is good.

Hit Points and Color Fills: Aesthetics and Accessibility
We are nearly done. Hang on; this next one looks uglier than it needs to:

```
#secondarynav li a {
    display: block;
    font-weight: normal;
    padding: 0;
    border-left: 1px solid #000;
    border-right: 1px solid #000;
    background: #e0861e;
    color: #000;
```

continues

```
    text-decoration: none;
    width: 100px;    /* False value for IE4-5.x/Win. */
    voice-family: "\"}\"";
    voice-family:inherit;
    width: 98px;    /* You get it. Good value for compliant
                        ➥browsers. */
    }
```

In the preceding rule, we're styling the anchor link and telling the link
to display block instead of inline. Combined with the line-height that was
established in #secondarynav li, the result is that the "button" is filled
with a particular color (enhancing aesthetics) and *the entire button is clickable*
(an important accessibility bonus for people who have impaired mobility or low
vision, as discussed in Chapter 14). Plus, the "button" really looks and feels like
a button.

We're also creating left and right borders to finish filling in the button, and
we're using the usual trickery to persuade IE5/Windows not to botch the box
model.

```
html>#secondarynav li a {
    width: 98px;    /* Be nice to Opera */
    }
```

Now (drumroll) for the final rule our button fiesta requires, which is a hover or
rollover effect:

```
 #secondarynav li a:hover {
    font-weight: normal;
    background: #c90;
    color: #fff;
    text-decoration: none;
    }
```

Once again, for accessibility and aesthetic reasons, the entire "button" will be
clickable, thanks to the display: block that was established in the earlier
link rule, which cascades down to the more specific hover rule shown here. This
rule tells the text color and background color to change in response to the user's
mouse cursor. We don't bother repeating the border-left and border-right
instructions because the single-pixel black border effects persist from earlier
link rules.

For the crowning touch, as we did when creating our hybrid layout in Chapter 10, we persuade the relevant button to present a "you are here" effect by inserting a page-specific embedded style in the <head> of the page:

```
<style type="text/css">
<!--
#secondarytop a:visited {
      font-weight: normal;
      background: #c60;
      color: #fff;
      text-decoration: none;
      }
-->
</style>
```

Refer to Figures **16.8** and **16.9**. The "you are here" effect can be seen in the daily report "button," with its darker background (#c60) and reversed-out text (#fff). The additional, user-activated rollover effect can be seen in Figure **16.9**.

16.8
A basic unordered list gets a beauty makeover courtesy of CSS. But wait, there's more!

16.9
There's the ubiquitous rollover effect. To the average citizen, these are standard navigation buttons. In fact, though, the whole thing is simply markup to which some style has been applied. Now you know.

On a technical note, the <!-- comments that surround our style sheet would be a problem if we were authoring in XHTML 1.0 Strict, but we're using Transitional. These comments would also be a problem if we were serving our page as application/xhtml+xml, but we're serving it as text/html. To understand why these elements would pose a problem in a strict XHTML environment, see http://devedge.netscape.com/viewsource/2003/xhtml-style-script/.

When the navigation bar we've just created combines with the banners, the search engine interface, and a style-switching widget we created while you weren't looking, the result is what you see in Figure **16.10**.

16.10
The sidebar is filled at last.

Finishing Up

There is more to the layout than can be covered in one chapter—even a big fat chapter like this one. There are accessibility enhancements made to form elements, including the Search form. There are our old pals Skip Navigation, tabindex, and accesskey. There's the design of a style-switching widget (visible in the center of Figure **16.10**) and the code it rides in on, taken from the open source A List Apart style switcher discussed in Chapter 15, "Working with DOM-Based Scripts." There is the need to actually create an alternate style [**16.11**], which largely, although not exclusively, consists of changing color values. And there are details like the "Externals" sidebar [**16.12**], which is hidden from view until the visitor decides to open it.

After having finished, there is the inevitable debugging, although there is actually little of it because browsers understand the CSS we've used. Still, a few problems do arise.

For instance, Apple's Safari browser initially suffers from an image latency problem after switching from the white layout to the orange layout [**16.13**, **16.14**]. To be fair to Safari, the browser was still in beta at the time of the redesign, and it managed to get the layout just about perfect aside from that flaw. Moreover, we were able to work around Safari's bug fairly easily.

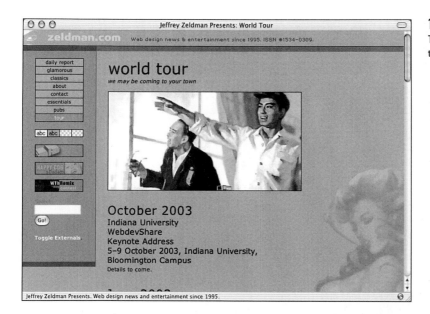

16.11
The alternate ("orange")
takes shape.

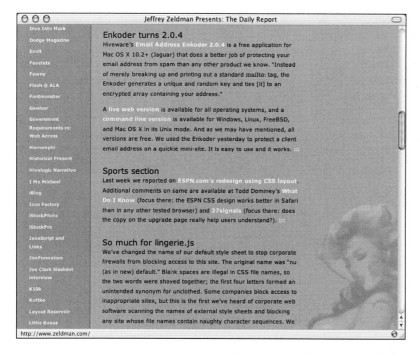

16.12
The orange layout with
the previously hidden
"Externals" sidebar
switched on. (See Chapter
15's discussion of showing
and hiding content via
the DOM.)

16.13

Here you can see the background image latency bug in Apple's Safari browser.

16.14

The bug is more obvious when the sidebar is viewed in isolation. There should be one color bar at the bottom of the sidebar. Safari has two. Contrast with Figures 16.2 and 16.11.

Here's what happened. The white layout, you'll recall, used a background image at the bottom of the sidebar [**16.4**, **16.10**]. The orange layout, as you have no way of knowing unless you've already gone online and checked out `http://www.zeldman.com/c/or.css`, uses no such background image. But when Safari switched to the orange layout, it incorrectly retained the white layout's background image.

The fix was simple: In a revision to the orange layout, we explicitly told all browsers not to use a background image in the sidebar. That did the trick. Figure **16.15** shows Safari's display after the CSS adjustment.

16.15
A quick CSS tweak solves Safari's problem. (Note: In Figures 16.13 through 16.15, an early version of the CSS style switcher is seen above the three banners and the Search field.)

Following is the original rule that we wrote for the orange layout:

```
background: #c60;
```

And here's the replacement that got Safari surfin' right again:

```
background-color: #c60;
background-image: none;
```

Other than Safari, no browser required this change. But this bug in Safari is easy to work around, and the change in rules is perfectly valid. No doubt the final version of Safari will be free of the glitch, but meanwhile, `background-image: none` compensates for the problem and does no harm. As with other web design methods, debugging of this sort is always the final step, although in the case of this redesign, the debugging, like everything else, took place in real time while readers watched.

We've now created a tableless CSS layout and a user-selectable alternative version, with not one scrap of presentational markup or anything resembling the insanity of sending each browser a different CSS file. The site loads fast, looks and works the same in all modern browsers, and is accessible to *any* Internet device. Our chapter ends here, but the site's redesign will continue. For instance, we plan to create an additional alternate layout that offers large or more easily resizable text. But that's another story, and it's time to stop listening to us and start thinking about the stories you want to tell.

Part III

Back End

Modern Browsers: The Good, the Bad, and the Ugly

As explained in Chapter 1, "99.9% of Websites Are Obsolete," when we refer to "modern" or "standards-compliant" web browsers, we mean browsers that understand and support HTML and XHTML, CSS, ECMAScript, and the W3C Document Object Model (DOM). These baseline standards help designers and developers transcend old-school methods (presentational markup and incompatible scripting languages) and the obsolescence they engender.

No browser yet released is *perfectly* standards compliant, and none is likely to be. But the dawn of the present millennium saw a crop of browsers that came pretty darned close to full compliance with core baseline standards. As updated versions of these browsers hit the market, they become more compliant and less buggy. They also continue to gain market share.

As of this writing, nearly all web users have updated to one of the browsers listed in the pages that follow or to a subsequent, improved release. This table lists only the most popular browsers and highlights only some of their features (and occasional drawbacks).

Compliant Browsers: The First Wave

Opera 7

Year Released: 2002

Supports HTML/XHTML?: Yes.

Supports CSS?: Almost all of CSS1 and most of CSS2.

Supports ECMAScript/DOM?: Yes, first version of Opera to do so.

Fun Facts: First version of Opera to support W3C DOM, the first truly "standards-compliant" version of Opera. The company has an excellent history of support for earlier standards such as HTML and CSS. Like previous versions of Opera, Opera 7 includes a clever Page Zoom feature to help make web text and web graphics more accessible to the visually impaired.

MSIE 5+/Macintosh

Year Released: 2000

Supports HTML/XHTML?: Yes.

Supports CSS?: All of CSS1, some of CSS2.

Supports ECMAScript/DOM?: Yes.

Fun Facts: Released in March 2001. First "standards-compliant" browser to market, first version of IE/Mac to correctly support JavaScript/ECMAScript, and first browser on any platform to correctly support CSS box model. Includes clever Text Zoom feature to help make web text more accessible to the visually impaired. Supports user style sheets.

Browser's Tasman rendering engine, which is responsible for improved standards support, is beginning to show its age. IE5/Macintosh's DOM support is good, but not as complete as one might hope. It's slow, and its occasional quirks drive some dynamic content authors crazy. Still, the browser supports basic DOM functions and is quite good overall from a standards point of view.

Netscape 6+

Year Released: 2001

Supports HTML/XHTML?: Yes.

Supports CSS?: All of CSS1, most of CSS2.

Supports ECMAScript/DOM?: Mostly yes, although some bits are odd, and dynamic repainting is slow compared to IE/Windows.

Fun Facts: Gecko-based browser built from the ground up to support web standards CSS, XML, XHTML, DOM, and ECMAScript. (Like Tasman, Gecko is a rendering engine designed to support core web standards. Tasman is for the Macintosh only; Gecko is for all platforms.)

Early Netscape 6.0 versions were a bit buggy. Later versions are better; versions 7.0 and higher are outstanding.

Includes Text Zoom for accessibility. Supports user style sheets and alternate style sheets. Also supports pop-up ad blocking, as of Netscape 7.01.

Mozilla 1.0

Year Released: 2002. Moz 1.0 released May 2002; original Mozilla builds date back to 1996 or so.

Supports HTML/XHTML?: Yes.

Supports CSS?: All of CSS1, most of CSS2.

Supports ECMAScript/DOM?: See DOM notes on Netscape 6+.

Fun Facts: Open source Gecko-based browser built from the ground up to support web standards. Used mainly by geeks but is consumer-friendly enough for your Uncle Bob. Includes Text Zoom for accessibility. Supports user style sheets and alternate style sheets.

Mozilla-based browsers include Chimera/Camino and Phoenix, but Mozilla does not live by browsing alone. You can use Gecko and the open source Mozilla code base to create new applications beyond the traditional desktop browser. (For instance, there's a TV set-top box based on Mozilla and Java.)

Safari

Year Released: Late 2002 (beta)

Supports HTML/XHTML?: Yes.

Supports CSS?: Appears to support most of CSS1, much of CSS2, although support is sometimes flaky.

Supports ECMAScript/DOM?: Mostly yes.

Fun Facts: Created by Apple Computer for its OS X users, based on open source KHTML engine. Light, fast, and accurate on most sites. Although it is still in beta as of this writing, Safari has already been adopted by millions of Macintosh users. Includes Text Zoom for accessibility. Also includes one-click Bug reporting button so that errors in CSS, XHTML, or scripting can be quickly fixed.

MSIE 6/Windows

Year Released: 2001

Supports HTML/XHTML?: Yes.

Supports CSS?: Most of CSS1, some of CSS2.

Supports ECMAScript/DOM?: Mostly yes, but with plenty of proprietary stuff as well. The proprietary stuff tempts some to code for IE6/Windows only. Doing so makes no sense unless you're building an IE-only intranet site. Even *then*, you might prefer to use the standard DOM, in case features or sections of your site are later moved to public web space.

Fun Facts: Most compliant version of IE/Windows. Currently the most-used browser on the web, in part because it's the only browser built into an operating system. Renders text stunningly when used in combination with Windows XP ClearType.

No Text Zoom or Page Zoom and no native support for alternate style sheets. Visually impaired users can make text more accessible by checking an Ignore Text Sizes on Web Pages option in User Preferences, but this all-or-nothing proposition is less sophisticated and less helpful than the Text Zoom or Page Zoom offered by other standards-compliant browsers.

IE/Windows users can change text size via an included browser widget, but some font-sizing methods are unaffected by this tool. (For instance, text set in pixels cannot be resized in IE/Windows.) By contrast, all text, no matter how it's specified, can be resized in IE5+/Macintosh, Mozilla, Netscape 6+, Opera, and Chimera.

MSIE 5.5/Windows

Year Released: 2001

Supports HTML/XHTML?: Yes, although with some omissions.

Supports CSS?: Mostly (but with some major bugs).

Supports ECMAScript/DOM?: Not really.

Fun Facts: Standards-wise, this was a good browser in its day, but its CSS bugs and scripting omissions make it less compliant than the other listed browsers. You can work around its CSS bugs as described in Part II of this book, "Designing and Building with Standards."

MSIE 5/Windows

Year Released: 1999

Supports HTML/XHTML?: Yes, although with some omissions.

Supports CSS?: Quite a bit, but with some major bugs and omissions.

Supports ECMAScript/DOM?: Not enough.

Fun Facts: Refer to comments on IE 5.5.

Netscape 4

Year Released: 1997

Supports HTML/XHTML?: Only partially.

Supports CSS?: Barely.

Supports ECMAScript/DOM?: Not at all (wasn't designed to).

Fun Facts: Released at the height of the browser wars, this once mighty browser was built to support proprietary code and markup instead of standards. Its CSS support was weak, wrong, and pitifully incomplete. For that matter, its support for basic HTML was no great shakes. It didn't support the DOM because the DOM hadn't been written yet— and probably wouldn't have supported it even if it *had* been written because during the browser wars, Netscape and Microsoft were convinced they could only "win" by inventing new technologies at the expense of standards.

Although most users have upgraded to Netscape 6+ or switched to a competing product such as MSIE or Opera, some have not upgraded for various reasons. The persistence of Netscape 4, with its wretched standards support, makes many designers and developers feel they must continue to employ outdated methods to "support" this ever-shrinking group of users. This book hopes to prove that you can support Netscape 4 users and everyone else while using standards.

MSIE 4

Year Released: 1997

Supports HTML/XHTML?: More than Netscape 4 but not by much.

Supports CSS?: More than Netscape 4.

Supports ECMAScript/DOM?: Not at all (wasn't designed to).

Fun Facts: Released at the height of the browser wars, MSIE 4 supported proprietary code and markup instead of standards. Nearly all IE 4 users have since switched to a more recent version, in part because Microsoft bundles the browser with the operating system. Upgrade from Windows 95 to Windows XP, for example, and you instantly move from IE 4 to IE 6. Thus, although IE 4 is scarcely "better" than Netscape 4 from a standards point of view (despite what Microsoft's PR department might have you believe), IE4 poses far less of a problem to developers because it is far less used.

Index

www.informit.com

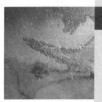

HOW TO CONTACT US

VISIT OUR WEB SITE

WWW.NEWRIDERS.COM

On our Web site you'll find information about our other books, authors, tables of contents, indexes, and book errata. You will also find information about book registration and how to purchase our books.

EMAIL US

Contact us at this address: **nrfeedback@newriders.com**

- If you have comments or questions about this book
- To report errors that you have found in this book
- If you have a book proposal to submit or are interested in writing for New Riders
- If you would like to have an author kit sent to you
- If you are an expert in a computer topic or technology and are interested in being a technical editor who reviews manuscripts for technical accuracy

- To find a distributor in your area, please contact our international department at this address. **nrmedia@newriders.com**

- For instructors from educational institutions who want to preview New Riders books for classroom use. Email should include your name, title, school, department, address, phone number, office days/hours, text in use, and enrollment, along with your request for desk/examination copies and/or additional information.
- For members of the media who are interested in reviewing copies of New Riders books. Send your name, mailing address, and email address, along with the name of the publication or Web site you work for.

BULK PURCHASES/CORPORATE SALES

The publisher offers discounts on this book when ordered in quantity for bulk purchases and special sales. For sales within the U.S., please contact: Corporate and Government Sales (800) 382-3419 or **corpsales@pearsontechgroup.com**. Outside of the U.S., please contact: International Sales (317) 428-3341 or **international@pearsontechgroup.com**.

WRITE TO US

New Riders Publishing
1249 Eighth Street
Berkeley, California 94710

CALL US

Toll-free (800) 571-5840. Ask for New Riders.
If outside U.S. (317) 428-3000. Ask for New Riders.

WWW.NEWRIDERS.COM